T0358533

Routledge Revivals

Labour and Politics in Nigeria

Originally published in 1974 and with a new introduction for the 1981 edition, this book is a clear and vivid history of the role of organized labour in the politics of Nigeria. It covers the period from the first General Strike of 1945 to the civil war and reintegration of the country. As well as providing an analysis of the characteristics and attitudes of Nigeria's wage earners, this study is concerned with their place in the wider political and social life of the country. The attempts of the trade unions to create a representative central labour organisation are considered, as is the internal structure of the unions themselves. The book also examines the relationship of the Unions with the political parties of the first Republic and later with the Military Government. The influence of the trade unions in the determination of wage rates is analysed. The book concludes with an overview of trade unions in other parts of Africa with which the performance and characteristics of organized labour in Nigeria are compared.

Labour and Politics in Nigeria

Robin Cohen

Routledge
Taylor & Francis Group

First published in 1974 and with a new Preface as a second impression in 1981 by Heinemann Educational Books Ltd.

This edition first published in 2024 by Routledge
4 Park Square, Milton Park, Abingdon, Oxon, OX14 4RN

and by Routledge
605 Third Avenue, New York, NY 10158. Reissued with permission of Hans Zell Publishers.

Routledge is an imprint of the Taylor & Francis Group, an informa business

ISBN 13: 978-1-032-70327-5 (hbk)
ISBN 13: 978-1-032-70329-9 (ebk)
ISBN 13: 978-1-032-70332-9 (pbk)
Book DOI 10.4324/9781032703299

Labour and Politics in Nigeria

ROBIN COHEN

Professor of Sociology,
University of Warwick

HEINEMANN

LONDON · IBADAN · NAIROBI

Heinemann Educational Books Ltd
22 Bedford Square, London WC1B 3HH
P.M.B. 5205, Ibadan. P.O. BOX 45314, Nairobi
EDINBURGH MELBOURNE AUCKLAND
HONG KONG SINGAPORE NEW DELHI
KUALA LUMPUR KINGSTON PORT OF SPAIN

ISBN 0 435 96150 0

Printed in Great Britain by
Biddles Ltd, Guildford, Surrey

Contents

Tables, Graphs and Charts

List of Abbreviations

AALC	Afro-American Labour Centre
AATUF	All African Trade Union Federation
ACSTWU	African Civil Servants Technical Workers Union
AFL-CIO	American Federation of Labour-Congress of Industrial Organizations
AFRO	African Regional Organization (of the ICFTU)
AG	Action Group
ANC	African National Congress (Zambia)
ANTUF	All-Nigeria Trade Union Federation
ATUC	African Trade Union Confederation
BTUC	Biafran Trade Union Confederation
CGT	Confédération Générale du Travail
CGTA	Confédération Générale du Travail Africain
CIA	Central Intelligence Agency
COLA	Cost of Living Allowance
CPP	Convention Peoples Party (Ghana)
ICFTU	International Confederation of Free Trade Union
IFCTU	International Federation of Christian Trade Unions
ILO	International Labour Organization (Office)
IULC	Independent United Labour Congress
JAC	Joint Action Committee
KFL	Kenya Federation of Labour
LUF	Labour Unity Front
MIT	Massachusetts Institute of Technology
MNR	Mouvement National Révolutionnaire (Popular Republic of the Congo)
NCNC	National Council for Nigeria and the Cameroons. Later: National Convention of Nigerian Citizens
NCTUN	National Council of Trade Unions of Nigeria
NEPU	Northern (later Nigerian) Elements' Progressive Union
NFL	Nigerian Federation of Labour
NFL	Northern Federation of Labour
NIPC	National Investment and Properties Co. Ltd.

NISER	Nigerian Institute of Social and Economic Research
NLC	Nigerian Labour Congress
NLP	Nigerian Labour Party
NNA	Nigerian National Alliance
NNDP	Nigerian National Democratic Party
NNFL	Nigerian National Federation of Labour
NPC	Northern Peoples' Congress
NSFL	Northern States Federation of Labour
NTUC	Nigerian Trade Union Congress
NTUF	Nigerian Trade Union Federation
NUT	Nigerian Union of Teachers
NWC	Nigerian Workers Council
NYM	Nigerian Youth Movement
OUP	Oxford University Press
PDG	Parti Démocratique de Guinée
RDA	Rassemblement Démocratique Africain
RILU	Red International Labour Unions
SWAFP	Socialist Workers' and Farmers' Party
TANU	Tanganyika (Tanzania) African National Union
TFL	Tanganyika (Tanzania) Federation of Labour
TUC	Trades Union Congress (Ghana)
TUC	Trades Union Congress (U.K.)
TUC(N)	Trades Union Congress (of Nigeria)
TUCN	Trade Union Congress of Nigeria
TUSC	Trade Unions' Supreme Council
UAC	United Africa Company
UCCLO	United Committee of Central Labour Organizations
UGTAN	Union Générale des Travailleurs d'Afrique Noire
UGTT	Union Générale des Travailleurs Tunisiens
ULC	United Labour Congress
ULCN	United Labour Congress of Nigeria
UMT	Union Marocaine du Travail
UNAMAG	Amalgamated Union of the United Africa Company African Workers
UPGA	United Progressive Grand Alliance
UPP	United Peoples' Party
USAID	United States Agency for International Development
WFTU	World Federation of Trade Unions

Short preface to the Routledge Revivals edition, 2023

Other than correcting some minor infelicities, the text to this book remains identical to the 1981 impression. Nigeria and the labour movement have changed greatly over the last four decades and I cannot hope to reflect their complex evolution in this current reprint. There are, however, some key moments that should be noted.

First, as I had already noted, the Nigeria government legislated into being the Nigeria Labour Congress (NLC) in 1978. Henceforth the NLC was to be the only legally-recognized trade union federation. The new federation comprised 1,500 affiliated unions, restructured into 42 industrial unions. This was a fundamental change to the somewhat chaotic and complex structures in the earlier periods described in this book. Despite the root-and-branch reform, there were some important continuities both at the local level and in the familiar faces that led the new body. For example, Wahab Goodluck became the founding president of the NLC, but we have met him before in these pages – when he was associated with the All-Nigeria Trade Union Federation, the Independent United Labour Congress and the Nigerian Trade Union Congress.

Second, although the government held fast for eight years in refusing to recognize any other federation, 'senior staff' (a rather loose category in Nigeria, essentially comprising what is often called 'white collar-workers' in the USA and UK) never accepted the NLC. Instead, they founded the (unrecognized) Federation of Senior Staff Associations of Nigeria which morphed into a consultative body called the Senior Staff Consultative Association of Nigeria. When the law was changed in 2005, once again allowing more than one national trade union federation, most of the Senior Staff unions formed a new Trade Union Congress of Nigeria (TUCN).

Third, the key reason why government intervened in 1978 to press the unions into one national body was to reduce the likelihood that unions would be 'political', by which was meant that the government wanted them to concentrate on their role in collective bargaining. However, this plan never entirely succeeded, notably when, in 2002, the NLC founded the Labour Party to represent workers in parliament and other political settings. Again, in 2023, the TUCN (representing senior staff) joined forces with the NLC to support Peter Obi's bid to become Nigeria's president, the first time it had ever taken so explicit a political stance.

Although he came in at third place (Bola Tinubu, the president-elect, scored 8.79 million votes to Obi's 6.1 million votes), the Labour Party had made a powerful showing. Peter Obi had united the unions behind him, had won in Lagos and Abuja (the Federal capital) and was a firm favourite with younger voters. Though it is always difficult to judge the accuracy of vote rigging claims in Nigeria (the practice and the accusations of electoral fraud are ubiquitous), it is probably true that Obi was more sinned against than sinning. It is also worth bearing in mind that the Nigeria's demography is tilting dramatically in the direction of a 'youthquake'. Adding these elements together suggests that organized labour will play an increasingly significant role in Nigeria's political future.

I trust that the reprinting of the book in the Routledge Revivals series will allow observers to gain both a better historical understanding of the relationship between labour and politics in Nigeria and find signposts indicating the possible evolution of the labour movement.

Robin Cohen.
Oxford, September 2023.

Introduction to the second impression, 1981

Since this book was first published in 1974, it is gratifying to be able to record the growth in African labour studies. At that time, I noted how national studies of labour movements had been replicated in several African countries. This trend has continued, but in some cases (Nigeria, Ghana, Zambia and Tanzania) much more careful attention has been paid to particular unions, particular industries or particular working-class communities within each country. Nigeria shows the fullest measure of this more specialized scholarly interest, as befits a country of its size, its population, its massive oil revenues and the consequently dramatic shifts in its infrastructural, agricultural and industrial development. As examples of such studies, it is possible to cite Raymond Smyke's and Denis Storer's study of the Nigerian Union of Teachers, Peter Waterman's numerous writings on the Lagos docks and Paul Lubeck's, Adrian Peace's and Gavin Williams's work on Kano, the Ikeja industrial estate and Ibadan respectively. All the authors mentioned above and elsewhere in this introduction have their works listed in the addendum to the bibliography of the present edition.

While a great deal of new information has now been made available by recent writers, it is also necessary to review briefly the theoretical and analytical advances that have been achieved or have been presaged in the current literature. First, although I had already noticed the emergence of a 'grassroots unionism', there is a much stronger shift in a number of studies to a worker-centred, anti-institutional view – a 'view from below', as a number of authors describe it.

For those who are committed to a worker-based view, I would add a note of caution to what is, in general, a welcome tendency. There is something of a danger in falling into what used to be called a 'Luxemburgist' position – one that stresses spontaneity and mass action without adequately portraying the class organs and wider institutions and structures that together constrain, inform and mediate class action. This is not to say, of course, that the pent-up anger of workers cannot sometimes explode into highly volatile forms of consciousness and action, which bypass the established workers' leadership and channels of representation. It was just such an explosion that scholars recorded in the early 1970s in Lagos and Kano. The strikes and other manifestations of dissent occurred, first, as a result of the backlog of wage demands and other grievances that had remained unsettled during the period of the civil war and, second, as a consequence of an industrial relations system basically run by periodic military decrees. Those whose work lies wholly within the context of localized factory or industrial estate need occasional reminders of the legal and structural limits that govern the overall dynamics of the political process as well as the peculiarities of the circumstances and time period that they have confronted.

To stress continuities rather than ruptures from below is not to ignore the important changes in the character of the trade union movement and the forms of wage bargaining (some of which are detailed below), but simply to point to the reassertion of familiar patterns and interest groups. In 1974/5 the Udoji commission, as other commissions depicted in earlier periods, settled wages by government review and a consequent 'demonstration effect', in the private sector, quite contrary to the government's formal adherence to collective bargaining and its later attempts to regulate labour relations through military decree.

In the period 1975–8 we can observe the trade unions trying to forge a single central organization, and partially succeeding, but it was one that was still subject to the centrifugal forces operating in earlier years. Again, we find the central government and the Federal Ministry of Labour pretending to benevolent neutrality but in fact strongly increasing their steady intervention in trade-union affairs. Finally, in 1979–80, with the return to civilian rule, the unions can once again be shown to have been as ineffective in capturing electoral power for themselves, but quite persuasive in identifying themselves and their supporters as a constituency in need of monetary assuagement by power-hungry politicians.

These continuities need more careful spelling out, but they are sufficiently clear to validate the original insistence on an historical account of the growth and development of organized labour and its relation to the political process. The second of the newer thrusts in studies of African labour has been precisely to deepen and elaborate a study of labour history as the basis for understanding the shifts and developments in worker consciousness, action and organization. Research in this tradition is included in the book edited with Richard Sandbrook, that coedited with Peter Gutkind and Jean Copans and a collaborative article co-authored with Arnold Hughes on Lagos workers in the pre-war period. My present regret is that, by confining my coverage to the post-1945 period in *Labour and Politics*, I underrepresented work on the history of railway labour, labour migration and forced labour in Northern Nigeria.

Another direction of attack on conventional scholarship has been that of those informally grouping themselves around the label 'political economy'. While I have been associated with the leading journal of this group, the *Review of African Political Economy*, this book made a partial contribution to the unfolding of the new perspective but failed to rise to the theoretical challenge demanded by the growth in radical scholarship of peripheral capitalist societies. Thus, even although in the pages of *Labour and Politics* the phrase 'political economy' was used and there is evidence of an appreciation of the links between the social structure, political processes and the means and forces of production, there is much too little at the level of praxis – that is, drawing from the inferences, descriptions and analysis a guide to the practices and interventions necessary to transform the conditions facing Nigerian workers.

The three analytical advances in the subsequent literature that I have identified – the trend to worker and shop-floor centred studies, the interest in labour history, and the revival of Marxist political economy – would all clearly have modified the design of the book had it been written a decade later. However, it is also important to indicate shifts in social reality as well as the apprehension of that reality. To do so completely would obviously require a more extensive revision – an enlargement of the book greater than a short new introduction will permit.

- First, I will deal with the major developments in respect of the central labour organizations, while reviewing somewhat more speculatively the changing texture of government-union relations.
- Second, I will describe the broad changes in Nigerian politics at the level of the state.

With respect to the structure of the trade unions and central labour organizations, the last eight years have seen major changes, effected mainly at the behest of the Federal government. The situation described in Chapter 3 of this book – with the existence of four central labour organizations (the ULCN, NTUC, NWC and LUF) – persisted intact until 1974, though there had been internal leadership tussles, particularly in the ULCN and the NWC. Some of the ideological rigidity previously shown was softened by the internal changes, but a most dramatic event served to propel the leadership of the trade unions together. In September 1974, J. A. Oduleye, the national treasurer of the ULCN and brother of S. O. Oduleye, general secretary of the LUF, died. To honour the dead and to express sympathy for his brother, all sections of the labour movement attended the funeral. The occasion seemed ripe to make yet another attempt at labour unity. A solemn affirmation, later known as the Apena Cemetery Declaration, was adopted by the leaders present at the occasion. They averred:

> Today, we are conscious of the necessity for the workers of Nigeria to come together and to remain under one umbrella. A brother, Mr J. A. Oduleye, dedicated to the movement, is dead. We have come in disparate groups to bury him. We feel ashamed that we had to come in groups. The finest thing would have been us coming as a group. This very occasion once more emphasizes the urgency for the building of a single centre for the workers of this country. Conscious of the historic mission of the labour movement, a movement that had never succumbed to any frontier, we here in Nigeria solemnly declare that we are now resolved to found a single national centre which shall protect, defend and promote the interests of the workers and of the community as a whole.

The Apena Declaration is undoubtedly one of the highlights of the workers' movement in Nigeria, but how far it represented an inevitable thrust towards internally generated unity is unclear. For 15 months, the four old organizations survived, as special conferences, steering committees and off-stage meetings about the allocation of offices took place. The historic merger was to take effect in mid-December 1975, under the name of the Nigerian Labour Congress (NLC).

Earlier in the month, a radical shift of government policy by the government of Murtala Mohammed (see below) was announced. Clearly, the prospect of a united labour movement, except one set up firmly under government direction, was not a body that the military welcomed. The police were ordered to raid the NTUC's Patrice Lumumba Institute and the ULC's Trade Union Institute, and they detained a hundred unionists. Mohammed also decreed that all foreign organizations other than the ILO and the Organization of African Trade Union Unity would be banned from Nigeria. There followed a set of changes at bewildering speed. The NLC was hesitantly launched on 18 December 1975, but only lasted two months before it was deemed unrecognized by the Federal Government. At the time of the launching, the brigadier opening the occasion calmly announced that the government was to institute a tribunal into the affairs of the trade union movement with a view to probing the activities of its prominent officers – including some just elected to serve on the NLC executive.

The findings of the Adebiyi Tribunal, in 70 volumes, represented a major source of evidence on the workings of the central labour organizations. With little attempt to assimilate them (which suggests a predetermined course of action) the government announced that the leadership of the trade unions lacked responsibility, was unaccountable to its membership and that some officers were selfish and dishonest. Eleven prominent leaders, including Michael Imoudu, Wahab Goodluck, S. U. Bassey, R. A. Ramos and J. U. Akpan, were banned from all further trade union activity. When it was indignantly pointed out that this was something for the workers, not the government, to decide and that the ban was, in any case, unconstitutional, the military simply issued another decree stating that the relevant provisions of the Constitution did not apply.

At the same time, it announced the appointment of a former Ministry of Labour official as administrator of the Nigerian Trade Union Movement. This office was occupied by Mr M. O. Abiodun, who immediately set about restructuring the existing 1,500 unions into 70 recognized unions, organized on industrial and trade lines, a reform that, as indicated in the book, had long been discussed in the trade union movement. Mr Abiodun also was charged with the task of preparing the foundation of one single central organization. The inauguration of this body, linking 43 of the recognized industrial unions, took place in Ibadan in February 1978, again with the name of the Nigerian Labour Congress. But although this body assumed the mantle of legitimacy of the December 1975 body, in fact it was a very different creature. Most of the old names had gone; the military had organized the inaugural conference; and the state was left holding the financial purse strings.

According to Brigadier Shehu Yar'Adua, the financial support given would not prejudice the independence of the Congress.

However, he immediately warned union leaders against 'unrestrained use of economic power, and exhibitions of intransigence, violence and blackmail in the conduct of trade union disputes'. It is easy to express scepticism of the capacity of a body born in such unpropitious circumstances truly to represent workers', interests, but in fact the early indications are that the reborn NLC has been quickly able to generate support at the state level and, somewhat to the military government's surprise, has borne a fang or two in their direction.

With the return to civilian rule after the elections of July 1979, the NLC may prove to be in an even stronger position to galvanize worker demands and grievances. To assess this prospect, it is necessary to summarize the major changes at the level of the state. Chapter 7 ended with an appraisal of military–union relationships during and immediately after the civil war. General Gowon's popularity, though waning, was still considerable among workers, and I was able to write, later in this book, that 'a good deal of trust was placed in his promise of a programme of economic and social construction after the war.'

Unfortunately, Gowon became trapped within the political machinations of the military satraps who had been created during the civil war. In addition to his political difficulties, there was simply a failure to deliver the goods promised in his economic and social policies. The huge benefits of the oil revenue ($7,000 million in 1974, compared with $2,000 million the previous year) had not been put to use, and apparently money alone could not relieve the scandalous congestion at the ports and the chronic inefficiency of the railways and food transport system. On 29 July 1975, Gowon was ousted from power by Brigadier Murtala Mohammed, one of the major field commanders during the war. The unions welcomed his accession to power.

Mohammed set about his task of reconciling the fractional interests of the business elite and the technical demands of the accumulation of state capital with energy and direction – qualities that were widely admired. Several military governors were fired; a firm programme for the return to civilian rule once again was announced; and seven more states were created in February 1976, as was a new internal federal capital, Abuja. Even the import and export of goods seemed to improve. On 13 February 1976, however, in an eruption of dissatisfaction within the officer corps, Lt-Col. Dimka arranged the assassination of Mohammed and one state governor. The coup had virtually no support within the army or outside and seems to have had the vague intent of restoring Gowon. Within a short time, LtGeneral Ilesegun Obasanjo had restored the status quo ante and had re-established the political trajectory set by Mohammed. An elaborate constitution was drafted (the academics and lawyers at last had their field day); an electoral register was compiled; and open civilian politics was once again permitted.

Due to the constitutional requirement for a party to show its federal character by having members on its executive for at least twothirds of the 19 states, only five of the 19 major political groupings were registered as parties for the July 1979 elections. Some of the left found itself organized in little tendencies that had no hope of registration – for example, lmoudu's Nigerian Workers' and Peasants' Vanguard Movement, launched in October 1978, or the Movement for the Eradication of Poverty and the Promotion of Justice. Others joined the big guns in Chief Awolowo's Unity Party of Nigeria (UPN) and Amino Kano's People's Redemption Party (PRP). As Richard Joseph noted, it is difficult to consider Awolowo's amalgam of Marxism, Fabianism, Christian humanism, Hegelianism and his own unique reflections as anything approximating socialism, but the PRP made a much more consistent appeal in class terms, referring directly to the need to remove traditional and comprador ruling groups and to transfer power to the representatives of the broad masses.

In the event, central power passed to a conservative coalition, the National Party of Nigeria (NPN), headed by Alhaji Shehu Shagari (later to become Nigeria's president). The PRP captured power in NEPU's old base in Kano (where it won 39 out of the 46 seats), while the UPN won nearly every seat in Lagos, Ogun Ondo and Oyo states, roughly old Action Group territory. If old figures and old alliances held true to form, so too did the promises previously of the politicians. Several state governments declared May Day 1980 as a public holiday to show their sympathy with Nigerian workers, while the Kano State government offered to pay ₦I02 a month as a minimum wage, an offer topped by the Lagos State government, which offered nearly double that amount. Even the conservative Shagari has put in a competitive bid of ₦100, despite the NPN Election Manifesto asserting the fetishized belief in 'meaningful collective bargaining', the 'protection of collective agreements', and 'freedom from state control'.

The pattern of the periodic politicized wage bargain depicted in Chapters 5 and 6 is once again in evidence, despite a civil war, 13 years of military rule and the organizational changes in the structure of trade unionism. The early 1980s look set for another stormy round of wage determination. While I have used this Introduction to comment on the major theoretical shifts in the literature and have updated the narrative in respect of changes at the level of the central labour organization and the state, the core of the account remains, I believe, reasonably valid. Certainly, I have been encouraged by reviewers and even more by the letters of students and unionists in universities, labour colleges and extramural departments in Nigeria, who have found the book useful and who have urged me to put the book back into print. Space forbids the reprinting of the extensive acknowledgements made in the 1974 edition but, unlike the legal disclaimers usually found in Nigerian newspapers, I am happy to say that 'all former debts remain valid.'

The reissue of this book also gives me the opportunity to record that two other scholars of the Nigerian labour movement are no longer with us – Wogu Ananaba and Bill Warren have recently died. Both will be sadly missed in the fraternity of labour scholars.

CHAPTER 1

Nigeria:
Polity and Society

Party Politics in Nigeria:
1945–66

Political associations of one kind or another have had a long history in Nigeria. Few of the earlier political organizations were fundamentally nationalist in character, in that they rarely demanded self-determination, but most were nationalist in implication in that they questioned the relationship of domination and subordination as between Europeans and Africans and challenged what were perceived as particularly onerous measures undertaken by the colonial government. The imposition of rates and taxes in Lagos at the turn of the century provoked popular discontent, a Political Union being organized in 1908 to defend Africans from the expropriation of their land and to champion the rights of the indigenes in general.[1] Again in 1923, when a small number of taxpayers in Lagos were accorded the right to elect three representatives to the Nigerian Legislative Council, the 'Father of Nigerian Nationalism', Herbert Macaulay, organized the Nigerian National Democratic Party to contest the election.

For the most part, however, prior to the Second World War political parties were either predominantly concerned with the parochial issues of Lagosian politics, or adopted such general and wide-ranging platforms (as did, for example, the inter-territorial National Congress of British West Africa), that they are more properly considered political movements than parties. As Ken

Post argues, the seminal period for the formation of new political parties was between August 1948 and August 1951.[2] During this period the nationalist politicians were engaged in a process of coming to terms with the early phases of Britain's decolonization process and the devolution of power promised by Governor Macpherson.

The most prominent party in the field was the National Council of Nigeria and the Cameroons (later the National Convention of Nigerian Citizens), which was founded in 1944 and led by Herbert Macaulay and Nnamdi Azikiwe, a controversial Ibo-born journalist. During the period 1944–8 the NCNC was, in Thomas Hodgkin's characterization, a 'congress' party – loose in structure, diffuse in goals, bringing together many small bodies and affiliates (including trade unions and tribal associations) and adopting an aggressive strategy towards the colonial power.[3] The proposed elections of 1951, though they were not to be conducted on anything near a universal suffrage, did, however, widen the basis of the franchise sufficiently to change the character of the NCNC to a more formally constituted electoral machine. The party leadership had been increasingly embarrassed in the previous few years by some of the more extreme proponents of the nationalist cause organized for the most part in the Zikist Movement. When the prospect of winning some degree of political power through constitutional means was held out, the NCNC became both less radical in its objectives and less national in the scope of its appeal. The major source of its support lay in the urban areas – in Lagos, Minna, Jos, Enugu, Aba, Port Harcourt, and Sapele – and in the *sabon garis* ('stranger quarters') of the North where Southerners had settled to trade and take up employment.[4] As well as being town dwellers, the supporters of the NCNC tended also to be drawn from a single ethnic group, the Ibo, who, while concentrated in their 'home' Region in the East, had migrated in large numbers to Lagos and other urban concentrations. (It should be pointed out, however, that the degree of ethnic exclusiveness in the NCNC was much less marked than in the parties that were to develop subsequently.) The 'Ibo abroad', as they were sometimes referred to, often developed strong intra-group ties organized most successfully in the Ibo State Union, whose President, not without significance, was the NCNC leader, Dr. Azikiwe. Other ethnic groups in Nigeria, especially during later periods of inter-ethnic hostility, often perceived the Ibo State Union and the NCNC to be inseparable arms in the struggle for Ibo ascendancy in Nigeria.

A discrete ethnic interest was also at work in the establishment of the Action Group (AG) in March 1950. Led by Obafemi Awolowo, who espoused the need for 'strong regional nationalist organizations',[5] the party attempted to enlist in its ranks anti-Azikiwe Lagosians apprehensive at the thought of the NCNC coming to power in the Western Region, traditional elements in the Yoruba countryside, and educated and professional people drawn from Ijebu, Oyo, and Ibadan Provinces.[6] The AG had strong links with a Yoruba cultural association, the *Egbe Omo Oduduwa* ('Society of the Descendants of Oduduwa', the supposed progenitor of the Yoruba people), but the practical aim of winning control of the Western House of Assembly in 1951 meant that the AG soon began to evidence a corporate identity distinct from that of the *Egbe*.

The pace of political activity in the North was to a large extent dictated by events elsewhere in Nigeria. Locked in a hierarchical system of social control, which was buttressed by the Islamic faith and the colonial government's doctrine of 'political untouchability' towards the emirate political systems, the traditional elements in the North were at one and the same time fearful of the forces for social change that the Southern-dominated parties represented, and determined not to be left behind in Governor Macpherson's schemes for constitutional revision. When an NCNC delegation toured the North in 1946 they aroused anti-Southern sentiments which both galvanized the ruling classes in the North into organizing themselves into a modern political organization, and made them conscious of the harbingers of change that were already present in Northern society. Thus, when artisans in Kano and Maiduguri made demands for wage increases, and workers in the Sokoto Native Authority, mainly of Southern origin, came out on strike for the same reason in September 1946, their protest was linked to the propaganda effect of the NCNC tour. Abubakar Tafawa Balewa, then an unofficial member of the Northern House of Assembly, angrily denounced the activities of the NCNC in a letter to the *Daily Times* (Lagos): 'Let the South know,' he declared, 'that we will never co-operate with that gang of agitators who are not even sure of what they are doing.'[7]

Balewa, together with Aminu Kano, then secretary of the Northern Teachers Federation, and the editor of a Hausa vernacular paper, *Gaskiya ta fi Kwabo*, articulated the demands of the 'young men' of the North for an organized expression of the Northern interest compatible with a modern political process. An instrument lay ready to hand in the form of the Northern Peoples' Congress (NPC), originally a cultural organization established by Balewa and others in 1949. At an emergency conference in September 1951 the NPC declared itself to be a political party. Although the transition to its new-found status came too late for the 1951 elections, as Ken Post points out, none of the members who were elected to the Northern House of Assembly were opposed to the interests that the NPC was founded to represent,[8] and some were active supporters of the organization.

While the NPC was careful not to alienate the favours of the emirs and other members of the Fulani ruling class, one of the most notable of whom, Alhaji Ahmadu Bello – Sardauna of Sokoto and direct descendant of the founder of the Fulani empire – became the NPC's President, more reformist and radical elements in the North grouped around Aminu Kano. Though himself a member of the Fulani aristocracy, his political vision encompassed a direct attack on the character of Northern society. The NPC was conceived of as a class instrument for continuing 'aristocratic privilege' and perpetuating 'an unscrupulous and vicious system of Administration.'[9] Aminu Kano and others in the organization he helped to found, the Northern Elements Progressive Union (NEPU) – whose birth in point of fact antedated the NPC's by over a year – consciously sought to identify with the aspirations of the *talakawa* (the 'common people'). They found the greatest source of their support in those areas of the North, like Kano and Kaduna, where the economic changes wrought by colonialism had produced a set of social groups no longer deeply bound by traditional bonds of obligation and respect to the Fulani emirs.

The four major parties that I have identified – the NCNC, AG, NPC, and NEPU – were not by any means the only political parties that developed at the time. Minor parties were formed to defend particular interests, personal or local, within each major ethnic group, as were parties concerned with opposing the political hegemony of the majority ethnic group within each Region. One of the strongest of these last was the United Middle Belt Congress, organizing, by and large, Nigerians in the 'pagan' and Christian North. While each of the small parties jostled for a place in the sun, the electoral returns of 1951 reflected the growing monopolization of political control in the North, West, and East, by respectively the NPC, AG, and NCNC. The NCNC not only obtained the greatest number of seats in the East, it also won five Lagos seats, including that won by Azikiwe himself. However, the overall control of the Western Region was in the hands of the AG. In the North, although several NEPU members reached the provincial electoral colleges, the overwhelming majority of the members of the Northern House of Assembly declared for the NPC after it became a political party.[10]

Throughout the period till 1959, when the crucial pre-independence elections were to be held on a near-universal franchise (women in the North were excluded), the major parties intensified their hold on the Regions of their strength, a process that was accelerated in 1954 when a further constitutional change firmly established Nigeria as a Federation. A bicameral legislature was set up in Lagos with equivalent legislatures in the three Regional capitals, Ibadan, Kaduna, and Enugu. The balance of power between Lagos and the Regions was set out in a painstaking manner with some powers being reserved for the centre, some on a concurrent list, and some reserved for the Regions. But the constitutional changes since 1954 (in particular) clearly had the effect of whittling down the powers of the centre in favour of the Regions.

As the 1959 elections approached the NCNC and the AG sought to find support in Regions other than the ones they controlled, by allying themselves to parties other than the dominant ones (the NCNC, for example, concluded a formal alliance with NEPU in 1954), or trying to win votes in their own names. Such support was vitally necessary to the AG and NCNC, as the allocation of seats in the Federal House of Representatives was based on population (*not* voters) and this gave the whip hand to the NPC, the Northern Region containing about half the country's population.

In the event, the 1959 elections confirmed the tendency towards one-party control in the Regions, so (until 1962 in the case of the West), a fairly simple pattern had emerged: three Regions, three ruling parties, three majority ethnic groups. At the Federal level, as a result of an alliance concluded after the 1959 election, the NCNC and the NPC shared governing power (with the NPC very clearly the dominant partner), while the AG constituted the official opposition. How loyal this opposition was to prove was another matter.

At its congress at Jos in 1962, the AG was dramatically split into two warring factions. The unity of the leadership was shaken by considerable corruption in the highest echelons of the party, a corruption that was to be confirmed by Justice Coker's investigating commission of enquiry. But more importantly, the exclusion from power at the central level had produced intense frustration among some sections of the party, and these now adopted a more radical stance. Simultaneously, the same pressures had produced an accommodationist group who were prepared to contemplate subservience to the NPC in return for some share of the benefits of Federal power. The importance of the centre, at this time, was, as Billy J. Dudley has pointed out,[11] reinforced by economic circumstance. The terms of trade for primary commodities had worsened, leaving the Regions (with the exception of the East) with recurrent deficits instead of their pre-1958 surpluses; the centre alone had responsibility for raising external loans, a monopoly which, after 1960, was extended to cover internally raised loans; and finally, the six-year plan, inaugurated in 1962, decisively placed development in the hands of the Federal government. The simmering conflict between the two factions of the AG became overt at the eighth congress of the party in February 1962, with Awolowo heading the group committed to a more radical social programme, and Chief Akintola surrounded by some rather hard-headed businessmen, pressing for appeasement with the NPC.[12]

Bitter in-fighting between the two groups, accompanied at one point by the unedifying spectacle of the Speaker's Mace being smashed during a fracas in the Western House, resulted in Akintola's faction gaining the upper hand in May 1963. The Federal government's declaration of a State of Emergency in the Region resulted in an interim administration established by the Federal government handing power to Akintola's group, the United People's Party, an action which was seen by the AG as blatantly exposing the partisan nature of the central administration's intervention. Akintola's control of the West was reinforced both by the defection of NCNC elements in the West to his camp, the joint party being called, apparently with unintentional irony, the Nigerian National Democratic Party (NNDP). Unmandated by popular election, and with little support in the Region as a whole, the NNDP continued to rule an increasingly turbulent West with the aid of its Northern allies.

Awolowo's faction had fared much worse. Towards the end of 1962 some elements in the party, organized in a Tactical Committee, had planned to overthrow the government by force. Twenty-five members of the party, Awolowo and other prominent leaders, were arraigned for treason. There is some doubt as to how seriously intentioned all the participants in the plot were, and as to what Awolowo's precise role was, but it is clear that some party militants had been sent to Ghana for paramilitary training and that plans for a coup had been devised. After a nine-month trial, twenty-one of the defendants, including Awolowo, were found guilty and sentenced to long periods of imprisonment.[13]

The creation of the Mid-West Region, carved out of the Western Region in 1963, also affected the balance of party control over the Regions. There had long been a Mid-West movement demanding a degree of autonomy, but the creation of a separate Region only became a political possibility after the AG had lost control of Akintola's faction in the West. The constitutional procedure for the creation of a new Region, which had become more permissive by a legislative amendment of 1961, required an affirmative vote of 60% of those on the area's electoral register and the approval of two Regional governments. So emasculated had the AG's power become, that it had little alternative but to advise its supporters in the Mid-West to vote 'yes' to the new Region. In the Regional elections in February 1964 that followed the affirmative plebiscite, the AG did not manage to capture a single seat in the Mid-West. It was apparent that where there was no ethnic sentiment to capitalize on, and where there was no 'bandwagon effect' to attract opportunist supporters to the party in power (the 50% share of the Mid-West seats that the AG captured in the 1960 Regional elections can be almost wholly attributed to this factor), the AG had little chance of retaining its appeal. True, many AG supporters had switched their allegiance to the Mid-West Democratic Front, an anti-NCNC grouping which had in some sense taken the AG's place, but the AG *had* run its own candidates and they were miserably defeated. By contrast, the NCNC retained its bedrock of support in its 'home' Region (having formed the government in the East since 1951) and had now made a fresh incursion into the Mid-West – capturing some 85% of the seats in the February 1964 election. In the few years since 1962 the AG had lost control of the Western Region, had its electoral strength in the Mid-West pared to insignificance, and suffered the indignity of having its top leadership languish in gaol or exile.

The replacement of AG rule in the West by an unpopular coalition beholden to the Federal government was bound to set the stage for a major confrontation. For what dependence meant to the Federal government was dependence on its dominant partner, the NPC. The formula, three parties, three regions, three major ethnic groups, indeed had only a surface symmetry, because one element in the triad had all along considerably more political resources than the other two. As the NPC could be expected to capture the overwhelming majority of Northern seats, the NPC had a freedom of action in the making and breaking of alliances that the other two major parties could not hope to achieve.

So important was the question of population to the determination of political advantage as between the parties, that this question provided the occasion for a conflict between the coalition parties at the centre. The decennial census was due to take place in 1963. The unofficial count conducted in 1962 indicated a redistribution of population in favour of the Southern Regions, and more particularly the Eastern Region. (Details of the successive counts are provided in Chapter 2.) The count was rejected as being unreliable at a meeting of the Prime Minister and the Regional Premiers, but what went on behind the scenes was a political haggling which effectively decided the distribution of population by political fiat. In the end (despite a challenge to the veracity of the figures by the Eastern government in the Supreme Court), the North showed only a marginal loss of seats. Out of a total of 312, the North was allocated 167 (a reduction of seven), the West received 57 (an increase of ten), the Mid-West 14 (a reduction of one), Lagos four (an increase of one), while the East had to settle for 70 (a loss of three).

For the NCNC the dispute over the census figures highlighted tensions between it and the NPC that had been smouldering for some time. The basic source of resentment was that the NCNC felt it had received insufficient benefits (in terms of the allocation of resources to the East, political office, etc.) from their alliance with the NPC. But there was also a real ideological disparity between the two parties – the NPC represented the forces of conservatism, traditionalism, and excessive regionalism, while the NCNC still retained within its ranks elements who were more committed to the pan-Nigerian aspirations of the founding fathers of the party, and some more radical social programmes. Too much should not be made of this difference, for the NCNC had by this time moved considerably away from its origins, but they were sufficient for the party to espouse some kind of woolly commitment to social welfare principles, which it described as 'pragmatic socialism'. As the party's leader, Okpara, was not slow to point out, the NCNC's ideology was not dissimilar to the AG's 'democratic socialism', the set of principles that the Awolowo section of the party had adopted after the Jos conference of 1962.

In a sense the drawing together of the AG and the NCNC, that was to follow, was a more 'natural' alliance than that between the

North and the East, in that the basic differences between the Northern and Southern Regions of the country (in terms of wealth, education, industrialization and western urbanization) had been obfuscated by the previous party alliances. Okpara heralded the entente between the AG and the NCNC by a strong attack on the NNDP, caustically describing it as '. . . the baby of the NPC set up in the West by the second Afonja of our time'. (Afonja with the help of the Fulani led a rebellion in Yorubaland in the nineteenth century which helped break the unity of the Yoruba empire.) For his part, Ahmadu Bello, the President of the NPC, announced in July 1964 that his party would have no further dealing with the NCNC for '. . . the Ibos have never been true friends of the North and will never be.'[14]

During the latter half of 1964 the alliances between the parties were becoming increasingly cemented as the Federal election in December of that year drew close. The nature of the alliances that were formed illustrates some of the basic features of Nigerian party politics at this time. The NPC could virtually govern by itself, but the need to maintain unrestricted access to the sea for the North's products meant that it would prefer to have a Southern ally, and if possible, a compliant one. This it had readily found in the NNDP. The two parties organized themselves into the Nigerian National Alliance (NNA), whose other allies consisted of minority groups in NCNC-controlled territory: the Mid-West Democratic Front (which resented Ibo control of the region) and the Niger Delta Congress (which pressed for minority self-determination). To this grouping were added 'ideological' dissenting parties like the Dynamic Party (a self-proclaimed totalitarian party) and the newly formed Republican Party (an Ibo group opposed to the established NCNC leadership), both of which had little support.

On the other side, the AG and the NCNC were joined by the Northern Progressive Front – itself a federated group comprising NEPU (ex-ally of the NCNC), and the United Middle Belt Congress (ex-ally of the AG). This alliance was christened the United Progressive Grand Alliance – UPGA. Some small parties of the left – whose problems are discussed later in this work – attempted unsuccessfully to join this alliance. The pillars on which the alliances rested were still essentially ethnic in character; where support could be gained outside the 'home' Regions this came primarily from minority ethnic groups seeking to escape their subordinate status, and only secondarily from small parties appealing to other than ethnic sentiment.

The election of 1964 turned out to be a fiasco. Intimidation, thuggery, and rigging took place to a much greater extent than in 1959. UPGA, who had in any case overrated their chances of electoral success, used the misconduct of the campaign to declare a partial boycott – thus ensuring an NNA victory at the polls. All told only four million voters turned out, compared to seven million in 1959, despite a large increase in the eligible electorate (20,000,000 as opposed to 9,000,000 in 1959).

The election led to a serious constitutional crisis when the President of Nigeria, Azikiwe, threatened to resign rather than perform his mandatory duty of appointing a Prime Minister from the winning party. For several days a complete impasse resulted, until finally – after the mediation of some members of the judiciary – the so-called Zik-Balewa Pact was announced, the former calling on the latter to become Prime Minister provided he formed a 'broad-based national government'. Within the UPGA camp Zik's move was regarded as a capitulation to the NPC and an act of treachery. Okpara had gone so far as to threaten the secession of the Eastern Region, but in the end he too was forced to recognize a *fait accompli*. A few marginal concessions were granted to UPGA. The constitution was to be reviewed and the machinery of elections re-examined. In addition a supplementary election was to be held in March 1965 in those constituencies where polling had not taken place. UPGA won nearly all of the seats at stake in this 'little election' (fifty-three out of fifty-five), but this was something of a phoney victory as the number of seats at stake was less than the NPC majority. Balewa did enlarge his cabinet to include seven NCNCers after this election (the cabinet also included fifteen NPC, seven NNDP, and three independents) but this was seen by UPGA militants as a token concession to the terms of the Zik-Balewa pact.

Later in 1965 the political cynosure shifted once again to the Western Region, where elections for the House of Assembly were due. This was to prove the last act in the interplay of party politics. For the AG, here was their long-awaited chance to vindicate their claim that Akintola's NNDP was a puppet administration installed by the NPC with the connivance of the Federal government. As in other elections, the incumbent party's control of the Regional administration was crucial to the outcome of the election in that it gave to the NNDP an edge in the techniques of rigging. As Walter Schwarz argues, 'The electoral game had now become a macabre battle of wits in which each side knew the other's tactics in advance, and was ready with counter measures.' So cynical had the participants' view of elections become, that a section of the electoral regulations made special provision for a new appointing procedure should an 'unopposed' candidate be murdered.[15] If December 1964 was tragedy, this was farce. Policemen discovered thousands of ballot papers in the illegal possession of the returning officers appointed by the Regional government. Sixteen NNDP candidates were returned unopposed though the AG had in fact offered contestants. The announced returns gave the NNDP a three-to-one victory, some of the radio announcements flatly declaring NNDP candidates elected, quite regardless of the actual returned count. The AG then proceeded to declare itself elected and appointed its own government, Adegbenro, the acting leader while Awolowo was in jail, being declared Premier.

Widespread rioting followed the official declaration of Akintola's victory, and he had to turn once again to the Federal government for support in maintaining law and order in his region. Some army units were already involved in this task when (or so it is widely believed) a deal was concluded between Akintola, Ahmadu Bello, and Balewa, to send in a number of army units to crush what by the end of 1965 was, in effect, a rebellion. It was partly as a defensive intervention against the use of the army in the task of suppression, that a number of young majors decided to effect a coup in January 1966. The character of the coup, and the subsequent military rule, are reserved for later discussion.

The Substance of Political Life

The interaction between parties and leaders in the period under review did not necessarily reflect all the elements in the informal political process. In reading the debates of the legislative chambers a certain ethereal quality pervades; but behind this lay real and pervasive social tensions which threatened, then finally overcame, the institutions of formal political debate. It is a truism that no social situation is totally disordered – given a longer time-span it is more than possible that the Nigerian political leaders would have evolved a system of containing, to a politically safe level, their competitive instincts. Indeed, in some areas bargaining between individuals, parties, and groups, had reached such a degree of Machiavellian refinement that Nigerian politicians enjoyed a great reputation for compromise. But if 'compromise' it was, it was compromise that was constantly played out at the furthest edge of brinkmanship, and compromise, moreover, that payed scant heed to the subterranean political realities that were daily becoming more manifest.

What were the basic sources of tension and conflict? Primarily, there never seemed to be enough wealth, social benefits, and political power to share among the political actors. Hardly an unusual state of affairs in any context, but within the Nigerian élite groups at times competition seemed to go beyond economic rationality or self-interest. Behind this intense rivalry a situational logic, of course, operated. A bourgeoisie, for the most part a newly emergent one, was suddenly faced with access to political power and the economic pay-offs that political power could bring. The Nigerian élite group was not, for the most part, a settled reservoir of second or third generation *riches*; rather its membership was highly socially mobile, with recruitment coming from a wide range of social origins. Abubakar Balewa was the descendant of a slave caste in Northern society; Nnamdi Azikiwe, though claiming a vague connection with Onitsha royalty, is the son of an army clerk;[16] Awolowo's father was 'a farmer as well as a sawyer [who] apart from his two brothers, . . . employed about a dozen other people in his lumber business'.[17]

Politics was a vocation for such men and there was a clear association between status mobility and the espousal of a nationalist cause. With telling, if somewhat sweeping asperity, Frantz Fanon has characterized the role of the colonial bourgeoisie in these terms:

> The national middle class which takes over power at the end of the colonial regime is an underdeveloped middle class. It has practically no economic power, and in any case it is in no way commensurate with the bourgeoisie of the mother country which it hopes to replace . . . The national bourgeoisie of underdeveloped countries is not engaged in production, nor in invention, nor building, nor labour . . . Its innermost vocation seems to be to keep in the running and to be part of the racket.[18]

The period of high opportunity that accompanied the colonial withdrawal was, however, both brief in duration and limited to the political and administrative structures and small areas of the commercial and industrial sectors. For the politicians and their associates to be 'part of the racket' was perhaps of lesser importance than their being seen to be part of the racket by aspirant groups whose avenues of mobility and economic advancement were increasingly being blocked. Among some members of the Nigerian élite the parade of socially derived wealth was so ostentatious, corruption and nepotism so open, that the sensibilities of those who had less, or those who had next to nothing, could not but be inflamed.

The sense of outrage and resentment applied widely, if not equally, to deprived individuals, ethnic groups, or groups representing a particular economic stratum. The sense of injustice felt by the deprived groups in Nigeria, had little to do with absolute poverty (though there was plenty of that about too); rather the awareness of insufficiency rose precisely at the point when the coffers of the regional and central governments were at their fullest, and expensive capital expenditure was beginning to be undertaken. This is, of course the well-known phenomenon of relative deprivation, where the perception of growing inequality is as important a galvanizing agent as total exploitation.

John Rex has argued in a very different social context that a status order may be subjectively understood in terms of three main images of the total society: 'These we may describe as the image of the occupational structure, the image of the community structure and the image of the educational and power structure.'[19] If, for the sake of this analysis, the term 'ethnic group' were substituted for 'community', we would have a simple, but perhaps effective, means of distinguishing the sources of grievance in post-colonial Nigerian society. The manifestations of inter-ethnic hostility can, for example, be explained partly in terms of the negative image of the ethnic structure that operated in the minds of members of the minority ethnic groups. The control of the Regional governments by dominant ethnically based parties, meant that a particular ethnic group was sitting on the most important source of booty. For the minority groups located within the dominant ethnic group's sway, there were three choices – ally with the dominant party and hope to receive crumbs from the master's table, ally with a rival dominant party which might weaken the competitive advantage of your immediate master in a central forum, and/or press for self-determination to escape your outsider status. How stark these choices were for minority ethnic groups may be gauged by an examination of the character of political associations. No less than 25% of eighty-one political parties outlawed after the coup of January 1966 specifically directed their appeal to ethnic sentiment, and this number excludes the many so-called 'Tribal and Cultural Associations'.[20] In effect, as between ethnic groups, a system of stratification was developing, measured by the closeness of the ethnic group concerned to the benefits of political power. For minority groups the negative image of the ethnic structure that they espoused was realistically connected with their image of the power structure.

Prior to independence the claims of the important political actors, and those groups who saw themselves as being disadvantaged by the ethnic, occupational, and power structures, were restrained by the normative rules of the game, to which the colonial government was able to demand at least a nominal compliance. To take only the special area of electoral behaviour, Ken Post's pessimistic judgement on the likelihood of a fair election being conducted subsequent to the 1959 election has been fully borne out by subsequent events. He writes:

> Faced with the task of organizing an election expatriate officials fell back upon the rules of the game as they knew them in Britain and were able to enforce some observation of these rules on the politicians. Yet this was the result of a particular situation at a particular time, and these conditions will not occur again. In a sense the Federal election of 1959 was the last great act of the British Raj.[21]

In the post-colonial period such equilibrium as the system was moving towards was threatened by the AG crisis of 1962. For Awolowo, after this time, if he was to have any hope of political office, had to appeal to the deprived groups – ethnic or economic (where they were not one and the same) – across the frontiers of the Regional power blocs. In essence, as Richard L. Sklar explains, this was what the AG split was all about:

> The 'Federal' faction, led by Awolowo, wanted the Action Group to identify its opposition to the Regional power groups that controlled the Federal government. The 'Regional' faction, led by the Premier, S. L. Akintola, favoured a general settlement with the other Regional power groups and the formation of a national government at the Federal level that would include all the Regionally dominant parties.[22]

If the logic of Awolowo's position as Leader of the Opposition forced him into the role of an outsider, this status had long been occupied by minority ethnic groups unable or unwilling to come to terms with the paramount Regional party in their areas. The most politically significant of these were the Tiv. So enraged had they become under NPC rule, that from 1960 onwards there were sporadic outbursts of violence that the forces of law and order were never fully able to suppress. In 1960 Tiv rioters systematically set fire to the houses of Chiefs, court members, and tax collectors, who had supported the NPC; an uprising that was intensified in February 1964, when the army and police units managed to put down rebellious elements only with a loss of several hundred Tiv lives.

For a time it looked as though the AG would have a central role to play in the energizing and channelling of the demands of the 'have-nots' in the political community, a prospect which was further enhanced by the *détente* with the NCNC, and the formation of UPGA. In retrospect it is clear that the 'progressive' camp overestimated its chances of success and underestimated (sometimes because of undisguised Southern contempt for the ability of Northerners) the capacity of the ruling groups for ruthlessness and resilience. The loss of the AG's electoral support and leadership did not make its bid for power any easier. Nor could UPGA fully seize popular initiatives on a trans-regional basis, because the NCNC was tarred with the same brush – of supporting its own Regional monopoly – in its home area. It can be doubted too whether Awolowo's shift to the left was a genuine ideological conversion, rather than a tactical position with a limited commitment.[23]

Where they did not come out in open rebellion, like the Tiv, the 'have-not' ethnic groups were generally constrained to play the game within the system of party alliances.

The deprived economic interest groups did not *necessarily* have the same constraints placed on their freedom of action – the wage-earners in particular had sufficient organizational strength to attempt to further their interests outside the major political parties. This book is partly concerned with both the capacity of the wage-earners to engage in independent political action, and the possibility of their doing so. Of course, it was not as simple as all that – the labour movement, I shall show, was split into factions, the origins of which were partly based on a choice of basic strategies: whether to ally with a major party or party alliance, whether to stay neutral, or whether to form trade union-dominated parties. Though a problem throughout the history of the movement, the dilemmas were especially acute in 1964 with the creation of UPGA. In that year the unions had engaged in a General Strike, discussed at length in subsequent chapters, which helped to dramatize and polarize political conflict along the lines of class conflict. In terms of the present theme of relative deprivation, the unions were flatly saying that their share of the national cake was too small, that they demanded a reordering of the occupational structure and that they would oppose any further depredations on the national wealth by the ruling groups. Whether to achieve their ends by linking their struggle to that of the 'progressive' politicians, or whether to go it alone was a problem which was not answered with a unanimous voice and one which in various forms had haunted wage-earner organizations throughout their development.

The excluded groups that I have briefly delineated – the ethnic minorities and those in the lower reaches of the occupational structure – were during the early sixties increasing their demands and claims on the political system, and, at points, their protests constituted serious threats to the continued power of the political élite. It was not, however, *their* alienation from the political system, but the alienation of groups within the higher levels of the power structure itself which ultimately ruptured the political system and the institutions of formal political discourse.

While (citing Ken Post) I have argued that the inherited rules of the game had largely been abandoned by the politicians in their electoral contests, there survived too, at least in some measure, an 'ideological residue' from the colonial period in the form of a system of values and norms which were supposed to govern relationships within the administrative, judicial and military apparatuses. Simply speaking, the values and norms flowed from the perceived purposes of the institutions concerned. Thus the bureaucracy was intended to be impartial in its recruitment and the execution of its duty as between different sections of the community, while its internal procedures were meant to be governed by the criteria of efficiency and merit. The judiciary was supposed to be independent of political pressures and subject only to its inherited standards and practices. The military was supposed to reflect a national rather than parochial or sub-national identity. Of course many people in these apparatuses did not follow the professed internalized norms of their institutions, nor again had the new rules of conduct totally eroded traditional dependency networks. Take, for example, the legal system in the North. Since 1906 the Emirs had exercised juridical powers co-extensive and concurrent with the local courts.[24] With the approach of self-government, an attempt was made to separate the judicial from the political authority – but with little success. The NPC either appointed or controlled many *alkali* (Islamic) courts, with the result that the judiciary was used to suppress the freedom of speech and action of the NPC's opponents. On a more general level, some individuals in the bureaucracy were justifiably accused of nepotism in appointments, and partiality in the distribution of social benefits. The point, however, is not that such conduct took place, but that there was just sufficient commitment by the higher strata of the power structure – in the army and bureaucracy – to values of legality and rationality, for them to resent bitterly the transgressions of the politicians, and the attempt of these men to manipulate political institutions for their own ends.[25]

For the military to take up their political cudgels in itself represented a violation of their rules of conduct, but intervention became plausible once other alienated groups had openly dissented (as in the Tiv riots, or the 1964 strike) and the breaking of the rules could be justified (at least to the satisfaction of the participants) as being in the national interest. Significantly the army had been called upon in at least three contexts (to control strikers, to put down the Tiv rebellion, and to suppress Akintola's opponents) to act as a support for the political élite. The climate of opposition, as well as the fact that the political élite had now exposed the shaky nature of its authority, gave the green light to a group of young majors in the army who were prepared to undertake direct action to 'stop the rot'. Though the army's near monopoly of firepower gave it the capacity to intervene, its interests should not be seen as separate from other elements in political processes: it may in fact be appropriate to consider Nigeria's present form of government as internal condominium between the military brass and the top bureaucrats – in a word, a 'bureaumilocracy'.

The Social Fabric of Urban Life

Many sociological studies of urbanization have highlighted the dichotomous styles of life found in village and urban societies. Life in a traditional setting is, it is argued, based on affectivity, consensus (Durkheim's 'mechanical solidarity') and informal controls, while the urban environment is thought to exhibit a high degree of impersonality, interdependence (Durkheim's 'organic solidarity') and formal controls over behaviour.[26] For the individual in an urban situation, his range of personal freedom is extended, in that he has more choice, but on the other hand the heterogeneity and competitiveness of urban life impose demands on him which may easily threaten his personal security. For a newly arrived migrant entering a wage-earning force, the strains of urban life may, it is thought, be especially acute. New modes of work discipline, the segregation of economic roles from other activities, a new concept of time (i.e. time related to output) may represent as rigid a break with ancient ways as do the more superficial features of urban life: the bright lights, the cinema, the football stadium, the dance hall, or the bar.

Few sociologists working in African cities would today regard the social changes accompanying urbanization as totally disruptive of older modes of social organization and social control. The negative view of the 'detribalized African' current alike among colonial administrators and white supremacists of the southern part of the continent, rested largely on their fear of the political attitudes the 'modern' African might adopt. Sociological models of a one-way change towards a more and more modern urban man have now largely been abandoned, primarily due to the influence of a group of sociologists and anthropologists studying social change on the Zambian Copperbelt in the 1950s and early 1960s.[27] Their collective position is perhaps best expressed by A. L. Epstein:

> The Copperbelt, then, has to be seen as a single field of social relationships which is composed of different sets of relations, each of which forms a distinct sub-system. At the same time, each sub-system enjoys a certain measure of autonomy: they do not react in the same way and at the same time towards the external stimuli making for social change. The various sub-systems are interdependent, but they

are not synchronized. Hence the contradiction whereby African urban dwellers give allegiance to tribal leaders in some situations and in others have moved away completely from representation on a tribal basis, is explained by the fact that these situations refer to different sets of social relations, and belong to different departments of social life.[28]

There is no doubt that the 'alternation models' of social change (as Philip Mayer has characterized them) developed by these writers have provided a major breakthrough in the analysis of African urban life. They have provided us with a new vocabulary to comprehend the plurality of the social and cultural worlds through which an urban African moves. His social identity is not presented as fixed or unchanging, nor is it moving in a unidirectional way. On the contrary, it is situationally specific, with 'selectivity' taking place as the urban African encounters various 'social fields' and participates in different 'social networks'. Leonard Plotnicov, in his study of the mining town of Jos in Nigeria, cites the Zambian studies with approval and argues that Africans in their day-to-day lives 'showed little inclination to maintain any role-consistency . . . A man must choose the proper social identity as frequently as the social context changes.'[29]

While a criticism of the alternation theorists need not be carried too far at this stage, it does seem that they have exaggerated the contextual relativism involved. Their perspective makes it difficult to identify the broader social and economic changes which would make it *more likely* for an African to, say, cling on to his ties with his village or settle permanently in the town, to participate in trade union activity or continue his fealty to a tribal association. We need perhaps to talk more about process and probability in the selection decision and identify more precisely the arenas in which we expect the social identity of an individual to be resolved in a particular way. None the less the perspective described forewarns the sociologist to expect to find traditional ways of life encapsulated in, adapting to, and existing parallel to, modes of living more commonly associated with urbanization.

The reservations that have already been expressed in adopting the ideal typical contrast between folk and urban ways are reinforced in Nigeria by the fact that there is no necessary correlation between the level of industrialization and the level of urbanization. This is by no means a unique situation. As W. E. Moore has pointed out, 'large cities have developed in many countries as "cultural" and government centres, as "overgrown villages of agriculturalists", as residences of absentee landlords, and as centres of trade'.[30] Only the category of 'residences of absentee landlords' is absent in Nigeria. Many, indeed nearly all, the towns or urban conglomerations among the Yoruba have some of the character of villages. Buchanan and Pugh had difficulty in classifying them as towns at all, arguing that:

> Many of these [Yoruba 'towns'] lack the basic services and functions which constitute the criteria of an urban area . . . and their population is often dominantly agricultural, working in the surrounding countryside during part at least of the year. They are, in short, more closely related to the 'urban villages' of the Spanish meseta.[31]

On the other hand, using purely statistical indices of urbanization, such as those used by Nigeria's census-takers, nearly half the total population of the pre-1967 Western Region were living in 'urban centres' of at least 5,000 people. Six towns, Ibadan, Lagos, Ogbomosho, Oshogbo, Ile-Ife, and Iwo, had populations of over 100,000 (using the 1952 census figures) and many others had populations exceeding 20,000. Considering population distribution alone, it appears that urbanism among the Yoruba exceeds that of Canada, France, Sweden, Greece, and Poland, and falls just below that of the United States.[32] The characteristics associated with urbanization in Europe and North America, such as the division of labour, and factory as opposed to agriculturally centred production, may, however, set up false standards of judgement. What is more relevant, as Akin Mabogunje has suggested, is that urbanization involves 'a recognition that somewhere around the chosen figure and within the cultural context of the particular country a town becomes generally distinguishable from a village'. Among the criteria he finds for distinguishing a Nigerian urban centre are the greater complexity of economic activities (including the carrying out of traditional crafts and trades), the greater intensity of trading activities, and the more complex forms of administration present.[33]

Most (88%) of the 'urban centres' defined by the 1952 census were in Western Nigeria. The Eastern States were thought to have about 14% of their population living in towns, while in the Northern States, the percentage of urbanized people was as low as 9%. In the Northern States early urban centres comprised the capitals of the Fulani emirates (Sokoto, Zaria, Katsina, and Kano) and the chief town of the Kingdom of Bornu, Yerwa. Kano was easily the largest of these, its importance being based on its centrality as a trading post – going back as far as medieval times. Its entrepôt character was reflected in the considerable ethnic heterogeneity and social diversity that was already present in the nineteenth century, a pattern that was repeated, though to a lesser degree, in other pre-colonial cities in the North. The growth in the older cities of the North between 1931 and 1952 (when the national censuses were conducted) was in some cases quite large – Zaria, Maiduguri, Katsina, and Sokoto almost doubled their populations. But these increases can be largely explained by natural growth and the development of *sabon garis* housing Southern migrants outside the walls of the traditional cities. More dramatic still were the increases in population in the cities that grew up in the North in response to economic stimuli – greatly increased after the Second World War – and the administrative needs of the colonial government. Over the period between the two national censuses, Kaduna more than doubled its population, while that of Jos increased sixteen-fold. The cosmopolitan character of Jos is especially marked, many Southerners having migrated there to work in the mines and allied industries and bringing with them their own social ties. Indeed Leonard Plotnicov maintains: 'the greater the distance of the homeland from Jos, and especially if it is in the South, the stronger the tribal union is'.[34]

The pattern of urban development in the East was dissimilar both to that found among the Yoruba peoples and to the more limited urbanization in the North. The early failure to develop large urban centres (as late as 1931, there were no cities of more than 20,000 people) was partly dependent on the character of Ibo and Ibibio social organization. This rested on the basic unit of the extended family, the structures above which had a limited social cohesion. Thus the kin-group comprised a series of fairly discrete extended families, while a village group comprised a number of distinct extended families. Above the level of the village group existed clans and sub-tribes, but these had little political meaning, and the largest political community (in the sense of limiting the perimeters of effective administrative control) was the village group.[35] Population pressures on the land forced a concentration in larger and larger units and also impelled a considerable out-migration, Ibos comprising a large proportion of the 'stranger' elements in Lagos, Sapele, Benin, and Calabar, and before the events of 1966, Kaduna, Zaria, Kano, and Jos.

The changes in the character of traditional urbanization as a result of the economic forces introduced by the European penetration and control were, in outline, of three main types: the physical form of Nigerian cities changed, their economic activities became wider and more diversified, and the socio-demographic composition of their population altered.[36] In the case of the village groups of the East, it is arguable that the set of changes that accompanied colonial government lent to them the character of an urban centre for the first time, but nearly everywhere else the changes were more subtle – grafting newer characteristics on to old forms of urbanization.

This is not to say that increased economic activities of the post-war period did not profoundly alter the old cities, but rather that we need to bear in mind a three-fold distinction between cities that retained much of their pre-colonial character, those which had a more or less even mix between the traditional and modern, and those which grew up mainly or exclusively as a result of the administrative, commercial, or industrial activities of the colonial power. Of course, this is a simple trichotomy based on what is in reality a range of variation. As Mabogunje has argued:

> Urbanisation in Nigerian towns has to be seen as a development spread out over a wide technological spectrum from pre-industrial to industrial. As national income rises, we can expect an increasingly substantial shift towards modern industrial technology which is bound to have great impact on the character of Nigerian cities.[37]

Of the cities that have been more affected by the European impact, and in some cases owe their very existence to that impact (and have therefore gone furthest along the road that Mabogunje describes), Kaduna, Minna, Jos, Enugu, Aba, Port Harcourt, and Lagos may be singled out. Most other Nigerian cities have fairly substantial modern areas e.g. Ibadan, Benin, Ife, Abeokuta, Kano, but continue to operate old or adapted forms of social institutions that owe little to the European intrusion side by side with institutions introduced by that intrusion. There remains a category of urban centres, like Sokoto, Katsina, Ede, and Oyo, which have, as yet, been little affected by the changes we have identified, particularly in respect of a significant alteration in the socio-demographic composition of the population concerned.

If, as I have argued, there is no necessary correlation between industrialization and urbanization, the differential impact of Western economic forces implies too that there is no necessary correlation between the extent of urbanization and the degree of social dislocation and disorganization. Ibadan may be taken as exemplifying a case of the survival of traditional networks in the contemporary situation. Despite considerable industrial activity, the establishment of a large university on the periphery of the town, and a considerable commercial presence, the city continues to house many farmers who customarily spend only three nights a week in Ibadan, the rest of their time being spent on their farms. In comparison to Lagos the growth of the city has been slight (2.8% per annum compared to Lagos's 9% per annum) and the number of non-Yoruba migrants small. A system of compounds or quarters persists, dividing the city into areas of indigenes, non-indigenous Yoruba, and other non-indigenous Nigerians (like the Hausa) as well as into segments based on the nature of the economic activity carried out. Only small sections of the city have a cosmopolitan character. Within the older areas of the city no special strains particularly characteristic of urban life are present, though there are often local political tensions between 'the sons of the soil' and the stranger communities, who are regarded as intruders. The presence in an urban centre of what are essentially village-type communities may relieve social tensions; it also, however, has its negative consequence in that the facilities and styles of life usually associated with urban life are simply not present. F. O. Okediji and O. Aboyade have described the 'core sector' of Ibadan in these terms:

> This area is unhealthy, filthy, crowded and highly susceptible to any epidemics . . . some houses have bathrooms, but what is regarded as a bathroom is no more than a small area fenced round with palm leaves. The floor is muddy, filthy, and odoriferous. The same bathroom is used by inmates for excretion purposes. Flies and mosquitoes breed with the utmost fertility . . . Goat dung and dogs' faeces are regular features of the premises.[38]

Survivals of a rural way of life are present in some degree in all Nigerian cities, the keeping of poultry and livestock and the undertaking of market gardening being the most common and visible signs of their existence. Such a phenomenon is partly the consequence of the pre-industrial heritage of many of the cities themselves and partly an attempt by migrants to recreate a rural style of life in their new surroundings. For some newcomers this represents a form of personal, psychological, and social retreatism; for the majority it is a more positive process of creating new urban associations based on older group, family, kin, and tribal bonds. The forms and character of these associations have been extensively documented in the literature,[39] and range from credit clubs, mutual aid societies, and syncretist cults, to improvement unions and 'tribal associations'. From the point of view of this study, I am interested in these organizations not so much as they serve to mediate the countryside/urban dichotomy but rather in so far as they provide an alternative focus of loyalty to other organizations, like the trade unions, which are organized on a non-ethnic basis.

The problem of competing loyalties is one which will be returned to frequently; here it will merely be noted that in the urban centres influenced by industrial or commercial growth post-dating European contact, new social groups of a distinct character began to emerge – unskilled labourers, production workers, skilled workers, a lower-level salariat, senior civil servants, university dons, etc. These new occupations, and the new organizations which were set up to service their needs, raised the possibility of cross-ethnic relationships being formed at work, at school, in the neighbourhood, or while participating in political and recreational activities.

As the alternation theorists have shown, the conflicting pulls of ethnicity and class in the urban context are both manifold and complex. These pressures demand an explanation that is both situationally specific and concerned with the behaviour over time of a previously demarcated social group or individual. Nevertheless it is important not to adopt an over-mechanistic alternation model, but rather to declare a bias as to how one sees the process of social differentiation working itself out. In this respect I would argue that tendentially, though not at equal rates or in equal measure, the circumstances of contemporary urban life are eroding the importance of traditional links and obligations as more discrete social groups become visible, conscious to some extent of their separate corporate identity and interests.

The group with which this study is concerned, the wage-earners, have, I believe, already advanced far along the road to self-expression and a political defence of their interests, but proof of this assertion must wait further exposition. Meanwhile some of the variations in class and ethnic relations may be indicated with reference to the organization, retention, and distribution of political power in pre-1966 Nigeria.

Ethnicity, Social Class, and Political Power

Who had most power in pre-1966 Nigeria? How was it gained, how was it sustained and who challenged it? To help answer these questions some key variables which are thought to provide the major determinants of inter-ethnic and inter-class relationships are elucidated.[40] Power, class, and ethnicity are closely related; they can be treated separately only as an analytical distinction. The justification for initially so doing lies in the need to consider the relationships individually in order to identify the importance of each in the process of social differentiation and political change.

In much of the literature on political development, 'national goals' are thought to comprise the reduction or elimination of largely pre-existing cultural cleavages through modern associational forms, and the prevention or retardation of class differentiation through the progressive bridging of the élite-mass gap.[41] Such a perspective is mystifying. It makes no clear distinction between the processes of social change that are altering societal relationships by virtue of their own internal dynamic, and those changes that are induced by the deliberate action of political actors. On the whole, aspirational and programmatic statements by African ruling groups and the normative concerns of academics themselves have been all too easily confused with social reality. Thus any number of noble sentiments by Nigerian politicians can be cited, without this enlightening us very much about their behaviour in office or the effects of their policies. 'Tribalism', the great swear-word of Nigerian politicians, was, it was claimed, to be eliminated. Workers, said one party manifesto, were to receive 'an equitable distribution of the national income' while rents and prices were to be controlled and low-cost housing and cheap means of transport were to be provided.[42]

To say that the politicians of the First Republic failed to subsume ethnic animosities into a broader sense of nationalism and failed further to redistribute income appreciably, or alleviate poverty and unemployment, tells us a little about their 'real' intent as well as their incapacity to confront adverse circumstances. It also, however, brings into focus the structural relationships in which the political process itself was imbedded. In Nigeria both ethnic and class relationships affect both mutually and singly the possession, retention, and devolution of power, and therefore both are aspects of a wider system of stratification, defined in M. G. Smith's sense as 'the principles that regulate the distribution of social advantage'.[43] The politicians weret hemselves a product of this system of stratification (and were therefore constrained by their class and ethnic allegiances) and were simultaneously active agents in trying to reinforce, perpetuate, or alter the regulative principles in their own interest. This interest was, naturally, not necessarily identical, nor perceived as being identical, with the national interest.

How did the ethnic system of stratification (more simply the ethnic structure) develop and affect the political process? Between ethnic groups there existed vast differences in political leverage which any one group (or more accurately its leaders) could bring to bear on the political system for the group's advantage. So great were these discrepancies that any realistic assessment of inter-ethnic conflict must take into account a ranking order between ethnic groups. The ranking order may be derived from several features of the ethnic structure.

First, the sheer size of the population and the extent of natural resources may invoke marked disparities between groups, particularly where electoral arrangements, like those favouring the North, bring this factor into prominence.

Secondly, the acquisition of social skills by each group may be vastly different. Under this rubric may be included the degree of sophistication in the production of agricultural wealth and the extent of commercialization and industrialization. Of further importance is the adaptability or receptivity of the group concerned to alien forms of social control. It has, for example, been argued that those societies that had an acephalous structure and low degree of centralization were more prone to adopt new social values and norms. Their movement along the westernization scale was easier as they did not have inhibitions of a traditional kind to deter them accepting western education – itself an important determinant of social mobility in the colonial order. Such considerations have been thought crucial in the case of the Ibo.[44]

Thirdly, a relationship of dominance and subservence may derive either from pre-colonial patterns of conquest (like that of the Fulani over the Hausa), or from an unequal division of labour where a particular ethnic group enjoys a monopoly of specialization in a valued skill or trade. Abner Cohen's study of the long-distance trade in kola and cattle between Northern and Southern Nigeria provides a convincing analysis of the attempt by the Hausa to continue their monopoly of the trade in the face of Yoruba competition:

> ... the Hausa developed and maintained their tribal exclusiveness. [Next] they built an internal organisation of political functions: communication, decision-taking, authority, administration and sanctions, and also political myths, symbols, slogans, and ideology. The principal aims of the whole system are (a) to prevent the encroachment of men from other ethnic groups into the trade, (b) to co-ordinate the activities of the members of the community in maintaining and developing their economico-political organisation, and (c) to maintain mechanisms for co-operation with other Hausa communities in both the South and the North, for the common cause.[45]

Fourthly, differential patterns of recruitment into certain occupations grew up in the colonial order. The Kru (imported from Liberia) were thought good manual workers, the Tiv good soldiers, the Yoruba good clerks, and so on. Other distinctions were determined by the coincidental geographical proximity of various groups to the areas of European settlement and penetration. In its simplest variant, those in the South of the country stood a greater chance of changing their life circumstances and becoming integrated into the colonial servitor sector than did those living in the hinterland.

Fifthly, and by far the most difficult factor to assess, is the adaptation of different ethnic groups to the new facts of political life. Take the case of the Hausa-Fulani. Though the NPC was formed later than the other two major parties in Nigeria, it was none the less more successful than the AG in retaining the unified character of its ethnic support, probably because it captured political control at both Regional and Federal levels. Control was then used to help disadvantaged Northerners to compete with better-educated Southerners. By contrast, the Yoruba were divided in their political allegiance as between the NCNC and AG prior to 1964, and the NNDP and AG after that date, despite the fact that all these parties claimed to represent Yoruba interests. It appears therefore that the ranking system of ethnic groups has consequences for, and is simultaneously partly the consequence of, the distribution of political power.

The struggle between ethnic groups in the political arena can be pictured either as an attempt to maintain the competitive advantage of the highest-ranking ethnic groups, or an attempt to displace the favoured groups by those of a lower rank. Seen in this light the political system of the First Nigerian Republic achieved only a highly precarious balance between the competitive claims of the dominant ethnic groups. The system was precarious in two major senses: (a) behind the liberal façade of formal political institutions and political debate lay a series of vicious struggles over the allocation and distribution of political office, the award of contracts, positions in the corporations and state boards, and the distribution of social and economic benefits; and (b) the pattern of dominant parties representing dominant ethnic groups and carving out the major benefits of political power was formed at the expense of minority ethnic groups which, added together, were a significant element in Nigeria's population.

A sense of relative deprivation led to virulent demands by minorities, only one of whose claims (in the Mid-West) was satisfied; and some of whose agitation – particularly in Tiv country – represented a threat to the authority of the Northern government. The need to use the army in the suppression of the Tiv riots also may have served to politicize the army itself, make it aware of its potential strength, and finally draw it into the orbit of ethnic competition. Paradoxically this was not demonstrated in the original January 1966 coup, where Major Nzoegwu was able to convince the men in his unit to strike a blow for 'Nigeria', but only later in July 1966 where rank and file elements saw a 'Northern interest' threatened, and again in September 1966 when Tiv soldiers brandishing rifles at a constitutional conference defended a 'minorities platform' by persuading the Northern delegation to reverse its stand on a fundamental constitutional issue.[46]

The result was – and this is one of the more visible aspects of Nigerian contemporary history since the coup – a considerable reallocation of the balance of power as between ethnic groups. Structurally, the new balance was reflected in the division of the country into twelve states in May 1967 and in the composition of the commissioners in Gowon's government, carefully selected by a process of ethnic arithmetic. In his own way, Ojukwu had also to recognize that the events of 1966 had shattered the tri-ethnic hegemony – his chief-of-staff, and some of his most important advisers were minorities' men. (Of course it was also in his political interest to present Biafra as a multi- rather than uni-ethnic state.)

The instances of inter-group conflict that have been cited demonstrate that possession of, or access to, political power can serve to overturn or cut across the other variables that determine ethnic group ranking. The balance of dominance and disability within the ethnic structure may indeed be subject to the outcome of inter-group conflict, as the present reduced circumstances of the Ibo demonstrate. But three reservations to this argument must be borne in mind. (a) It may be some time before a reallocation of ethnic power at the political level takes effect in terms of the ratio of educated persons, the number of prized jobs, the extent of capital accumulation and other indices of increased ethnic status. (b) The description of inter-ethnic conflict has been oversimplified to the point where it appears that groups acted collectively, as if with one voice. In practice this is far from the case. Customarily Nigerian politicians entered into a transactional, almost mercenary, relationship with their followers under which leadership was confirmed in exchange for tangible favours; while between the leader and his followers there was a whole range of brokers and fixers, i.e. essentially *class* actors, who interpreted and cemented the relationship while simultaneously taking their own cuts.[47] It is also the case that consciousness of ethnic identity and its behavioural expression varied considerably between different elements within each ethnic group.

If the character of the ethnic structure in Nigeria cannot be discussed apart from the political process, the same qualification applies to the class structure. The political process is here widely conceived to include the impingement of the *external estate* (the key foreign and commercial interests, the ex-colonial power and other powers which have strategic or economic interests in Nigeria) on the internal distribution of power. The external estate can influence not only the class structure, but may also affect the ethnic structure – I have shown already how the decolonization settlement favoured the ruling group in the North and how the differential regard for the supposed capabilities of various ethnic groups slotted different ethnic groups into various tiers in the occupational structure. As regards the relation of the external estate to the class structure, its influence was mainly seen in the social character and nature of the ruling group and the higher levels of the administrative and military apparatuses. These groups I shall henceforward refer to explicitly as the *political class*[48] and the *intendant class*.

The major activity of the political class in Nigeria was an

attempt to use the benefits of political power to redress their insecure economic and social position. Their insecurity was derived partly from their weak and pliant position in the neo-colonial order (Balewa, in particular, was widely regarded in Nigeria as being little more than a Western lackey) and partly through their inability to capture permanently the internal sources of political control. The political class attempted to overcome their disabilities by fusing with and conscripting the small commercial bourgeoisie (traders, transporters, and land speculators) and the professional elements (lawyers, doctors, etc.). Banks were used to finance the major political parties, while government contracts were awarded to party supporters where the claims of the external estate did not obtrude. Wealth obtained from the holding of political office was used to acquire land, houses, or small service industries. Public or semi-public corporations were set up, and some of these were rapidly transformed into little more than legalized syndicates of get-rich-quick opportunists. These activities, though they ultimately failed to leave the same personnel in office, do define a tendency to use the benefits of office to solidify a class interest, a tendency which is visible, to a lesser extent, in the armed branch of the political class, i.e. the present military rulers.

An intervening group between the working class and the political class is what I have called the intendant class, a term used to refer to state functionaries, middle-level bureaucrats and supervisory personnel. Though partly organized by the trade unions, in for example, the National Union of Teachers or the various Civil Service Associations, this group has a peculiarly conservative character in that it includes people who are structurally linked to the *status quo* in a much more rigid sense than the working class proper, in that their primary function is to service the state apparatus and the interests of the external estate.[49] Though this does not exclude their acting occasionally in harness with other organized labour, their interests are ultimately linked to the viability of the state in its present form. Such disagreements as the intendant class have with the political class relate not merely to the unfair expropriation of wealth by the last group, but also to differences of attitude with regard to the adoption of legal-rational demands, efficiency, meritocracy, and other standards of social behaviour derived from external models. A good example of this is the advice that the top judiciary and constitutional advisers transmitted to President Azikiwe during the 1964 election crisis, to the effect that any insistence on his assuming the role of Commander-in-Chief of the armed forces was illegal.[50] The intendant class owes its social character to its training – in public administration, organization theory, managerial techniques – acquired in western educational institutions or local institutions heavily influenced by western standards. Paradoxically, the intendant class, while holding to formal legal rational demands, acts as a parasitical class, creaming off the resources of the state without having much in the way of increased national production to show in return. Though its parasitical character has to some extent been concealed by the partial acceptance of family and kinship obligations (it acts partly therefore as a network for the distribution of wealth), theoretically, as its corporate interests become clearer, its acquisitive character will become more apparent.

A full elaboration of the nature of the working class, its place in the economy, and its groping towards consciousness and self-assertion must await discussion in Chapter 2. In this brief depiction of the class structure, little more can be indicated than the basic social forces with which the working class must interact and within which working-class institutions, like the trade unions, are set. A full class analysis of Nigerian society would involve too a discussion of the rural social structure, but since the relationship of the working class as a whole to the countryside is intermittent, no systematic consideration has been given to the impingement of rural-based social forces on the town- and factory-centred activities of organized labour.[51]

No picture of urban life is complete, however, without mentioning the conditions of the so-called 'unemployed' element, large numbers of whom obtrude in nearly every African landscape. As a social category, the parameters of this group are particularly difficult to determine. It may include members of the working class who are temporarily out of work, those who are partially or spasmodically employed, those who seek jobs for the first time, and those who have accommodated themselves to a socially disapproved livelihood as thieves, pimps, or prostitutes. Peter Gutkind's portrayal of the Lagos outcast neatly captures the bitter flavour of his plight:

> Many exist on the most casual and irregular work and generally sleep out. Such men will be found at the bus parks, the markets, the parking areas, the docks, in the bowels of slums, near building sites or stores hoping to earn a few pence a day. Younger juveniles try to earn some money helping the drivers park their cars and look after

the vehicles. Many wait for hours outside warehouses and shops hoping that they will be given a head-load to carry. Others wait at the lorry parks at the docks to pick up a few hours work. When new building construction commences, within hours hundreds of young and old will gather at the site. Not infrequently the police has to be called to disperse or control the crowd; when the foremen have hired all the men they need, the rest walk away slowly in a dejected manner to begin the eternal round of visiting other places.[52]

Peter Worsley has argued that the unflattering Marxist epithet, the *Lumpenproletariat*, which has been used to describe this group, itself conditions the view that the unemployed are incapable of cohesive political action and that, on the contrary, within the sub-proletariat (which term he prefers) there resides a considerable pool of revolutionary talent which could be tapped by revolutionary activists.[53] This view of the *Lumpenproletariat* depends partly on the assumption that the working class in poor countries have been inducted into the ranks of the privileged few, that there is a marked social distance between wage-earners and those without full-time employment, and that it follows that the latter are the 'true' urban underclass. Although no special attempt was made to test this hypothesis, such evidence as is cited in the study as to the actual progress of strikes and worker demonstrations shows that the working class continue to a large extent to recognize their social obligations to their kin among the unemployed and that the interests of these latter and the interests of organized labour are not necessarily contradictory. This does not, however, discount the possibility that any further success that the wage-earners may have in maintaining or increasing their real wages may involve a disjunction of interest between the two groups.

Thus far I have sketched the features of the ethnic structure and indicated (with the exception of the working class) the major components of the urban class structure. Both in turn have been related to the power structure of the society, as it was revealed in the political process of Nigeria prior to the assumption of power by the military. Theoretically, four major variants of class and ethnic relations were possible.

(*a*) A situation where the ranking along both class and ethnic hierarchies coincided i.e. where a division of skills in the occupational structure corresponded neatly to the status of the ethnic group involved in that occupation.

(*b*) A situation of conflict between class and ethnic membership, where ethnic identity predominated. Two particular strata may be identified as being likely to have had a conflict-outcome of this nature – the lower echelons of the political class, particularly Regional and Federal legislators, found that they had constantly to take cognizance of the basis of their electoral support, which was essentially ethnic in character, and the intendant classes within which the institutional legal-rational demands, including merito-cratic principles, were constantly in conflict with traditional systems of reciprocity.

(c) A situation of conflict between class and ethnic membership where class identity came to the fore. This situation assumes a poly-ethnic stratum linked by economic or other ties, which characteristically vitiated the attractiveness of ethnic sentiment. The strata in which this outcome was most likely to occur were the political and the working classes.

(d) Finally, there are many situations where a conflict between class and ethnic membership was unresolved, or could have gone either way depending on political and social circumstances.

This is the situation envisaged by the 'alternation' theorists and such variegated responses were replicated throughout the social structure. Detailed empirical work would, however, be needed to assess the particular 'mix' involved in any one situation, or the likelihood that the conflict-outcome would debouch towards the (b) and (c) variants noted above.

I conclude, however, by reasserting the view that class and ethnicity must be considered together, as a group of intersecting and interrelated matrices the deepest of which were connected with the possession and distribution of political power. One caveat should be noted. The discussion has tended to concentrate on the state or the urban environment as the forums for competition within which ethnic and class groupings were stratified with respect to their positions of dominance and disability. This has tended to disregard the nature of the class structure *within* each ethnic group, and to pay only scant attention to inter-ethnic hostility within each class. The post-1966 history of Nigeria is essentially that of the inter-ethnic tensions in the political class, which were barely contained by the wheeler-dealing of party politics, gaining full expression and leading ultimately to the secession of Biafra. While it would be untrue to argue that the working class fragmented along ethnic lines quite as dramatically as did the political and intendant classes, it is none the less the case that the unions were in no position to arrest the pressures of ethnic politics in the country at large and were themselves profoundly affected by secession.

That a degree of working-class solidarity survived despite these pressures can be explained by reference to the structural position of the workers, to the degree to which they espoused a separate corporate identity, and to the history of working-class institutions, which themes are treated below.

NOTES

1. Coleman, J. *Nigeria: Background to Nationalism* (Berkeley and Los Angeles: University of California Press, 1963), p. 180.
2. Post, K. W. J. *The Nigerian Federal Election of 1959* (London: OUP for the Nigerian Institute of Social and Economic Research, 1963), p. 26.
3. Hodgkin, T. *African Political Parties* (Harmondsworth: Penguin, 1961), pp. 51, 53.
4. Post, K. W. J. op. cit., 1963, p. 29.
5. Cited in ibid., p. 29.
6. Sklar, R. L. *Nigerian Political Parties* (Princeton: Princeton University Press, 1963), p. 102.
7. Cited in Dudley, B. J. *Parties and Politics in Northern Nigeria* (London: Frank Cass and Co., 1968), p. 22.
8. Post, K. W. J. op. cit., 1963, pp. 42, 43.
9. NEPU document, cited in ibid., p. 73.
10. Sklar, R. L. and Whitaker, C. S. 'Nigeria', in Coleman, J. S. and Rosberg, C. G. (Eds.) *Political Parties and National Integration in Tropical Africa* (Berkeley and Los Angeles: University of California Press), p. 608.
11. Dudley, B. J. 'Federalism and the Balance of Political Power in Nigeria', *Journal of Commonwealth Political Studies*, 1966, 4 (1).
12. *See* Mackintosh, J. P. *et al. Nigerian Government and Politics* (London: Allen & Unwin, 1966) p. 445 et seq.
13. Further details of the background to the trial can be found in Sklar, R. L. 'The Ordeal of Chief Awolowo', in Carter, G. M. (Ed.) *Politics in Africa: Seven Cases* (New York: Harcourt, Brace & World Inc., 1966) pp. 119–65.
14. Both quotes from Mackintosh, J. P. op. cit., p. 564.
15. Schwarz, W. *Nigeria* (London: Pall Mall Press, 1968), pp. 180, 181.
16. Jones-Quartey, K. A. B. *A Life of Azikiwe* (Harmondsworth: Penguin, 1965), pp. 43–5.
17. Awolowo, O. *My Early Life* (Lagos: John West Publications, 1968), pp. 18–19.

18. Fanon, F. *The Wretched of the Earth* (London: MacGibbon & Kee, 1965), p. 122.
19. Rex, J. *Race Relations in Sociological Theory* (London: Weidenfeld & Nicholson, 1970), pp. 94, 95.
20. *Nigeria Year Book, 1970* (Lagos: Times Press Ltd., 1970), pp. 42, 43.
21. Post, K. W. J. op. cit., 1963, p. 439.
22. Sklar, R. L. 'Contradictions in the Nigerian Political System', *Journal of Modern African Studies*, 1965, 3 (2), p. 205.
23. In my view Richard Sklar overdraws Awolowo's shift in position. He maintains: 'Few developments of recent Nigerian history have excited more wonderment than the transformation of Chief Awolowo from a moderate "Fabian" socialist into a fervent opponent of neo-imperialistic privilege.' Sklar, R. L. ibid.
24. Dudley, B. J. op. cit., 1968, p. 15.
25. For a similar argument, on which this view is partly based, *see* Post, K. W. J. and Vickers, M. *Conflict and Control in an Independent African State: Nigeria 1960–1965* (London: Heinemann, 1973).
26. Breese, G. *Urbanisation in Newly Developing Countries* (Englewood Cliffs: Prentice Hall Inc., 1966), Chapter I.
27. I refer primarily to the works of Mitchell, Epstein and Gluckman in e.g. Mitchell, J. C. 'The Kalela Dance', *Rhodes-Livingstone Paper*, No. 27 (Manchester: Manchester University Press, 1957), Epstein, A. L. *Politics in an Urban African Community* (Manchester: Manchester University Press, 1958) and Gluckman, M. 'Anthropological Problems Arising from the African Industrial Revolution', in Southall, A. (Ed.) *Social Change in Modern Africa* (London: OUP, 1961).
28. Epstein, A. L. op. cit., 1958, p. 234.
29. Plotnicov, L. *Strangers to the City: Urban Man in Jos, Nigeria* (Pittsburgh: University of Pittsburgh Press, 1967), pp. 7, 8.
30. Moore, W. E. 'The Social Framework of Economic Development' in Braibanti, R. and Sapengler, J. J. (Eds.) *Tradition, Values and Socio-Economic Development* (Durham, North Carolina: Duke University Press, 1961), p. 74.
31. Buchanan, K. M. and Pugh, J. E. *Land and People in Nigeria* (London: University of London Press, 1965), p. 63.
32. Bascom, W. 'Yoruba Urbanism: A Summary', *Man*, 1958, No. 253, p. 190 and Mabogunje, A. *Yoruba Towns* (Ibadan: Ibadan University Press, 1962), p. 19.
33. Mabogunje, A. op. cit., 1962, pp. 3, 4.
34. Plotnicov, L. op. cit., 1967, p. 67.
35. Coleman, J. S. op. cit., 1963, pp. 28, 29.
36. Mabogunje, A. *Urbanisation in Nigeria* (London: University of London Press, 1968), pp. 116–35.
37. ibid., pp. 312, 313.
38. Okediji, F. O. and Aboyade, O. 'Social and Economic Aspects of Environmental Sanitation in Nigeria: a Tentative Report,' *The Journal of the Society of Health, Nigeria*, 1967, 2 (1), p. 10.
39. *See* e.g., Little, K. *West African Urbanisation: A Study of Voluntary Association in Social Change* (Cambridge: Cambridge University Press, 1965), Wallerstein, I. (Ed.) *Social Change: the Colonial Situation* (New York: John

Wiley & Sons Inc., 1966) Parts IV and VI and Banton, M. *Wes African City* (London: OUP, 1957).

40. The section that follows is largely derived from a more general discussion on the nature of African class relations in Cohen, R. 'Class in Africa: Analytical Problems and Perspectives' in Miliband, R. and Saville, J. (Eds.) *The Socialist Register 1972* (London: The Merlin Press, 1972) pp. 231–55.

41. A good example of this perspective may be found in Coleman, J. and Rosberg, C. G. They write: 'For our purposes national integration is regarded as a broad subsuming process, whose major dimensions are (1) political integration, which refers to the progressive bridging of the élite-mass gap on the vertical plane in the course of developing an integrated political process and a participant political community, and (2) territorial integration, which refers to the progressive reduction of cultural and regional tensions and discontinuities on the horizontal plane in the process of creating a homogeneous political community.' *Political Parties and National Integration in Tropical Africa* (Berkeley and Los Angeles: University of California Press, 1964), pp. 8, 9.

42. United Progressive Grand Alliance. *Forward with UPGA to Unity and Progress: a Clarion Call to all Progressive Forces* (UPGA Election Manifesto, 1964), p. 11.

43. Smith, M. G. 'Pre-Industrial Stratification Systems', in Smelser, N. and Lipset, S. (Eds.) *Social Structure and Mobility in Economic Development* (Chicago: Chicago University Press, 1966), p. 42.

44. Ottenberg, S. 'Ibo Receptivity to Change' in Bascom, W. R. and Herskovits, M. J. (Eds.) *Continuity and Change in African Cultures* (Chicago: Chicago University Press, 1959), pp. 130–43.

45. Cohen, A. *Custom and Politics in Urban Africa* (London: Routledge & Kegan Paul, 1969), p. 184.

46. The issue concerned the continuance of the country as a Federation (which the soldiers favoured) as opposed to the splitting up of the country into more or less autonomous units (which the Northern delegation initially favoured). Personal information from a participant at the conference. *See also* Federal Republic of Nigeria, *Memoranda submitted by the Delegations to the Ad Hoc Conference on Constitutional Proposals for Nigeria* (Lagos: n.d., but 1966).

47. For a good discussion of this theme, *see* Bailey, F. G. *Stratagems and Spoils* (Oxford: Basil Blackwell, 1969), Chapter 3.

48. One of the difficulties in selecting terminology is to modify the accretion of meaning that attaches to a particular term. For James O'Connell the political class comprises in Nigeria the first-on-the-scene nationalist leaders, professions and businessmen, communal champions and local opinion leaders. 'The Political Class and Economic Growth', *Nigerian Journal of Economic and Social Studies* 8 (1) March 1966. I exclude the last category, and include military élites and conjoint rule by bureaucratic and military élites.

49. The intendant class may usefully be compared to the group that the Africa Research Group designate Nigeria's 'middle class' one of whose determining characteristics, so the ARG argue, is that they are a group 'whose productive relations are determined mainly by the social organization of

consumption'. Africa Research Group, *The Other Side of Nigeria's Civil War* (Cambridge, Mass: April 1970), p. 6. I disagree, however, with the ARG's use of the term 'middle class', with their conception of how class was created and with their rather broader inclusions under the rubric.

50. Schwarz, W. op. cit., p. 173.

51. For an analysis, in the Marxist tradition, which examines the total social structure, urban and rural, in Western Nigeria *see* Williams, G. 'The Social Stratification of a Neo-Colonial Economy: Western Nigeria' in Allen, C. and Johnson, R. W. (Eds.) *African Perspectives* (Cambridge: Cambridge University Press, 1970).

52. Gutkind, P. C. M. 'The Energy of Despair: Social Organisation of the Unemployed in Two African Cities: Lagos and Nairobi', *Civilisations* 17 (3) 1967, pp. 186–211 and 17 (4) 1967, pp. 380–402. This reference, pp. 390–1.

53. Worsley, P. 'Fanon and the "Lumpenproletariat" ' in Miliband, R. and Saville, J., op. cit., pp. 193–230. For an opposing view *see* Cohen, R. and Michael, D. 'The Revolutionary Potential of the African Lumpen-proletariat: a Sceptical View', *Bulletin of the Institute of Development Studies*, March 1973.

CHAPTER 2

The Economy and Employment

On the Political Economy of Nigeria

Post-1945 Nigeria exhibited some of the classical features of a colonial economy. Giant expatriate firms, notably the United Africa Company (a subsidiary of Unilever), John Holt's, and the Union Trading Company, had long held a grip on the export of Nigeria's primary products and on the import of manufactured goods from the industrialized world. By the late 1930s the UAC alone was responsible for more than 40% of the import–export business, though it is worth noting that the metropolitan-satellite axis was not so rigid as to prevent penetration of the Nigerian market by non-British firms which in 1939 and 1949 respectively accounted for 37% and 40% of her imports.[1] Exports, reserves, investments, and after the period of welfare colonialism had begun, aid, were, however, enmeshed in the colonial nexus. In addition to these forms of economic hegemony, European ownership and control of the banks, insurance houses, and shipping agencies, was nearly total, a situation which persisted to a large extent into the post-colonial period.[2]

A decisive shift in the colonial government's attitude of permissiveness to the operations of British and European capital in the area came during the Second World War, when the government established an official monopoly of the export and marketing of primary products. This was a forerunner of the post-war Marketing Boards whose operations were intended, it was said, to stabilize prices in the interests of the peasant producer. Certainly the worst effects of the wild fluctuations of the world market prices on the peasant's income were moderated. But the government itself depended on the same commercial firms which had penetrated the pre-war economy (organized, after 1945, in the Association of West African Merchants), to act as licensed buying agents for the agricultural produce. Against such oligopolistic competition indigenous businessmen had little chance of attaining the 'commanding heights' of the economy, although there are several notable examples of locally engendered small-scale commercial enterprises.

The colonial state had, however, provided a new and potentially rich source of capital accumulation in the surpluses that were generated by the official Marketing Boards. The access to, and distribution of, the funds generated by these surpluses were to provide one of the most glittering prizes of the nationalist politicians, the control of which represented in some measure an alternative form of bourgeois endeavour from that associated with the Puritan entrepreneur of early western capitalism. Though new sources of government revenue were to become available in the late sixties from the discovery and exploitation of oil, Nigeria's basic wealth lay up till recently in the strength of her agricultural sector.

In the early sixties it was estimated that agricultural exports represented some 80–5% of all exports, and provided nearly 60% of the gross domestic product.[3] The size of the contribution of the rural sector may indeed be understated in that, as John Henderson has remarked, '. . . it is difficult to assign a market value to products which never find their way to the market'.[4] Despite a steady increase in manufacturing, transport, commerce, and mining, in the years following the Second World War, the 'modern' sector of the economy remains small. In the early sixties manufacturing provided at most 8% of the GNP[5] despite having grown over a fifteen-year period to 1964 much faster than the agricultural sectors of the economy (see Table 2.1). Agricultural growth remained static at about 2% per annum over the period of the first Plan (1962–68) while its share of the GNP dropped marginally from about 60% to 55%.[6]

The phenomenal growth rate in manufacturing (which was maintained despite political instability and the dislocations of the war during the period 1963–8),[7] depended on the growing investment of overseas companies in the manufacture of a large range of locally made products – textiles, tyres, enamelware, cement, paper products, plastics, beer, cigarettes, etc. In colonial times, the use of foreign capital to finance industrial development was to be expected, but the post-independence government also endorsed an open-door investment programme. Not only was there a political predisposition for such a policy, the post-independence Nigerian governments also buttressed their support for foreign capital with legislative incentives – including import duty relief, the development of low-rent industrial estates, pioneer industry tax exemptions, and industrial loans.

TABLE 2.1

Commodity Output in Key Sectors, 1950–64

Sector	Growth Rate p.a.
Agriculture for domestic use	2·5
Export crops	5·0
Fish, Livestock, and Forestry	2·5
Small-scale industry	3·0
Large-scale manufacturing	15·0
Modern construction*	7 0

Source: W. A. Lewis, *Reflections on Nigeria's Economic Growth* (Paris, Organisation for Economic Co-operation and Development, 1967) p. 11.

* Excludes land development and non-concrete housing.

In terms of its direct economic return to the country, the wisdom of allowing foreign capital entry on such generous terms can be seriously questioned. The total value added by large-scale industry to the national income was estimated in 1963 to be some £45 million out of a national income of £1,185 million.[8] Benefits accrued to the Nigerian economy in the form of wages and salaries paid to Nigerian employees (often a small amount owing to the capital-intensive nature of the industries established), the taxes on foreigners' incomes, the income tax on firms, the profits on the part of the capital locally owned, and finally the income generated by the purchase of local goods and services. As against these benefits, the heavy bias in the structure of investment towards capital emanating from the external estate (Table 2.2), allowed the expatriation of the major portion of the amortization, interest and profit.

The persistence of this pattern of domination by foreign capital investment has continued into the late sixties, half the total and well over half of industrial private capital coming from abroad.[9] As the authors of the new (1970–4) plan recognize, trade unions are among the few institutional groups that might stand out against the perpetration of a neo-colonial status. They also, however, used the opportunity provided to state again the familiar argument that

TABLE 2.2

Sources of Investment, 1963*

	£ million	% of Total
Foreign	38·75	68
Nigerian public sector	12·45	22
Nigerian private sector	5·56	10
	56·76	100

Sources: Federal Government, *Industrial Survey*, 1963. W. A. Lewis, *Reflections on Nigeria's Economic Growth* (Paris, O.E.C.D., 1967) p. 27.

* Excludes loans, supplier's credits, and all sources of finance other than paid-up capital.

trade unions in some way appropriate an unfair share of the nation's wealth by acting on behalf of their members.

Particularly in a neo-colonial situation, a responsible trade union movement can serve as a healthy countervailing force against foreign investors who often dominate the growing points of the national economy. In both political and economic terms, Nigerian trade unions have, on the whole, been responsive to the problems of economic development and social change. In the process, they have done much to benefit their members. Even the poorest paid industrial worker is far better off than the average peasant farmer and infinitely better than the urban unemployed. This is not often appreciated by the self-seeking trade unionist.[10]

The crucial issue as to whether the working class is benefiting financially at the expense of other sectors of the economy will be discussed further at later points in this study. Certainly one of the assumptions of this view rests on the acceptance of the notion of the state as a neutral arbiter, serving the interests of the nation as a whole and selecting economic policies that are designed to serve this end. But neither the present anticipated role of foreign capital that the planners envisage nor the past experience of the use of such capital by the Federal and Regional governments give much credence to the notion of a referee state.

The new plan also contains a heady statement that 'The uncompromising objective of a rising economic prosperity in Nigeria is the economic independence of the nation and the defeat of neo-colonialist forces in Africa,[11] but one is hard put to discover any concrete suggestions for limiting foreign penetration of the economy. R. S. Bhambri, while considering the new plan an 'impressive document', pinpoints this contradiction in the planners' position.

> Though the Planners are concerned about the dominance of foreign firms in the burgeoning industrial sector and have declared their intention of changing this situation by public control and participation in some industries, no serious attempt is made to implement this decision. Only limited financial resources have been set aside for industrial investment by the governments . . . In the incorporated sector, the proportional importance of foreign private investment is likely to increase. Evidently, the Planners have no intention of taking their rhetoric seriously. After paying ritual homage to the idea of controlling the 'commanding heights', the Planners have in a realistic manner decided to reduce the proportion of resources devoted to public sector programmes compared to the first Plan.[12]

Part of the explanation for this change of strategy is that the authors of the 1962–8 plan were wildly optimistic in expecting that half the public sector capital investment would be derived from external sources, but the reduced expectations of the public sector derive too from the experience of public sector performance under civilian rule. Although there are some exceptions, the development corporations set up by the Regional governments generally displayed a mixture of bad planning, inefficient management, and corrupt administration. Where the enterprises established were not uneconomic to begin with, the depredations of political appointees soon took their toll. Many of the older-established public corporations (such as the Railways, the Electricity Corporation, and the Water Boards and Corporations) provided basic infrastructural requirements and did not have to be justified in terms of a strict cost-benefit analysis. The setting up of other, newer bodies, such as the Dams Authority, which was responsible for overseeing the construction of the Kainji Dam, could also be justified in terms of the long-term returns. There remained, however, a large category of Marketing Boards and Development and Housing Corporations whose operations revealed how important they were as spheres of influence and patronage for the political class rather than as cost-controlled economic enterprises.

The depredations of socially derived wealth through such agencies were one of the most important sources of grievance for trade unionists who felt that under the circumstances they could hardly be asked to hold down wage demands for the sake of 'national' development. James O'Connell has suggested that given the pressures of domestic politics, Nigeria, like many other countries, may not have the capacity to implement a plan that serves the nation equitably. As in Gunnar Myrdal's 'soft state', he suggests that, 'it is for the time being too much to expect to find in most countries a positive will-to-plan'. Even individual policies, like import controls, may save foreign exchange, 'but the economic gains made through such policies must be measured against wider issues such as the appearance of ineffectiveness in governing and the corrupted integrity of public servants'.[13]

While the integrity of the public sector was prone to atrophy as it assumed more control of the economy, the features of the 'soft state' were seen too in the attempts of the public sector to aid indigenous entrepreneurs in their competition with the foreign companies. According to Sayre P. Schatz, 'in the decade following World War II, when the foundations of present development strategy were laid, Nigerian business played an extremely modest role in the modern economy . . . [even] in 1962/3 net private investment financed by domestic sources was only 3·7% of net domestic product and this included . . . substantial outlays by foreign-owned companies incorporated in Nigeria.'[14]

In what areas, then, did Nigerians successfully compete? Existing industries in Nigeria fall into two main categories. First, about half the industries are raw-material orientated and include such diverse enterprises as abattoirs, cotton ginneries, and tin smelters (in the Northern states), rice mills, soap factories, oil extraction, and palm oil mills (in the Eastern states), and rubber processing, sawmills, and canneries (in the West and Mid-West). Second, there is a group of industries that is market-orientated and comprises enterprises like brewing, cigarette-making, furniture and metal fabrication, tyre and textile production, cement, asbestos, and bitumen processing, and assembly plants for bicycles, motor vehicles, and electrical appliances. Although Nigerians attained a measure of participation in the raw-material orientated industries, those enterprises which are market-orientated are heavily dominated by the external estate and foreign-trained management. The lack of Nigerian involvement in these industries cannot be attributed to a cultural impediment or the lack of a

'Protestant ethic'. Indeed, as John R. Harris and Mary P. Rowe have argued:

> Theories of entrepreneurship as a manifestation of social deviance or theories of underdevelopment related to a lack of entrepreneurial spirit are inapplicable in Nigeria. Nigerians appear to be actively seeking material awards, and entrepreneurship as such is socially honoured . . . Nigerians are alert to profit opportunities and can find the necessary capital for industrial projects which seem to be within their capability to exploit.[15]

What appears to have happened is that Nigerians were excluded from certain areas of profitable investment either through a traditional oligopolistic control inherited from the colonial days (the predominance of a few companies in the wholesale and retail distribution of exported goods is of central importance), or because, generally speaking, only foreign companies had the necessary expertise and financial backing to engage in enterprises which begin to make profits only after a number of years. Where finance on any scale was available to Nigerians, it was closely linked to the capture of political power by élite groups. Companies were indeed often run as extensions of a political party, while conversely, access to political power, particularly at the Regional level, was used as a means to finance private investment, or more usually, private consumption. The most extensive documentary evidence of these trends can be found in the detailed four-volume report of the Coker Commission which castigated, in no uncertain terms, the AG administration in the West. Though any quotation from the report must be highly selective given the wide range of its investigations, the case of the National Investment & Properties Co. Ltd. (NIPC), neatly exemplifies the party/business link. According to the Commission:

> Abundant evidence has been produced before us to prove that the NIPC Ltd. belongs to the AG, that no one of the shareholders who are also the only directors of the company ever paid a penny for his shares of £25,000 in the company and indeed that payment for all the shares was made through funds diverted from the NIPC Ltd. on the pretext that this money was being paid on . . . building contracts . . . We are satisfied that the present financial plight of the NIPC Ltd. has been brought about by the substantial amounts of monies (described by the Company in their books as loans to the AG, but in the books of the AG as special donations) being paid out of its funds to the AG.[16]

Sayre P. Schatz's study of the Regional loans boards in Nigeria during civilian rule also illustrates how rational economic calculations designed to test loan-worthiness were abandoned under the influence of political considerations. He cites a White Paper which investigated the activities of the Northern Nigerian Development Corporation and showed that where the loan recipients were not themselves prominent Northern politicians, applicants had to have acquired political influence if they were to succeed. The NNDC varied its rate of interest whenever it deemed it appropriate and in some cases did not charge interest at all.[17]

Those Nigerian entrepreneurs who were less close to the sources of political patronage tended to invest in areas which demanded a relatively small capital outlay and a relatively quick return. Their success in transport and construction, even against strong competition from Lebanese-owned companies, and the development of several import-substitution industries in the period of rigid import restriction during the civil war, are proof enough that an entrepreneurial spirit is not lacking.

It has been argued that for Nigerians to gain sufficient expertise to compete with the expatriate companies, investment from the public sector should be directed towards fostering small enterprises, which both contribute more to the national income than do the foreign-dominated enterprises and (as they are less capital-intensive) provide greater employment opportunities.[18] As W. Arthur Lewis asserts:

> Given the private enterprise system, the only way to industrialise Nigeria adequately is to produce a large class of Nigerian entrepreneurs with industrial experience. Small enterprise is the university where this class receives its training. Thus, looking ahead, it is more important to lay the foundations of an industrial class by helping small entrepreneurs than it is to build a few large factories – all the more so when 70 per cent of the value added by large factories accrues to foreigners.[19]

Though superficially attractive, Lewis's argument too readily assumes that the structure of the economy will permit Nigerian entrepreneurs skilled in small-scale industry to pass on to large-scale industry without at least running the risk of antagonizing entrenched expatriate interests. In the past some expatriate concerns, like the United Africa Company, have allowed some of their operations, particularly the retailing of the products they handled, to become indigenized. Foreign interests have both become more diversified and have ensconced themselves in less politically sensitive areas like banking or insurance, or enterprises at present beyond the technical or financial scope of local businessmen. It is doubtful too whether the small-scale enterprises that Lewis has in mind can provide a training ground for the skills he wishes to develop. The technology used is simple, working conditions are harsh, and the scale of operations too minute to teach anything of relevance to the conditions of factory production. Lewis has also identified the lack of entrepreneurial capacity and technical skill as the major impediment to industrialization. Entrepreneurship is not, however, lacking in Nigeria. Sayre P. Schatz has indeed specifically discounted both the shortage of entrepreneurial capacity and the shortage of capital as being the central impeding factor and instead considers environmental problems – a lack of adequate markets, suppliers, equipment etc. – as the greatest obstacles to successful indigenous business expansion.[20]

Whatever the prospects of indigenous enterprise succeeding, the discovery and exploitation of oil and natural gas in the late sixties has dramatically altered the character of Nigeria's economy. The proportion of the country's revenue derived from agricultural pursuits has already shown a big drop, and if the projections are accurate, oil revenues may soon account for over half the total available for government spending.[21] The oil revenues may, as Peter Kilby argues, free Nigeria from the 'binding constraints of inadequate domestic saving and deficient foreign exchange earnings',[22] but bar a few linkage industries planned at the terminals, it is unlikely to have any immediate effects on the structure of industrialization, or on the creation of employment.

Any permanent shift in the basically dependent character of Nigeria's economy depends largely on a massive reorientation of the government's investable surpluses towards locally owned industry and the limitation on the incursions by foreign capital. With its reservoir of human and natural resources, Nigeria is better placed than most underdeveloped countries to resist the vicious cycle of poverty and stagnation and raise the living standards of its people. But it would be foolhardy to be optimistic about Nigeria's economic potential becoming realizable and distributed with any degree of parity. Distribution of personal income is highly inequitable and there are wide disparities in inter-regional and inter-sectorial development.[23]

Moreover, under the present form of dependent capitalist development there seems little prospect of reducing consumer expenditure and the proportion appropriated for government expenditure on its own administration – both of which would be necessary for capital formation to rise appreciably. The £96 million allocated to capital expenditure on Defence and Security under the new Plan is itself a significant index of the extent to which the military are beginning to act as a political class in their own right. The annual budget allocated to the armed forces has actually increased subsequent to the collapse of Biafra, while authoritative press statements by army officers indicate that they intend maintaining the large army built up specifically for the purposes of the civil war. Underdeveloped countries are constantly at the mercy of international market forces and subject to the depletion of wasting resources like oil and mineral deposits. Nigeria is no exception to this condition, and if the benefits of the present economic boom are seen by aspirant groups to be slewed towards ultimately non-productive ends, like building up a military machine, one might expect a considerable loss in the military government's political legitimacy and capacity to govern.

The Labour Force

One of Nigeria's greatest economic assets lies in its human re-sources, the population being about double that of all the French West African territories added together, and about seven times as large as that of Ghana. The overall labour force can be considered as a repository from which are drawn the particular members of the labour force that concern this study. This section attempts, therefore, to assess the size, distribution and utilization of the labour force – by no means an easy task in view of the lack of reliable census figures. The last generally accepted population figures were those gathered in the 1952/3 census, which gave Nigeria a population of nearly 32 million. An attempt to conduct a recount in 1962 ended in a political fiasco, when each of the Regions, anxious to secure increased representation in the Federal

Parliament, inflated their population counts. By the new count, although the North showed an increase of 30% on the 1952/3 figures, it now no longer had an absolute majority of the country's population. The population in the Eastern Region had apparently increased by 71%, and in several Eastern divisions the increase was even more dramatic, ranging from 120% to 190%. The official enumerator accepted the Northern figures, but, with obvious justification, rejected those of the East as being falsified. In the event, the Northern political leaders rejected the Northern total as being an underestimate, and demanded another head count. One Northern Provincial Commissioner 'called on all Chiefs and Councillors to join in the forthcoming arrangements to make the census

TABLE 2.3

Population Estimates for Nigeria, 1952, 1962, 1963

Old Regions	1952	1962 (unofficial)	1963
North	17,573,000	22,500,000	29,777,986
West	6,400,000	10,880,000	12,811,837
East	7,497,000	13,492,000	12,338,646
Federal Territory of Lagos	272,000	675,000	675,352
Total:	31,742,000	47,547,000	55,613,821

Sources: Annual Abstracts of Statistics. Various Government Estimates.

a success.'[24] His plea did not go unheard in the North, for over seven million more people were now discovered and the percentage increase on the 1952/3 figures now jumped from 30% to 67%, thus ensuring for the North the majority of seats in the Federal Assembly.[25] The population estimates in the three successive counts are listed in Table 2.3.

Unless we are to believe the argument that the 1952/3 figures were gross underestimates, the overall figure suggested in the 1962 count probably represents the most feasible, if still high, growth rate (though the Eastern figures were clearly inflated). The figure of 55·6 million, though unlikely in 1963, is, taking into account the rising birth rate and falling death rate consequent upon improved medical facilities, not far from the truth towards the end of the sixties. The figures showing the geographical distribution of the population as shown in the 1963 census (see Table 2.4) may be open to some doubt in view of the political chicanery accompanying the count. The estimates have also been regrouped according to the twelve-state structure introduced by the Federal Military Government on 31 May 1967, but do not indicate population movements consequent on the disturbances of 1966 and the civil war itself. The statistics on the sectorial distribution of the labour force are probably less unreliable, in view of the lower absolute numbers involved and the separate issue of questionnaires to employers. A sample survey of the labour force was conducted in

TABLE 2.4

Distribution of Population by State, 1963 Census

State	Population	Area in sq. miles	Persons per sq. mile
North-Western	5,733,297	65,143	88
North-Central	4,098,305	27,108	151
Kano	5,774,842	16,630	347
North-Eastern	7,893,343	105,300	75
Benue-Plateau	4,009,408	38,929	103
Kwara	2,399,365	28,672	84
Lagos	1,443,568	1,381	1045
Western	9,487,526	29,100	326
Mid-Western	2,535,839	14,922	170
East-Central	7,227,559	11,310	639
South-Eastern	3,622,591	11,166	324
Rivers	1,544,313	7,008	220
Total:	55,769,956	356,669	*Average:* 156

Source: Government Estimates, *Nigerian Year Book 1969*, p. 21.
Note: Discrepancies in the sources have been removed in this table.

1966/7, but some doubt must be expressed as to the representativeness of this sample. In general I have used data based on the 1963 census; any statistics cited after this date should be treated with caution.

Of great consequence to the potential productive capacity of the country is the age distribution of the population, which is heavily weighted with young non-productive persons. While it should be remembered that young Nigerians are far more likely to engage in productive activities in trading or farming than their counterparts in industrialized countries, the comparative figures are nevertheless startling. Nearly 44% of Nigeria's population is below the age of fifteen which compares with 24% of the population in the

United Kingdom and about 26% in the United States of America. As T. M. Yesufu argues, the age structure of the population means that:

> Nigeria needs to invest relatively more of her wealth than the advanced countries in order to develop and maintain schools, health and social welfare facilities for its young population, and generally for the development of its manpower resources. Thus the propensity to consume is high, while savings and investment tend to be further depressed owing to non-productive expenditure to support a high rate of non-productive persons.[26]

Of the remaining 56% of the population, when exclusions are made for retired persons, for university and secondary school students, and for the non-participating members of the female population, Nigeria's actual labour force is half the population or less, of the order of 28 million. By the latest reliable estimates, the occupational structure of the labour force includes 19·5 million (70%) involved in agriculture and allied pursuits, 4 million (15%) engaged in commerce, about 1·8 million wage-earners, and just under three million people who are self-employed as traders, craftsmen, transporters, etc.[27]

For our purposes, the figure of 1·8 million wage-earners is most significant. Though still a small percentage of the labour force (6·4%) and an even smaller percentage of Nigeria's population (3·2%), the new figure indicates a phenomenal growth in wage employment since 1939 when the first estimates were made. At that time the wage-earning population was reckoned at 182,000, which included 25,100 employed in the Cameroons plantations (the Cameroons, at that time being jointly administered with Nigeria).[28] In the last twelve years the number of wage-earners has nearly trebled, though this rate of increase has nowhere near kept pace with the demand for wage employment. The distribution of the wage-earning force over the various sectors of the economy has been tabulated from those establishments employing ten or more workers which responded to statistical questionnaires issued in 1961, 1962, 1964, and 1965 (Table 2.5).

The large disparity between the total wage employment tabulated in the employment returns (765,000 persons) and the current estimates of 1·8 million persons can be explained on three scores. First, the earlier figures are probably underestimated;[29] secondly, small establishments employing less than ten persons (which in the East alone employed an estimated 28,721 in 1962)[30] are excluded

TABLE 2.5

Reported Employment by Industry Group (1961, 1962, 1964, 1970) and by Type of Employer (1964)

Industry Group	Dec. 1961 Total	Dec. 1962 Total	December 1964 Total	December 1964 Government (a)*	December 1964 Non-Government (b)†	1970 Estimates only to nearest 1,000 Total
Agriculture, forestry, and fishing	37,254	31,308	35,116	17,876	17,240	70,000
Mining and quarrying	27,347	47,817	51,035	216	50,819	55,000
Manufacturing	34,263	53,125	61,864	3,716	58,148	145,000
Construction	89,303	100,793	78,020	28,006	50,014	105,000
Electricity etc.	11,248	16,545	14,939	4,614	10,325	20,000
Commerce	37,551	38,925	45,165	855	44,310	55,000
Transport, storage, and communications	42,737	49,831	58,068	17,851	40,217	50,000
Services	143,172	180,461	217,327	147,308	70,019	265,000
Total:	422,875	518,805	561,534	220,442	341,092	765,000

Sources: Adapted from the *Annual Abstract of Statistics* (Federal Office of Statistics, 1966) Table 3.1, p. 22. 1970 Figures from *Second National Development Plan 1970–1974* (Federal Government Printer, n.d.) p. 329, Table 6. (Projected from 1965 data).

* Includes Federal, Regional, and Local Governments.

† Includes Public Corporations, Commercial, and Voluntary Establishments.

from the survey; thirdly, the coverage of establishments employing over ten persons is incomplete: the 1965 Establishments Survey, for example, only had about a 75% response rate.

Despite the incompleteness of the figures, one significant feature can be derived from the 1964 breakdown, that is the high proportion of wage-earners working for the public sector. Even with workers in the public corporations excluded, the percentage employed by the government is almost 40%. With the corporations included – and, in any case, these are identified in the minds of most workers as part of the government – the percentage is closer to 60% and may be more. The significance of this percentage should be obvious. The government's position as the prime employer means that it is in a crucial position in the determination of wages and in generally setting the standards for industrial relations, a theme that is elaborated in Chapter 6.

Despite the large increases in the wage-earning sector, unemployment of the labour force is a persistent and growing problem in the Nigerian economy. 'Unemployment' is itself a problematic concept. Individuals may be employed on a part-time basis, unemployed only seasonally, underemployed, or simply describe themselves as unemployed when what they mean is that they have not yet found employment that meets their job expectations. Far then from being a 'hard' statistical category which can be gauged accurately from the unemployment registers of the Ministry Labour Exchanges, a description of an unemployed person should ideally involve both an objective index of the under-utilization of an individual's labour power (where his skills and training could be used in a more productive capacity) and a subjective index of the individual's perception of being unemployed or underemployed.

The very opaqueness of the term unemployment has led Keith Hart and John Weeks virtually to abandon the notion altogether and to speak instead of employment in the 'informal' sector as opposed to employment in the 'formal', i.e. salary and wage-earning, sector.[31] While such a distinction is useful in counteracting the culture-imported notions of unemployment that have often been applied in underdeveloped countries, the perception by both the social actors and decision-takers involved, that an 'unemployment problem' exists, is also an important datum. The dislocative effects of a precarious urban life appear to many to be less onerous than the potentialities or possibility of employment in the formal sector, and the number of 'applicants' and job-seekers continues to rise. Whether their assessment is rationally based or not, governments in many poor countries appear also to believe that the increase of numbers of urban dwellers not in the wage sector may disrupt a precarious political equilibrium, especially, as was feared in Nigeria, where these may be added to by demobilized soldiers.

None the less, such attempts as have been made in Nigeria to alleviate the problem, through the development of small industry or through making rural life more attractive, have either not been seriously undertaken or have met with general failure. The announcement in the 1970–4 Plan that a National Youth Corps is to be set up, with an initial intake of 2,000 youths in four camps, is, in the context of the overall problem, a drop in the ocean.[32] T. M. Yesufu has, however, strongly argued the case that if 'unemployment' continues to rise it may be necessary to slow down the rate of growth in order to ameliorate the situation:

> . . . economic policies designed merely to ensure a high rate of growth of the national product are no longer adequate for Nigeria; and it cannot now be taken for granted that measures which promote economic development will of themselves necessarily create enough job opportunities for the masses of the unemployed. The acceptance of the employment objective as a cornerstone in Nigeria's economic and development policy has therefore become imperative. This implies that employment creation must be a conscious objective of the development planners even if it means a reduced overall growth rate in the short run.[33]

Contributing to the failure of the supply of jobs in the formal sector to keep pace with the demand is the tendency for large-scale industry to be capital-intensive (a refinery in Port Harcourt for example costing £13,000,000 employs only 350 people, while a flour mill in Apapa employs 100 workers). While such low labour inputs are the general feature of a dependent capitalist economy, low labour intensity in the petro-chemical industry and oil extraction are built into the nature of the productive process itself. Two additional reasons for the failure of manufacturing to create employment opportunities may be mentioned. (a) Foreign-owned enterprises may be more interested in utilizing their machinery in setting up a production line than they are in solving Nigeria's employment problem. (b) It may in fact be cheaper for industrialists to set up capital-intensive industries. This is because Nigerian labour is only apparently cheap and the low absolute cost has to be set against the high cost of training and supervising a largely unskilled labour force. Over two-thirds of the labour force could be so categorized in 1962, as Table 2.6 demonstrates.

A special area of difficulty is integrating into the formal economy the large number of school-leavers whose aspirations, it is suggested, may have been realistic a decade ago, but are now unrelated to their job opportunities.[34] Unemployment levels are thought by Nigerian planners to be highest among school-leavers who have acquired a primary school education but fall below a School Certificate or its equivalent, this group accounting for 59%

TABLE 2.6

Division of Labour Force by Skill, 1962

Occupation	No.	% of Total
Professional and administrative	32,793	6
Minor professional, clerical, skilled, sales	134,667	26
'General' (unskilled) labour	351,345	69
	518,805	100

Source: *Annual Abstract of Statistics*, Table 3.4, 1964 (1962 figures).

of all unemployed persons.[35] The age distribution of the assumed unemployed group is also heavily sloped towards young people, as Table 2.7 shows. The geographical distribution of officially estimated unemployment showed in 1963 a countrywide rate of urban unemployment of the adult labour force running at 14·6% with towns in the Northern States and Western State (with the significant exception of Abeokuta) showing rather lower rates of unemployment than those of the Eastern States, the Mid-West State, and Lagos (Table 2.8).

An International Labour Office Survey particularly concerned with unemployment among school-leavers in three villages in the Western State indicated that 'the group made little or no attempt to offer to labour jobs for example on major construction works such as dams, road-building, and similar unskilled work, mainly for status reasons'.[36] Over 57% of the group had, however, tried to look for jobs in the Lagos conurbation. Both the ILO study and the attempt by Nigerian Planners to set up a National Youth Corps (referred to earlier) are based on the assumptions that Nigerian school-leavers are totally immune to market forces and educated 'out of their background'. The Second National Development Plan specifically proposes measures to remove young people from the labour market and 'sublimate their energy and talent into more socially desirable channels'.[37] That these assumptions may be exaggerated or not universal throughout the country, may be inferred from some comparative data collected in Ghana. There, Margaret Peil found that aspirations were in many cases tied to job prospects, that aspirations varied regionally and that where aspirations were unreasonably high, job *expectations* were not. Contrary too to the conventional view that school-leavers are not

TABLE 2.7

Age Distribution of Assumed Unemployment, 1966–7

Age	% Share of total unemployment
15–17	19·6
18–23	50·2
24–29	16·5
30–35	7·1
36–40	2·3
41–45	1·7
46–50	1·7
51–55	0·8

Source: Labour Force Sample Survey 1966–7. Adopted for Federal Republic of Nigeria, *Second National Development Plan,* Table 3, p. 312

prepared to get their hands dirty, Dr. Peil found that the most coveted jobs were mechanic, electrician, clerk, factory worker, and teacher (in that order), and that many school-leavers in the Volta Region expected to farm.[38]

Evidence such as that produced by Margaret Peil shows that school-leavers may be more responsive to market forces than previously assumed and, as Keith Hart and John Weeks argue, may not in any case be totally unemployed – but employed instead in the informal sector. Thus, in addition to 'hidden' unemployment which economists have told us to expect, we may find too the phenomenon of 'hidden employment'. While this conception does not totally 'abolish' the unemployment problem it does question the spectre-like proportions that the problem has assumed among economic planners. Many school-leavers have not yet broken into the wage-sector of the Nigerian economy, but what sort of social universe confronts those who are already there?

TABLE 2.8
Official Estimates of Unemployment, 1963

Old Region	Town	Estimated unemployed adults	
		Number	*% of Labour Force*
Federal Territory	Lagos	50,776	15·5
North	Kaduna	4,790	10·8
	Kano	5,859	5·7
	Zaria	6,143	10·0
	Bukuru	7,275	23·7
	Jos	1,563	19·7
	All Northern towns shown	25,630	10·6
East	Enugu	15,413	19·5
	Onitsha	17,421	26·3
	Port Harcourt	11,236	16·1
	Aba	9,746	21·1
	Umuahia	1,197	15·4
	Calabar	5,710	14·4
	All Eastern towns shown	60,723	17·6
West	Ibadan	20,979	3·6
	Ife	18,357	19·7
	Oshogbo	11,828	12·5
	Agege	3,928	23·3
	Abeokuta	25,854	34·6
	Mushin	5,780	14·6
	All Western towns shown	86,126	11·6
Mid-West	Benin	6,599	15·4
	Sapele	6,318	21·7
	Warri	3,163	22·9
	All Mid-Western towns shown	16,080	17·8

Source: National Manpower Board, *Urban Unemployment Survey, 1963* (Lagos, Mimeographed, 1963), Table 2. Reproduced in F. O. Fajana, *Wage Differentials and Economic Development In Nigeria 1947–1967* (Ph.D. thesis, University of London, 1971) p. 266.

The Social Face of Industry
and the Employment Relationship

According to Clark Kerr and his collaborators, the worker, in the early stages of industrialization, is:

> . . . more prone to absenteeism, prolonged and sporadic withdrawal from industrial work, wild-cat stoppages, naked violence and destruction of machines and property . . . The worker may protest not necessarily by strike action, but by lack of attention, co-operation and morale. Violent fights, flare ups, machine or parts breakage, theft, the use of narcotics . . .[39]

How far does this characterization of a neophyte work force apply to Nigeria's workers? In my view only in a very limited way. Despite the comparative focus of the influential Kerr study, the material was largely derived from studies of the economic history of western nations where the wrench from the countryside to an urban factory-based mode of production was more complete than that in many African countries. As Margaret Peil has argued in her study of *The Ghanaian Factory Worker*, '. . . industries in today's developing countries are usually in cities where workers in many factories and in non-industrial employment are all living together'.[40] In examining wider aspects of the 'industrial man' thesis she argues that the nature of the work experience does not play as central a role in the Ghanaian context as it did in the early stages of western industrialization:

> Structural formation of Ghanaian society is proceeding rather slowly, and the workers appear to be well adjusted to the society as it is today rather than anticipating the modern, industrial society which may one day appear. Early socialization and contacts outside the workplace are more important in shaping attitudes and behaviour than is work experience.[41]

As regards the other aspects of Kerr's argument, it is true that it would not be difficult to find a number of instances of 'anomic' behaviour in Nigeria's labour history[42] and it is possible too that workers with little experience of harsh factory conditions (like, say, those obtaining in the textile mills of the Northern States) may be prone to an anti-industrial mode of behaviour. It is true too that many unskilled workers use drugs, though not narcotics, regularly.

The eating of kola nuts, a mild stimulant, is, for example, a socially acceptable, indeed often socially required, form of drug-taking. In addition rolled marijuana (locally called hemp) is widely smoked, customarily as a means of relaxation after a hard day's work. Among employees this is virtually exclusively an activity of unskilled workers – wage- and salary-earners above this level having acquired western tastes in drug-taking, notably in the consumption of manufactured beer.

In general, however, studies on groups of workers that have been carried out in Nigeria show striking evidence of a full acceptance of the work ethic. Whether this derives from the social and economic security that the trade unions, improvement unions, tribal associations, and mutual aid societies provide, or from the fear of the loss of a livelihood, is uncertain, but W. H. L. Bispham argues persuasively that in Nigeria 'There is now a ready-made labour force fully willing to work in industrial conditions, and, as far as the evidence goes, capable of doing so . . . despite stresses . . . the fact remains that the men are there and it is the jobs to which they are anxious to commit themselves that are not.' [43]

Bispham also points to a striking degree of double-think involved in the depiction of the African workers. The very indices of the internalization of the industrial ethic that are used – such as a measure of labour turnover – are used in the under-developed world to show 'low labour commitment', while the same phenomenon in the industrialized world is often approved of as increasing 'labour mobility'. In any case it has been empirically shown that the rate of labour turnover is not vastly dissimilar from that expected in the technologically advanced countries.[44] Moreover, the extent of absenteeism and labour turnover is often used to indicate the lack of conformism to the industrial process, quite without reference to the prevailing factory conditions, the wages paid and the job security *offered*. What would thus be a response of any wage-earner to intolerable working conditions is misinterpreted as low commitment.

Several studies have now shown that where reasonable conditions prevail job satisfaction and productivity are high and absentee rates low.[45] In Nigeria, H. Dieter Seibel has conducted two carefully researched surveys on Nigerian factories, the Nigerian Textile Mills in Ikeja and the Guinness beer factory. Though considerable variations existed in, for example, the average length of time stayed in each job (the Textile Mills' fifteen months to Guinness's ten months) and the average wage (£11.5.0 to

Guinness's £13.3.0) both indicated low absenteeism and little job dissatisfaction.[46]

Despite the Nigerian worker's acceptance of the norms of new productive relationships, this is not to say that he does not experience hardships and articulate grievances, both of the kind that reflect wider social and political tensions operative in the society, and those which may be conceived as special or characteristic features of his day-to-day employment relationship. It is these more narrowly considered relationships that I am concerned with here.

One such issue relates to the degree of Nigerian participation in the management of the economy. The overwhelming dominance of expatriate and Lebanese capital and management in the private sector of the economy has already been described. This has meant that the number of Nigerians who have access to supervisory positions within private industry is severely limited. With the coming of independence the demand for Nigerianization in the civil service and public corporations was given added incentive. Barring the attachment of a few specialized experts to individual ministries, and the remnants of the British administration in the Northern States, the process of Nigerianization in the public service is virtually complete. Private industry was similarly pressured by the politicians and trade unions to follow suit, so far with little demonstrable effect. The Lebanese-owned firms are notably remiss in this respect; but most other expatriate firms have tended to fob off demands for Nigerianization by appointing a few Nigerians to sinecurial positions on management boards, or elevating a small number of Nigerians to junior supervisory positions. The more radical ideologues of the unions are especially contemptuous of those Nigerians who have accepted titular boardroom appointments. A correspondent in a trade union newspaper describes their role as 'perfidious', and characterizes their functions in these terms:

> The typical 'oyinbo dudu' is given a high-sounding title and a fabulous salary with little responsibility. His main qualification is the ability to pass damaging information about government functionaries and fellow Nigerians in private industry, who have the integrity to distinguish between loyalty to country and loyalty to employer. It is surprising in spite of all the evidence, that up to now we do not seem to realize the crucial nature of a clear-cut government policy on Nigerianization in expatriate firms. I say critical because no country can be really free when all the top jobs in the private sector

are held by expatriates – and usually expatriates of the wrong type, who in nine cases out of ten are unsympathetic to our economic plans and problems.[47]

Some trade unionists see the domination of foreign capital as explicitly involving Nigeria in a neo-colonialist relationship, and argue for the nationalization of the major industries. According to Wahab Goodluck, a Nigerian Trade Union Congress (NTUC) leader:

> In 1960 when Nigeria threw off the yoke of British colonialism, like a ravenous pack of economic wolves the U.S. monopolies, the West German capitalists, the sly, cunning Israelis and a host of others descended on Nigeria's virgin economic field each helping himself to the best picking.[48]

For the worker on the shop-floor the social distance between himself and the management means that, as T. M. Yesufu has remarked, 'labour-management relations in Nigeria have for long partly assumed the character of race relations'.[49] A columnist in the NTUC newspaper who writes under the pseudonym of 'Ombudsman' is loud in his charges against racialist managements. While complaints of this kind may not be representative of larger expatriate concerns, where working conditions and job security are usually better than in Nigerian or Lebanese-owned concerns, Ombudsman's column usually contains two or three items concerning racialist managements every week. Two examples may illustrate the sort of grievance involved:

> (i) . . . the workers of a renowned Indian furniture factory in Mushin . . . made me to understand that their managing director, Mr. J. is very fond of using abusive words on them. I am reliably informed that the managing chief substituted such words as 'bastard', 'fool' and 'blackie' for greetings.
>
> (ii) Over to you Mr. Stores Chief (of a Chinese-owned machine tools store) . . . I must confess that I am learning for the first time, that is if you can confirm it, that you freely abuse yourselves as part of 'culture' in your part of the world? . . . One thing is clear and that is that you abused the African workers simply because you feel they deserve the abuse being Africans. And that tends to show that you're a racist.[50]

The racial factor is an important catalyst in strikes and other industrial disturbances that are concerned with 'dignity' questions. Workers appear to have a strong operational concept of social justice, which includes an assertive (though hazy) definition of workers' rights, and an insistence on the correct forms of address by supervisory personnel. In this respect the cultural isolation of the expatriate community provokes labour-management disharmony, especially when supervisors insist on addressing their workers in a clubhouse pidgin which, as T. M. Yesufu has noted, is usually 'devoid of the finer points of politeness and good humour'.[51] The lack of communication between workers and management was one of the most important precipitating factors in an attempt to assert workers' control in a plastics factory in Lagos early in 1969. 'Participant' observation of the strike revealed that the idea of seizing the factory had entirely spontaneous origins – none of the workers I spoke to appeared to be aware of the European anarcho-syndicalist tradition or the moves towards worker democracy in some of the East European countries. The workers, besides demanding better wages and medical facilities, complained of the arrogance of the Syrian and Lebanese management and the 'frequent dismissal of African workers on flimsy excuses'. The plan to 'sack the management and take control of the company' was described by the secretary of the Metaloplastica (Nigeria) Ltd. African Workers Union as a 'prize for their long suffering'.[52] Several workers were apparently thinking of marketing the goods they would continue to produce in the management's absence, but the plan did not meet general acceptance and the management was able to reassert its control after making some concessions to the demands of the workers.

Another illustrative case of the congruence of racial 'dignity' and political issues reinforcing an economic grievance concerns the workers of the Federal Palace Hotel in Lagos. In a rather extra-ordinarily phrased petition addressed to cabinet ministers indivi-dually and dated January 1962, the union attacked the (then) Lebanese management for *inter alia* 'Greekinizing all their com-panies instead of Nigerianizing', for practising racial discrimina-tion and 'South Africanism', for bribing ministers, for using 'forced labour' and for 'gross neglect of African Personality'. The petition is long, so one (literal) extract must suffice to give its flavour:

> The first impression each guest has on entry to the Federal Palace Hotel is the Grecian Goddess fountain, with a bowl, throwing out water. As one of the able receptionists at the Hotel, the regular question from the guests is, 'Is that lady a Nigerian?' On reply, they shrug, mimicking their lips. My Hon. Sir, this monument is a national disgrace, slight and challenge to all the inhabitants and nationalists of this peaceful, hospitable and well guided nation . . . it would be

shameful, suicidal and disgraceful for any of us to sell out our National interests, dignity and personality at the alter of Mescandes Cars, Plots and Money from the Directors of this establishment; and paying noctrial visits, either in person or their wives. We are not saying that our Ministers are coarsed and bought over, but it pains us more than our Ministers to hear the Directors boost that our Ministers are in their pocket . . . Telling our foreign guests that they have got a hand in the Government of our land.[53]

The management was also accused of a 'divide and rule policy' in that most of the Ibo workers (who were apparently thought more militant) were transferred elsewhere, while the Yorubas who were employed in their stead were cautioned not to join the trade union. While the workers' protest against this supports my general position that class solidarity usually cuts across ethnic loyalties in the lower-paid sector of the economy, inter-ethnic relationships in employment are complicated by the differential regard for certain classes of work based on ethnic stereotypes. The problem has a dual origin. On the one hand, as has been argued in Chapter 1, on the basis of unvalidated prejudices the European companies and colonial administration regarded some ethnic groups as 'more suitable' for certain types of work. Sometimes, however, discriminatory employment patterns were based on more rational grounds, e.g. those with a greater exposure to western education (first the Yorubas, then the Southerners as a whole) were recruited for minor administrative posts. On the other hand, some ethnic groups had traditional aversions to certain forms of work that were thought to be unbefitting or demeaning. Herbert A. Tulatz provides an interesting example where traditional attitudes influenced the decision of a group of Lagos nightsoilmen not to continue in employment. Customarily, nightsoil work in Lagos and in other towns was performed by a group of Egbe workers. They had long been subjected to the ridicule of the people of Lagos and this was felt in their home villages to reflect badly on the status of the whole group. When a strike occurred late in 1959, the Egbe and Yabba Descendants' Union in Lagos took the opportunity to demand that their co-villagers down tools on pain of a £20 fine. The district head, the Elegbe of Egbe in like manner warned all his subjects to give up this 'shameful and dirty work'. The social ostracism proved too much to bear for the 200 Egbe workers, all of whom struck solidly, and sought alternative employment.[54] Other aversions to manual work based on traditional attitudes have been described in the case of the Mid-Western workers.[55]

The division of labour based on traditionally accepted ethnic 'preserves' may in fact provide part of the explanation of the generally amicable inter-ethnic relations in employment. Where, however, an upward socially mobile ethnic group has challenged what another ethnic group regards as its preserve, a good deal of discord occurs. This is especially noticeable in Yoruba-Ibo tensions over civil service appointments from the early decade of this century. In the 1920s it was estimated that Yorubas had over 40% of the total educated persons in prestige occupations, while only 11% of these valued jobs were filled by Ibos.[56] In subsequent decades the percentage of educated Ibos rose dramatically and seriously threatened the Yoruba hegemony of professional occupations. Ethnic competition in the intendant class and among professionals was given constitutional sanction by the acceptance of the Macpherson Constitution in 1951, by which the structure and organization of the civil service was regionalized. Inter-ethnic hostility was further intensified when the Northerners demanded a share in civil service appointments commensurate with their political power. The determining factor in inter-ethnic competition in the public service was that the logic of the devolution of political power to the Regions clashed with the meritocratic principles that were supposed to govern recruitment and promotion in the services. It is hardly surprising that an educated Southerner resented having to accept the authority of a less-qualified Northerner, or that acrimonious cynicism about posts, that were only in theory open to all ethnic groups, was widespread.

While ethnic tensions to some extent percolated down to all levels of employment, inter-group friction was primarily manifested in the higher and middle echelons of the intendant class in public employment, and in those types of employment that were directly under political patronage (for example, the Regional corporations). Wage, as opposed to salary earners, were never infected with the ethnic virus to as great an extent; and often indeed held positive and complimentary attitudes towards other ethnic groups.

As evidence for these assertions we may cite some of H. Dieter Seibel's findings in the factories he studied. In the Nigerian Textile Mill a clear majority of workers stated that although they liked their own ethnic group best, they preferred working in mixed gangs. One commented, 'You learn a lot from other tribes,' while another justified his preference by saying 'I believe in one Nigeria.' Some non-Yoruba said of the Yoruba 'I am in their land

and they are kind to me,' while a non-Ibo said of the Ibo that 'they don't discriminate', 'they read the Bible'. The most positive stereotype was that of the Hausa, who were variously character-ized by the non-Hausa as 'better', 'honest', 'sincere' and straight-forward'. In the Guinness factory that Seibel studied over 40% of the workers there maintained that they had no preference for any one ethnic group in leisure activities,[57] findings that were substan-tially repeated in a larger sample (509 workers in ten industrial firms in Lagos and Ibadan) that Seibel used in an article on inter-ethnic relations. He writes:

> I started from the hypothesis that ethnic feelings among Nigerian workers are very strong. . . This hypothesis has been falsified . . . I found that attitudes and actual behaviour are more in favour of ethnic heterogeneity than ethnic homogeneity – not only at the working place but to an increasing extent during leisure.[58]

In this author's own smaller survey (further details of which are reported in Chapter 4 and tabulated in Appendix I) a question designed to see what influence the prosecution of the civil war and the expression in the media of bitter inter-ethnic sentiments had had on the attitudes that Seibel noted, was phrased as follows: 'Would you be prepared to work side-by-side with Ibos after the war is over?' All but one of the sixty-nine respondents answered affirmatively and although the question simply called for a Yes/No answer, some added indignant comments such as 'Why not?' and 'why do you ask this question?' (Appendix I, Question 76) An overwhelming majority (73%) were also willing, if asked, to send money to workers in the war areas. And this despite the fact that there was currently operating a 5% levy on the workers' wages in the interests of the Federal war effort. Of course, expressing willing-ness to contribute does not itself tell us how many would actually respond if the hat were passed round, but it does indicate a certain feeling of identity with fellow workers in their moment of plight. I also had occasion to interview a group of Ibadan workers whose union was organized by an Ibo general secretary, most of whom were of the opinion that an Ibo would be likely to achieve better results for their union than would a member of another ethnic group. This attitude typifies an often striking ambivalence in the use of ethnic stereotypes. On the one hand, those who are already predisposed towards anti-Ibo sentiment, cite the supposed 'go-getting', 'acquisitive' qualities of the Ibo as validating evidence of their prejudices. On the other hand these same qualities are cited with approval where Ibo are thought to provide useful functions. Often positive regard for the Ibo is expressed at the expense of the person's own community; the Yoruba in particular evinced attitudes of 'self-hatred'.

While I would argue that factory-floor relationships between ethnic groups are generally amicable, this generalization by no means excludes the possibility that tensions present or fomented at other levels, particularly in so far as ethnic hostility is used in the struggle for power, will feed back into the industrial situation and occasionally override class loyalties derived from a common work experience. As has been argued earlier, work experience is not so determinate as totally to condition roles that are focused on experiences outside the working relationship, and where the society itself is undermined by ethnic tensions workers cannot help but be affected to some measure by this.

Another issue generating tensions in the employment relationship concerns the question of grading. Differential pay scales and conditions of service for different parts of the country were inherited from the colonial government, but some differentials are also expressions of status differences that were accorded recognition in the post-independence period. Nurses trained in the United Kingdom, for example, were paid on a different scale from those trained in Nigeria, though the indigenously trained nurses claimed an equivalence in academic standards. The Commission set up by the government to review wages and salaries in 1964 recommended that the regrading of posts be considered as the issue was repeatedly raised by petitioners:

> Although grading does not form part of our terms of reference, the claims for regrading, for the creation of new posts, and for the adjustment of disparities in grading as between persons performing the same kind of duties in different parts are numerous . . . so important is this issue that we respectfully request that the Government should regard it as a matter of top priority that grading teams be set up to review all the claims.[59]

Following the report of the grading team that was set up in response to the Commission's request,[60] a great deal of trade union energy was spent in trying to remove the many anomalies that the grading team brought to light.

While questions of racial discrimination, Nigerianization, interethnic tensions and status differentiation, provide the social backdrop to employment conditions and act as galvanizing forces for the unions, essentially these issues are of secondary importance compared with the number of unembellished wage demands that the unions present. The nature of these demands and their relationship to the wider political forces in play are reserved for later discussion.

NOTES

1. Kilby, P. *Industrialisation in an Open Economy: Nigeria 1945–1966* (Cambridge: Cambridge University Press, 1969), pp. 59–65.
2. For a discussion of the shifting metropolitan-satellite relationship in the post-colonial period *see* Ojedokun, O. 'The Changing Pattern of Nigeria's International Economic Relations: The Decline of the Colonial Nexus, 1960–1966', *The Journal of Developing Areas*, 1972, 6, pp. 535–54.
3. Sokolski, A. *The Establishment of Manufacturing in Nigeria* (New York and London: Praeger, 1965), p. 30.
4. Henderson, J. P. 'Wage Negotiation and Legislation in Nigeria', *Seminar Paper* (Economic and Agricultural Development Institute, Michigan State University, 1964).
5. Lewis, W. A. *Reflections on Nigeria's Economic Growth* (Paris: Organization for Economic Co-operation and Development, 1967), p. 23.
6. Federal Republic of Nigeria, *Second National Development Plan, 1970–1974* (Lagos: The Government Printer, n.d.), p. 104.
7. Bhambri, R. S. 'Second Development Plan: A Selective Appraisal', *Nigerian Journal of Economic and Social Studies*, 1971, 13 (2), p. 183.
8. Lewis, W. A. op. cit., pp. 9, 26.
9. Estimates from Bhambri, R. S. (Unpublished seminar paper, Ahmadu Bello University, 1971) cited in Waterman, P. *Neo-Colonialism, Communism and the Nigerian Trade Union Congress* (M.Soc.Sci. dissertation, University of Birmingham, 1972), p. 10.
10. Federal Republic of Nigeria, *Second National Development Plan*, p. 259.
11. ibid., p. 32.
12. Bhambri, R. S. 'Second Development Plan', p. 193.
13. O'Connell, J. 'Political Constraints on Planning: Nigeria as a Case Study in the Developing World', *Nigerian Journal of Economic and Social Studies*, 1971, 13 (1), pp. 48, 49.
14. Schatz, S. P. *Economics, Politics and Administration in Government Lending* (Ibadan: OUP for the Nigerian Institute of Social and Economic Research, 1970), p. vii.

15. Harris, J. R. and Rowe, M. P. 'Entrepreneurial Patterns in the Nigerian Sawmilling Industry', *Nigerian Journal of Economic and Social Studies*, 1966, 8 (1), p. 67.
16. Federation of Nigeria, *Report of the Coker Commission of Inquiry into the Affairs of Certain Statutory Corporations in Western Nigeria* (Lagos: Federal Ministry of Information, 1962), Vol. IV, Paras, 7, 8.
17. Schatz, S. P. op. cit., pp. 51, 52.
18. A pioneer survey of small industry in Eastern Nigeria by Peter Kilby indicated that this small-scale industry (employing less than ten persons), which had been undocumented in employment surveys, employed three times as many persons as large-scale industry. *See* Kilby, P. *The Development of Small Industry in Eastern Nigeria* (Enugu: Ministry of Commerce in Eastern Nigeria and USAID, 1962).
19. Lewis, W. A. op. cit., p. 28.
20. Schatz, S. P. 'Economic Environment and Private Enterprise in West Africa', *The Economic Bulletin of Ghana, 1964*, 7 (4).
21. Kilby, P. op. cit., 1969, p. 16; *West Africa* (London) 26 September 1970, p. 1111.
22. Kilby, P. loc. cit.
23. For a wide-ranging discussion of these issues see Teriba, O. and Phillips, O. A. 'Income Distribution and National Integration', *Nigerian Journal of Economic and Social Studies*, 1971, 13 (1) pp. 77–122. *See also passim*, chapter 6, for some remarks on the wage structure.
24. Cited in Mackintosh, J. P. *et al. Nigerian Government and Politics* (London: Allen & Unwin, 1966), p. 552.
25. For a discussion of the political issues surrounding the census see ibid., pp. 547–9 and pp. 551–6. Further discussion of the census figures can be found in Aluko, S. A. 'How Many Nigerians? An Analysis of Nigeria's Census, Problems 1901–1963', *Journal of Modern African Studies*, 1965, 3 (3), pp. 371–92.
26. Yesufu, T. M. *Labour in the Nigerian Economy* (Lagos: Nigerian Broadcasting Corporation, October Lectures, 1967), p. 5.
27. ibid., p. 6. Based on Reports of the National Manpower Board published for the most part in the mid-sixties.
28. *See* Orde-Browne, G. St. J. *Labour Conditions in West Africa* (London: HMSO for the Colonial Office, 1941).
29. The estimated number of strikers in the General Strike of 1964, for example, almost equalled the number said to be employed in these sectors in the same year. Not even the unions boasted a 100% turnout.
30. Kilby, P. op. cit., 1962.
31. Hart, K. 'Informal Income Opportunities and the Structure of Employment in Ghana' (Brighton, Institute of Development Studies Conference Paper, September 1971); Weeks, J. 'Employment and the Growth of Towns' (African Studies Association Conference Paper, University of Birmingham, September 1972) and seminar presentations by both writers to the Centre of West African Studies, University of Birmingham.
32. Federal Republic of Nigeria, *Second National Development Plan*, p. 262.
33. Yesufu, T. M. op. cit., pp. 8, 9.
34. *See* Callaway, A. 'Unemployment among African School Leavers', *Journal of Modern African Studies*, 1963, 1 (3), pp. 351–71.

35. Federal Republic of Nigeria, *Second National Development Plan*, p. 312. Figures from a 1966/7 Labour Force Sample Survey.
36. Calcott, D. 'The Background and Conditions of Unemployed School Leavers in Three Rural Towns of the Western State of Nigeria', *Working Paper No. 61* (Geneva, ILO for the Ministry of Economic Planning and Social Development, Western State, 1967).
37. Federal Republic of Nigeria, *Second National Development Plan*, p. 314.
38. Peil, M. 'Aspirations and Social Structure: A West African Example', *Africa*, 1968, 38 (1), pp. 71–8. Caroline Hutton in her Uganda study found a 'general lack of hostility to farming' among school leavers. Hutton, C. 'Unemployment in Kampala and Jinja, Uganda', *Canadian Journal of African Studies*, 1969, 3 (2), pp. 431–40.
39. Kerr, C., Dunlop, J. T., Harbison, F., and Myers, C. A., *Industrialism and Industrial Man* (Cambridge: Harvard University Press, 1960), pp. 30, 208, 209.
40. Peil, M. *The Ghanaian Factory Worker: Industrial Man in Africa* (Cambridge: Cambridge University Press, 1972), p. 220.
41. ibid., pp. 219, 220.
42. For some documentation on this see Hughes, A. and Cohen, R. *Towards the Emergence of a Nigerian Working Class: the Social Identity of the Lagos Labour Force, 1897–1939* (Occasional Paper, Faculty of Commerce and Social Science, University of Birmingham, Series D, No. 7, November 1971) pp. 21–36.
43. Bispham, W. H. L. 'The Concept and Measurement of Labour Commitment and its Relevance to Nigerian Development', *Nigerian Journal of Economic and Social Studies*, March 1964, 6 (1), pp. 55, 56.
44. Report of the Sixth Inter-African Labour Conference, March 1961. CCTA/CSA Labour VI (61) 35.
45. Kilby, P. 'African Labour Productivity Reconsidered', *The Economic Journal*, June 1961, vol. LXXI, pp. 273–91.
46. Seibel, H. D. *Labour in a Nigerian Industrial Firm* (Mimeographed, April 1964). The author expresses his thanks to Mr. N. Rigos, the Manager of Nigerian Textile Mills, for allowing him to see a copy of this report; and *Industrial Labour in Nigeria* (Mimeographed, Nigerian Institute of Social and Economic Research, 1964).
47. Alase, T. A. 'Nigerianisation . . . Here's Contra Move from Alien Firms', *Advance* NTUC newspaper, 17–23 November 1968. ('Oyinbo dudu' – white lackey – literally: white black).
48. Goodluck, W. 'Neo-colonialism and the Nigerian Crisis', *Advance*, 16–22 March 1969.
49. Yesufu, T. M. *An Introduction to Industrial Relations in Nigeria* (London: OUP for Nigerian Institute of Social and Economic Research, 1962), p. 100.
50. *Advance* (i) 'Even a Labourer deserves Respect', 25 February–2 March 1968. (ii) 'There's No Room for Racism Here, Mr. Chinaman', 7–13 July 1968.
51. Yesufu, T. M. op. cit., 1962, p. 101.
52. *New Nigerian* (Kaduna) 25 February 1969.
53. 'Petition by the Federal Palace Hotel African Workers' Union', January 1962. Copy in author's possession.

54. Tulatz, H. A. *Die Gewerkschaftsentwicklung Nigerias* (Hanover: Verlag für Literatur und Zeitgeschehen, 1963), pp. 21, 22.

55. Wober, J. M. *Psychological Factors in the Adjustment to Industrial Life among Employees of a Firm in (Sapele) Southern Nigeria* (Edinburgh: Department of Social Anthropology, September 1966).

56. Coleman, J. F. *Nigeria: Background to Nationalism* (Berkeley, Los Angeles: University of California Press, 1963), p. 143.

57. Seibel, H. D. *Labour in a Nigerian Industrial Firm* and *Industrial Labour in Nigeria*.

58. Seibel, H. D. 'Some Aspects of Inter-Ethnic Relations in Nigeria' *Nigerian Journal of Economic and Social Studies*, 1967, 9 (2), p. 227.

59. *Report on the Commission on the Review of Wages, Salaries and Conditions of Service of the Junior Employees of the Governments of the Federation and in Private Establishments* (Lagos: Federal Ministry of Information Printing Division, 1964), Para 16, p. 5.

60. *Report of the Grading Team on the Grading of Posts in the Public Services of the Federation of Nigeria* (Lagos: Federal Ministry of Information, April 1966).

CHAPTER 3

Fusion and Fissure: Nigeria's Central Labour Organizations

Excepting only some short periods of time, the Nigerian labour movement, since the inception of the first central organization in 1943, has nearly always been divided into mutually hostile groupings. From that date the trade unions have witnessed the setting up of some twenty-five union centres or federations, five substantive – but unsuccessful – attempts at establishing a single central organization, and many more occasions when walk-outs and splinter groups have frustrated moves towards unity. This situation is unusual in Africa, for with the exception of some of the union centres in colonial French Africa, where metropolitan divisions were replicated, nearly all African countries, especially since independence, have seen a tendency towards the development of a single central body, often engineered or supported by the dominant political parties. The general absence of governmental or party intervention in the Nigerian case has allowed free play to some of the factors that divide the Nigerian labour movement: personality differences; the structure of the movement itself; its relationship to the international unions, the political parties, and the Government; and ideological and tactical wrangles. In this chapter an attempt is made to plot the fragmentation of the labour movement, to set its development in a wider societal and political framework, and finally to provide an analytical insight into the continuing disunity.

'Conservatives and Radicals': the Early Central Bodies

Trade union organization in Nigeria, though often sporadic and short-lived, dated almost from the beginnings of wage-labour in the country. The legal sanction to organize was, however, restricted and was only fully granted by the colonial government in April 1939, when a Trade Union Ordinance passed the previous year came into force. The formal recognition of the right to organize and bargain collectively, together with the increased pressures on the economy due to the war, provoked a sudden increase in the pace of unionization – forty-one unions were registered by the end of 1941. The rising cost of living and the government's wartime propaganda regarding the strategic importance of Empire products led to an increased political awareness among the wage-earners in Lagos. Agitation for a Cost of Living Allowance (COLA) culminated in 1942 in a march of railway workers to Government House, led by Michael Imoudu, the fiery leader of the Railway Workers' Union, and a subsequent confrontation with Governor Bourdillon at the Locomotive Yard. For his part in the agitation Imoudu was imprisoned in Benin (where he organized a strike of prisoners) and then banished to Auchi for 'threatening the peace of the colony'.

The COLA agitation and the growing number of new unions led to a demand for some co-ordination at the central level. A federation of four government unions calling itself the African Civil Servants Technical Workers Union (ACSTWU) had existed since 1940. Many workers felt, however, that this body had not taken a sufficiently militant stand during the COLA agitation and thought that it was too unrepresentative in composition. This body nevertheless assumed the task of piloting the formation of a new central organization. Under its leadership a group of unions – the Federated Trade Unions of Nigeria – met in November 1942 and in turn undertook to arrange a congress of union delegates with sufficient authority to constitute themselves into a central body.

A congress of thirty-one unions, including nearly all the largest, met in July and August 1943 and formed the Trade Union Congress (of Nigeria) (TUC).[1] Messages of support flowed in from a number of participating unions. The Congress published a quarterly bulletin, *The Nigerian Worker*, edited by Obafemi Awolowo, then Secretary of the Motor Transport Owners' Union and an aspiring journalist, politician, and lawyer. With the help of the Department of Labour, the TUC started a series of trade union summer schools – the embryo of the Workers' Educational Association of Lagos.

Despite its links with the Department of Labour, its educative character, and the staid urbane nature of most of its leadership, the Congress took overt political stands. It demanded labour representation in the Legislative Council (perhaps as a counterweight to the representation of shipping, banking, and mining, interests), while its constitution announced that one of its objects was '. . . to press for the nationalization of mining and timber industries, township transport and other important public services'.[2] The representative character of the new centre was given official standing when the government, anxious to keep a paternal eye on any new organization, accorded it official recognition, and inaugurated a series of monthly meetings between the council of the TUC and the Commissioner of Labour.

For Nigerian wage-earners the end of the War brought new economic pressures. The workers claimed that they had minimized their wage demands because of the War, and that the cost of living had gone up by 200% since 1942 (when the last increase to government workers was granted). Their claims were actively supported by the nationalist press, especially Nnamdi Azikiwe's *West African Pilot*. Reflecting the urgency of the new demands, a General Strike, more fully discussed elsewhere, began in late 1945. The leadership of the TUC revealed little unanimity in their attitude towards the strike. The President was also the president of the union that was instrumental in calling the strike; others in the TUC tried unsuccessfully to revoke the strike order, cowed by the government's declaration that the wartime regulations were still in force and that the strike was therefore illegal. One section of the TUC – the All-Nigeria Government Technical and General Workers' Federation and the Nigerian Union of Teachers – formed a body within the TUC to present a reasoned case on behalf of the strikers to the Tudor Davies Commission set up by the Colonial Government to investigate the causes of the strike and to make recommendations as to the possible revision of wage rates. This body, the Supreme Council of Nigerian Workers, was recognized by the Tudor Davies Commission, not entirely equitably, as a 'body sufficiently rational and sufficiently responsible to voice the opinions of Nigerian Labour as a whole'.[3]

Henceforth the government, shocked and surprised by the virulence of labour agitation, cast a rather wary eye over the activities of the TUC. By the end of 1946 it had fifty-six affiliates and claimed some 42,000 members. Open dissension between the more conservative and more militant leaders of the Congress was avoided until the annual conference of 1948, where a conflict broke out over the question of the affiliation of the TUC to the National Convention of Nigeria and the Cameroons (NCNC), the party led by Nnamdi Azikiwe, trying at this time to spread a protective umbrella over all organizations that could be instrumental in effecting a colonial withdrawal. During the 1945 strike Azikiwe's group of papers had given valuable support to the strikers and many of the labour leaders saw the nationalist struggle and the cause of the labour movement as indissolubly linked. Imoudu sat on the Executive Council of the NCNC, and many other labour leaders, especially those who were connected with the Zikist Movement, a left-wing and black-conscious pressure group working within the NCNC, had their feet in both camps.

By 1948 strains were beginning to appear in the relationship. Some of the more moderate labour leaders were swayed by the colonial government's injunctions to keep the labour movement out of politics, a policy common to all British territories, but accentuated in Nigeria after the General Strike of 1945. More important, both Azikiwe and the more conservative labour leaders were becoming increasingly disenchanted with the activities of the Zikists. Founded in 1946, the Zikists had within their ranks a liberal sprinkling of radical opinion – some Fabian socialist, some communist, some racialist – all of which found a happy milieu in the labour movement. At the 1948 Conference the more conservative group showed its hand, proposed a motion to disaffiliate from the NCNC, and carried the conference with it.

The radicals – who included Imoudu, F. O. Coker, and Nduka Eze – were nonplussed. Some talked of founding an independent workers' party, others organized a Committee of Trade Unionists which in the first place attempted to influence the TUC to reverse its decision. When this failed, the radicals formed the Nigerian National Federation of Labour (NNFL) in March 1949 as a rival body to the TUC. The aims of the new centre were nothing if not aspiring. The leaders proposed to: '. . . press for the socialization of important industries in the country with a view to realizing

Socialist Government where the identity of the working class would not be lost' and, ultimately, 'the achievement of a world-wide parliament of the working classes'.[4]

In 1949 a dramatic event brought the two factions closer again. Coalminers striking at the Enugu colliery were fired on by the police, who killed twenty-five strikers and wounded fifty-one others. Nationalist sentiment was outraged. Richard Sklar, commenting on the shootings, maintains: 'No previous event ever evoked a manifestation of national consciousness comparable to the indignation generated by this tragedy.'[5] The two sections of the labour movement, while maintaining their organizations intact, came together in the National Labour Committee, which in turn co-operated with the National Emergency Committee, an inter-party, inter-ethnic, inter-class organization that was to survive for less than a year. Nduka Eze, a Zikist radical and a member of the NNFL, described the event in these terms:

'The radicals and the moderates, the revolutionaries and the stooges, the bourgeoisie and the workers sank their differences, remembered the word "Nigeria" and rose in revolt against evil and inhumanity.'[6]

The nationalist sentiment engendered by the Enugu incident redounded to the benefit of the radical wing of the labour movement. But the main strength of the radicals and the conservatives alike lay not in the viability of the centres, but in the growing militancy of the individual unions they organized. Nduka Eze, in particular, had gained control of the executive of the Amalgamated Union of the United Africa Company African Workers (called UNAMAG) which by 1950, with 18,000 members, was the second largest union in the country and by far the largest organizing workers in the private sector. The TUC had lost support owing to its image of a government 'sponsored' centre, while the NNFL had not yet gained sufficient organizational coherence to attract affiliates. In its annual report of 1950/1 the Department of Labour claimed that: 'By the 31st March, 1950 the majority of the registered trade unions, including most of the largest, were outside both organizations.'

Within the Department of Labour the need for a strong representative centre was recognized and in March 1950 the department organized 'peace talks' to bring the two centres together. In May 1950 the merger took place and a new centre, the Nigerian Labour Congress (NLC), was formed. It was an unhappy marriage right from the start as far as the ex-TUC leaders were concerned. The new body was dominated by the leadership of the NNFL – Imoudu became President, F. O. Coker Deputy President, and Nduka Eze took the post of General Secretary, thus adding to his position of influence. At its congress in June the NLC immediately took steps to affiliate with the World Federation of Trade Unions (WFTU) internationally, and with the NCNC internally – the last issue being the cause of the split in 1948/9. Many independent unions, including the well-organized Nigerian Union of Teachers, refused to transfer their assets to the new body. The ex-TUC leaders were resentful of the takeover and feared and distrusted the Zikist radicals. Eze in particular secured their disapprobation after his circulation of a tract entitled 'Call for Revolution'. The Zikists' increasing commitment to violence, together with the attempted assassination of the Chief Secretary to the Government by a labourer in the Posts and Telegraphs Department, induced the government to ban the movement. The conservatives' attitude and the government's ban had little effect on Eze who, in August 1950, led his union, UNAMAG, in a highly successful strike, gaining for the workers a $12\frac{1}{2}\%$ increase in their cost of living allowance.

Four months later, in December, a disastrous reverse was suffered by the radicals in the labour movement. Eze attempted to call out all the mercantile workers in a country-wide strike. The strike was badly planned, badly timed, and badly led. Even the radicals in the NLC's leadership refused to lend their wholehearted support, and the strike was broken, the strikers victimized.

The NLC practically disintegrated under the shock of this event, but two underlying factors were in any case threatening the dominant position of the radicals in the labour movement. The NCNC leadership, increasingly aware of the possibility of transforming itself into a ruling political class, grew progressively more disillusioned with the more revolutionary organizations that it spawned. Concurrently, the British were beginning to hold out a sufficiently attractive devolution of power for party leaderships in the West and North to organize themselves as the recipients. In this situation the Zikists and other radicals in the party were an embarrassment to the NCNC. The strike of December 1950 set the seal on it as far as Azikiwe was concerned. The *West African Pilot* carried an item in January 1951 deploring communist infiltration into the NLC and in the same month Eze was expelled from the NCNC 'cabinet', on grounds of 'disloyalty and breach of trust'.

Despite his attempt to form a Freedom Movement committed to revolutionary socialism, Eze's expulsion from the NCNC marked the demise of his importance in the labour movement.

The second underlying factor contributing to the weakening of the position of the radicals was the impingement of the international federations' concerns on the local labour movement – a factor that was to prove a constant impediment to trade union unity in the future. After the ICFTU split from the WFTU in January 1949 the two organizations began increasingly to compete for the allegiance of colonial unions. While the rump of the WFTU came under the predominant leadership of the Russians, who saw colonial unions as allies in a wider anti-imperialist struggle, the ICFTU was for the first few years of its existence divided in its attitude to African trade unionism. The British unions, closely tied to the policies of the Labour government, stressed the virtues of non-political unionism and notions of trusteeship. The American unions, on the other hand, were much more concerned to push the ICFTU into an anti-colonial stance in order to further American cold war aims.[7] Ultimately it was the Americans who were to gain the upper hand, but even in the early fifties international rivalry affected the Nigerian labour movement. The NLC had secured a certain amount of financial support from the WFTU and the French Confédération Generale du Travail; during 1950 and the early months of 1951 the ICFTU in its turn held out promises of scholarships, and financial and international support, to the more conservative elements in the labour movement, already unhappy at the dominance of the radical leadership in the NLC.

In March 1951 a clash came to a head. An ICFTU delegation touring West Africa arrived at Lagos airport and some trade unionists, including H. P. Adebola, who was subsequently to play an important role in the movement, met them. The militants also turned out to boo and heckle, and clashes occurred between the two sides. For a while the pro-ICFTU unionists organized loosely in the Committee of ICFTU Affiliated Unions in Nigeria, but most of the conservatives were reluctant to lend their support to this body (probably because they each wished to peg a claim to the leadership) and for the next year and a half effectively no trade union centre existed.

A more fundamental reason for the failure to generate any mass enthusiasm for the establishment of a virile central organization was that little or no support was forthcoming from the nationalist politicians who were increasingly preoccupied with the problems of winning regional power. The unions on their part, damaged by their display of impotence in 1950, were uncertain as to how to respond to the new forms of ethnic nationalism.

From ANTUF to the Ibadan Conference

Although at least one attempt was made to revive the NLC, nothing was achieved until July 1952 when, at the initiative of the Railway Workers' Union, a conference was called to consider the establishment of a new centre. The conference met with wide support – forty-eight unions were represented and the working committee that was elected reflected a wide range in their backgrounds and opinions. Unionists such as H. P. Adebola (General Secretary of the Nigerian Railway & Ports Authority Workers' Union), who were later to become prominent in the ICFTU-orientated section of the labour movement, were represented, as were Imoudu and those radicals whose reputation had survived the débâcle of 1950. In August 1953 a new union centre, the All-Nigeria Trade Union Federation (ANTUF) was formed with an initial membership of about twenty affiliates. The programme of the Federation included certain demands pushed through by the radicals; one clause, for example, referred to the establishment of a 'political wing of the workers movement (political party) with a view to realising a socialist government', while another called for 'the state ownership of major industries', but some of the aims were vague and conciliatory. It was hoped 'to encourage the spirit of oneness and collective security amongst all working peoples': workers were to obtain 'social and economic security', and so on.[8] With Imoudu as President and Gogo Chu Nzeribe (of the Union of Posts and Telecommunications Workers) as General Secretary, the militant elements had won significant control of the leadership of the Federation. However, unity was only made possible by the resolution of one of the problems that had provided disagreement in the past, i.e. the question of affiliation with a political party. Imoudu's own union had decided the issue for him, when in 1952 they voted that none of their officials should hold office in a political party. In fact, co-operation with the established political parties at this stage was, in any case, unrealistic. The foundation of ANTUF coincided with a constitutional conference in London which effectively regionalized political power. The politicians neither needed the support of the labour movement against the colonial power, nor was co-operation with the radical elements in the unions feasible after 1950.

At first the government refused to recognize the new organization and at the second annual conference tried to infuse the more moderate elements into the leadership. The potential for a new split remained. As with the NLC, the moderate elements did not yet have a sufficient hold on a substantial section of the labour movement to press their claims, but from the beginning they levelled accusations against the leadership to the effect that it was communist infiltrated. N. A. Cole (of the Nigerian Union of Nurses), H. P. Adebola, and L. L. Borha (General Secretary of the Locomotive Drivers' Union), at first attempted to take over the leadership of ANTUF and when that failed looked clandestinely, then overtly, to the ICFTU for support and patronage. Their efforts to change the character of the organization were unsuccessful, as ANTUF was extremely popular among the workers. In 1956 it organized forty-five unions with some 181,000 members (out of a total organized labour force of 200,000) thus embracing the overwhelming majority of organized workers. Only six registered trade unions, including the National Union of Teachers and the Association of Local Government Employees, remained outside the centre. The leadership also showed a good deal of prescience by affiliating, by decision of its second congress, neither to the WFTU nor to the ICFTU, thus making the accusation of communist infiltration more difficult to sustain. The solidarity of the Federation was also increased by the widespread militancy among workers in the years 1955–6.[9]

Those trade unionists who were hostile to the leadership of ANTUF lent a certain amount of support to an organization set up in April 1956 called the Council of ICFTU Affiliated Unions (apparently the successor organization to the Committee of ICFTU Affiliated Unions referred to earlier), while remaining in their executive positions in ANTUF. The Council later gained adherents in the Nigerian Civil Service Union and the Enugu Council of Labour, both formally independent. The anti-radical group consisted of both the old style 'conservative' unionists such as N. A. Cole, organizing the salariat and white-collar unions, and more 'professional' unionists such as H. P. Adebola and L. L. Borha who sold their organizational talents to skilled and unskilled workers alike. This group had been loosely described as 'moderate' – but what they primarily had in common was a doctrinaire anti-communist bias.

At the fourth annual conference of ANTUF in November 1956 the moderates felt strong enough to submit a motion calling for the affiliation of ANTUF with ICFTU. The motion was rejected, despite the efforts of a delegation representing the Gold Coast TUC who were then strongly allied with ICFTU. According to an account by a trade unionist hostile to ICFTU, the Ghana delegation 'campaigned with delegates for affiliation with the ICFTU and spent hundreds of pounds'.[10] Despite being re-elected to the executive, six days later H. P. Adebola tendered his resignation, charging the executive with being communist inspired. This was quickly followed by a request to the executive by N. A. Cole, L. L. Borha, and two others, to remove Gogo Nzeribe from his post as Secretary-General on the charge of being communist 'inclined'. When this request was rejected they joined Adebola and set up a new body called the National Council of Trade Unions of Nigeria (NCTUN), on 17 April 1957.

Despite its affiliation internationally to the ICFTU, the NCTUN claimed itself 'independent of any external influences', and maintained that it intended to organize 'free and democratic trade unions'.[11] Their rivals in the ANTUF did not agree with their analysis. They saw conspiracy at work from four directions. First, from the government, whose Minister of Social Welfare and Labour, Chief Festus Okotie-Eboh, granted immediate recognition to the new body without ascertaining its representativeness. Secondly, from the Commissioner of Labour, George Foggon, and British TUC advisers who had influenced the Ministry decision. Thirdly, from the leadership of the NCNC. Here an explanation by digression is necessary. A sub-committee of ANTUF meeting in 1955, whose membership included Imoudu, S. U. Bassey, and Wahab Goodluck (two new faces who were to dominate radical unionism subsequently), had recommended the formation of a Nigerian Labour Party. The party was duly formed in March 1956, and its leaders argued that the NCNC were anxious to thwart any attempt by the new party to gain a mass-based body of support. Finally, the machinations of the ICFTU were seen to be at work not least through the spread of ICFTU sponsored unions in other parts of Africa, notably Ghana. In a petition addressed to the 1958 conference of the International Labour Organization, ANTUF spelled out its objections to the new body. The petition, designed to prevent the conference's accepting the credentials of the NCTUN's representative, L. L. Borha, talked of 'subtle methods and mercenary means' on the part of the ICFTU. Far from helping the NCTUN to organize 'Free and democratic unions', they claimed:

> the ICFTU has become the antithesis of freedom and democracy, and has been responsible in the main for the diabolical activities of the few dissident elements known as the NCTUN. It is therefore the general impression of Nigerian workers that the ICFTU is an imperialist-International Organisation purposely designed to serve the material interests of Colonial [sic] possessing-Countries, and that its main policy is to mislead Colonial workers in their fight against Colonialism, industrial and economic oppression.[12]

The rival organizations survived for two years, but by 1959 agitation was once again growing at a rank and file level for the government to set up a commission to review the wages and salaries of workers in the public sector. The need to present an undivided case to the Mbanefo Commission that was set up, and also a widely held but vague feeling that, as independence was approaching, Nigeria should emerge into nationhood with an undivided labour movement, produced another attempt at trade union unity. For the first time since 1943 pressure from below was an important factor in influencing the union leadership to work together at the central level. After months of discussions and negotiations, together with the friendly intervention of the Ministry of Labour, ANTUF and NCTUN agreed, at a merger conference held at Enugu in March 1959, to come together to form the Trade Union Congress of Nigeria (TUCN). While the Annual Report of the Department of Labour for 1958-9 sardonically noted: 'It is by no means certain that the ideological differences have been completely resolved,' in some areas a genuine attempt at compromise was made. ANTUF leaders undertook to withdraw their attacks on the Ministry of Labour concerning their allegation that the Ministry inspired the formation of the NCTUN and also agreed, as S. U. Bassey wrote later, that the two organizations 'should make a joint statement denouncing communism as an evil not desirable in the Nigerian Trade Union Movement, and should further declare a positive resistance against any attempt to overtly or covertly [allow] the infiltration of this ideology into this movement'.[13] For its part the NCTUN revoked its affiliation to the ICFTU, and it was decided, in the interests of unity, that the new centre should have no international ties.

In the voting for the executive of the TUCN, M. Imoudu (ANTUF's nominee) narrowly beat N. A. Cole of the NCTUN into the office of the Presidency. When the voting for the General Secretaryship was taken, the ANTUF-sponsored nominee, S. U. Bassey, did not fare quite so well; and L. L. Borha was elected. Claiming rigging, the ANTUF delegates walked out of the conference, leaving the rest of the delegates to elect a NCTUN-dominated executive. Imoudu, hoping that his own influence could be set against the rest of the executive, and conscious that union members would be angered at yet another split in the labour movement, publicly maintained that the elections were fair and free.

A few months later the quarrels about leadership were set aside in the face of the discovery by the ANTUF group (which had continued to exist as a pressure group within the TUCN) of some extraordinary correspondence.[14] If authentic, the letters showed that the British TUC and the ICFTU were attempting to effect an affiliation with the TUCN through the NCTUN members on the executive, and behind Imoudu's back. One letter, addressed to L. L. Borha, documented a financial commitment by the ICFTU:

> I feel that assistance should not be withheld . . . at least the ICFTU should help the TUCN financially. We are therefore transferring to you a sum of £200 for each of the months of August, September and October, out of which the salary of the General Secretary of the TUCN is to be paid in accordance with an earlier commitment on our part.

Another memorandum, purportedly written by the Geneva representative of the ICFTU to its General Secretary in Brussels, indicated that the ICFTU was prepared to break up the TUCN and revive the Committee of ICFTU Affiliated Unions should it not succeed in gaining the TUCN's affiliation.

There followed a singular sequence of events. Imoudu, angered by a refusal to let him inspect the financial dealings of the Deputy President, and mandated by a request from two-thirds of the affiliated unions, called for a conference to be held in Lagos in April 1960. The central working committee of the TUCN maintained that any decision on a conference was to be made by the executive acting collectively, and not by Imoudu alone. They had arranged for a simultaneously timed conference to be held in Kano; and called on Imoudu to attend or be faced with suspension. Imoudu, with dubious constitutionality, replied by sacking the working committee.

The two conferences duly met, and drew their support from the old groupings: those who had previously been in ANTUF went to Lagos, the ex-NCTUN delegates went to Kano. The Kano conference held to its claim of legality, and retained the name – TUCN. Not to be outdone, the Lagos conference set up a centre called the Nigerian Trade Union Congress (NTUC). With regard to the relative strengths of these two bodies, the TUCN claimed eighty-eight affiliated unions with 86,200 members, the NTUC said its affiliates numbered forty-six unions with 48,500 workers, while some 197 unions with 142,000 members remained outside both congresses.

The TUCN now openly reverted to its former affiliation (previously under the name of NCTUN) with the ICFTU, while in Lagos the conference of the NTUC was strongly influenced by the appeals of John Tettegah, representing the Ghana Trade Union Congress, to join the newly established All African Trade Union Federation (AATUF) – a Pan-Africanist body largely led by the Ghana unions and set up to counteract the influence of the ICFTU. The affairs of the Nigerian labour movement should, at this moment in time, be seen in a wider perspective. Though previously an ardent affiliate of the ICFTU, the Ghanaian TUC, in keeping with the ideological proclivities of Nkrumah, was preaching a persuasive Pan-Africanist message, and backing this moreover with hard currency. To some individual leaders in the Nigerian labour movement, particularly those excluded from the TUCN leadership, the Ghanaian bait had considerable attraction. This factor goes a long way towards explaining the support that Imoudu was able to gain for his Lagos conference.

Now that the need to compromise in the interests of unity was no longer important, the NTUC leadership radicalized its programme. The leaders demanded the immediate introduction of a unitary constitution, the resignation of British personnel employed in the army and police force, the nationalization of the major industries, and the creation of an African liberation fund. The NTUC hurled vituperative allegations at the leadership of the TUCN. They had split the labour movement by their secret affiliation with the ICFTU; they had sold out the interests of the airways workers when, during a strike in 1959, they had agreed to the payment of a loyalty bonus to strike breakers; they had failed to make adequate representation to the Mbanefo Commission (discussed later) reviewing wages and salaries.

Finally, a personal element entered into the rivalry. During a workers' demonstration in 1959 against the European manager of the railways led largely by Imoudu, H. P. Adebola was acquitted in a court case when he presented an alibi, while Imoudu and the other leaders were sentenced to various terms of imprisonment. Imoudu still talks with great bitterness about this incident and of the sarcastic label that the workers applied to Adebola – 'Alhaji Alibi'.

The TUCN replied in kind. Imoudu was attacked for being a 'splitter' and the TUCN claimed that the NTUC was being manipulated by the Ghana TUC: they were enraged by Tettegah's press statement that he knew of no union in Nigeria other than the one led by Imoudu and Bassey. Characteristically, the TUCN programme stressed co-operation with the government, which they urged 'to come to an agreement about their consultative status in all activities of the state which were concerned with industrial, social and economic matters'.[15]

In continental terms the period immediately after 1960 – when independence came to many African countries – was one of intense rivalry between the internationals for the support of African unions. The fundamental differences in the Nigerian labour movement, and the lack of structural unity, meant that the groops were too weak to resist such pressures, even if they had the will to do so. In T. M. Yesufu's judgement each of the two groupings was 'in fact a puppet of one or more foreign organisations and run almost completely with money from foreign sources'.[16] The exact amount of money that was given in grants-in-aid at this stage is impossible to discover: it is in the nature of the transactions involved that the accounts kept by the Nigerian centres concealed the amount of financial dependence on international bodies. Certainly the WFTU now channelled its contributions through AATUF, and Tettegah's visits to Lagos, in common with his peripatetic travels through Africa, had a significance other than the simple expression of workers' continental solidarity. The TUCN's affiliation with ICFTU was strengthened in December 1960, when a conference in Tunis decided to set up an African Regional Organization (AFRO), H. P. Adebola being elected to the Presidency of the executive committee.

For the next two years, despite attempts at mediation by the Federal Minister of Labour, K. O. Mbadiwe, and even by the Oba of Lagos, His Highness Adele II, to whom some workers had turned in despair, the rival sources of foreign support and the internal differences kept the two groups in a state of continual bickering. In March 1961 the local unions organizing in Enugu, tired of the obscure in-fighting among the Lagos leaders, set up a body called the Eastern Nigeria Trade Union Congress, which in turn was built up on the foundations of an earlier body, the Enugu Council of Labour. The organization was not set up in direct competition with the other centre, for the individual unions represented continued their affiliations with the NTUC or the TUCN, or were independent of either. Similar inter-organizational bodies, such as the Port Harcourt Council of Labour and the Calabar Council of Labour, were later to be set up in the Eastern Region. All of them reflected a feeling that the struggles between the Lagos leaders were irrelevant to the interests of the workers, and that much could be gained by presenting a united front to the Regional government or the individual employer in the East.

The Ibadan Conference and its Aftermath

In August 1961 the Federal government initiated perhaps its only attempt at participatory democracy, when it arranged a conference called the All Nigeria Peoples' Conference, bringing together a number of individuals from the universities, the government, and special associations, to discuss the performance of the Nigerian government since independence. Among other matters it discussed, the conference looked at possible ways and means of reconciling the trade union centres. A Labour Reconciliation Committee, consisting of well-known politicians and academics, spent arduous hours with the leadership of the TUCN and NTUC trying to iron out their differences and draw up a mutually acceptable constitution. The climax of this intense attempt at reconciliation was to be a conference of all registered trade unions in a large hall at the University of Ibadan. There a common leadership was to be elected, and the question of foreign affiliation decided by a vote of the conference delegates. The months before the conference were spent in the usual atmosphere of acrimonious charges and counter charges. The TUCN, in a memo to the Labour Reconciliation Committee, proposed to retire Imoudu on the grounds that he had become 'a capillary attraction for dissensions and splits in the labour movement'. Imoudu replied at a press conference on 30 January 1962 by flourishing a letter said to have been written by Irving Brown of the AFL-CIO to another American trade unionist, Mr. George McCray, at the TUCN offices in Lagos. This, said Imoudu, indicated that the TUCN was being infiltrated by the CIA. *The West African Pilot* supported Imoudu in his charges and claimed that it was clear that 'foreign labour interests will leave no stone unturned to win the hearts of Nigerian workers'. *The Daily Telegraph* (Lagos), on the other hand, considered Imoudu's press conference 'a calculated attempt to wreck all that the . . . All Nigerian Peoples' Conference had taken pains to build'.[17]

The conference was postponed for a month to allow tempers to cool, but both the TUCN and the NTUC went to the Ibadan conference with a good deal of apprehension. Each set of leaders were offering themselves for re-election on a broader basis than that on which they had originally gained their prominence. No one could be sure whom the delegates to the conference would oust and whom they would retain in office. In the case of the TUCN the established leadership had been severely criticized by its own Assistant General Secretary, Nneamaka Chukwura, who in an internal memo violently attacked their financial dealings. He demanded an explanation for the disappearance of £8,000 that he claimed was paid to the TUCN coffers in the previous three months and charged that, 'In the past and under the traditional pretext and guise of "prestige fight" and "ideology", scientific crooks and swindlers have cleverly bulldozed and defrauded us.'[18]

When the seven-hundred-odd delegates to the conference assembled in Ibadan on 3 May 1962, in accordance with the carefully worked out peace formulas of the Labour Reconciliation Committee, a motion proposing the dissolution of the NTUC and the TUCN and the setting up of a United Labour Congress (ULC) came before the conference. In the proceedings that followed, according to the accounts of several participants, money changed hands with extraordinary blatancy in order to buy the votes of the delegates. There were angry disagreements over procedures and the organization of the conference. On the third day both sides attempted to pack the hall with delegates whose presence was unauthorized by the chairman (each accredited delegate had a signed entrance ticket). Delegates from moribund and nonexistent unions dutifully lined up for each vote. When the votes were counted on the vital issue of international affiliation, the number of voting delegates had swollen to 1,025, the majority of whom came out in favour of affiliation with the ICFTU. The NTUC group, who themselves had earlier insisted on taking the issue to a vote, were enraged at the result. About four hundred extra unionists had apparently appeared since the conference opened. Who had allowed them admission? Or had the voting figures been rigged? The NTUC group demanded that the figure of 1,025 be checked by the number of delegates actually present in the hall. When the chairman, a senior politician, refused on the grounds that some delegates had dispersed, he was accused of collaboration with the TUCN and of being under the influence of the Americans.

The NTUC group walked out, staged a noisy demonstration on the university campus and formed the Independent United Labour Congress (IULC) – unaffiliated internationally, but, in a phrase that was to be repeated on many occasions later, 'having fraternal relations with international trade unions of the socialist bloc'.

The net effect of the Ibadan conference not only returned the position to the *status quo ante*, but also increased the acrimony between the ULC and the IULC, subjected the leadership of both groups to the recriminations of the rank and file – who had been hoping for much from the conference – and provoked disagreement within each leadership over the tactics that had been employed at the conference. For as long as the two groups could convincingly hurl abuse at each other, the dissension within each group could be contained.

The ULC, which was recognized by the Federal government in June 1962, pushed the 'red scare' for all it was worth. The IULC, they said, was communist led, communist inspired, and communist directed. John Tettegah, the Ghanaian trade union leader, had no business in attending the conference; he was seeking to subvert the Nigerian Labour Movement and should be banned from entering the country. The ULC's place as 'the most favoured' union centre was acknowledged when the Federal government responded to this request and banned Tettegah.

For its part the IULC 'discovered' yet another letter, this time purportedly from H. P. Adebola, the newly elected President of the ULC, to George Meany, the President of AFL-CIO. Although almost certainly a forgery, the letter is interesting in the charges it puts forward. The letter 'sustained' the IULC charges against the impartiality of the chairman; 'identified' a plot to poison Nigerian –Ghanaian relations by the spreading of a malicious rumour that John Tettegah, leader of the Ghana TUC, had arrived with a band of thugs ready to beat up TUCN delegates; and 'documented' the financial transactions involved, Adebola allegedly charging Meany £1,000 to cover the expenses involved in 'convincing' delegates.[19] On a more bizarre level Sam Bassey of the IULC accused the TUCN delegates of imbibing alcohol 'as fish would drink the waters of the ocean' and the American State Department of buying canvas shoes for 'bare-footed teenagers' who could thereby be more accurately represented as accredited delegates.

Ribaldries of this nature accompanied deepening rifts between and within the sections of the labour movement. The first manifest breakaway group was set up in December 1962 when N. Anunobi and N. Chukwura took their unions out of the ULC, set up the Nigerian Workers' Council (NWC) and affiliated internationally to the International Federation of Christian Trade Unions (IFCTU). Both leaders had been excluded from nomination as delegates to the ILO conference the previous June, despite their prominent position in the ULC hierarchy (as the ULC was the government recognized centre, it had, at the time, the responsibility of nominating workers' delegates to the Conferences of the ILO). Some resentment may have been felt over their exclusion, for although they had voted with the TUCN delegates at the Ibadan conference, both Anunobi and Chukwura (as has been seen) had been in disagreement with the other ULC leaders for some time. Despite Anunobi's position in the ULC, he had also for some months held the position of Assistant Secretary in the Pan-African Workers' Congress in Brazzaville, the African organization of the IFCTU. Both leaders had an antipathy to any brand of communist ideology, and would not have thought of defecting to the IULC (as their behaviour at the Ibadan conference indicates), even if we assume the unlikely proposition that the IULC leadership would have accommodated them. The affiliation of the NWC to a largely Christian international should not be taken too literally – although both leaders are Christian by conviction, many of the workers they organized were Muslims. Anunobi and Chukwura can be thought of as being 'in the market' for a split. When the IFCTU was forthcoming with promises of aid and support, it made their break from the ULC possible, although Chukwura himself later argued to me that the formation of the NWC provided a 'necessary challenge to the other centres'.

Within the IULC a bitter struggle for power developed among the forceful personalities that controlled the centre. The prominent trade unionists who walked out of the Ibadan conference with Imoudu included Ibrahim Nock – a Northern trade unionist whose influence reflected the growing strength of organized labour in the Northern textile mills; S. U. Bassey and Wahab Goodluck – whose opinions were more rigidly Marxist than most others in the IULC and whose personal ambitions were anything but invisible; Side Khayam – who, while a radical student in England, was recruited as General Secretary to the Nigerian Union of Seamen by some Nigerian seamen he met at Liverpool; and Amaefule Ikoro – who was elected General Secretary of the IULC (Imoudu was its President).

The pond was too small for all the big fish. The first to leave was Ibrahim Nock, who in December 1962 announced the formation of the Northern Federation of Labour (NFL) with himself as General Secretary. Nock claimed that he had affiliated his organization to the International Confederation of Arab Trade Unions.[20] In fact, for a long while the NFL represented little more than a personal following of Nock, who was trying to ingratiate himself with the NPC, from which he hoped to receive a measure of patronage and support. It says much for Nock's persistence that he transformed the paper existence of the NFL to the point where three years later, in June 1965, a delegates' conference was held in Kaduna which claimed to represent some 6,000 to 7,000 workers. It is also possible, though I have found no concrete evidence to substantiate this, that some NPC politicians played on the ethnic suspicion of Hausa workers in order to persuade them to join Nock's union. However, it would be inaccurate to infer from what evidence is available that the prime motivation for the setting up of the NFL was a desire for ethnic separatism – moving closer to the locus of regional power is a more likely explanation of the creation of the NFL.

The next crisis to strike the IULC was a confrontation between Goodluck, Bassey, and Khayam, on the one hand, and Imoudu and Ikoro on the other. Ostensibly the argument was over the use of funds that had been paid to the Congress by the Ghanaian TUC. In fact, the dissent represented a take-over bid by Bassey and Goodluck and an ideological conflict between them and Imoudu and Ikoro. Bassey and Goodluck had forged ties with Dr. T. Otegbeye, a medical practitioner, who, later in 1963, set up a Marxist party, the Socialist Workers' and Farmers' Party, which differed only on peripheral ideological grounds with Moscow (and never obviously enough to cut off a source of funds). Imoudu and Ikoru were more disposed to think of the working-class struggle in national or Pan-African terms and attacked Otegbeye and his allies in the IULC for regarding the struggle of Nigerian workers as some kind of sideshow for an international conflict led by the socialist countries. Although their position was far from articulate, Imoudu and Ikoro had some allies in a group of left-wing intellectuals who had disagreed with Otegbeye on these (and other) grounds.[21] These ideological differences were multiplied by the contempt in which Bassey and Goodluck held Imoudu's organizational abilities. The conflict between the two factions was already apparent at an IULC conference in 1962, but a showdown was forced the following year when Bassey and Goodluck, with the connivance of Khayam, stage-managed a demand from Khayam's Seamen's Union that they head a 'caretaker committee' to be set up because of Imoudu and Ikoro's alleged mismanagement of the IULC. They transformed their take-over into a *fait accompli* by the simple device of getting into the offices of the centre and changing the locks.

In August 1963 Bassey and Goodluck called the First Revolutionary Congress of the faction; reverted to the name NTUC; and became General Secretary and President respectively, while Khayam was elected Deputy President. Imoudu and Ikoro responded by setting up their own organization, the Labour Unity Front (LUF). They claimed not to have founded another central organization at all, but rather a body that would have as its main aim the achievement of labour unity. The structure of the new organization, at least, validated their claim. The LUF represented a loose confederation of unions either estranged from the other central bodies, or, like the Nigerian Union of Teachers, traditionally unaffiliated. The LUF was held together by the strength of the individual unions that comprised it – notably the NUT, Imoudu's Railway Union, and Gogo Nzeribe's Posts and Telegraphs Workers' Union – by Imoudu's own personal popularity, and by little else.

Whatever claims it had to being simply a means to effect labour unity, the net result of its existence was to create another competing source of allegiance for individual unions.

To JAC and Beyond

Paradoxically, the centrifugal tendencies evidenced in the labour movement coincided with a period of widespread dissatisfaction among the wage-earners in the country, and a demand for effective labour agitation in order to raise wages. Since 1959 the important leaders of Nigeria's unions had taken precious little account of the feelings of the rank and file. The characteristic remoteness of the centres to the membership is discussed elsewhere, but it is none the less true that workers' dissatisfaction occasionally forced a temporary unity of the leaders, as later events were to show. The demand for fatter wage packets was, as well as being a reflection of the inflationary pressures on the economy, a protest about the relative deprivation of the working and intendant classes *vis-à-vis* the members of the political class. The politicians' claims were becoming more obviously fraudulent, their corruption more open. Among many of the workers it was felt that labour unity had to be achieved before the bulk of the national wealth was spent in conspicuous consumption, transferred to overseas bank accounts, or dissipated on wasteful and ill-conceived governmental projects.

In order to maintain their positions, the labour leaders could not but react to the pressure from the rank and file. The ULC published an open letter in July 1963 reproaching the political leadership for the 'splendid prospects that heralded and marked the celebration of independence . . . becoming increasingly confused and darkened by the statements and doings of politicians and governments. The Workers [the statement went on] are baffled and fearful, disillusioned and frustrated.' [22] The NTUC for its part inaugurated a discussion group on wages in August 1963 with which the other union centres decided to co-operate. Finally, a meeting of all registered unions in Lagos under the auspices of the ULC was called on 12 September 1963; this endorsed the ULC's call for a general revision of wages and prepared the setting up of a Joint Action Committee (JAC) to embrace all the labour centres.

The formation of JAC, which was to play the crucial role in organizing labour agitation for the next nine months, showed that co-operation between the different factions in the labour move-ment was possible when time and occasion demanded it, but right from the beginning some of the leaders of JAC saw it as a tem-porary alliance, rather than as a prelude to the permanent achieve-ment of labour unity. JAC demanded that the government set up a high-powered commission of enquiry to investigate the conditions of the workers, and threatened strike action if its demands were not complied with. The government temporized – misled by the violent in-fighting of the labour leaders, it underestimated the widespread sense of grievance. The government's confident assumption that JAC would collapse within a week proved mis-placed when on 27 September 1963 JAC called a General Strike. Confined at first to Lagos, the strike spread within two days over most of the country and involved, in a curious official phrase, 'more than 34,513 workers'. (JAC claimed that 50,000 workers participated.) The strike was timed to coincide with Nigeria's assumption of the new status of a Federal Republic on 1 October 1963 and the installation of her first President. The solidarity of the workers was reinforced by their disappointment at not receiving cash bonuses for the occasion – a current rumour in Lagos had fed this belief. With foreign dignitaries arriving daily to unserviced hotel rooms, the political embarrassment of the government was acute. It capitulated, and ordered the setting-up of a wage com-mission. Six months after it had called its first strike, the JAC demanded publication of the commission's report within seven days, or, its ultimatum declared, another General Strike would commence. The government effectively invited strike action by publishing the report (which, as the JAC leaders suspected, was substantially favourable to the workers) simultaneously with a White Paper that rejected or diluted most of its findings. Incensed by the cavalier treatment that was accorded their demands, JAC called a General Strike (the full background and implications of which are reserved for later discussion), which lasted fourteen days and all but paralysed the modern sectors of the economy and administration.

Labour unity had paid off, and the concessions which were

gained as a result of the strike meant that JAC was held in such high regard by the wage-earners that it was difficult for any of the union leaders to withdraw. For the radicals in the NTUC and the LUF, JAC's success was evidence that it should be transformed into a permanent body (those leaders who had a record of industrial militancy could assume that they would be prominent in the leadership). Adebola and Chukwura demurred, and maintained that JAC was formed for a limited purpose only. Since this purpose had been achieved, it should be dissolved. A correspondent in the *West African Pilot* had pessimistically noted that JAC operated without a constitution, with no programme, minutes or records 'and above all no hope except in the mere sentiments of the workers and the publicity of the newspapers . . .'[23] The lack of a permanent secretariat meant that after September 1964 the central meetings of JAC in Lagos became more and more infrequent, although the regional organizations in the East and the West continued to have some vitality.

The opportunity for the moderate leaders to withdraw from the organization formally came with the Federal elections of December 1964. In the elections the labour leaders were hopelessly divided on what political line to adopt. As has been described in Chapter 1, two major coalitions had emerged to contest the elections. The NNA combined the forces of NPC and the NNDP, together with some minor parties; while on the other side the NCNC had deserted its coalition partner in the Federal Government and allied itself with the AG, the Northern Elements' Progressive Union (NEPU), and others, to form UPGA. As the election campaign progressed, it became clear that the NNA was prepared to use any means at its disposal to prevent UPGA from being returned to office. Electoral irregularities and intimidations were widespread; prior to the elections NNA declared that they expected eighty unopposed seats in the North, the majority of which UPGA had in fact decided to contest. At the last moment UPGA decided to call a boycott of the elections as a protest against the conduct of the campaign. Regarding the boycott as a tactical blunder, the NCNC in the Mid-West asked their supporters to turn out – but elsewhere the boycott was effective, thus making certain a NNA victory. The LUF and NTUC leaders, in support of UPGA, decided to sponsor a strike in the name of the JAC against the rigging of the elections. At the decisive meeting Adebola, who was in the chair, went along with the strike demand, only to denounce it as 'political' some days later when it was clear that the constitutional crisis involving

Balewa and Azikiwe that followed the elections was being patched up and that he would have to mend his fences to retain his favoured position with the political establishment. The election strike, which provided the first occasion on which workers were called out for a purely political issue, was a fiasco.

The failure of the strike, and Adebola's timely disassociation from it, provided him with a golden opportunity to withdraw from the JAC. Chukwura followed his lead, and two weeks after the strike the ULC and the NWC set up their own central organization – the Supreme Council of Trade Unions – leaving the rump of the JAC to the radicals. Although the regional organizations of JAC in the West and East lingered on for a while, the passions and recriminations that followed the elections effectively foretold the disintegration of the JAC in Lagos. Within a short while the Supreme Council of Trade Unions fell into oblivion: its formation can be regarded as a defensive gesture by Chukwura and Adebola in case the NTUC-controlled JAC revealed some hidden teeth.

After the Coup

For another year no further initiative with regard to labour unity was taken. The coup of January 1966, which was initiated by a group of young majors and taken over by the establishment figure of Major-General Ironsi, provided yet another opportunity for an attempt at reconciliation. The young majors had been motivated by much the same demands as had provoked the 1964 strike and the attempted boycott of the 1964 elections – the coup was broadly populist in character and expressed the same contempt for the corrupt politicians of the establishment parties. Although Ironsi was very much a man of the old régime, he too, at least to some extent, had to go along with the groundswell of popular opinion. One of his first political acts was to call the labour leaders together and suggest that they make yet another attempt to form a single central organization. Proposals as to the character of the body were drafted by the NWC who suggested that a Nigerian Trade Union Federation (NTUF) be formed without destroying the assets and liabilities of the old bodies. Given certain concessions from the other trade union centres, the NWC maintained that it was prepared to renounce its affiliation to the IFCTU. The proposals by the NWC met initially with a favourable response from the LUF and the NTUC. The ULC, whose organizational strength had been grown at the expense of the other organizations and whose income from international sources had increased substantially, turned down the idea of the Federation on the grounds that non-trade unionists had been instrumental in the formulation of the proposals. On 17 February 1966 the ULC issued a press statement defining its position:

> The presence of the Labour Party and SWAFP representatives in the so called exploratory meeting summoned on the platform of the NWC furnishes an absolute proof that the meeting which ought to be an industrial one was used by some politicians for the political manoeuvres in complete disregard and violation of the undertaking given to the Supreme Commander and Head of the Federal Military Government in a meeting with labour leaders. The ULC is purely an industrial and not a political organisation.[24]

Although the NTUF was little more than a loose alliance, the NWC, LUF, and NTUC retained a form of commitment to it for a few months after its formation. The ULC's newspaper, *The Nigerian Worker*, sardonically but correctly predicted in February 1966 the ephemeral nature of the new organization: '. . . the ULC assume that these strange bedfellows shall trudge along in the prescribed rut and forever do the expected thing.' A short while later the NWC withdrew from the NTUF and the centre broke up. According to an account in the NTUC newspaper, *Advance* (May 1966), the ULC had contacted the IFCTU in Brussels (to which the NWC was affiliated) and indicated to them that the NWC was flirting with the communist section of the Nigerian labour movement. The NWC, it was argued, decided to revert to its independent status when the IFCTU threatened to cut off its aid and scholarship programmes. Certainly in terms of anti-communist bias and the moderation of their attitudes the NWC leadership had a natural affinity not with the NTUC, but with the ULC. By October 1966 Chukwura was praising the editor of *The Nigerian Worker*, the ULC newspaper, for the 'courage and moral fortitude with which you have resisted and continue to resist the dazzling buts and magic trappings of partisan politics – the very bane of some past and present organs of many trade union organizations'.

The massacres in the North during 1966 placed the unions in a delicate position. Among those hardest hit by the ethnic disturbances were Eastern workers who provided the mainstays of trade union organizations in the North. With the flight of these workers to the East after the September 1966 killings, the trade union centres in Lagos tried to give limited support to their claims for compensation. For the ULC the dilemma was particularly acute, as they did not want to endanger their favoured position with the Federal Government. Like the other union centres in Lagos, in early 1967 the ULC tried desperately to prevent Colonel Ojukwu from declaring secession. A telegram in the ULC files from L. L. Borha, the General Secretary, pleaded with Ojukwu: '. . . in the spirit of what and not who is right, the ULC appeals to you and through you to our brothers and sisters of Eastern Nigeria for a give and take attitude in finding a solution to the present stalemate, believing instead Nigeria is the last hope for lasting peace and prosperity to which posterity is entitled. May Nigeria not disintegrate under a military regime.'

When the Eastern Region of Nigeria seceded from the Federation on 30 May 1967, the unions in the East renounced their affiliation to Lagos and were gradually drawn into a Biafran Trade Union Confederation (BTUC). For a while the NTUC affiliates listened to their instructions from Lagos to remain outside the organization, but when their half-heartedness was interpreted as hostility by the Biafran regime, they knuckled under. The BTUC was headed by Ben Udokpora, a former Secretary of the ULC in the East, and after secession given the title of Ojukwu's 'Labour adviser'. The formation of the BTUC was, as well as a product of the secessionist movement and part of an incipient Biafran nationalism, a reflection of the gradual regionalization of the labour movement in the East which was manifested as early as 1961.

On the Federal side the trade union centres all united behind the military government, with the ULC, anxious to dissociate itself from the action of its affiliates in the East, being conspicuously obsequious in its declarations of loyalty to the Federal Government. The NTUC's position on secession and the war that followed placed it for once in the Federal Government's good books. Ojukwu, like Tshombe, was identified as the pliant client of his neo-colonial masters. He was being used to destroy from within a country that could seriously threaten western imperial interests.

Despite this identification of interest between the different centres on the Federal side, it is a testimony to the crystallization of organizational interests that had taken place as a result of the Ibadan conference of 1962 that throughout the war period the centres retained their autonomy virtually intact.

The exception to this statement was the formation of a merger body between the LUF and the NFL, (now called the Northern States Federation of Labour (NSFL) announced in January 1968. The LUF-NSFL was to be a prelude to a further abortive merger between the LUF and the NTUC.[25] Although great publicity attended the proposed merger, and the NTUC and LUF set up a committee to work out a basis for unity, the entente foundered in the depths of a personal quarrel between the two leaderships.

The only other development of note during the civil war was the creation, in December 1968, of a small body called the Nigerian Federation of Labour (not to be confused with the Northern Federation of Labour) which originated as a split from the NTUC. The General Secretary of the new body, Mr. Edet Bassey Etienam, who was on the NTUC executive, announced in the *Daily Times* (24 December 1968) that his new federation 'would serve as another devastating blow to our detractors who would not take kindly to this positive development'. Etienam also declared that all the leaders of the NTUC had been sacked and that he had formed a caretaker committee to take over the affairs of the Congress. Bassey and Goodluck have dismissed Etienam's caretaker committee as 'a one-man affair', a charge that appears accurate from the sorry little press conference he held at a Lagos hotel, where he told the assembled newsmen that he had to withhold the names of others in the NTUC who supported him 'for tactical reasons'. As no other defectors from the NTUC had emerged several months after the formation of the NFL, Etienam's tactics seem a trifle obscure.

At the end of the war the Biafran centre disappeared, and left the Lagos-based centres, particularly the ULC and the NTUC, trying to reactivate their affiliates in the Eastern States. The NTUC was more fortunate than the other union centres in this respect, as many of its pre-war affiliates were located in the 'minorities' area of Biafra, namely the Rivers and South-Eastern States. These areas had reverted to Federal control fairly early in the war and during 1969 Sam Bassey and others expended a good deal of energy reactivating organized trade unionism in the area. The ULC was not so fortunate. Shaken by a struggle for leadership, by the defection of its Western district secretary and hamstrung by its own ideological conservatism, the ULC did not succeed in capitalizing as much as the NTUC on the fresh wave of wage demands that the end of the war brought.

The behaviour and performance of the unions under wartime conditions is discussed more fully elsewhere, but it can be noted here that the exigencies of the time produced one more attempt at presenting a united front against the major employer of labour, namely the state. This was the creation in August 1970 of the United Committee of Central Labour Organizations (UCCLO), a body which drew its representation equally from the NTUC, ULC, NWC and LUF. Faced by widespread militancy among workers, and this despite the prevailing legal restrictions on strike activity, the Federal Military Government appointed a wage commission under Chief Adebo, Nigeria's permanent representative at the United Nations. UCCLO was set up solely to co-ordinate the submissions of the unions to this commission. It demanded that the Commission should recommend a restoration of their members' purchasing power which 'for many years consistently impoverished by a sharp rising in the cost of living [was now] debilitated by the harrowing effects of the thirty months Civil War in which the country was embroiled'.[26]

For the advocates of labour unity the limited purpose for which UCCLO was formed was yet another opportunity lost. Michael Imoudu, angered at the failure of the leaderships of the four major centres to set up a permanent body, emerged out of retirement to call a well-attended rally in Lagos at which a Nigerian Workers' Unity Committee was launched. The old warhorse trumpeted that 'Labour unity is an historical imperative' and that 'Self-appointed labour leaders have championed the workers' cause, but only to my disappointment and to your disunity.'[27] But if an historical imperative was at work, the dialectic moved in a strange and wondrous way. Certainly the leaders of the NTUC, LUF, ULC and NWC did not feel themselves bound by historical necessity, for after the dust settled on the Adebo commission's report, Nigeria still had four central labour bodies.

The Failure to Unite:
an Analytical Perspective

Attempts to explain the origin and persistence of the fragmentation at the centre have ranged from over-facile statements about personality differences, to more sophisticated attempts to find a deeper (usually ideological) explanation. The behaviour and acrimonious statements of the labour leaders themselves would seem to confirm the simplistic interpretation. For Bassey and Goodluck, as Goodluck told me, Imoudu is 'too undisciplined' to work with; as has been noted above, Chukwura has spoken of 'scientific crooks and swindlers' in the labour movement; Adebola has been accused of opportunism or cowardice by the other leaders; while he himself spent a good deal of time and energy initiating an appeal to ULC unions to institute a £50,000 libel claim against NTUC officials. It is also usually the case that the rank and file of the trade unions are also prone to think of the differences in the labour movement in terms of the personalities of the top leaders. Invariably the names of the prominent leaders are more familiar to workers than the names of the organizations that they lead. This is no doubt partly because of the frequent changes of names of the organizations compared, until recently, with the relative stability of the leadership; but it also represents a real tendency for individual unions to cluster round a leader whose public image conforms most strongly to their own dispositions. Thus, according to the qualities that are sought, one leader is characterized as 'honest', another as 'responsible', a third as 'militant', and so on.

These personality differences provide a partial explanation for the divided labour movement and they certainly add fuel to the flames, but they can be more fairly regarded as the surface manifestations of less obvious causes of disunity.

For one thing, the proliferation of small unions, and their divisions into industrial, house, craft, and departmental units, has meant that union officials are rarely in a position to organize one union full-time. The general secretaries not only seek to sell their services to as many unions as possible, they also often use their control of individual unions to sell their support to a union centre. Amalgamation of smaller unions or union centres would both decrease the bidding advantage of ambitious general secretaries and decrease the number of 'top dog' jobs available to them. It was in response to pressures of this kind that, at one unity conference, a proposal to establish six posts of Assistant General Secretary was suggested, so that all could be accommodated. But elasticity of this kind clearly reaches a maximal point where the employment claims of trade union officials can no longer be met.

The trade union leaders' quest for financial security has also drawn in a network of international federations and foreign unions willing to sponsor their allies in the Nigerian movement. Genuine ideological empathy between the donors and recipients cannot be ruled out, but in general the past behaviour of union leaders, and the disbursements of funds received from the international bodies, would seem to indicate that the leadership has a predominantly instrumental attitude towards foreign support, rather than being too concerned about the political colouring of its money. Christopher Allen, in his study of Gambian trade unionism, documents the 'farcical' situation of the Gambia Labour Union which simultaneously was affiliated to the AATUF, but received no money from it, received scholarships from individual East European unions, and was affiliated to the ICFTU, receiving in a two-year period over £2,000 from it.[28] WFTU, AATUF, the AALC, ICFTU, and IFCTU, all play the market for allies, and give remarkably generous assistance to their associates (though the more canny, like the AALC, impose rigid institutional controls over the spending of funds). Several instances can be found where the policy of the internationals had had directly deleterious effects on trade union unity. The ICFTU, for example, was, with some justice, accused of sponsoring a clandestine group in the 1959 TUCN, despite a conference decision of the body not to be involved in international entanglements. Similar accusations of interference with the affairs of the Nigerian unions can be made against the other international bodies. Though it is difficult to separate cause and effect in every case, it is probably true to assert that the activities of the international bodies both helped to sow the seeds of disunity and reinforced existing divergences. At the very least the patronage and support that the foreign unions lent to their favoured allies in Nigeria ensured the survival of some organized groupings in the labour movement that might otherwise have been swallowed up by mergers or takeovers

Another important divisive issue has been the relation of the trade unions to party political activities. The 1948 conference of the TUC provided the first occasion when the link between the centre and a political party (in this case the NCNC) provoked dissent on the question of affiliation and led to a bifurcation into two camps. There are many strands to unravel in subsequent party/union relationships, but basically three tendencies appeared. One was a feeling of disenchantment with the established political parties and a corresponding desire to set up worker-orientated or worker-dominated parties. The formation of the two Nigerian labour parties (in 1956 and 1964), SWAFP, and other small left-wing parties can be cited in this regard. A second tendency manifested itself in a formal commitment to non-partisanship, which often meant in practice giving tacit support to, or concluding an opportunistic alliance with, the dominant party of the day. The decision of several leaders of the NTUC and the ULC to stand on the electoral tickets of the major parties during the 1964 Federal election is evidence of this tendency. Finally, one central body, the NFL, fashioned an umbilical relationship to the NPC. It was partly created and maintained by the party, and became a faithful servant to its policies. The NFL's position represented the final compromise of a union centre to the regionally based party system that had developed in Nigeria; but the divergences of interest among the other centres also reflected their difficulty in reconciling the idea of a national class-based organization with an ethnically based power structure.

Government attitudes towards the trade unions have also helped to perpetuate divisions. At the Federal level the unstable coalition of regional and ethnic interests during the civilian régime found considerable difficulty in enunciating a national interest even on such basic issues as economic development and foreign policy. Similarly, in their policy towards the unions, the Federal government, unlike many other African states where one-party control of the state apparatus dictated a trend towards centralization and incorporation of all politically significant organizations, was unable or unwilling to compel organized labour to unite, or to impose a rigid control of trade union activities. Periodically, however, the government has threatened state intervention to end the fragmentation of the labour movement – and, with the increased national responsibilities that the Federal Military Government had arrogated to itself during the war, there is just a possibility that legislation to this effect may be implemented. Such intervention as there has been so far has either been half-hearted (for example, the nature of Ironsi's admonitions to the union leaders) or only partly lent the authority of the Federal government's support. In its role as the largest employer of labour in the country it was in the interests of the government to keep the other side of the negotiating table at loggerheads; it would perhaps not be going too far to assert that successive governments have connived to maintain the *status quo*.

But this assertion must be set in the context of a default of any consistent policy directives regulating the relationship between the unions, the Ministry of Labour, and the larger governmental apparatus. Ministry of Labour officials on occasions acutely felt the pressures of their ambiguous position between the demands of the political class on the one hand and the legal-rational impulses of the intendant class (to which they themselves belonged) on the other. But by and large the Ministry of Labour has been given considerable rein in its handling of trade union affairs. This has not prevented a good deal of criticism from a section of the labour movement for its failure to maintain a strictly neutral stance towards the various central bodies. Some ideological residue of the colonial government's preference for a 'non-political' union has remained within the Ministry; it was often manifested when the questions of governmental recognition of a centre, or the nomination of a workers' representative to ILO conferences came to the fore. In so far as accusations of the Ministry's partiality for the more conservative section of the labour movement could be convincingly sustained, the Ministry's self-cast role as impartial arbiter between the centres was undermined, while simultaneously an atmosphere was created which lent support to conspiracy theories regarding the government's position.

To explain individual splits in the movements, all the above factors – personality differences, the structure of the movement, its relationship to the international bodies, the parties, and the government – have to be considered: though not all of these factors were present in every case, nor again were they of equal significance. On some occasions the most divisive issues seemed to have been settled, and most of the apparent prerequisites for unity were present. For example, the factor of international affiliation was removed in the unity conference of 1959, when it was agreed that the new centre should be independent of any foreign connection – yet even before the attempt at secret affiliation was discovered the two warring factions were meeting clandestinely and acting as pressure groups within the centre. During the strike of 1964 all the trade union leaders sank their differences in the Joint Action Committee, and Imoudu and Adebola 'shed blood' together in a dramatic march across the Carter Bridge. A few months later the Joint Action Committee existed only in name. Again, immediately after the first coup in 1966, and after the end of the civil war, when parties no longer existed as a factor, it was found impossible to effect unity.

Is it then possible to detect a consistent pattern in the personalities involved, the interests represented, and the ideologies propagated within the labour movement which would provide the underlying explanation of the persistent disunity? Robert Melson has suggested[29] that, despite the alignments and realignments, two predominant groups are evident in the movement. The first comprised, in Melson's terms, 'youth', i.e. Marxists and anti-regionalists who sought affiliation with the WFTU, the second consisted of 'neutralists' (in the sense that they avoided prior commitment to any one political party) and accommodationists who sought international support from the ICFTU. This perceived dichotomy has a measure of validity – indeed, it finds popular expression in the characterization of LUF and NTUC as 'radical' or 'left-wing' and the description of the ULC and NWC leaders as 'moderate', 'conservative', or 'right-wing'. But it isolates two divisive issues (international affiliation and the attitude to the regional political structure) over and above all other factors that provoke disunity. Here, while it is acknowledged that two basic tendencies are apparent in the labour movement, it is proposed to discard conventional terminology that plots positions along a left-wing/right-wing continuum (for many of the leaders clothed themselves in more than one ideological garb) and to regard the divergence of attitudes in terms of a cluster of ideas and modes of expression that are characteristically found in two basic groupings. In the contemporary context these are represented in the programmes of the NWC and ULC on the one hand, the NTUC and LUF policies on the other, but the historical progeneration of these two 'clusters' can be located in earlier intra-movement struggles: in the differences between the 'conservatives' and 'radicals' of the early central bodies, in the differing attitudes to affiliation with the NCNC, in the degree of overt political colouring that the various centrals proclaimed. The outcome of these series of disagreements can be noted in tabular form, as follows:

LUF, NTUC LEADERSHIP	NWC, ULC LEADERSHIP

Customary Mode of Address

'Comrade'	'Brother'

Attitude to Strikes

A necessary recourse to deal with a stubborn management. A means of increasing the consciousness of the workers by struggle. ('Militant')	A regrettable recourse; to be used only when all the mechanisms of collective bargaining are exhausted. It is possible to have a meaningful dialogue with management. ('Responsible')

Attitude to Government

Government basically represents colonial bourgeois or neo-colonial interests; workers should not be surprised if their interests are ignored. ('Hostile')	Government represents the national will, and there is every expectation that it will consider the interests of the workers. ('Favourable')

Attitude to Ministry of Labour

The Ministry is an arm of the government; its intervention in the affairs of the movement is not always disinterested. ('Suspicious')	The Ministry considers the wishes of the workers, employers and government equally; it is truly neutral. ('Strongly favourable')

Attitude to Political Parties

The major political parties have promised the workers much, and given them little; they represent selfish ethnic interests; workers therefore need their own parties to represent their interests. ('Exclusivist')	Individuals may lend support to any party they choose. Unions should avoid involvement in partisan politics. ('Neutralist')

Attitude to Class

Class antagonisms are endemic and inevitable. Employers and workers are locked in an irreconcilable struggle. ('Conflictist')	Class lines are not clear and there is every possibility of reaching accommodation between worker and employer. ('Collaborationist')

Although the attitudes and ideologies of the centres are discussed again elsewhere, several caveats to this schema should be noted here. The attitudes expressed by the groups are typical, not universal. Secondly, an individual union or an individual worker may not hold the attitudes of a centre to which he is attached. As the fusion and fissure of the centres takes place customarily without widespread discussion and involvement from below, this does not provide an objection to the basic dichotomy presented here. Finally, special factors which have been enumerated, such as international affiliation, personality differences, etc., must be adduced to explain the splits within the two basic groups. These factors may also explain the immediate cause for any one split.

Ultimately the divergent ideas of the leaders are related to their class origins, their life experience, and the tactics and strategies that have been forced upon them during the course of their union struggles. These ideas have now, however, assumed the status of 'a material force' which constantly impedes any moves towards trade union unity. It is possible that a strong central government may legislate to bring one body into existence (forbidding external affiliations may be one compelling device). Equally, as in 1964 and in 1970, the workers may force the union leaders into a temporary alliance by pressure from below. But as long as no constraints of this kind operate, it can be confidently predicted that any settlement between the union centres will remain a temporary expedient and not a permanent condition.

Summary Chart of Central Trade Union Organizations

Date of Formation	Name of Organization	Comments
1941	African Civil Servants Technical Workers Union	Offices held by L. A. Nkedive and M. Imoudu.
November 1942	Federated Trade Unions of Nigeria	Offices held by T. A. Bankole and S. Coker. Arranged conference to set up TUC.
August 1943	Trades Union Congress (of Nigeria) TUC(N)	Office held by Bankole, N. A. Tokunboh, and F. O. Coker.
1946	Supreme Council of Nigerian Workers	Part of the TUC, set up to present a case to the Tudor Commission.
1948	Committee of Trade Unionists	Led by Imoudu, F. O. Coker, and N. Eze. A pressure group within the TUC set up to try to reverse the decision to disaffiliate from the NCNC.

March 1949	Nigerian National Federation of Labour (NNFL)	Same leadership as above. Set up as a rival to the TUC
1949	National Labour Committee	Part of the National Emergency Committee set up after the Enugu shootings. Members from NNFL and TUC
May 1950	Nigerian Labour Congress (NLC)	Merger of NNFL and TUC dominated by radicals – Coker, Imoudu, and Eze. Affiliated internationally to WFTU
1951	Committee of ICFTU-affiliated Unions in Nigeria	Led by U. Agonsi. Had covert support from conservatives in NLC
August 1953	All Nigeria Trade Union Federation (ANTUF)	Led by Imoudu and G. C. Nzeribe. Set up after the collapse of the NLC. Unaffiliated internationally.
April 1956	Council of ICFTU-affiliated Unions	The successor to the Committee of ICFTU-affiliated Unions. Support from N. A. Cole, H. P. Adebola, and L. L. Borha, who retained positions in ANTUF
April 1957	National Council of Trade Unions of Nigeria (NCTUN)	Led by Borha and Cole. Affiliated to the ICFTU
March 1959	Trade Union Congress of Nigeria (TUCN)	Led by Imoudu and Borha. Merger of ANTUF and NCTUN. Contested affiliation with ICFTU
April 1960	Nigerian Trade Union Congress (NTUC)	Offices held by Imoudu and Nzeribe. Split from the TUCN
March 1961	Eastern Nigeria Trade Union Congress	Local organization having members in TUCN and NTUC

Date of Formation	Name of Organization	Comments
3 May 1962	United Labour Congress (ULC)	Led by Adebola and Borha. Merger of TUCN and NTUC Affiliation with ICFTU
5 May 1962	Independent United Labour Congress (IULC)	Led by Imoudu and A. N. Ikoro. NTUC personnel splitting from ULC 'Fraternal relations' with WFTU
December 1962	Nigerian Workers Council (NWC)	Offices held by N. Anunobi and N. Chukwura. Affiliated to the IFCTU Split from ULC
December 1962	Northern Federation of Labour (NFL)	Led by I. Nock. Claimed affiliation to the International Confederation of Arab Trade Unions. Split from IULC
August 1963	Nigerian Trade Union Congress (NTUC)	Take-over of IULC by W. Goodluck and S. U. Bassey.
September 1963	Joint Action Committee (JAC)	Temporary alliance of all trade union centres.
January 1965	Trade Unions' Supreme Council (TUSC)	Defensive alliance by ULC and NWC against the radicals in the JAC
February 1966	Nigerian Trade Union Federation (NTUF)	Merger between LUF, NTUC and NWC. Short-lived.
May 1967	Northern States Federation of Labour (NSFL)	Change of name from Northern Federation of Labour.
June 1967	Biafran Trade Union Confederation (BTUC)	Branches of the centres in the East secede from Lagos.
January 1968	The Labour Unity Front-Northern States Federation of Labour (LUF-NSFL)	Merger between these two organizations.
December 1968	Nigerian Federation of Labour (NFL)	Small breakaway from NTUC by E. Bassey Etienam.

August 1970	United Committee of Central Labour Organizations (UCCLO)	Alliance of NTUC, ULC, LUF, and NWC. Leaders include W. Good-luck, Y. Kaltungo, A. A. Ishola, and J. Uzor.

Source: Reprinted from Robin Cohen, 'Nigeria's Central Trade Union Organization: a Study Guide', *Journal of Modern African Studies,* 9 (3), October 1971, 457-8.

NOTES

1. Some difficulties of nomenclature exist in describing this body. Contemporary documents refer variously to the Trade Union Congress, the Trade Union Congress of Nigeria or the Trade Union Congress (Nigeria). I have adopted the simple expedient of calling the body established in 1943 the TUC to contrast it with a body established in 1959 called the TUCN.

2. Yesufu, T. M. *Problems of Industrial Relations in Nigeria with Special Reference to the Administration of Workmen's Compensation* (Ph.D. thesis, University of London, 1960), p. 98.

3. *Report of the Tudor Davies Commission into the Cost of Living and the Control of the Cost of Living in the Colony and Protectorate of Nigeria* (HMSO for the Colonial Office, No. 204, 1946), Para 5.

4. November, A. *L'évolution du mouvement syndical en Afrique occidentale* (Paris and The Hague: Mouton, 1965), p. 53 and Dept. of Labour, Nigeria, *Quarterly Review,* March 1960.

5. Sklar, R. L. *Nigerian Political Parties* (Princeton: Princeton University Press, 1963), p. 77.

6. Eze, N. *Memoirs of a Crusader* (1952) cited in Sklar, R. L., op. cit., p. 77.

7. See Davies, I. *African Trade Unions* (Harmondsworth: Penguin, 1966), pp. 190-5.

8. Dept. of Labour, Nigeria, *Quarterly Review,* March 1960 and November, A. op. cit., p. 54.

9. For further details *see* Woddis, J., *Africa: the Lion Awakes* (London: Lawrence & Wishart, 1961), pp. 129-30.

10. Bassey, S. U. *Review of the Development of the Nigerian Trade Union Congress, 1941-1967.* (Mimeographed, n.d.), p. 5.

11. Dept. of Labour, Nigeria, *Annual Report*, 1956–7.
12. Cited in Yesufu, T. M. *An Introduction to Industrial Relations in Nigeria* (London: OUP for the Nigerian Institute of Social and Economic Research, 1962) p. 150.
13. Bassey, S. U. op. cit., p. 6.
14. Stylistically and logically the contents of these letters ring true. One, with an authentic letterhead, has been examined by me. It should be noted, however, that these letters were the first in a series of 'secret correspondence' that one group in the movement claimed were authentic, and the maligned group claimed were forgeries.
15. Nigerian Employers' Consultative Association, Lagos, *Newsletter* (No. 9, November 1960), pp. 11–13.
16. Yesufu, T. M. op. cit., 1962, p. 155.
17. *West Africa* (London) 17 February 1962.
18. Memo by Chukwurah (February 1962) in my possession.
19. Incidentally, assuming the plot to poison Nigerian–Ghanaian relationships was a fabrication, it nevertheless reflected a nice sense of political reality. By 1962 Ghana's Pan-Africanist ambitions were placing her in an increasingly isolated position in Africa. In Nigeria in particular there was a good deal of resentment at the Ghanaian assumption of a leadership role that was 'rightfully' Nigeria's. Driving an Anglophone wedge into Nkrumahist ambitions could also be said to reflect accurately American policy at the time. *See* Post, K. W. *The New States of West Africa* (Harmondsworth: Penguin 1968), pp. 172–5.
20. *Daily Times* (Lagos), 28 December 1968, and Lynd, G. E. (pseud.) *The Politics of African Trade Unionism* (London: Praeger, 1968), p. 127.
21. Most of the Nigerian left had been organized in the Nigerian Youth Congress, a body which was launched by ex-Zikists on the eve of independence. It was in this body that a conflict between Otegbeye (who in 1963 was President) and another group of Marxists, including Eskor Toyo, broke out. The group around Eskor Toyo supported Imoudu and Ikoro, and in 1964 launched a Nigerian Labour Party to counteract the influence of the Socialist Workers and Farmers Party. Further discussion of these small left-wing coteries and parties can be found in a subsequent chapter.
22. Ananaba, W. *The Trade Union Movement in Nigeria* (London: C. Hurst & Co. 1969), p. 232.
23. *West African Pilot* (Lagos), 20 May 1964.
24. Press statements signed by Acting General Secretary of the ULC. ULC files, 1966.
25. *See Daily Times* (Lagos), 12 January 1968. The NFL changed its name to the NSFL after the creation of the twelve-state structure in May 1967. Ibrahim Nock became a commissioner in the North Central State, but remained as the *éminence grise*. The merger between the NSFL and the LUF was not a happy one; a LUF leader informed me in late 1968 that the NSFL had threatened to withdraw from the body if the salaries of its officers were not paid by the LUF. Subsequent to this point the fortunes of the NSFL declined considerably.
26. United Committee of Central Labour Organizations, *Equitable Demand for Economic Growth and National Prosperity* (Ibadan: Government Printer, 1970), p. 1.

27. *Morning Post* (Lagos), 29 October 1970.
28. Allen, C. 'African Trade Unionism in Microcosm: the Gambia Labour Movement, 1939–67', in Allen, C. and Johnson, R. W. (Eds.) *African Perspectives* (Cambridge: Cambridge University Press, 1970) p. 425.
29. Melson, R. F. *Marxists in the Nigeria Labour Movement: A Case Study in the Failure of Ideology* (Ph.D. thesis, Massachusetts Institute of Technology, 1967).

CHAPTER 4

Trade Unions in Nigeria: Their Leaders and Their Members

The Structure of the Trade Unions

The complex history of the attempts to create a central trade union organization has been described in the previous chapter. Underneath the level of the surviving central organizations are the numerous 'primary' unions, the vast majority of which are affiliated to one or other central organization. The numbers of claimed affiliations vary considerably according to the fortunes of the central organization and the period of time that is examined. In a few instances more than one central body claims a particular union as its affiliate. This usually happens during a factional split in an individual union, where one official claims that a previous affiliation holds good and another that the union has changed its allegiance to a rival central body. The pressures of competition by the central unions may indeed provoke the factional dispute in the first place. Ambiguity also arises in the problem of 'aspirational affiliation'. Quite frequently either the individual union or the central body claims a link when what they mean is that they hope to achieve one. None the less the relative importance of the various central organizations can be indicated to some extent by the number of unions each central body claimed to have as affiliates. (Table 4.1) These figures have been modified by cross-checking doubtful cases with officials of opposing central bodies, and I believe them to be a substantially accurate assessment of the situation in late 1968

TABLE 4.1

Claimed Affiliates of the Five Central Organizations, 1968

Centre	No. of Affiliates Claimed
United Labour Congress	240
Nigerian Trade Union Congress	209
Labour Unity Front/Northern States Federation of Labour	28
Nigerian Workers Council	112
Nigerian Federation of Labour	3
	592

The numbers of claimed affiliates shown are, however, misleading in some respects. Many of the affiliates listed by the NTUC were unions based in the East, most of which were moribund owing to the war situation. The number of affiliates of the Labour Unity Front belies the strength of their organization in terms of membership, as its adherents included three large unions – the Railway Workers' Union, the Nigerian Union of Teachers, and the Posts and Telecommunications Workers' Union (though the NUT was substantially an independent body in its own right). The Nigerian Workers' Council, by contrast, organized a large number of small unions. The situation since the end of the war remains somewhat obscure. The NTUC does appear to have successfully reactivated most of its affiliates in the Eastern States and enlisted a number of new allies. My impression is, however, that it still plays second fiddle to the ULC – only slightly in terms of the number of unions affiliated, but more clearly in terms of the number of workers, as the ULC has been more successful in trying to amalgamate unions in the same industry group. (The delay by the Registrar of Trade Unions in accepting such amalgamations also, incidentally, confuses the statistical picture.) The NWC for its part was racked by a leadership shake-up and lost unions as a consequence of the departure of N. Chukwurah and his replacement as general secretary of the centre by Mr. J. U. Akpan. In an interview with Mr. Akpan in January 1972 he claimed that the NWC organized 'about a hundred unions', most of which were in Lagos and Ibadan.

In addition to the gains and losses that the centres have experienced since the civil war there seems to be a growing number of unions established in the last few years which are unaffiliated or not yet affiliated to a central body. The growth of registered unions has been quite dramatic, especially from the early sixties onwards. From 14 registered trade unions with a membership of 4,649 in 1940, the trade union movement had grown to 873 unions with 655,215 members in September 1971.[1] But only a little over half the membership are organized in unions of over 5,000 members. The increase in overall growth has been paralleled by a corresponding increase in the large number of unions organizing 51–250 members that are registered each year; these amounted to 365 in 1971. Unions organizing less than 1,000 workers constitute 85% of the registrations, while over 50% of all unions have less than 250 members. The size distribution of the trade unions and the distribution of membership in the various sizes of unions is indicated in Table 4.2. Two features of the latest figures may be noted. (*a*) The number of very large unions increased by only one since 1964/5, despite recent attempts to amalgamate unions in one industry group. (*b*) The number of members recruited does not seem to have kept pace with the number of unions created since 1964/5. This may, however, be partially explained by the increase in the number of unions which have not returned their membership figures.

The difficulties of centralizing and amalgamating the small trade unions, even in similar occupational categories, can be attributed to eight major reasons.

First, the legal provisions for the registration of new unions are extremely permissive, any group of five or more persons having the right to constitute themselves into a union. This factor is especially important in making it easy for any disgruntled faction of a union to split and create a new union.

Second, within the civil service and public corporations, Nigeria already exhibits complex hierarchical structures, involving differing incomes, styles of life, and functions, that might be more characteristic of a highly industrialized society. The distinction between white- and blue-collar workers is especially acute when the acquisition of a pen-pushing job comes replete with an increased status and highly developed attitudes of snobbery, as is the more basic accepted dichotomy between 'general labour' and

TABLE 4.2

Trade Unions by Size, Number, and Membership, 1963–5, September 1971

Size	Total Number of Registered Trade Unions				Total Membership Stated			
	1962/3	1963/4	1964/5	Sept. 1971	1962/3	1963/4	1964/5	Sept. 1971
50 and under	62	105	91	138	2,779	26,940	2,855	4,469
51–250	167	180	231	365	22,880	26,588	30,155	47,087
250–1,000	79	93	139	239	39,278	46,914	70,607	112,364
1,000–5,000	52	45	47	77	92,401	94,016	91,376	154,016
Over 5,000	15	12	21	22	166,865	158,332	322,915	337,279
Membership not known	60	67	22	32	—	—	—	—
Total:	435	502	551	873	324,203	352,790	517,911	655,215

Sources: Ministry of Labour, *Annual Report* 1964/5, Appendix VIII, p. 59. Author's calculations from Ministry of Labour files.

workers outside this category. Unions such as the Airways African Senior Staff Association and the Ewekoro Cement Works General Workers' Union, clearly indicate the accepted demarcation between skilled and unskilled workers, while the word 'association' rather than 'union' is sometimes used to describe organizations of managerial and supervisory staff. Where complex grading systems exist, as in the civil service or the public corporations, there is invariably a multitude of trade unions organizing the different income and status layers.

Third, small unions are a result of the diffusion of industrial enterprises to areas widely separated geographically and badly served by the communications network of the country. T. M. Yesufu has called attention to pockets of timber and rubber establishments in the Benin, Delta, and Ondo, provinces whose remoteness from any means of transport made organization at the local level a *sine qua non*.[2]

Fourth and fifth, ethnic and Regional considerations have occasionally played a part in promoting union factionalism, or in creating rival foci of interests. More recently unions have begun to organize within the boundaries of the State governments established by military decree in May 1967. In the first nine months of 1971 seventeen unions registered with the name of a State government included in their description. They included the Kwara State Washmen's Association and the Western State Stone, Sand and Gravel Blasters and Diggers Union. As regards ethnic differences, these have only been of minor importance. An early example of a trade union formed purely on an ethnic basis was the Ibo Timber Labourers Union registered in 1945 with 1,128 members, and destined to survive for less than a year. No union registered in recent years has indicated an ethnic identity in its title, though some very localized unions, like the Idapometa Bricklayers' Association, would naturally tend to organize an ethnically specific group. Ethnicity was, however, occasionally a factor in promoting factionalism, as in the splinter groups which broke away in the early sixties from the Nigerian African Mineworkers' Union, the first major trade union on the Jos Minesfield. Two breakaway groups were the Northern Mineworkers' Union, which was overwhelmingly Hausa, and the Middle-Belt Mineworkers' Union, which was predominantly Birom. The splits also, however, coincided with political differences. The three unions' political links were as follows. (a) The Northern Mineworkers' Union was essentially a sponsored union of the Northern Peoples' Congress. This can be seen most clearly in the overlap of personnel. Alhaji Dan Ladi, as well as being general secretary of the union, combined the roles of secretary of the local NPC and *employer* of the unionists he organized. The President of the Northern Mineworkers' Union was also simultaneously the Provincial President of the NPC. (*b*) The Nigerian Mineworkers' Union (a fusion between the Nigerian African Mineworkers' Union and another breakaway union, formed in 1961) consisted primarily of Ibo supporters of the NCNC/Northern Elements Progressive Union alliance; while (*c*) the Middle-Belt Mineworkers' Union lent their support to the AG/ United Middle-Belt Congress alliance. A further explanatory factor lies in the division of skills between the Ibo-dominated Nigerian Mineworkers' Union, which comprised the skilled, technical, and clerical, workers; the Hausa-dominated Northern Mineworkers' Union whose members were semi-skilled or unskilled labourers; and the Birom-controlled Middle-Belt Mineworkers' Union whose membership consisted of a less stabilized unskilled labour force.[3] While other examples of ethnicity intruding into union affairs can be given, ethnicity is rarely the single explanatory factor in a split,[4] and Jos provides a unique case of the congruence of ethnic rivalries, political tensions, and differing levels of skill. Unions organizing on the basis of a purely Regional and now State loyalty are a more potent explanation for the persistence of the small trade unions. Unions such as the Northern Watchmens' Union (with 600 members), the Northern Nigeria Rural and Medical Workers' Union (with 960 members), the Mid-Western Regional Telephonist Union (with 40 members), and the Eastern Nigeria Private Cinema Operators Workers' Union, all attest to the influence of Regional sentiment in the period before the civil war. Since 1970, there have been a number of small unions organized on a State-wide basis. Both the South Eastern State Motor Stevedores and Catering Workers' Union, and the Mid-Western Nigeria Vulcanizers' Union, for example, have a membership of less than 50.

Sixth, at a more macro-level of analysis, Regional pressures were structurally entrenched in the constitutional arrangements of Nigeria after 1951. This meant that it was often in the interest of organized labour to operate on a Regional level (even though there may not have been separate Regional organizations created), particularly when negotiations with the Regional government were being undertaken. While the State governments are unlikely even to have comparable power to the old Regional governments, as their financial resources and administrative viability expand they will become fairly large employers in their own right with whom the unions will have to negotiate.

Seventh, the attitude of Nigerian employers is extremely important in promoting the formation of a multiplicity of 'house' or 'company' unions. Examples of this type of union are legion: the Oxford University Press Workers' Union, the Nestlés Workers' Union, the Taylor Woodrow Workers' Union, are but a few examples of what is the predominant type of union in the country. Even within single companies there have been cases of the decentralization of union organization to the plant or branch level, as for example in the case of the John Holt Rubber Factory and Allied Workers' Union, Ologbo, the rest of the company's workers being organized in the Holts African Workers, Union of Nigeria. In general, however, within each company of national importance, is a Nigeria-wide organization of its workers. The C. Zard African Workers' Union, J. Allen African Workers' Union, K. Chellerams and Sons (Nigeria) African Workers' Union, and the UAC and Associated Companies African Workers' Union, are some of the many national company unions, the last providing an interesting example of how employers' attitudes can influence the structure of unionism. House unions began organizing in the UAC in 1945, and in 1947 the secretary of one of the company's unions, Nduka Eze, succeeded in forming an Amalgamated Union of UAC African workers. After a successful strike in 1949, Eze, who was by now the General Secretary of a Mercantile Workers' Union (organizing other company unions in addition to the UAC) and the Nigerian Labour Congress (the radical central organization referred to in Chapter 3), called a nation-wide general strike against all foreign firms. The strike was broken, and for four years (until 1955) the company recognized no labour representation other than management-sponsored joint consultative committees. In 1955 a house union was recognized in a Lagos branch, but it was not until two years later that the company acceded to a request to form an amalgamated company union.[5] The UAC's attitude towards the unions is typical of a good many employers. Employers are hostile to any tendency towards 'movementism', suspicious of any trade union organizer who is not an employee of the company, and tend to adopt a positively favourable attitude to unionism only when the leadership can be characterized as 'responsible' (or, in a more cynical formulation, 'pliable'). Naturally enough, many managements have been less than enthusiastic in recognizing large unions whose officials would be likely to have a greater independence from management pressures.

Eighth, and finally, the problems of union centralization are related to the prevailing type of trade union leadership. In the vast majority of cases the aggregate income that the general secretaries can expect to receive from organizing several small unions is greater than the income they would receive from an amalgamated union. An important set of exceptions to this statement concerns the unions which were granted check-off orders after 1961, when a non-compulsory check-off system was introduced. An analysis of the financial returns by sixty-two unions which operated the check-off system in 1966 showed that the salaries and allowances of trade union officials jumped from £26,500 to over £44,500 within a year, while the payment of grants to members totalled only 2·5% of the unions' incomes.[6] In addition, any move towards amalgamation would probably mean the displacement of general secretaries organizing relatively inefficient or small trade unions: consequently the fear of job insecurity is an important motive for resisting any such move. It may also be the case that union members would feel more 'in control' of a local general secretary compared to a union bureaucracy physically far away from their place of work.

The structural features of Nigerian trade unions can also be examined in terms of the five various types of organization that are registered under the Trade Union Act. (a) Of the 873 organizations registered in September 1971, a few are employers' organizations which qualified under the provisions of the Trade Union Act: while (b) some are modern Craft Guilds like the Gboyin Tailors' Union (with 500 members), or the Mainland Cycle Repairers Union. It is in practice extremely difficult to differentiate between those guilds that register under the Trade Union Act and the great many 'unions', 'societies', and guilds that do not. Organizations of corn millers, shoemakers, bakers, mechanics, leather-workers, blacksmiths, carvers, weavers, tailors, and many others, proliferate in Nigeria. Some describe themselves as unions, but are more strictly co-operative societies. Many, however, that are not listed by the Registrar of Trade Unions would appear to be technically qualified for registration under the Trade Union Act.[7] (c) There is next a category of Craft Unions which differ from the guilds in that they organize employees in a single (or related) occupation regardless of the establishment in which they are employed. The All Nigerian

Union of Electrical and Allied Employees and the Western Nigeria Painters' Union are examples of this type. (*d*) By far the largest group of unions are those described as Industrial Unions in the sense that they organize all the employees in a particular industry or service regardless of their grade or occupation. The majority of these Industrial Unions (about 80%) are house and company unions, although in the last few years there has been a vigorous effort by the central organizations to amalgamate company unions of one particular type of industry into larger units. The

TABLE 4.3

Types of Registered Organizations, 1954, 1971

	1954 % *of Total*	*Jan. 1970–Sept. 1971* % *of Total*
Employers' Organizations	6	5
Craft Unions	32	19
Industrial Unions	42	46
General Unions	3	1 (?)
Guilds	17	27*
Unclassifiable	—	2
	100	100

Sources: T. M. Yesufu, *An Introduction to Industrial Relations in Nigeria* (OUP for NISER, 1962), p. 42.
List of Registered Trade Unions, Ministry of Labour files.

* Various Drivers' Unions, difficult to classify because of the varieties of part-ownership, have been included in this category.

ULC in particular successfully merged six motor transport unions into a body established in 1968 and called, if not colloquially, the Nigerian Motor Drivers, Mechanics, Clerical and Allied Transport Workers' Union.[8] Similarly the Northern States' section of the ULC have negotiated a merger between eleven textile workers' unions, though when I interviewed the trade union secretary responsible for the proposal in December 1968, the Registrar of Trade Unions had refused to recognize the merger on the grounds that the mills at Aba and Asaba (shut down because of the war) would not be able to participate. (*e*) There are very few General Unions in Nigeria which group workers irrespective of the industry or occupation in which they may be employed, the

Public Utility Technical and General Workers Union being the most notable.

The Ministry of Labour has not published a breakdown of the type of registered organizations for many years, and it is not always easy to classify them simply by looking at the names of registered unions. None the less, such an attempt has been made by analysing the registrations from the period January 1970 to September 1971. This in turn has been compared with the figures compiled by T. M. Yesufu based on the 1953/4 returns (Table 4.3).

The Leadership of the Trade Unions

The role of the general secretary in the Nigerian labour movement has always been a controversial one. Ministry of Labour reports are full of admonitions about the fecklessness and inefficiency of union leadership, and several government reports have indicted union officials for absconding with union funds. The Fitzgerald Commission of 1949, enquiring into the Enugu coal mine shootings, did not bother to conceal its contempt for the secretary of the Colliery Workers Union:

> We are not at all impressed by the evidence which he has submitted concerning the sum of over £1,500 which he received personally out of a levy of little more than £2,000 subscribed . . . His behaviour at best showed a greater interest in his own financial improvement than was consistent with his devotion to the cause of the miners, and at worst exposed him to the charge that he deliberately used his position to enrich himself at the expense of the union's funds. [9]

Thomas Hodgkin, while allowing that the individual concerned drew 'no very clear distinction between trade union funds and his private purse', considers that his patriarchal and traditional style allowed him to present himself as dominating the mine management much as he had dominated the union, and extract considerable wage increases as a result. [10]

The attitudes of contemporary general secretaries are also ambivalent. Although many of them express vehement pro-labour sentiments, very few have a broader ideological commitment, say to a radical political party or a socialist system of government.[11] The ULC District Secretary in the Midwest State, for example, claimed: 'What we need is not the stirring up of class consciousness by more of strikes, agitations, and sabotage, but the reinforcement of our democratic influence in society by the expansion of our trade union education work.' (Interview, February 1968.) In like manner Mallam Kaltungo, the District Secretary of the ULC in the Northern States, now the President of the ULC, argued that 'the workers would make a mistake in trying to set up a dissident political party. This will be to the detriment of the workers' interests.' (Interview, December 1968.) While such attitudes might be expected of ULC officials because of the more conservative character of its ideology, despite the previous connection of the NTUC with the Socialist Workers' and Farmers' Party several NTUC secretaries expressed their doubt about linking their trade union work with a broader political movement. (Of course it should be remembered that this was only a theoretical possibility as political parties had been banned by the Military government.) One NTUC secretary maintained, 'Oh, I disagree with Goodluck on ideology. We must organize workers from the bottom upwards if we do not wish to go cap-in-hand to government. Not all this talk of workers' party.' (Interview, March 1969.)

The militancy of trade union organizers seems largely related to their commitment to a professional expertise. In this respect, W. A. Warmington has provided a suggestive analogy of the role of the general secretary. They are, he considers, to be regarded as professional consultants undertaking to act in the interests of their clients in much the same way as a solicitor would.[12] General secretaries have a style of their own, and even in-group jargon; some, for example, referring to the unions they organize as their 'portfolios'. Although this may be apocryphal, one general secretary was said to have held twenty-eight 'portfolios' simultaneously; certainly organizing five or six unions is not uncommon. Several persons interviewed were boastful of their successes in 'capturing' unions organized by their personal or ideological rivals. One mournfully claimed that his union was 'pinched' while he was imprisoned for his political views. His rival did not deny this charge but maintained that far from the erstwhile general secretary being detained on political grounds, he had been tried for fraud. Individuals were derogated as being 'loud-talkers' or 'politicians'. 'You tell me which union X has?' one challenged me (I didn't know, as my previous respondent had been particularly vague on this score). The check-off unions notwithstanding, in general the more unions the general secretary organizes the greater is his income, and moreover, if one union dispenses with his services he has a few more to fall back on. On the other hand the union rank and file see every reason to use the services of a general secretary who has demonstrated his capability in negotiating for another union.

The general secretaries are likely also to have little understanding of the exact nature of the work of their members, and consequently may be unable to appreciate special problems or grievances that may arise from particular working conditions. This was especially brought home to me by talking to a union organizer in Jos. Sent up from Lagos six months previously, he had not yet seen the inside of a mining compound, despite the fact that the majority of workers he organized were miners. The lack of contact between workers and general secretaries is also reinforced by physical separation; most of the general secretaries have their offices in the centre of the town rather than at the place of work. The management is also more likely to resent the idea of officials outside the plant organizing 'their' workers, and most of the larger establishments have attempted to sponsor their own 'company' unions. Workers are, with some justification, suspicious of the paternalist character of some of these unions; and the term 'company union' is usually used pejoratively.

The general secretary's role is characteristically a function of the nature of the disputes that are engendered, and in this respect Peter Kilby has given an admirable description of the way grievances are typically generated:

> A major claim or grievance arises: mobilized by individuals from the artisan and craftsmen ranks, members begin paying their union dues and the services of a professional trade union secretary are recruited. After a few preliminaries (perhaps including statements to the local press), the professional secretary confronts the management and threatens strike action if the claim is not conceded. If in the end, perhaps after a short strike, the claim is not granted the services of the secretary are terminated; equally, if successful the absence of any energising discontent is soon reflected in a decline in dues and the exit of the general secretary for want of remuneration – unless, of course, he can manage to generate a new dispute.[13]

I think Kilby exaggerates the universality of this pattern and the extent to which general secretaries 'exit' – usually they keep the union concerned 'on their books' without being particularly active in its day-to-day organization. But Kilby is right to point out that this frequently found pattern of disputes tends to mean that the 'strong man' secretary survives, and that he retains his position through his qualities of bellicosity and intransigence. Even where the general secretary signs a collective agreement with the management, he sometimes finds himself repudiating the agreement if the membership decides he made concessions too easily or has 'sold out' to the management.

The Department of Labour realized at an early date that collective bargaining had little prospect of success unless it could train a group of trade union officials that would be prepared to work within the norms of compromise and negotiation that are characteristic of the British model of industrial relations. Several unionists were sent on scholarships to study the operation of trade unions in the United Kingdom, either to the TUC or to Ruskin College, Oxford. While providing the individuals concerned with an excellent opportunity to advance their own educational qualifications, as far as the Nigerian unions were concerned, the scheme backfired grievously, for none of the early recipients returned to work in the unions. Of the six officials who went to the United Kingdom in 1950, three joined the civil service on their return, two took up appointments in private industry, while one remained in England to study law.[14]

Those leaders who remained in the labour movement during the 1950s moved into the positions of dominance at the level of the central trade union organizations. All the leaders of the four rival trade union centres which had developed by 1963 – Imoudu and Ishola of the Labour Unity Front (LUF), Adebola and Borha of the United Labour Congress (ULC), Chukwura and Anunobi of the Nigerian Workers Council (NWC) and Goodluck and Bassey of the NTUC – had one important characteristic in common. Their claim to leadership was based not so much on educational attainment (all, with one possible exception, have not completed their secondary education) as on a history of militancy and long service as officials of important unions and central bodies.

After 1962 their authority in the labour movement was paradoxically both reinforced and undermined by the greater intrusion of foreign trade union international bodies into the affairs of the Nigerian labour movement. On the one hand, while all the

'Lagos leaders' retained their positions (usually as general secretaries) in the primary unions they organized, they now had independent sources of income. The ULC affiliated to the International Confederation of Free Trade Unions (ICFTU), the NWC to the International Federation of Christian Trade Unions (IFCTU), and the NTUC had 'fraternal relations', then affiliated openly, to the World Federation of Trade Unions (WFTU). Only the LUF remained unaffiliated. Control over the purse strings from their international sponsors provided the Lagos leaders with renewed sources of patronage and influence. The lower-level cadres could often be relied upon to legitimize the power of the Lagos leaders, provided scholarships, the chance of foreign travel, grants of equipment, and supplementary grants of money, were forthcoming. Regional secretaries of the ULC, the richest of the four centres, were given car allowances and a small salary in addition to the income they derived from their union 'portfolios'. The NWC, for which I have reliable figures, received an annual grant of £20,000 from the African regional organization of the IFCTU before 1970, and £10,000 yearly after that date. This was apart from an extra grant given to finance the purchase of land in Lagos for the building of a Labour College. The centre had three cars in Lagos and one car each for the use of organizers in the Northern and Western States.

While providing a source of patronage, outside funds also exposed the Lagos leaders to charges that they were self-seeking and interested only in maintaining a flow of income from outside the country. Richard Sandbrook has argued that in Kenya, union conflict was often expressed in terms that would accord with the precognitions of the international sponsors:

> The ideological vocabulary of political and union conflict can thus be partly explained by the actors' need to demonstrate their fidelity to International sponsors. In fact, there were very few conversions to a new political faith. More frequently there was a cynical attempt to exploit the apparent naïveté of American, Russian, East European, and Chinese donors, who actually interpreted Kenyan political and trade union conflict in terms of East–West rivalry. The main effect of the foreign money . . . was to increase the venality of those into whose pockets it eventually passed.[15]

While a similar process of ideological formation is observable in Nigeria, the degree of locally engendered ideological disagreement is perhaps greater than in Kenya. None the less, the attachment of the Lagos leaders to competing sources of foreign support could not but have a deleterious effect on the cause of labour unity. All the Lagos leaders tried to outbid each other in verbal contortions designed to demonstrate how dear the cause of unity was to their hearts. Wahab Goodluck (NTUC) maintained 'If leaders have a common front, no employer can have the gut to treat workers with a levity and hope to remain in business.'[16] H. P. Adebola (ULC) declared: 'There must be unity at all costs even if there will be a plebiscite to determine the most popular central organization,'[17] while N. Chukwurah claimed that, 'We of the NWC firmly and sincerely believe in genuine unity in the labour movement, but our main contention is that it must be unity won through negotiation and not compromise.'[18] Despite reiterated protestations of this kind there remains a widespread cynicism among the lower cadres of leadership and the rank and file as to their sincerity. The readers' columns of the newspapers regularly carry letters from disgruntled trade union members. One reader complained: 'It appears that the leaders are intentionally making it difficult to form one central body hence they make the unity calls to camouflage [sic.] the working masses . . . Because the leaders are supreme than the masses, there is nothing the poor workers can do. Even though it is known that in trade union the masses are supreme to the leaders.'[19]

Certainly workers are intensely conscious of the benefits that they gained from the temporary unity of the centres during the 1964 strike, and many tend to lay the blame for the break-up of the co-ordinating body squarely on the shoulders of the Lagos leaders. A significant proportion (41%) of the respondents in the University Workers' Survey (reported fully later in this chapter), held the trade union leaders partially responsible for the lack of labour unity. 'Union leaders like too much money and do not care about the welfare of the workers', 'leaders are untrustworthy', 'leaders in Nigeria get money from other countries and have no time to look into workers' complaints', 'leaders are fighting for themselves and not for the common people' are samples of the responses in this category. Asked whether they trusted the Lagos leaders, only 9% of the workers interviewed answered an unequivocal 'yes'; the rest answered 'sometimes' (56%) or 'never' (35%). (Appendix I, Question 25.)

Some radicals, who saw the political crisis in the country as providing an opportunity for the labour movement to assert its political power, are especially scathing about the role of the Lagos leaders. Eskor Toyo, whose position is left of all the trade union centres including the pro-Moscow NTUC, for example, writes:

> General Ironsi did invite trade union 'leaders' to unite and, it is said that he urged them: 'Unite and participate in my government.' But the opportunist and mediocre professionals that infest the trade union movement shrugged off the opportunity with callous abandon. Had the opportunity been seized the country might have been saved the carnage and anguish of July 1966 and subsequent months. But, of course, the fate of the masses means nothing to the pack of mediocre clerks that call themselves 'labour leaders' in Lagos. Since January the opportunity of worker–army dual power has existed in the country, but the blind and selfish professionals of the labour movement have preferred to amble along their own individual blind and crooked paths like lame rascals.[20]

Although the small group of radicals that concern themselves with the problems of the labour movement have very little support among the rank and file, it is clear that since 1964 there has been a growing groundswell of opinion within the trade unions against the dominance of the Lagos leaders. This was manifested in July 1969 when H. P. Adebola was ousted from the presidency at the annual conference of the ULC by Yunusa Kaltungo, where Kaltungo was able to use the distrust of the Lagos leadership in his bid for power. Six months previously he had told me: 'as regards labour unity, there is no problem in the North where we work together. The problem is in Lagos. They should let us come down from the North and help them in Lagos.' In December 1969 Chukwurah and Anunobi were displaced from the leadership of the NWC while the veteran unionist Michael Imoudu was excluded from the LUF representation to the United Committee of Central Labour Organizations set up in 1970 to present a case to the Adebo Commission. Only the NTUC leaders remained in the positions they had held since the early sixties.

Dissatisfaction with the old leaders appeared to emanate from the level of leadership immediately below that of the central organization leadership – the regional and district secretaries, assistant general secretaries, and other administrative officials in the central organizations. This group of leaders, although they are general secretaries at one and the same time, are primarily the bureaucrats and co-ordinators of the central bodies. They are also partly the creation of the Lagos leaders themselves. As the assistance from the foreign international bodies increased, the Lagos leaders were obliged to use some of the money to set up training institutes and provide seminar courses for their own trade union officials. In 1963 the NTUC established the Patrice Lumumba Institute of Political Science and Trade Unionism (now called the Patrice Lumumba Labour Academy) financed by Soviet money and offering courses in Basic English for Workers, Basic Anthropology for Workers, Economics for Workers, Scientific Socialism (Marxism–Leninism), Political Economy, Marxist Philosophy, and 'some other working class courses'. The ULC with the active assistance of the Afro-American Labour Centre (AALC) has since 1966 been operating the Trade Union Institute for Economic and Social Development, offering short courses for trade union officials in Industrial Relations, Trade Union Law, Economics, etc. Its Directors have been American trade unionists nominated by the AALC. The NWC with the assistance of the IFCTU acquired land preparatory to building a proposed Labour College.

The staff and the products of these institutes gradually moved into a position where they could challenge the authority of the Lagos leaders. Reinforcing the central bodies' own educational efforts are the occasional courses run by the Ministry of Labour and by the Extra-Mural Departments of the Universities of Ibadan and Lagos, and these have also increased the level of sophistication of union functionaries. This level of trade union leaders can usefully be thought of as forming part of the lower ranks of the intendant class. Their conflicts of interest with the Lagos leaders may (at a different level) be considered analogous with the conflicts between members of the higher ranking intendant class and the politicians – in that their views both represent, in some measure, the ethic of efficient and rational organization.

While this shift in the leadership pattern of the centres has been presented in terms of the growing bureaucratization of the unions, sole emphasis should not be placed on this interpretation. The leadership struggles of recent years have analogies with those of the early sixties (especially in terms of personal rivalries); where they differ is that the new leadership is trying to offer a new kind of credibility to workers and foreign sponsors alike. This credibility rests not so much on their past history of militant action and popular support as on their ability to internalize the language of industrial economics and collective bargaining.

Membership and Recruitment

What support do the unions derive from persons employed in the formal sector of the economy? Of the estimated 1·8 million wage-earners in Nigeria, the unions claimed to organize some 655,215 workers in 1971. In terms of their geographical distribution (derived from the lists of registered trade unions) organized labour is concentrated in eight urban centres – Lagos, Ibadan, Port Harcourt, Kano, Kaduna, Jos, Benin, and Enugu (especially before the war), and in the Sapele–Warri–Burutu cluster in the Mid-West State. There appear to be few trade unions organized outside these areas, though some of the bigger trade unions – like those organizing the workers in the public corporations and the Nigerian Union of Teachers – have branches or members in most of the smaller towns and villages. Divided into industry-groups, there is apparently no special predisposition for workers of one or other category to be interested in trade union activity. The distribution of trade unions by broad industry groups can be tabulated from the 1965 data (Table 4.4). Other than some increases in employment in the petro-chemical industry and in construction, which are bound to swell union membership in these areas, the proportions of organized labour in the various industry groups are likely to have remained much the same since 1965.

The number of unionized workers looks impressive when one takes into account the large number of part-time, spasmodic, or seasonal workers, as well as wage-earners working in small firms employing less than ten workers, all of whom would have little inclination towards joining a trade union. The claimed total becomes more explicable when one considers the grounds on which membership of a union is claimed. Only in 85 out of 631 unions (1966 figures) where the check-off system is operative, are union dues the prime determinant of membership. In the other unions, membership may be judged by the number of workers who have contributed a token sum to the union coffers, or by the number of workers who gave vocal expression to their support for the union, or, finally, by the numbers who have supported a strike called by the union. Very often, the hat will be handed round after the cessation of a successful strike action, or before the undertaking of strike action that looks to the membership as if it may succeed.

The contribution to union dues then becomes, as it were, a payment for services rendered to the union membership by the union leadership.

The large number of new members that join the unions after a successful strike is dramatically evidenced by the overall jump in membership of more than 165,000, after the 1964 general strike.

TABLE 4.4

Union Membership by Industry, March 1965

	No. of members	% of total membership
1. Community Services	133,208	25·4
2. Transport	102,089	19·5
3. Manufacturing	78,438	15·0
4. Mining and Quarrying	55,990	10·8
5. Agriculture, Forestry, and Fishing	33,854	6·5
6. Services (not otherwise specified)	28,470	5·4
7. Construction	27,993	5·3
8. Government Services	27,930	5·3
9. Wholesale and Retail Trades	11,387	2·1
10. Electricity, Steam, and Gas	8,419	1·6
11. Banks, Insurance, and Financial Institutions	8,197	1·6
12. Communications	7,936	1·5
	523,911	100

Source: Compiled from the *Annual Report* of the Ministry of Labour 1964/5, Appendix IX, p. 60.
Notes: 1. There is a discrepancy of 6,000 members between the total presented here, and the accepted total for 1964/5 of 517,911.

2. All labour statistics in Nigeria must be treated with caution. There is a further discrepancy in that the numbers of union *members* found in the manufacturing industry is larger than the *total reported employment* in manufacturing. (*See* Table 2.5.)

An increase in membership is also apparent when a wage commission is set up (as with the Adebo Commission in 1970), and the prospect of a favourable wage settlement looks bright.

The increase is shown in the following table (Table 4.5) and graph, which also illustrates the point negatively, i.e. in the periods where there was a low strike incidence (between 1942–5, in the early 1950s and during and just before the civil war) there was little growth in the membership figure, 1952 indeed showing a drop of nearly 9,000 members.

By and large then, the trade union member in Nigeria should be seen as an intermittent participant, who will turn to the union either when he has a high expectation of receiving an immediate

TABLE 4.5

Annual Registration of Unions and Members, 1940–September 1971

Date	No. of Unions	No. of Members	Date	No. of Unions	No. of Members
1940	14	4,629	1956	270	198,265
1941	27	17,521	1957	298	235,742
1942	80	26,275	1958	318	254,097
1943	85	27,154	1959	347	259,072
1944	91	30,000	1960	360	274,126
1945	97	41,000	1961	402	281,124
1946	100	52,747	1962	435	324,203
1947	109	76,362	1963	502	352,790
1948	127	90,864	1964	551	517,911
1949	140	109,998	1965	615	519,000*
1950	144	144,389	1966	631	520,164
1951	124	152,230	1967	674†	530,000*
1952	131	143,282	1968	696†	540,000*
1953	152	153,089	1969	721†	550,000*
1954	177	165,130	1970	809†	600,000*
1955	232	175,997	1971 (Sept.)	873	655,215

Sources: Ministry of Labour, *Annual Reports.* J. I. Roper, *Labour Problems in West Africa* (Penguin, 1958), p. 107. H. A. Tulatz, *Die Gewerkshaftsentwicklung Nigerias* (Hanover, 1963) p. 127. Author's calculations from Ministry of Labour files.

* Weak Data: Estimates.

† Calculations made 1971 List of Registrations, Ministry of Labour files. There are discrepancies between the number of unions added shown here, and the figures suggested by the Ministry (*See* Ministry of Labour, *Annual Report* 1965/6 Para. 115 p. 23.) In all these cases I have used my own figures.

return for his support, or when he feels impelled by moral necessity and social pressure to reward the union when it has taken up the cudgels on his behalf. The intermittent interest of most trade union members in the affairs of the union can be seen in the conduct of union meetings which, with few exceptions, tend to be ritualistic obeisances to democratic control, rather than genuine attempts at representative democracy. Regular attendance at meetings is unusual, and those who do attend the meetings may lack the sophistication to challenge the union leadership on procedural or constitutional issues. David Smock, in a study on the Nigerian Coal Miners' Union, has described how the general secretary of the union, one E. A. Bassey, succeeded in controlling the running of the union's annual conference. According to Smock's account, Bassey called points of order when he wanted to stop a hostile or over-verbose speech, or dismissed suggestions as unconstitutional when he was the only one who possessed one of

Graph of Annual Trade Union Recruitment, 1940–September 1971

Sources: As for Table 4.5.

the few copies of the constitution. Free discussion only took place when there was open contradiction of Bassey's point of view from a powerful member of the executive, or when Bassey indicated that he did not care which way the issue went.[21]

Union elections, even where they are regularly held, tend to be little more than a public demonstration of the legitimacy of the trade union leadership. This should evince little surprise considering the customary lack of communication between the trade union leadership and the rank and file. In essence a system of communication requires a sender, a message, a channel, and a receiver. Where the trade union leadership is anxious to preserve its control over information, where there are few union publications to inform members of what the leadership is doing, and where the rank and file is uninterested in receiving regular information, there is little doubt that an unscrupulous leadership will try to exploit the lack of communication to retain its control of the union.

The low level of information available to the membership can be illustrated by the response to a questionnaire issued to a group of seventy members of the University of Ibadan Workers' Union. 31% of the respondents had never spoken to the general secretary of their union directly, despite the fact that the union's active membership was less than 300 and the general secretary lived opposite the main gates of the university. (Appendix I, Question 15.) A much higher proportion of the persons interviewed (61%) had no idea to which of the central labour organizations their union belonged. (Appendix I, Question 16.) The high proportion of 'don't knows' to this question is probably related to the fact that the general secretary of the union, on his own authority, switched his allegiance from the NTUC to the ULC. It is an indication of his contempt for democratic procedures that he apparently did not even bother to inform the whole union executive, let alone the membership, of the change. It should be added that the general secretary was voted out of office thirteen months after this survey was conducted. From a second-hand report, however, his removal seemed more a result of his lack of militancy than of his non-adherence to democratic principles.

Too great a stress on the capacity of the leadership to manipulate the membership, however, underestimates the large number of occasions when the leadership has suddenly found its authority undermined and the union split into rival factions. Often such a circumstance will arise out of interests external to the membership. Two central organizations, for example, may each gain adherents on the union executive, and the union will split over an affiliation issue (there are, as has been mentioned, several unions whose affiliation is claimed by two or more of the central bodies). There are, none the less, many instances where the membership will call a mass meeting to remove an errant official. One such reported case concerned the Barclays Bank Workers' Union whose central executive had, out of union funds, presented a gift of a genuinely needed car to the general secretary of the Nigerian Union of Bank Insurance Allied Workers. The management of Barclays Bank were, according to a press account, flooded with letters withdrawing check-off forms, several mass meetings were held, and the executive was called upon to resign and call fresh elections to put an end to 'such an illegal spending of other people's funds'.[22]

Rather than attributing the attitudes of the membership towards their union to ignorance or apathy, it is more accurate to consider that members neither wish nor feel themselves competent to exercise a day-to-day control over the actions of their leadership, who have, within wide limits, the capacity to manage union affairs as they consider best. Workers have, however, strong attitudes on the performance expected; if the leadership exceeds its wide limits of accorded power, or refuses to go along with a generally felt demand, the workers will exercise their ultimate power of removal without the slightest hesitation.

The low level of participation in union affairs can also be related to the limited role that trade unions play in the social experience of the individual workers. Unlike in Britain, where trade unions historically provided a range of social activities and benefits for their members (working men's clubs, burial societies, old age and sickness benefits etc.), unions in Nigeria are simply one of a myriad network of competing affinities. Tribal unions, improvement organizations, or religious bodies, all provide social outlets for their members, and trade unions are generally relegated to their purely economic function. As T. M. Yesufu writes:

> The workers own tribal organization, or 'improvement' union in the town provides benefits in desperate cases, financially assists those who want to get married, pays the burial expenses of a deceased parent, makes a present on the occasion of a new babe, honours the worker elevated to a chieftaincy, and repatriates the destitute. Some tribal organizations award scholarships to the young educated worker or to the children of others. It is this that explains the seeming paradox that whereas the worker will not regularly subscribe to the

funds of a trade union (apparently because he is too poor) he does pay regular subscriptions to the fund of his tribal 'union'; and the contributions here are usually higher than those required by the trade union . . . Thus the trade union is caught in a vicious circle; it is deprived of funds because the services which it ought to render are provided by non-industrial organizations supported by the workers, and it cannot provide rival services because it has not funds.[23]

The fact that few workers expect the union to provide social benefits and amenities can be shown from the response to a question in the University Workers' Survey asking why membership was sought (Table 4.6).

TABLE 4.6

Workers' Reasons for Joining their Union

Question: Why did you join your union? (*give reasons*)

	%
To fight for workers' rights	42
To fight for better wages	33
'United we stand, divided we fall', and variants	8
Job security	7
Thought it compulsory	4
For help when in difficulties	2
No definite motive	4
	100
	N = 98

Source: Appendix I, Question 37.

In sum, the trade union member sees the union as providing a highly circumscribed set of services. When the union fulfils these expectations, the members are prepared to demonstrate their support by joining the union, paying dues, and going out on strike. In other circumstances the member shows a measure of indifference to union affairs commensurate with his sceptical attitude to the leadership and his continued attachment to non-industrial associational interests.

Some Workers' Attitudes:
a Report on a Survey

To evaluate the attitudes of a group of union members, and assess
the degree to which they express a corporate interest, cannot but
be a hazardous task. Class consciousness does not have the character of an instantly discoverable presence or absence, but rather is a
function of the objective conditions affecting wage-earners as a
group, the workers' perceptions of these conditions, and the degree
of success that organizations of workers have in coping with the
effects of these conditions. I concur with the Marxist position that
the basic datum separating a mass (or a statistical category) from a
class, is activity conducted on behalf of, or preferably by, the
group concerned. The sharper and more sustained the activity (is
it, for example, special representation, occasional conflict, or
permanent struggle?), the more clearly visible is the transition, to
paraphrase Marx's words, from a class of itself, to a class for itself.
In this sense, the evolution of class consciousness and the expression of political attitudes by Nigerian workers cannot be considered
in isolation from the history of the activities of organized labour.
Yet this is precisely what the survey method demands. Bounded by
time and circumstance, a survey of this character can only hope to
elicit a few 'ideological residues' of past experience and some
immediate and hastily considered responses to issues that the
workers may have given little thought to. It cannot provide
anything but the vaguest guide to future attitudes, let alone to
future behaviour.

These limitations, as well as those deriving from the small
sample and other methodological weaknesses, should be borne in
mind by the reader in gauging the value of the survey results
provided below. In Appendix I there is a note on methodology
and a tabulation of all the responses. Those statements that are
reported in the text below are followed by parenthetical references
to the Question and Response number in Appendix I. The survey
was carried out in one union in early 1968, a period of relative
labour quiescence induced largely by the appeals of the Federal
government not to 'rock the boat' during the conduct of war
operations in the East. As against this surface tranquillity, it should
be borne in mind that there were considerable complaints by the

workers at the imposition of a compulsory savings levy of 5% to pay for the costs of the war, over and above the 10% deductions that went to the National Provident Fund.

The sample population comprised seventy members of the Ibadan University Workers' Union (whose secretary claimed a 'committed' membership of 280 persons), who were stratified by skill and then more or less randomly selected. The population shared a roughly even spread of ages with a weighting towards younger (20–29 yrs.) workers (Question 1). Many (34%) earned between £14 and £20 a month (Question 3) while a considerable proportion of workers were Yoruba (41%), the only other ethnic groups represented in any numbers being Ibo (10%) and Bini (9%) (Question 5).

Considering the weighting towards young workers, the population was on the whole remarkably stabilized, 61% claiming that they had resided in Ibadan for ten years or more and a further 17% from five to ten years (Question 6). An explanation for this probably lies in the job security that the university offered as well as good conditions of work for most workers. Other indices of stability were that 13% were born in Ibadan while 47% were sending their children to be educated there. This last high figure is probably to be explained by the provision of schooling facilities at Abadina, the workers' compound on the university campus. On the other hand 81% claimed to send money 'home' (Question 11), and some 56% of these remitted 10% or more of their income (Question 12), while a large percentage (73%) professed that they themselves, or their immediate families, had the use of land rights (Question 9).

Two questions designed to elicit further information on the population's stability produced ambiguous responses. Although 63% avowed that they would retire to their birthplace and only 11% to Ibadan, an examination of individual respondents showed that some indigenous Ibadans placed themselves in the former category, while 5% out of the 11% were people who were born elsewhere, but had decided to stay in Ibadan (Question 8). Similarly a question concerning the number of occasions when the birthplace was visited produced many (57%) who were prepared to visit only once or twice a year (very few of these responses can be accounted for by cost of travel or inaccessibility due to the war), and 10% who stated that they never visited home (Question 10).

The educational attainments of the group are listed in Table

4.7. Despite what seems to be, by local standards, a very well-educated labour force, a considerable number of workers (43%) did not read newspapers, though it is more than possible (this was not tested) that the price deterred many people who nevertheless listened to newspapers being read aloud to them during their work breaks. A notably high number of the group (15%) did, however, read the weekly trade union newspaper, *Advance*, the rest of the newspaper readers (29%) taking privately owned newspapers (overwhelmingly the *Daily Times*) or Government-owned papers (13%), mainly the *Morning Post* (Question 27).

TABLE 4.7

Education of Respondents

Lower Primary	19%
High Primary (Standard VI)	40%
Secondary	21%
No schooling	13%
Technical Training (exclusive of other education)	7%
	100%
	N = 70

Source: Question 19.

Besides these questions concerned in 'profiling' the sample, specific series of questions were directed to evaluating the attitudes of workers to their fellow workers and the unions, to questions of 'class' differentiation, and to their attitudes concerning politics. The degree of interest in their own union was moderately high – 69% had spoken to their general secretary, though not always on union matters, while 59% had exercised their vote, at least once, at a trade union meeting, including, that is, informally convened meetings. (Questions 14 and 15.) Three other questions concerned with the worker's knowledge of his union, and the labour movement brought responses listed in Table 4.8.

The large number not knowing the centre to which their union was affiliated is partly explained by the particular circumstances of the University Workers' Union and the vacillations in loyalty by the general secretary, referred to earlier in this chapter. But the responses indicate that the general secretary could, because of the

TABLE 4.8

Knowledge of Trade Unions

	% Yes	% No	
Knows to which centre his union is affiliated	39	61	N = 70
Can name leader(s) of the NTUC	70	30	N = 70
Can name leader(s) of the ULC	78	22	N = 69

Source: Questions 16, 17, 18.

lack of knowledge of the membership, have a considerable discretion in the question of affiliation. In two open questions on labour unity and on what means should be used for improving the position of workers, the respondents demonstrated a considerable awareness of the issues involved (Tables 4.9 and 4.10).

The general acceptance of a corporate interest revealed by these answers is perhaps noteworthy in view of the fact that 49% of the sample belonged simultaneously to a tribal association (Question 13). This fact, together with the response of 91% who did not consider that ethnic factors entered into the election for union office (Question 32), demonstrates that workers are, through a process of 'situational selection', able to compartmentalize their roles according to the circumstances involved. Interestingly enough, the proportion of workers who stated that they would, if

TABLE 4.9

Workers' Views on Labour Disunity

Question: Why are Trade Unions not united? (Give reasons)

	%
Leadership struggles	41
Ideological differences	17
Government foments or provokes disunity	11
Some unions support government, some do not	10
Other reasons	10
Unions *are* united in goals and spirit	5
No reasons/don't know	6
	100
	N = 121

Source: Question 26.

need be, ask for a loan from their union and fellow workers, as against their relations, broke more or less even (Question 34).

The next series of questions was an attempt to measure attitudes towards 'class' identity and differentiation. The difficulty in framing valid questions here was most marked since local *English*

TABLE 4.10

Workers' Views on how Their Group Position Could be Bettered

Question: How can workers improve their position?

	%
Striking	34
Fostering labour unity	24
Having labour representative or party	11
Replacing present leaders	9
Working harder	7
Take over government	6
Supporting government of the day	2
Don't know/other	7
	100
	N = 86

Source: Question 28.

linguistic development had brought into common usage only the terms 'big men' and 'common people'. Pre-testing had included a number of other differentiating concepts including the words 'masses', 'élite' and 'working men', which it became clear were not readily understood by the respondents. I ended up using the categories, 'same as', 'more important than', 'a big man', 'less important than', into which workers were asked to classify their general secretary, an army officer, and a civil servant (Table 4.11).[24]

While the responses to these categories were, perhaps predictably, vague, the possession of political power by the officers undoubtedly increased their prestige, it being, prior to 1966, very difficult to recruit Yoruba and others represented in the survey to a military career. The lower social estimation that is accorded to the 'civil servants' is probably a reflection of the inadequacy of the category, as many quite junior public employees are wont to describe themselves as 'civil servants'.

Most workers had heady aspirations for their children, some

94% believing that they would be in a better job than themselves (Question 35), a response which would seem to argue that social mobility was still seen as relatively open.

Finally, a group of questions was framed to look at the workers' attitudes to politics. Questions in this category showed that, despite the fact that 24% claimed to be not interested in *party* politics (Question 23), nearly all workers displayed a considerable measure of political cynicism: 93% thought that they were not getting a fair share of national wealth (Question 24) while 45% were prepared to countenance the notion of a workers' political party (Question 31). Although the question called only for a straight alternative answer, several who said they were not in favour mentioned the past failures to establish a labour party with any electoral support and others again referred to the practical problems involved in recruiting support from the electorate.

A sophisticated analysis of the political attitudes of Nigerian workers has been provided by Robert Melson[25] who sees their political attitudes as being governed by the 'cross-pressures' of

TABLE 4.11

Workers' Classification of Social Position of Others

Regards as:	General Secretary	Army Officer	Civil Servant
Same sort of man	31%	21%	38%
More important man	50%	51%	31%
One of the 'big men'	6%	25%	19%
Less important man	13%	3%	12%
	N = 68	N = 65	N = 68

Source: Questions, 20, 21, 22.

ethnicity and class. He accepts as a general proposition the view that the Nigerian worker will tend (like workers in other countries) to support his ethnic group when it is threatened, but pays particular attention to those workers 'who claimed to support a labour party while *at the same time* supporting ethnic parties'.[26] These 'inconsistents' are divided into 'descriptive' and 'prescriptive' inconsistents. The former claim to support a labour and an ethnic party simultaneously, the latter claim to support a labour party (perhaps because they feel they should do so) but in practice support an ethnic party. Dr. Melson's series of non-probabilistic sample surveys was carried out largely during the last six months of 1964, when at the beginning of the period he was able to assess the support for a labour party immediately after the stirring events of the June 1964 General Strike, and at the end of the period he could examine what support remained as the Federal elections of December 1964 drew near. He found clear evidence that (a) the 88% who indicated some support for a labour party had dropped to 41% in October–December, (b) the 5% who had indicated in July that they would support an ethnic party (only) had increased to 41% later in the year, (c) the percentage which was cross-pressured in July (69%) had dropped to 19% by the time the elections were due. 'In effect,' Melson concludes, 'this meant that in a four-month period, the labour party lost up to half its support.'[27]

While some reservations may be expressed on methodological grounds – Dr. Melson tested *different* workers and the results cited are based on samples of fifty-eight and seventy-two workers – the results are stark enough to support Melson's conclusion that the large number of inconsistents belied the real strength of the support for a labour party and gave an illusory picture to those who were trying to organize workers politically on the basis of class solidarity.

One of the difficulties in evaluating the continuing relevance of Melson's findings is that the declining support for a workers' political party in 1964 might have been a function of the particular character of the labour parties then existing and the circumstances surrounding the December election. Neither the Nigerian Labour Party nor the Socialist Workers' and Farmers' Party was a particularly inspiring body, in terms either of leadership or of organization, and, as will be seen in Chapter 5, the election results were distorted by the partial boycott carried out by the United Progressive Grand Alliance. It is sheer speculation to surmise what would have happened had the labour parties been able to campaign on a wider basis and develop a national platform expressing a working-class interest, but what must have been clear to the workers was that the labour parties and individual labour leaders were themselves constrained by the pressures of ethnic politics. This was demonstrated for example when SWAFP tried unsuccessfully to forge an electoral alliance with UPGA, and when several labour leaders stood on the platform of the major parties. Workers may well have felt that the self-proclaimed leaders of working-class interests were behaving in much the same way as any of the other politicians of the First Republic and were equally deserving (or undeserving) of their support.

In the University Workers' Survey considerable cynicism was reserved for the politicians generally, few of whom were trusted by the respondents. Army officers, by contrast, were considerably more favoured, though evidently workers had reservations about their military leaders too (Table 4.12).

TABLE 4.12

Attitudes to Politicians and Army Officers

	Yes	*No*	*Sometimes*	
Do you trust politicians?	6%	83%	11%	N = 70
Do you trust army officers?	26%	39%	35%	N = 69

Source: Questions 29, 30.

The most voluble reaction to all the questions concerned one asking about the respondents' notion of socialism. Some confessed ignorance, 'As I am illiterate I cannot say,' commented one. Several others saw the state of socialism as some kind of hedonistic paradise involving, as one saw it, 'making friends, going to movies, dances, footballing etc.'. But a good number had a clear understanding of what was involved, their responses being listed in Table 4.13.

What generalizations can we draw from this brief venture into empirical sociology? First, that in groups of workers, like our sample, that are relatively stabilized, a self-conscious identity of a kind has already been established. This may not necessarily manifest itself though participation in, and extensive knowledge of, trade union affairs, but it does find a limited degree of expression in the comparison of the workers concerned with other workers, and in the measure of social distance that workers accord to other groups in the social system. Second, the workers concerned have an unexpectedly high measure of political sophistication in understanding political issues and are prepared to adopt political stances of a fairly radical nature. That these may not translate to a continued support for a labour party, however, has been shown by Robert Melson's study. Third, the results would seem to confirm the view that a 'working class' in the sense that the term would be used in an industrial environment is clearly in the making. An

element of consciousness is revealed, there is a measure of understanding of the group interest, there is critical awareness of the
workings and failures of the organizations that represent workers,
and a 'world view' of the place of the group in Nigerian society

TABLE 4.13

Workers' Notions of Socialism

Question: Some people talk of Socialism. What is it?

	%
Fair distribution of wealth	27
To be friends, trust each other, to be polite, hospitable, brotherhood	26
Taking care of the poor	13
Everybody treated on merit	9
Workers in control of government	9
Everybody enjoys life	8
No clear notion, doesn't know	8
	100
	N = 158

Source: Question 38.

that broadly resembles the group's real social position. At the very
least, the attitudes revealed show a substratum of workers' opinion
that could, under favourable conditions, be used and amplified
by organizations concerned with representing their interests.

NOTES

1. The statistical services of the Ministry of Labour were placed under severe
strain during the period of the civil war. The publication of *Annual
Reports*, in any case subject to a long time-lag, ceased in 1964/5, the following year's report (1965/6) being published in 1971. The *Quarterly
Reviews* have been published up to October–December 1967. No further

reports are available at the time of writing (January 1973). I was fortunate, however, in gaining the assistance of Ministry of Labour officials in looking at their files until the early months of 1972. Separate acknowledgement to the officials concerned has been made in the preface to this book. However, there remains a data gap particularly in the period 1966–70 which could not be adequately filled by the statistics made available to me.

2. Yesufu, T. M. *An Introduction to Industrial Relations in Nigeria* (London: OUP for the Nigerian Institute of Social and Economic Research, 1962), p. 80.

3. A basic antagonism between the Biroms and the other ethnic groups on the Minesfield was noted as early as 1941 in a Colonial Office report. The indigenous Biroms were characterized as 'extremely primitive wearing little or no clothing and resenting any appreciable measure of control ... The "pagans" are, however, despised by the more sophisticated Hausas, Yoruba, Fulani, etc. of the Christian and Mohammedan Communities.' Orde-Browne, G. St. J. *Labour Conditions in West Africa* (London: HMSO for the Colonial Office, 1941), p. 54.

4. Billy J. Dudley has, however, documented the case of the Nigerian (Northern) Electricity Supply Corporation African Workers Union which at a conference at Bukuru in 1959 split into Hausa, Middle-Belt and Southern factions. Dudley, B. J. *Parties and Politics in Northern Nigeria* (London: Frank Cass, 1968), p. 241.

5. For further details of UAC company unions *see* Kilby, P. 'Industrial Relations and Wage Determination: Failure of the Anglo-Saxon Model', *The Journal of Developing Areas*, July 1967, 1 (4), pp. 507, 508.

6. Yesufu, T. M. *Labour in the Nigerian Economy* (October Lectures, Nigerian Broadcasting Corporation, 1967), p. 29.

7. A discussion of the craft enterprises and their organization in Ibadan can be found in Callaway, A. 'From Traditional Crafts to Modern Industries', *Odu*, July 1965, 2 (1), pp. 28–51. Callaway has even discovered a union of worn-out tyre traders.

8. *ULC Information* (March 1968).

9. *Report of the Commission of Enquiry into the Disorders in the Eastern Provinces of Nigeria, November 1949* cited by Yesufu, T. M. op. cit., 1962, p. 89, who also gives two instances of trade union officials being indicted for forgery and stealing.

10. Hodgkin, T. *Nationalism in Colonial Africa* (London: Frederick Muller, 1956), p. 137.

11. This, and other categorical statements in this section, are based on a series of intensive interviews held with twenty-seven general secretaries in all the major areas of organization in the Federation except Enugu and Port Harcourt. The quotations used in this section are reproduced verbatim, though it has sometimes been necessary to preserve the anonymity of the official concerned.

12. Warmington, W. A. *A West African Trade Union* (London: OUP, 1960), p. 135.

13. Kilby, P. op. cit., 1967, p. 509.

14. Yesufu, T. M. op. cit., 1962, pp. 95, 96. Other prominent ex-trade union officials whose ideological proclivities and educational attainments

would have made them competent to work a system of industrial relations based on collective bargaining, left the labour movement. They include M. A. Tokunboh (now Permanent Secretary of the Ministry of Establishments), Ayo Ogunsheye (once a Professor of Adult Education and now a private businessman), Adio Moses (now personnel manager for an oil company), and J. M. Johnson (at one time Minister of Labour).

15. Sandbrook, R. 'Patrons, Clients, and Unions: the Labour Movement and Political Conflict in Kenya', *Journal of Commonwealth Political Studies*, 1972, 10 (1), pp. 24, 25.

16. *Daily Sketch* (Ibadan), 20 May 1969.

17. *New Nigerian* (Kaduna), 3 June 1969.

18. *Morning Post* (Lagos), 18 April 1968.

19. *Morning Post* (Lagos), 14 October 1968.

20. Toyo, Eskor *The Working Class and the Nigerian Crisis* (Ibadan: Sketch Publishing Company, 1967), pp. 43, 44.

21. Smock, D. R. *Conflict and Control in an African Trade Union: a Study of the Nigerian Coal Miners' Union* (Stanford: Hoover Institution Press, 1969), pp. 63–74.

22. *Daily Times* (Lagos), 10 February 1968.

23. *Daily Times* (Lagos), 14 April 1959, cited by Sklar, R. S. *Nigerian Political Parties* (Princeton: Princeton University Press, 1963), p. 496.

24. I am indebted for this suggestion to the surveys carried out by Robert Melson in connection with his doctoral work *Marxists in the Nigerian Labour Movement: A Case Study of the Failure of Ideology* (Ph.D. thesis, MIT, 1967). *See also* the methodological note in Appendix I and the references to Dr. Melson's published discussion of workers' political attitudes below.

25. Melson, R. 'Ideology and Inconsistency: The "Cross-Pressured" Nigerian Worker', *American Political Science Review*, 1971, LXV (1), pp. 161–71.

26. ibid., p. 161.

27. ibid., p. 164 and Tables 1 and 2 oc. cit.

CHAPTER 5

The Unions as Political Agents

Political and Economic Unionism: a False Dichotomy?

The highly political nature of trade union activity in under-developed countries has often been commented upon. Walter Galensen, for example, writes:

> It should be apparent that the outlook for non-political unionism in the newly developing countries is not very bright. We may expect rather a highly political form of unionism with a radical ideology. Indeed so strong is the presumption that this will be the prevailing pattern, that, when it is absent we may draw the conclusion that unionism is in fact subordinated to the employer or the state i.e. that we are dealing either with company unionism or a labour front.[1]

With regard to trade unions in Latin America, R. J. Alexander maintains: 'From its inception organized labour in Latin America has been highly political. Virtually all important trade-union groups of the area have been closely associated with one or other political party or with the government.'[2] Similar generalizations about the political character of unions in Asia and Africa have been made; indeed it is often asserted that in the underdeveloped countries a form of unionism *sui generis* has developed or is about to emerge.[3] This is usually described as 'political unionism' and is often contrasted both with the 'economic' or 'business' unionism that is supposed to operate in the industrialized west and some-times with the 'productionist' unionism that operates in the Soviet Union and other centrally planned economies. In like vein the *modus operandi* of political unionism is referred to as 'political bargaining' as opposed to the method of 'collective bargaining' enshrined in the ILO principles.

The contrasting models of unionism can be regarded as ideal types which, while having only a limited basis in reality, none the less offer patterns of contrast in the nature of union behaviour within and between individual countries. The tenor of the conventional argument can, however, be shifted somewhat if the political element in union behaviour is accepted as a given datum and the element of 'unembellished' economic demands is explained within a broader political process. Take, for example, economic or business unionism in America which is often held up as a 'pure' version of this type. The first, and most obvious political assumption on which such a depiction rests, is that the legitimacy of the unions' bargaining power is recognized and integrated into a political *status quo* that acknowledges the structure of industrial capitalism as an acceptable political value. Secondly, it is assumed that this legitimacy will be similarly recognized by the majority of employers and given legal sanction by the important decision-making bodies. Given that these conditions operate in the United States, American unions have not yet totally 'renounced' politics in favour of a purely economic role. Unions in America have always performed important lobby functions on behalf of their membership – the very recognition of their rights to exercise their economic bargaining power (the Norris–La Guardia Act of 1932) was only achieved through intense political activity. In the 1940s, the CIO, through its Political Action Committee, tried, with some success, to get out the mass vote to promote candidates and policies favourable to labour. In 1948 both the AFL and CIO campaigned vigorously to secure Truman's re-election. The American unions are non-political only in the sense that they organize primarily around 'bread and butter' issues, they reject the notion of a Marxian class struggle, and (through the success of their other political activities, primarily their voting power) they have found it unnecessary to set up a workers' party to obtain their ends. In Britain, despite the stress on collective bargaining as a method of conducting industrial relations, the organic connection between the TUC and the Labour Party makes nonsense of the notion of a non-political labour movement, while the commanding influence of anarcho-syndicalist and communist ideologies in the French unions also discountenances any such notion.

Thus, even in the economic unionism of the industrialized west, from which the 'political unionism' of the underdeveloped countries is typically regarded as an aberration, there intrude strong political features in union behaviour. For unions in underdeveloped countries, a number of historical and social factors increase the political influence, or the predisposition towards political activity, of the labour movement. Included in these is the degree of politicization of the unions derived from their connection with the nationalist movements (this varied greatly and was probably stronger in Asia than in Africa); the strategic position that the unions have in the modern sectors of the economy and polity; the relative weakness of authority and legitimacy of the political systems in which unions operate; the labour movements' propaganda strength and influence outside the union structure; and the political attitudes that are distilled from the life-situation of workers newly wrenched from traditional forms of social control and to which the unions give expression. Though not all these factors are significant in every labour movement in Africa, Asia, and Latin America, it is probably true to assert that unions in these areas have a political influence quite disproportionate to their membership, finances, or apparent organizational viability.

But paralleling this measure of political influence is an industrial and economic weakness, and this weakness, too, explains the political content of their activities. For collective bargaining to operate successfully (and fairly) some kind of parity of power must exist between the employer and employee at the bargaining table. In its ultimate form the parity will represent the equality of a zero-sum game, with the employer standing to lose as much in terms of profits as the workers would in terms of their wages and job security. Such a parity rarely exists, save under exceptional circumstances. Abstracting, for the moment, the wider political process which may encapsulate an ideology of harmonic social control, and considering only an industrial environment, such an exceptional circumstance may occur where the labour force is highly skilled (i.e. more difficult to replace), and where in consequence the union side would have added leverage against the management. In underdeveloped countries, on the other hand, a huge pool of surplus labour is almost always available, thus making the threat of the withdrawal of labour a largely impotent one. Further, the concentration on extractive, service, and simple processing industries, demands a low level of skills. Where one man would do as well as another, the power of the management to hire and fire is substantially increased. The union in an under-developed country is, in short, in an inherently unequal position. To rely solely on collective bargaining in these circumstances is simply unproductive – not unnaturally the unions cast about for additional or alternative systems of bargaining in order to redress the imbalance between themselves and the management.

They find these alternative systems of bargaining primarily in the political sphere. In the industrialized west, involvement in the institutionalized political process has often been an important element in gaining legal recognition of the right to organize and strike, in regulating the conditions of employment, and in implementing progressive social legislation. Although lobbying and the participation in formal political structures is likely to be of importance in many countries, the value of union intervention on these lines will vary according to the electoral strength of the union vote, the degree of autonomy of the legislature, and the 'responsive capability'[4] of the political, system. In most African countries, however, a working-class vote is numerically too insignificant to attract the support of political candidates campaigning solely on a labour platform, even in the few cases where open electoral systems and independent legislative processes obtain. Nor can the unions be relied on to bring out a solid working-class vote, for, as has been shown earlier in the Nigerian case, the worker is cross-pressured by his traditional allegiances, which feelings tend indeed to determine the general pattern of voting.[5] So political participation usually takes other forms.

The nature of union political participation may be derived in part from Bruce Millen's suggestions as to what constitutes the typical patterns of political unionism.[6] First, leadership goals tend to be broad and diffuse, involving a major restructuring of the society, an attack on élite privileges, and in the most radical case some kind of exegesis of proletarian power. In contrast to this pattern, the American unions (say) present a range of highly circumscribed goals organized primarily around an individual establishment; where the state is involved at all, it is regarded as an agency of reform from which concessions are to be sought within the prevailing economic system. As C. Wright Mills writes, 'The unions are less levers for change of that general frame [the political economy of the U.S.] than they are instruments for more advantageous integration with it. The drift their actions implement . . . is a kind of "pro-capitalist" syndicalism from the top.'[7]

Second, there is often a tendency towards 'movementism' with the trade unions themselves being regarded as partial means to achieve a greater end. Unions in poor countries will often claim to speak on behalf of the 'toiling masses' or 'the common people' and seek to represent their activities as being necessary for the greater good of most. The tendency towards movementism may take one of several forms – the trade unions may set up a political party, informally take on the characteristics of political parties, or enter into an alliance, temporary or symbiotic, with a party. It may also take the form of the presentation of a 'united front', including in its structure peripheral organizations such as women's organizations, student groups, or coteries of intellectuals.

Third, union behaviour is more likely to be associated with mass action – in the form of a riot, demonstration, or rally. In this respect I. Tedjasukmana's description of the behavioural characteristics of the Indonesian trade union movement may be generalized to many other unions in Asia and Africa:

> [The] structure bears the marks of simplicity, flexibility, mobility and other prerequisites of a fighting organization. The administration of the union is dynamic, unbusinesslike and sometimes illogical. The behaviour of the unions, which betrays their political nature, is subject to spontaneity, emotion, impulses and outbursts of enthusiasm or rages and of a fighting spirit.[8]

For the union leaders, public demonstrations act as a spectacle designed to increase the level of class consciousness among the work force; for the workers, they act as a reassurance that the leadership is vigorous and dynamic. The use of mass action by unions can, as Myron Weiner has remarked with regard to India, be represented as 'a kind of Gresham's law . . . in which militant unionism drives out responsible unionism'.[9] The lack of well-defined and accessible channels of political communication contributes to the inclination to use mass action, but this tendency is also related to the fact that there are few intervening and mediating agencies between unions and government. At the most obvious level this is because the government is by far the most important employer of labour in nearly all underdeveloped countries; but a direct union/government relationship reflects too the characteristic features of a 'soft state' – a weak bureaucracy, atrophied or non-existent political parties, and a political class structurally dependent on an external estate.

Taken together, the tendencies to escalate a union grievance into a political issue, to encompass a broad set of goals, to regard the union as part of a larger movement, to use mass action, and to enter into a direct relationship with the government, all provide indices for evaluating how 'political' a particular union is. But these indices are not universal throughout underdeveloped countries, nor exclusive to them (witness the International Workers of the World in America). Many unions in Africa may choose (or be forced) to work within the system, hoping to gain concessions from co-operation and collaboration with the governmental authorities; other unions, whether through a realization of their own political impotence or as a result of a lack of responsiveness in the system, may direct their demands in the form of threats, latently or overtly inimical to the workings of the political system itself. In some cases the union may attach itself to an opposition political party or find itself being considered a counter centre of legitimacy even against the wishes of the leadership. A strike initiated for narrowly industrial objectives may become a political symbol for a wider discontent expressed by persons not necessarily within the union structure at all. Unions within a particular political system may differently incline to one or other model. Again, one union may oscillate between using the bargaining styles associated with economic unionism and those that are thought more characteristic of political unionism. It is, further, by no means unlikely that a union may choose to bargain at the level of the workshop and in the political arena simultaneously.

It should be apparent, then, that there is no 'pure' political unionism any more than (as has been argued earlier) there is a pure form of economic unionism. 'Political unionism' becomes therefore not a generic description flowing *pari passu* from the aims, structure, and leadership, of some abstracted 'typical' union, but on the contrary is a condition closely related to the prevalent political and economic system. The relative intensity of political bargaining in industrialized and unindustrialized countries alike is thus not a contingent occurrence. It is dependent on the degree to which the necessary conditions exist which make economic unionism, collective bargaining, or other forms of worker protest, possible or preferable tactics for union struggle. Different union organizations may also, as I shall indicate in the case of the Nigerian central bodies, have different perceptions of this bargaining environment and may as a consequence adopt different strategies to cope with it.

How the Union Centres see the Government

In this section the stated views, in pamphlets, union documents, and newspapers, of three major centres – the ULC, NWC, and TUCN, are examined. The statements of the leaders of the LUF have been so infrequent as to be thought not worthy of inclusion.

In terms of the personnel and character of the body, the ULC had, as was shown in Chapter 3, an earlier identity as the TUCN, the change of name (and little else) dating from the aftermath of the abortive 1962 Ibadan Conference on labour unity. The 'Independence Manifesto' of the TUCN clearly stated what it hoped its relationship with the government would be:

> ... the TUCN considers it a compelling obligation on the part of the Federal and Regional Governments ... to accord it *full consultative status* at all levels of State and national activity in the industrial, social and economic fields. On its part, the TUCN fully accepts its obligations to the values of Nigeria and expresses its readiness to give reasonable co-operation in the patriotic task of building Nigeria into a truly great and democratic welfare State.[10]

From the beginning the organization tried consciously to integrate itself into the political structure and processes that already existed in Nigeria, hoping through influence or 'working inside the system' to ameliorate conditions for the workers and to place itself in an advantageous position *vis-à-vis* the other union centres. Paralleling this internal movement towards integration with the authorities was an external association with the ICFTU (predominantly an American-dominated organization after 1953 and until the late sixties when the large American unions withdrew their support). Though the external affiliation of the Nigerian unions should not perhaps be taken too seriously as an index of their ideological predispositions, the possibility of patronage and support being rather more important than ideological empathy, the connection with the ICFTU did reinforce the 'conservative' character of the ULC in a number of areas. Besides the connection with Brussels, it should be noted that the ULC had connections with several other external union organizations. (a) AFRO, the African Regional Office of the ICFTU which had set up its head-quarters in Lagos. The office acted as a clearing-house for

ICFTU funds, housed a small research unit, and distributed a newspaper. There exist connections in personnel and informal liaison between AFRO and the ULC. (b) The African Trade Union Confederation (ATUC) set up in 1962 in Dakar mainly to act as a counterweight to AATUF, i.e. those unions from the 'Casablanca Group' of countries whose major voice was Ghana's. Though having no formal links with the ICFTU, ATUC derived its overwhelming membership from ICFTU-affiliated unions.[11] The ULC's leaders, Borha in particular, were office-holders in the body, but it had an effective presence only for a short while. (c) The AALC, the major agency that USAID and the AFL-CIO use to channel support to African unions, particularly after the former's disenchantment with the ICFTU. The AALC is probably the most effective instrument for training union leaders in Nigeria, and is responsible for nearly the whole of the ULC's educational programme. (d) The ULC also had friendly relations with the Israeli Histradut, and some German and Canadian unions which offered scholarships and training in their countries.

Though the media were different, the message was much the same. Great stress was laid on the phrase 'free and independent unions', one of which the ULC was supposed to be. Though usually explained to mean freedom and independence from party or governmental control, in practice the phrase also meant freedom from communist influence. Gradually, as the influence of the American training programme made itself felt, the ULC leadership grafted on to its own ideas preferences for a check-off system and the fostering of industry-wide unions with which collective bargaining could take place. The more sophisticated or perhaps better-trained leaders saw themselves as in the 'personnel management' or 'human relations' business, helping to explicate and make palatable the basic 'harmony of interest' between management and labour. At the plant level this involved a commitment to join consultation, collective bargaining, and the building up of local union bureaucracies. That this policy did not meet with entire success is revealed by the apparent 'misunderstanding' that some unionists had of the functions of unions:

> ... in most cases it was revealed that the instigation of communist inspired NTUC chaps was responsible. It was proved that while the trade union leaders preach the true principle of free trade unionism – most of the union leaders believe in this ideal – some evil minded communist inspired chaps go round under cover promising the union members improvisation of full time secretaries free, and free service

... The only way to overcome this menace is the enforcement of check-off.[12]

It is possible that besides counteracting the influence of the 'communist chaps' the potential for receiving a regular income also induced the ULC leaders to advocate the check-off system. At the level of government relations the handouts of the ULC constantly stress the desirability of institutionalizing conciliation, mediation, and arbitration procedures,[13] and of developing a permanent consultative status with the Government. Francis Luyimbazi, a research officer at AFRO's offices in Lagos, published an article bemoaning the fact that the government seemed to have little interest in the advice of the unions because, he thought, it 'attach[ed] undue importance to the possession of university degrees and diplomas and refuses to believe that anyone not so endowed can make a useful contribution to national planning'.[14] The ULC leaders were further enraged when the government did not bother to invite trade union participation in an internationally-attended conference on national reconstruction and development that took place during the civil war. Alphonsus I. A. Okwese, the Acting Secretary (Administration) of the ULC, complained:

> Whatever was responsible for this nebulous omission, this most unforgivable affront on the integrity of the entire working class of this country stand condemnable ... It is possible that what led to this type of attitude ... is that there are still some people today in official circles who look upon the labour movement with disdain.[15]

The plain fact of the matter is that the ULC gained precious little from the government despite its 'most favoured' position. On occasions the Ministry of Labour lent its tacit or overt support in the matter of sponsoring delegates to international labour conferences; the ULC leaders found it easier to travel abroad; and once or twice the government let it be known which side it backed in the movements towards labour unity, as it did in the Ibadan Conference of 1962. The ULC was often in fact in an unenviable position – having to reconcile its collaborationist principles and the demands of its backers on the one hand, and the rank and file pressures and competitive bids from the NTUC on the other. The ULC's attitude to the government has, as a consequence, oscillated in response to these pressures.

As early as 1961 the ULC (in its earlier manifestation as the TUCN) had attempted to set out an elaborate and reasoned claim for an increase in wages. The presentation of this, the Zudonu Committee Report, was described as 'Operation Square Deal'.[16] The total indifference of the government to this claim, and the rebuffing of a ULC delegation to the Minister of Establishments in May 1962, led to a considerable revision of the ULC's strategy in dealing with the federal government, the first fruits of which were manifested in the 1st Annual Delegates Conference held in May 1963. Though few overt differences within the ULC came to the fore, the differences in strategy revealed by the reports of the President (Adebola) and the General Secretary (Borha) were considerable. Whereas Adebola still adopted the tone of a humble petitioner, praising Azikiwe as 'a Socialist of great calibre' and Balewa as 'a God-fearing gentleman' and suggesting that the ULC 'need[ed] to co-operate rather than to indulge in shouting outworn slogans of Imperialist Agents, Neo-colonialists, etc., etc.',[17] Borha's report was of a much more radical temper. For him the Nigerian worker had an 'unfulfilled but legitimate expectation for a worthy place in the national scheme of things . . . he is wandering about and feeling betrayed by the promises of his political comrades and friends who today hold in their hands of power and sit in judgement over his destiny'. Referring to the government consideration of their wage demand, Borha commented that, 'we no longer feel enthused by the continued exchange of platitudes on the subject. We feel it is time we prodded the Government into definite action.' Borha also, for the first time in the ULC debates, drew a distinction between the government 'as employer' and the government as, 'the authority of state, which has a dire responsibility to protect wage-earners in all sectors of wage employment from the ravaging effects of rising prices and the oppressive maladjustments in the colonial wage structure which regrettably, still obtains in independent Nigeria'.[18]

Although views of this kind come to the fore when there is a general build-up in pressure for a wage review, the ULC has only bowed to this pressure on occasions. For the most part it continued to adhere to its programme of non-partisanship in politics and co-operation with the incumbent government. According to a ULC policy paper:

> Union leaders all over the country, especially those under the guardianship of the ULCN, have come to uphold the fact that, like leaders of free independent and democratic trade unions the world over, they must co-operate with the Government of the day without any prejudice however to the right of the union members.[19]

This policy was accentuated after January 1966 and until the end of the civil war when the pressures for patriotic gestures were all the greater. In May 1966 Adebola went as far as stating that 'It is my duty and responsibility to remind you of your obligations as workers. All forms of laziness, malingering, loiterings and malpractices must cease and Nigerian workers must remember that they are no longer working to sustain white men, but that they are working to sustain their fatherland.'[20]

The attitude of the Nigerian Workers' Council to the Government is not substantially different from that of the ULC. Although the centre had on occasions entered tactical alliances with the 'radicals', e.g. after the 1962 Ibadan conference and in 1966, these were temporary in character and, as the discussion of the origins of the centre in Chapter 3 demonstrated, personality differences and the opportunity to seek out new sources of international patronage were in any case a major explanation as to why the centre was created.

Like Adebola, the general secretary of the NWC lent his extravagant support to the new military government. According to the NWC newsletter, 'The workers of Nigeria have nothing but praise and high regard for the present régime and all that it stands for,' but the Council also hoped that the government would take seriously 'our humble but genuine sincere hints and counsel'. Perhaps less unequivocally than the ULC – the NWC had never attempted to attain as favoured a place with the government – the NWC leader was able to condemn the pre-1966 politicians for doing 'nothing except enrich themselves and install an administration whose order of the day was favouritism and nepotism coupled with tribalism and its related evils'.[21]

N. Anunobi, the previous president of the NWC, despite a former attachment to the NTUC, had been acting since the early sixties as something of a one-man band on behalf of the IFCTU, and its regional organization, the Pan African Workers' Congress, in which he held office. As the IFCTU affiliation began to bear fruit in the form of money to rent a fairly large building as the NWC headquarters, the NWC increased its commitments to the principles of the parent body, in Europe perhaps readily understood by the phrase 'Christian Social Democracy'. Transposed to the Nigerian context, these principles found expression in such phrases as 'the social well-being of workers', 'the acceleration of the rate of industrial development in our country', and the 'eschewing of violence and bitterness', all citations from NWC publications. The tone of moral finger-wagging and earnest advice that pervades nearly all the NWC's pronouncements is captured in an editorial on the 'Economic Development of Nigeria':

> It is most amusing [*sic*.] and disappointing to observe that while much endless noise is made about Nigeria's development programme, very little or nothing is being done to develop the main and premier instrument of production – the worker . . . No matter how well-intentioned and sincere, any Government which neglects the social development of the masses as represented by its labour force is definitely placing obstacles in its way to economic growth and prosperity.[22]

The section of the labour movement led by S. U. Bassey and Good-luck had few illusions that the government could be *persuaded* to support the demands of the unions. At the First Revolutionary Convention of the IULC (later to become the NTUC) in August 1963 a policy paper on the Political Struggle of the Working Class bluntly stated that: 'Your parliament does not represent the material interest of the working class of Nigeria.' It went on to argue that:

> Independence has not brought democracy to Nigerian workers and farmers. This is because the type of democracy preached and prac-tised by the Nigerian Government is the democracy for the few rich Nigerians, the Emirs, the Obas their families and supporters . . . The existing major political parties are parties of the rich and feudal aristocracy. They are dominated, controlled and financed by the agents and representatives of the rich classes. They only use the people, the workers and farmers, as ladders to climb into power.[23]

The General Secretary of the IULC, Bassey, advocated the calling of a national strike – a prospect which the compiler of the Policy Statement on Trade Unions and Industrial Relations welcomed. According to this document 'The pompous, show business juju priest outlook of the employers and capitalists are meant to frighten and to deceive the workers. Underneath it all is cowardly pretence, braggadoccio and naked tomfoolery. The only place to test the truth of the statement is in the field of practice, in actual struggles.'[24]

The NTUC has always sought to use the strike weapon as a means of increasing the consciousness of workers and as an attempt to polarize industrial conflict along the lines of political conflict. It also includes in its programme a commitment, directly in contra-diction to the policy of successive Federal governments, to the state ownership of the major industries and more grandly, the establishment of a socialist society in Nigeria.[25]

The NTUC, in its programme and organization, has features that resemble the characteristics of political unionism that have been described earlier in this chapter. The goals of the leadership include a major restructuring of the society, not simply in terms of the nationalization of industry but also, for example, in terms of an attack on 'Northern Feudalism', a call for the abolition of Native Authorities and the institution of popularly elected councils at a local level, and the extension of the franchise to include women in the North.[26] Next, the NTUC exhibits a tendency towards 'movementism', particularly in so far as it established links with, and was partly responsible for the creation of SWAFP, immediately after the meeting of the First Revolutionary Convention in 1963. For the ideologues of the NTUC, the political and economic struggles against the prevailing system are inseparable.

The Policy Paper on Politics presented to the Second Revolutionary Convention in 1965 argued that:

> We must henceforth use our economic power, whenever necessary to secure our political objectives. Having secured political power, we can then use it to alleviate our economic burden and secure a greater measure of social justice. That is the only way. You can not remove the source of social injustice by limiting the activities of trade unions to mere economic, bread and butter, issues.[27]

The Leninist language is perhaps appropriate to a centre which has strong connections with WFTU. What was to be initially described as 'fraternal relations' with the WFTU was later changed to outright affiliation, but not before the NTUC had made considerable capital in its slanging matches with the ULC on labour unity, concerning the latter's organizational dependence on the ICFTU.[28], The message of the NTUC, and until 1966 when parties were banned, SWAFP, was carried in the weekly newspaper *Advance*, the opening issue of which declared:

> Founded on the bedrock of the general truths and principles of Marxism–Leninism, basing the activities on the objective realities of our society, guided always by the true interests of the working people and linked with their struggles, the SWAFP is sure of leading the workers and poor farmers of Nigeria to victory over their class enemies.[29]

Finally, the NTUC's organizational weakness predisposes it to adopt frequently the tactics associated with political bargaining.

Unlike the ULC, the NTUC has very few unions operating a check-off system. Its grass-roots organization is usually weak and this is true particularly of its Northern affiliates. Peter Waterman has observed that few copies of the NTUC paper arrived in Kaduna and none were sold. NTUC officials in the Northern States moreover expressed open resentment of their isolation from Lagos, where at least one supposedly full-time secretary of a Northern NTUC union continued to be based.[30] The NTUC tends to come to the fore when wage-bargaining at a national level takes place with government-appointed wage commissions, while it is far more inclined than the ULC to use rallies, demonstrations, and marches as platforms for the exposition of its views. Not surprisingly also, the leadership comes into conflict with the authorities far more frequently – the general secretary and President of the centre were gaoled early in 1971 and detained for over a year for advocating further strike action to implement the decisions of the Adebo Wage Commission.

Having contrasted the collaborationist-type unionism of the ULC and NWC with the political-type unionism of the NTUC, it is nevertheless an overstatement to split organized labour into two clearly defined camps. The sentiments of the leadership, and their perceived relationship with the government of the day, do not always mean very much to the 'professional' general secretary or his rank-and-file membership. At the local level, Nigeria's trade unions seem to function in much the same way, quite regardless of their attachment to one or other of the trade union centres. In fact, as we have seen in the case of the Ibadan University Workers' Union, the membership may not be aware to which centre their union is affiliated. If the public protestations of the union centres cannot be taken as a certain index of how their affiliates will behave, what do the sharp discrepancies of opinion between the ULC and the NTUC leadership signify? Partly they provide ideological validation designed for foreign consumption, and partly they legitimize previous stances taken by the leadership in inter-centre disputes. But occasionally the centres seem trapped in the coils of their own rhetoric, particularly when they seek to capitalize on, or not lose support during, a spate of workers' grievances that emanates from below. The dynamics of the inter-action between rank-and-file demands and leadership responses can be appraised to some degree by examining the two General Strikes that Nigeria has experienced.

A Conflict Situation:
the General Strikes of 1945 and 1964

In the early years of the Second World War wage-earners had considerable difficulties in maintaining their living standards. The cost of living in Lagos rose precipitously, John Weeks estimating that real wages had fallen to 68% of the 1939 level two years later.[31] The war years generally were marked by a rapid increase in the rate of urbanization (the population of Enugu alone increased by 400%) and the growth in numbers of wage- and salary-earners (from 183,000, to 300,000 in 1946).[32] The increased organizational activity among wage- and salary-earners was reflected in the number of new unions created, the spread of unionization into areas outside Lagos, and the creation of the first Trade Union Congress in 1943.

The political consciousness of the wage-earners was aroused by a number of instances of direct action during 1941 and 1942 (in the form of walk-outs, demonstrations, and marches) associated with the demand for a Cost of Living Allowance (COLA). The government, acting also perhaps, as John Weeks argues,[33] in response to short-term labour shortages in Lagos, granted an interim increase to its employees in 1941, and in 1942 accepted a recommendation from a government-appointed committee for an increase of 50% in the Cost of Living Allowance.

Declining real wages were again manifest over the period 1942–5, when, so the unions rather hyperbolically claimed, the cost of living had gone up by 200%. To this basic economic grievance were added others of a more specifically political character. The first was that an accusation of racial discrimination could convincingly be sustained against the colonial government, which had given European civil servants increased bonuses after the war, while leaving unchanged the allowances for African government workers. The second was a feeling based on a number of issues, that the government had behaved in a high-handed fashion towards its employees. An order in 1942 under the General Defence Regulations made strikes and lockouts illegal for the duration of the war, an action (though general to British colonies) which was interpreted as an attempt to curb labour militancy precisely when it was gaining most ground. The banishment of Michael Imoudu, the railway workers' leader, for his part in the 1942 disturbances gave the labour movement its first hero and provided one of the *causes célèbres* of the nationalist movement.[34]

Equally important was the feeling on the part of the wage- and salary-earners that they were *entitled* to an award to cover the rise in the cost-of-living. This claim was based on a speech by Governor Bourdillon in July 1942 when he announced the awards of that year. He had publicly promised that the award would be subject to review if a rise or a fall in living standards should make it necessary. The Tudor Davies Commission, which was set up to look into the demands of the 1945 strikers, specifically isolated this broken promise as a cause of the strike. The commission pointed out that although the trade unions in June 1944 had demanded that the government promise be honoured, 'The Government made its first constructive attempt to take cognizance of that request in August 1945. In the interval the strike occurred and the cause of the strike was Government dilatoriness and its lack of sympathy in handling its employees.'[35]

Without the political ineptness of the colonial government, it is possible that the strike could have been averted; certainly this factor increased the support and strength of purpose of the strikers. An exchange of letters between the African Civil Servants Technical Workers' Union (ACSTWU), which was to act as a co-ordinating body in the strike, and the Chief Secretary of the Government, is instructive in revealing the extent of the insensitivity of the Lagos government. When the ACSTWU wrote to complain that government control of prices was inadequate, that rents had quadrupled and the government cost-of-living index was a 'mysterious jumble of metaphysical figures',[36] the Acting Chief Secretary replied (six weeks later) in terms not unlike those of Marie Antoinette:

> Unless the public is willing to do without or reduce their consumption of commodities which are scarce, or to substitute other commodities for them . . . no benefit will result from increasing COLA.[37]

During the war the government stressed the strategic importance of Empire goods as a reason for holding down wage demands, but apparently remained quite oblivious of the increased awareness of the wage-earners that their labour was being used to uphold an international economic system with whose purpose their interests were not necessarily coincident. The Nigerian TUC had made several contacts with overseas bodies like the Negro Labour Victory Committee and the Council on African Affairs in New York, as well as with the Fabian Society and the British Trade Union Congress.[38] These contacts no doubt contributed towards 'the wide range of literature produced and published in the UK and elsewhere concerning colonial administration and colonial economic patterns which was put in as evidence by the trade unions' with which the Tudor Davies Commission pronounced itself 'impressed'.

The government also committed a grave political miscalculation, perhaps because of the inexperience of the Acting Governor, Whitely. Hoping to remove the sting from the workers' demands, he ordered that Imoudu be released. Instead Imoudu returned to Lagos, only to be fêted by the Lagos crowds and in time to play a leading role in the strike. Among Imoudu's backers were Azikiwe's NCNC and his two dailies, the *West African Pilot* and the *Daily Comet*. The alignment of the NCNC with the more radical sections of the labour movement reflected, as Robert Melson has argued, the uncertainty of the nationalist leadership as to what tactics were necessary to oust the colonial power.[39] Violence had not by any means been ruled out at this stage (in fact Zik was to talk of the possibility of violence as late as 1948) and this made it all the more necessary for the NCNC to maintain contact with leaders like Imoudu who had a sizeable following among the masses. Although the strike also gained the support of other nationalists such as Macaulay and Awolowo, some of the politicians fought shy of too close an association with the 'hotheads' in the unions. The Nigerian Youth Movement, predominantly led by élitist Yoruba Lagosians, with which Zik broke in 1941, attempted to make contact with a more moderate group in the labour movement in the TUC and a faction of the African Civil Service and Technical Workers Union, and once the strike began, pressed for an early settlement. The NYM's newspaper, *The Daily Service*, was conspicuous in omitting any mention of Imoudu's role in the strike.[40]

The course of the strike may be briefly described. On 21 and 22 June 1945, the technical employees, and labourers in the Railways, Marine, Public Works, and Printing Departments, and Lagos Municipal workers, came out. The ACSTWU, (with twenty-two unions representing a claimed 90,000 members) although led by a moderate president, T. A. Bankole, had been pressed to formulate the first set of strikers' demands – a minimum daily wage of 2/- and a 50% increase in COLA. The union reserved its right 'failing the grant of same in full for the workers of Nigeria to proceed with their own remedy with due regard to law and order on the one hand and to starvation on the other'.[41] An attempt by some of the ACSTWU leadership to postpone the strike for fourteen days was decisively repudiated at two mass rallies on 21 June, with Imoudu and other militants coming to the fore. The established leadership in the TUC and ACSTWU made two attempts to halt the strike and restore their control but both the 'Strike Reconciliation Committee' and the 'Maja Peace Committee' (organized by the president of the NYM) failed woefully to capture the minds of the workers.[42]

The hard line of the strikers owed much to the attitude of the government, which successively threatened the strikers with a forfeit of wages, attempted to run a skeleton railway service with the aid of the management and Port Harcourt prison labour, took on 900 blackleg labourers, ordered the arrest of nine leaders suspected of being responsible for the derailment of a train, and finally banned the *West African Pilot* and the *Daily Comet*. Zik's newspapers had repeatedly supported the most militant position. *The Pilot* ran a long eulogistic series on the trials and tribulations of Imoudu in exile, and Zik himself gratuitously offered his advice to the government in his personal column 'Inside Stuff' on 8 July. Responding to the government's threat to close his paper down, he published a column entitled 'If I Were Governor of Nigeria'. The comment began 'From September 1939 to December 1944 the cost of living had increased with no corresponding increase in wages; I would make an analysis and recommendations as follows'. Blank spaces followed.[43] The banning of Azikiwe's *Pilot* and *Daily Comet* and his flight to Onitsha, in response, so his supporters said, to a government plot to assassinate him, gave an enormous boost to his standing as a national hero (though it later provided ammunition for his more cynical opponents who claimed that no such plot existed). It became one of the conditions of a return to work that the ban on Zik's papers be lifted.

Though the strike was not entirely solid, and was confined nearly totally to the South, most of the workers concerned had stayed out for thirty-seven days and many had stayed out for forty-four days. Although the stoppage involved (according to an official source) only 32,600 workers at any one time[44], as James Coleman points out, 'It was not the number of strikers that made the work stoppage significant, but the fact that most of them were performing services indispensable to the economic and administrative life of the country.'[45]

The strikers won a significant victory in that they only returned to work once the government conceded to their demands that there should be no victimization, that the contemplated legal proceedings against arrested strike leaders should be withdrawn, that the newspaper ban should be lifted, and that an impartial enquiry should be set up to consider their grievances. In the submission of evidence to the commission headed by Tudor Davies, the more moderate leaders recovered some of their prestige. An *ad hoc* body, called the Supreme Council of Nigerian Workers, comprising the Nigerian Civil Service Union, the ACSTWU, and other largely white-collar unions (including National Union of Teachers, which had previously stayed outside the central bodies), submitted detailed evidence to the commission. While the commission castigated the government in no uncertain terms, it was also clearly interested in lending its weight to the building up of the moderate leaders, predominantly representing the white-collar unions, at the expense of the section following Imoudu. It recognized the Supreme Council as 'fully representative' and issued dire warnings that unless the trade unions received 'help and encouragement from Great Britain to develop along proper trade union lines' they would drift 'finally and irrevocably into the hands of the politicians'.[46] The commission concluded in visionary terms. The British Empire required a larger purchasing power for its people: 'By this means the Colonies can become busy hives of activity, filled with eager, ambitious and loyal workers; this is the ideal of an ever expanding colonial development.'[47]

Despite the recognition of the Supreme Council by the commission, the establishment leadership of the unions had lost considerable support among the workers by their attempt to postpone, then settle, the strike. Zik editorialized against the Civil Service unions and the TUC, and dismissed the last as 'a sort of Cinderella, subject to the vagaries of the colonial administration'.[48] For sections of the labour movement and the NCNC, the cause of the workers was seen as linked to that of the nationalist movement. 'Indeed', in James Coleman's judgement, 'the strike served as a dramatic opening of a new nationalist era.'[49] Imoudu was accorded high status in the nationalist leadership, co-opted on to the executive of the NCNC and toured the countryside with the NCNC Pan-Nigerian delegates in April 1946. The link between the labour movement and the NCNC survived for only a short time, and eroded as the decolonizing process got under way and the colonial government was able to use the attractions of political office to woo the leaders of the NCNC on to the path of constitutional activity. But the strike had at least raised the possibility of co-operation between the unions and more populist-inclined politicians. It also demonstrated that given the fusion of a basic economic grievance with a galvanizing political issue, the unions could bring considerable pressure to bear on the central political authority. In this respect the remarks of the Tudor Davies Commission assume a prophetic character:

> It is apparent that the influence and power of the Nigerian Trade Unions for good or ill should not be underestimated, for if their organisational strength – financial and numerical – is small what may be termed their operational strength is great.[50]

The General Strike of 1964 replicated, at least in three respects, the lessons of 1945. First, it was clear that given a reasonable unity of purpose the unions could represent a fairly formidable political force. Second, their ability to act together depended largely on a favourable coincidence between political dissatisfaction and economic grievance. Finally, the issue most likely to galvanize the unions to action was an increased perception of social inequality combined with governmental insensitivity and arrogance in handling their demands. The similarity to the 1945 situation was quite marked despite the fact that the central government had in the meantime become indigenized. Much of the rhetoric of the strike leaders concerned itself with pinpointing the analogies in attitudes and behaviour that the political class had with the former colonial administration.

How then did the unions manage temporarily to set aside their differences in 1964 to present a common set of demands? The period since independence had seen a constant strengthening of the economic bonds between members of the political class, whose depredations from the public till, so the unions argued, were preventing any meaningful redistribution of wealth. The perception of this political trend and the frustration of being able to do little about it was common to nearly all workers and trade union leaders of whatever centre, despite the fact that this unity of outlook may have been masked by the internal wranglings of the unions.

The unions had indeed been agitating for some time for an increase in wages. The ULC, for instance, had drafted an elaborate report in 1961, which was described as 'Operation Square Deal' and suggested extensive changes in the wage structure.[51] But the pressure for militant action to back a wage claim really got under way in 1963 when the NTUC leaders explicitly pressed for a General Strike. Within the ULC too, much more radical noises were being made, the Eastern District Council of the Centre having adopted a resolution in August 1963 which advocated the setting up of a Political Action Committee for 'the furtherance of workers' power and influence in the national politics of Nigeria' and co-operation with 'other organisations, political or otherwise, that subscribe to the principles of a social welfare state in Nigeria'.[52]

The two organizations came together in a wages committee, which then transformed itself into a twenty-man 'Action Committee' with equal representation from both sides.[53] The name was changed to Joint Action Committee when it was later enlarged to include the Nigerian Workers Council, the Nigerian Union of Railwaymen (Federated) and other neutralist unions. These last two had been brought together to co-operate with the Joint Action Committee by the Labour Unity Front.

The first act of the JAC was to issue a call to the Federal Government to set up a governmental enquiry into wages and salaries with the threat that if this were not done, the union would call out their members on 27 September 1963. The unions showed a measure of political astuteness by timing the strike nearly to coincide with Nigeria's assumption of republican status and the installation of her first President. The day before the proposed strike the Minister of Labour moved a little way towards meeting JAC's demands, by appointing a committee to look into their claims. Against government opposition, JAC was determined to link the claims of the workers in the private sector with those working directly for the government, a bone of contention which was resolved when the government knuckled under in response to increasing stoppages of work. It finally included in the terms of reference of the Morgan Commission a requirement that the Commission should examine the need for 'a general upward revision of salaries and wages of junior employees in both government and private establishments'.

The next seven months were devoted to the presentation of memoranda to the commission, submission of evidence, and the testimony of witnesses. The JAC memorandum, drafted with the help of some sympathetic academics and some radical ideologues on the fringes of the labour movement, combined elaborate statistical evidence with a strong attack on the 'promised master-servant relation expressed not only in a prestige income structure but in social snobbishness',[54] and a claim for a minimum annual wage of £180. JAC also, unusually for Nigerian centres, managed during this period to set up several viable Regional branches, the one in the West being particularly active.

The government almost certainly calculated that JAC would disintegrate and it delayed over the publication of the report. Many of the workers suspected (and this was confirmed to them by a member of the commission who leaked the general findings) that the delay was due to the report's being substantially favourable to the workers' case. Finally, in May 1964 the Joint Action Committee issued an ultimatum declaring that there would be a General Strike unless the commission's report was published. This the government did on 27 May, but made no statement as to the acceptability or otherwise of the findings. One trade union leader, Mallam Inuwah of the ULC, described the presentation of the report without the White Paper as 'a wrapped parcel given by an angry father to a hungry child whose patience cannot endure for another fortnight'.[55] Four days later the General Strike began, the solidarity of the strikers being measurably stiffened by the publication a few days *after* the strike had started of a Government White Paper which severely reduced the wage recommendation and in almost contemptuous terms rejected many of the commission's other suggestions.

It is an indication of the government's lack of perception as to the seriousness of the situation that the Minister of Labour calmly flew to New York to attend a conference on youth problems, just as the strike was beginning. Despite repeated telegrams from his own ministry, the Minister showed a measure of reluctance to interrupt his American sojourn. The Prime Minister also failed to realize the determination of the strikers and the widely held sense of grievance. He issued a Canute-like order to the strikers to return to work without having either the credibility or power to enforce this order. The strike involved perhaps 750,000 workers, many of them not unionists, and spread over the whole countryside. In contrast to 1945, the tin miners in Jos also joined the strike. Besides the wage- and salary-earners, a large measure of support came from other sources. Many domestic servants refused to work, while, in the towns, a number of unemployed joined the workers at political rallies and mass meetings.[56] In a moment of farce H. P. Adebola threatened to call out the nightsoilmen on the grounds that, as he announced: 'What is worth doing is worth doing well'.[57] From several personal accounts of the course of the strike, it appears that the nightsoilmen needed no special urging to down tools.

Balewa's call for a return to work without offering any concessions on the proposals outlined in the White Paper, provoked a large measure of derision at the mass meetings. Workers chanted 'Balewa must go' and a good number of explicitly political demands were interjected during the course of the demonstrations. In his retrospective assessment of the situation Wahab Goodluck argued that, 'in its development (the strike) had raised possible political action which with a developed marxist–leninist party could have led to a proletarian revolution'.[58] There are many 'ifs' in this position, but certainly thoughts of seizing political control were very much in the minds of some trade union leaders. At a rally immediately preceding the strike, on 30 May, Michael Imoudu had the crowd shouting 'NO! NO!' to an appeal for restraint from the Minister of Labour and went on to declare 'This is a test case between the workers and the government. The strike will lead us to take over the reins of government from them.'[59] Akoi Achamba, another JAC member, was even more explicit: 'We will take over the government without apology . . . Army or no Army, Police or no Police, there is no harm in a citizen of this country trying to rule this country.'[60]

In fact the strikers in Ibadan at least were able to come to an amicable deal with the police, a situation that occurred elsewhere in the country. One private informant described how, in a large British-owned motor distributor's workshop in Ibadan, the police constables played football with the strikers while the sergeant was left to score nice legal points ('They did actually report for work, sir') with the management. That this co-operation may have been widespread was indicated in a demand by H. P. Adebola that the police should be included in the wage settlement.

The government only began to negotiate seriously once the Balewa call produced an even greater solidarity among the strikers. The economic advisers to the government warned about the serious economic consequences of allowing the strike to drag on (they eventually assessed the cost of the strike to the country at 2·5 million pounds), and finally a reconciliation committee was set up under the chairmanship of the Minister of Finance, Chief Festus Okotie-Eboh, with which JAC decided to co-operate.

The wage settlement that followed more or less fell between the government's White Paper and the Morgan Report's recommendations. The detailed wage settlement is not of immediate concern here;[61] what was important was that the result was widely felt to be a victory for the unions. When the dust had settled, certain salient political implications could be drawn.

Workers could no longer be put off by general moral injunctions to the effect that it was necessary to hold down wages in the interests of 'development'. The 1964 strike at first represented the claims of a group who did not necessarily articulate a mass populist will against the government, but rather sought to get their own share (though a rather smaller share) of the benefits of economic growth. As the strike progressed, however, it began to raise political possibilities of a more fundamental order. Many workers during the strike were not simply begging for their share of the national cake, but were explicitly threatening the political system itself. The government had also undermined any credibility it still retained as to its preparedness to concede to democratic pressures.

After the 1964 strike and the election in December 1964, political violence, always present in the system, became a real possibility for those wishing to effect political change. The government had also displayed a considerable degree of ineptness and powerlessness in the face of the strikers' demands. The support of the army and police force in particular was now in question. Both the army and the police had been called out to suppress the strikers and, in Lagos, police with army auxiliaries were ordered to defend the Carter Bridge against a march to Government House that the government had declared illegal. Significantly for later events, the army had been used to suppress a political demand to which they were not entirely unsympathetic. The police indeed had openly abetted the trade unions. Though one can only argue this point of view with the benefit of hindsight, it seems clear that the 1964 strike helped provide a staging ground for the army's own intervention eighteen months later. Not only was the government's legitimacy undermined, the precariousness of its hold on the political system was clearly underlined. It would not perhaps be stretching credulity too far to assert that some young majors in the Nigerian armed forces clearly perceived this fact.

Party/Union Relations (1943-64) and Alternative Strategies for the Unions

Though, as has been shown in Chapter 3, there are many reasons to explain the fragmentation of Nigeria's labour movement, one of the most consistent sources of disagreement has been the perceived choice of different political strategies available to the unions. One option was to attempt to effect a structural link with the existing major political parties, another to attempt a stance of neutrality in party politics, while a third rested on the assumption that workers needed to create a political identity separate from the established political parties.

As regards the first option, we have already seen how in 1945 the NCNC, conscious of the need to secure a popular base and uncertain as to what tactics would be necessary to displace the colonial government, supported the demands of the strikers and how, in their turn, the more radical unions were prepared to see their economic struggle as part and parcel of the anti-colonial movement. This link was certainly the most significant of all major party/union alliances in that it provided a platform for a common campaign in the Zik-owned press and in public demonstrations and rallies. But too much should not be made of this alliance. Within the Trade Union Congress there were powerful dissenting voices questioning the advisability of too close a link with the NCNC and these gained the upper hand at the TUC conference in March 1948, forcing the 'radicals' out to create the Committee of Trade Unions. H. P. Adebola's speech at the 1948 Conference argued the case for disaffiliation in the following way:

> . . . Unwarranted association with non-labour political parties tends to diminish the enviable positions which workers should occupy in the scheme of things. Instead of political parties soliciting for support of workers, the workers are soliciting for support of political parties where ideologies are at variance with those of the labouring class. Instead of affiliation I recommend full collaboration . . . not to tie ourselves so that in the face of any disagreement we may be able to part company without embarrassment.[62]

Although Adebola's phrase 'full collaboration' was probably masking a deeper distaste for any kind of organizational link with

the political parties, he was right in pointing to the possible divergence of ideological aims. For, within the NCNC itself, such a
heterogeneity of political opinion existed, that, as Richard Sklar
maintains, during the period 1944–53 when Zik was in charge of
the party's fortunes, 'he made comparatively little effort to create a
disciplined and cohesive organization'.[63] The failure of the NCNC
leadership to live up to the expectations of the more radical of its
activists, particularly the Zikists, was always a source of bitter
disillusionment and frustration to them. One plea from the heart
was recorded by the Zikist Mokwugo Okoye, who was expelled by
the Annual Convention of the NCNC in 1955:

> By your vindictiveness, shallowness and poltroonery, you have lost
> some of the noblest characters that a Nigerian nationalist movement
> has produced over the years . . . I trust that our country shall yet
> produce able, true and brave sons and daughters who can effect her
> deliberations and usher in the socialist millenium we all visualise
> today.[64]

But by 1955 few in the leadership of the NCNC were contemplat-
ing the socialist millennium – they were much more concerned
with the problems of retaining Regional power and evolving some
kind of *modus vivendi* with the Action Group and the NPC at the
federal level. As Ken Post writes of this period, 'Considerations of
patronage, the distribution of amenities and sheer administrative
expediency came more and more to dominate the thinking of the
party . . . The whole crucial period from 1951 to 1959, then, was
marked by a trend away from principles and towards pragmat-
ism . . .'[65]

The aura of the NCNC and its leader, Azikiwe, as the leading
champions of the nationalist struggle, was never quite dissipated by
events subsequent to the 1945–51 period, and many workers continued to give at least a minimum allegiance to the party by voting
for it – but the connections with the trade unions were henceforth
tenuous. They comprised a few initiatives by the NCNC to win
trade union support during the time of election campaigns and in
the competition the party gave to AG control of the West in the
early fifties. A few trade union leaders were also nominated as
NCNC candidates.

Like the NCNC, the Action Group was founded on a sprinkling
of political opinions; Richard Sklar considers that even in the early
stages one can distinguish left, right, and centre groupings. The
left-wing element was originally organized in the United Working

People's Party, established in June 1952. The group included some familiar names: Gogo Nzeribe, the leader of the Post and Telegraph Workers' Union; S. G. Ikoku, who was later to be associated with the treason trial of 1962; Ayo Ogunsheye, a former trade unionist whose Ruskin Scholarship had elevated him to university teaching, and other intellectuals at University College, Ibadan. Sklar suggests that this group 'edged the party to the left, becoming Fabian thinkers themselves, in the process'.[66] The importance of the left-wing elements was substantially increased, however, when after the 1962 split in the party (described in the first chapter) the Awolowo section of the party adopted a social programme much more radical in content than Chief Akintola's section of the party would ever have been prepared to countenance. For their part the unions never seriously considered, nor ever were in a position to effect, a formal alliance with the Action Group, though there was always a considerable amount of personal contact with individuals in the Action Group. For example the unions' case to the Morgan Commission was drafted with the help of some AG intelletuals.

As to the NPC, the party had a staunch ally in the Northern Mineworkers' Union whose president combined the role of employer and Provincial President of the NPC. The Northern Federation of Labour, under Ibrahim Nock, also kow-towed to the wishes of the NPC despite the association of its leader with the IULC at the 1962 Ibadan Conference. The denunciation of the 1964 strike by the leader of the NFL during a television interview severely damaged what support the centre had been able to build up, while the few benefits that the leadership were able to secure for themselves in patronage can hardly be said to constitute a convincing demonstration of the benefits of a close union/governing party relationship. While the workers organized by the NFL certainly benefited from the Northernization policy of the NPC, the NFL cannot claim to have influenced this policy significantly.

By and large, as far as the governing parties were concerned the period from 1951-64 was marked by preoccupations other than the fostering of formal bonds with the union or union centres, despite the fact that at key points, like elections or large-scale agitation over wages, the parties showed themselves anxious to attract working-class support. A more blatant and conscious attempt to seek allies in the unions occurred in 1964, as the federal election of December approached. Many political actors, especially those in UPGA's camp, believed that the election would be a closely fought affair, and the unions had just demonstrated in the June General Strike that they had access to a considerable political constituency. The NNA made its play directly to the union leadership, if on a somewhat crude level:

> The governments of the Alliance will give workers' leaders an opportunity to make their contribution to the normal conduct of their country's affairs. To this end they will be encouraged to play an active part in business through appointments to committee boards and corporations.[67]

By contrast, UPGA was prepared to commit itself to much more explicit reforms. The Manifesto of the Progressive Alliance promised that:

> Members of [the labouring] class will receive full returns for their labour by the overhauling of the present colonial wages and salary structure to guarantee to the workers a minimum living wage and to ensure an equitable distribution of the national income.[68]

UPGA further promised that, if elected, it would control rents and prices, set up low-cost housing schemes and provide cheap transport for the workers. That several trade union leaders were convinced of the sincerity of the UPGA promises was shown by the calling of a political strike by the still-surviving JAC in support of UPGA's boycott of the election. The strike was supported in Lagos and in the East by a fair number of workers, but by and large it was a failure, for unlike 1945 and 1964, there was no immediate economic grievance to galvanize the full support of the rank and file.

The 'election strike' of December 1964 strengthened the hands of those in the unions who had all along been committed to the principles of non-partisanship in politics. These, as we have seen, were predominantly found in the ranks of the ULC, whose leaders, while holding rigidly to the non-partisan formula, nevertheless individually saw no reason why they should not stand as candidates on the platform of the major parties (Adebola and Borha were elected as NNDP and NCNC candidates respectively). While the neutrality stance conformed to one of the basic ideological principles of the ULC and its precursors, in a sense neutrality was not an option at all during the period 1951–64, but simply a reflection of the lack of interest of the governing political parties in contracting alliances which might prove politically embarrassing and in any case were seen as politically unnecessary.

A more positive response to the increasing tendency of the

parties to retreat to their Regionalist bases and set up a system of patronage of which the unions were but a small part, was the attempt by union leaders or left-wing ideologues to create political parties or movements which directed their appeal to class rather than ethnic sentiments. In an intermediate category is a party like NEPU, which made specific appeals to subordinate groups and social strata, including organized labour, but which was not necessarily concerned with implementing trade union objectives. Some parties or political associations which in personnel, aims, or organization, have connections with the unions actually predated the period of Regionalism, but most were formed during 1951-64. Scattered references to these worker-orientated political groups have been made in several places: listed overleaf (*see* chart) are most of the developments along these lines, together with some comments on their composition and electoral appeal (if any).

Any further possibility of establishing a separate political base for organized labour suffered a decisive reverse by the insignificant showing of SWAFP and the NLP in the elections of December 1964. But it may perhaps be tentatively argued that the profusion of the attempts to establish such parties or pressure groups may be taken as symptomatic of an ideological ferment and a growing realization that it may be possible to use the distinct socio-economic interest of the wage-earners as a political base.

The failure to do so hitherto may be related to three major causes. First, the leadership of several of these minor political parties was of a distinctly indifferent quality, for example, a number of unionists expressed to this author contempt for Tunji Otegbeye's SWAFP, considering that it was little different from the major parties ('They only have a different paymaster', commented one general secretary; incidentally in the NTUC). Second, workers in Nigeria are widely dispersed, only forming a narrowly considered geographical constituency in a few places. Elsewhere, the pattern of multi-class occupation described in Chapter 1 obtains. In Lagos, the greatest area of concentration, it is virtually only Yaba and Surulere (where low-cost housing has attracted many workers) that can be described as working-class districts. Thirdly, in the period after 1951 the locus of disposable economic resources and therefore of political patronage was firmly based in Regional governments which could therefore be dominated by ethnically based parties. It is possible that the breakdown of the Regional power structure in the period since 1967 may, however, have significant effects on the future patterns

Summary Chart of Worker-Orientated Political Groups

Date	Group	Comment	Electoral Support
1930	Nigerian Labour Organization	Set up by J. A. Olushola in response to 'growing unemployment'.	—
1931	African Workers' Union/Nigerian Labour Party	Set up by I. T. A. Wallace Johnson, radical Sierra Leone journalist.	—
1948	Labour Party	Decision by Imoudu, Coker, and radicals, to set up LP after the 1948 TUC conference – formed instead the NNFL, which dominated the NLC (see below).	—
1950	NLC/NNDP Market Women's Guild	United Front largely organized by NCNC.	Alliance won 18 out of 24 seats in Lagos Town Council Election, October 1950.
1951	Freedom Movement	Organized by ex-Zikist, M. C. K. Ajukchuku.	—
1951	'League'	Comprised Freedom Movement and Peoples' Committee for Independence. Joined by N. Eze.	—
1951	CPP of Nigeria and the Cameroons	Successor Group of Freedom Movement and two other 'Committees'.	
1952	United Working Peoples' Party	Left element in the AG.	—

1956	Nigerian Labour Party	Established by Imoudu (Pres.) and Bassey (Gen. Sec.). Party is 'against regionalisation in any shape or form'; for 'the establishment of adequate uniform wage fixed in agreement with the unions'.	
1960	Nigerian Youth Congress	Established by Otegbeye (Pres.), Organized most of the Nigerian left.	
1961	Nigerian Peoples' Party	Started by Nzeribe. 'The Party of the Nigerian Working Class – of the workers, women, farmers and peasants, youth, students and progressive businessmen, intellectuals and professionals.'	
1963	Socialist Workers and Farmers Party	Founded by Otegbeye. Linked to the NTUC. 'Experience has shown that the struggle for total independence and socialism may take any forms ranging from parliamentary to armed struggle.'	Obtained 2,206 out of 1,848,270 votes cast in Dec. 1964. (Boycott distorted returns.)
1964	Nigerian Labour Party	Set up by Eskor Toyo and Imoudu to contest seat in December 1964.	Imoudu contested Lagos North but boycott distorted results. Little chance anyway.

Sources: On pre-war organizations *see* Hughes, A. and Cohen, R. *Towards the Emergence of a Nigerian Working Class: the Social Identity of the Lagos Labour Force* (Occasional Paper, Faculty of Commerce and Social Science, University of Birmingham, Series D. No. 7, November 1971); on 1948 Labour Party *see supra* Chapter 3; on the Market Women's Guild, Freedom Movement, 1951 League and CPP of Nigeria *see* Sklar, R. L. *Nigerian Political Parties* (Princeton: Princeton University Press, 1963) p. 84, p. 81 and p. 82; on United Working People's Party *see supra*, this Chapter; on 1956 Nigerian Labour Party *see Programme and Constitution of the NLP* (Lagos: Salaho Press, n.d.); on the Nigerian Youth Congress *see supra* Chapter 3, footnote 21; on the Nigerian Peoples' Party *see The New Nigeria Programme* (Lagos: the NPP, n.d.); and on SWAFP *see*, for this quote, *SWAFP Manifesto* (Lagos, 1964), p. 36.

of political organization, including the possible emergence of a more broadly based populist party.

What political influence the unions have had in the past has not, however, been derived from their capacity to act as totally independent political agents. Their political influence has to be considered (*a*) in the context of a bargaining environment that produced in part of the labour movement behaviour patterns associated with a model of 'political unionism', (*b*) as an interaction with other agents in the political process which occasionally felt the necessity to recruit the support of organized labour and listen to its demands, and (*c*) as an outcome of the politicization of the wage bargain itself. This last theme merits separate treatment in the next chapter of this study.

NOTES

1. Galenson, W. (Ed.) *Labor in Developing Countries* (Berkeley and Los Angeles: University of California Press, 1963), p. 3.
2. Alexander, R. J. *Organized Labor in Latin America* (New York: Free Press, 1965) p. 7.
3. Though not by any means a complete list of references, arguments along these lines may be found in Galenson, W. (Ed.) op. cit., 1963; Galenson, W. (Ed.) *Labor and Economic Development* (New York: John Wiley & Sons, 1959); Millen, B. H. *The Political Role of Labor in Developing Countries* (Washington: The Brookings Institution, 1963); Kassalow, E. M. *National Labor Movements in the Post-War World* (Evanston, Illinois: Northwestern University Press, 1963); Deyrup, F. J. 'Organised Labor and Government in Developing Countries: Sources of Conflict', *Industrial and Labor Relations Review*, 1958, 12 (1); and Gamba, C. 'New Paths in Industrial Relations in Developing Countries', *Journal of Industrial Relations*, 1965, 7 (3).
4. Almond, G. A. and Powell, G. B. *Comparative Politics: a Developmental Approach* (Boston and Toronto: Little Brown & Co., 1966), pp. 201, 202.
5. As Ken Post writes with regard to the Nigerian electorate: 'For most electors the choice between candidates was not one to be made individually, but as a member of a community . . . How then are we to define community? Primarily it may be suggested, as the place to which

a man felt himself to "belong", where he had both rights and obliga-
tions, where his ancestors were buried, where his family had land.' Post,
K. W. J. *The Nigerian Federal Election of 1959* (London: OUP for the
Nigerian Institute of Social and Economic Research, 1963), p. 377.

6. Millen, B. H. op. cit., p. 9 et seq.
7. Mills, C. Wright, in Kornhauser, A. *et al. Industrial Conflict* (New York:
   McGraw-Hill, 1954), p. 151.
8. Tedjasukmana, I. *The Political Character of the Indonesian Trade Union Movement* (Ithaca: Cornell University Press, 1958), p. 43.
9. Weiner, M. *The Politics of Scarcity* (Chicago: University of Chicago Press,
   1962), p. 84.
10. 'Workers of Nigeria', *TUCN Manifesto* (1 October 1960), p. 3. Italics
    added.
11. See Legum, C. *Pan-African: a Short Political Guide* (New York: Praeger,
    1965), pp. 88–92.
12. 'The Problem of Union Leaders in Nigeria vis-à-vis Government', *ULC
    Document* (Mimeographed, 1967), p. 4. Copy in my possession.
13. See e.g. *ULC Information* (Monthly Newsletter of the ULC), March 1968,
    1 (7).
14. Luyimbazi, F. 'Trade Unions and Economic Planning in West Africa',
    Civilizations, 1966, 16 (2), p. 201.
15. *ULC Information*, May 1969, 2 (4), p. 5.
16. Ananaba, W. *The Trade Union Movement in Nigeria* (London: C. Hurst &
    Co., 1969), p. 228.
17. 'Presidential Address', ULC, 1st Annual Delegates Conference, May 1963,
    p. 5.
18. 'General Secretary's Report' ULC, 1st Annual Delegates Conference, May
    1963, pp. 2, 10, 11.
19. 'The Problem of Union Leaders . . .', ULC Document (Mimeographed,
    1967) p. 4.
20. *The Nigerian Worker* (ULC Monthly Newspaper), May 1966.
21. *The Voice of Labour* (NWC Monthly Newsletter), May 1966.
22. *The Voice of Labour* (NWC Monthly Newsletter), February 1967.
23. 'The Political Struggle of the Working Class', *Policy Paper*, 1st Revolutionary
    Convention, Yaba, August 1963, p. 4. My thanks go to Peter Waterman
    for providing me with a set of documents relating to the conventions of
    the IULC and NTUC. A sustained analysis of the NTUC ideology is
    provided in Waterman, P. *Neo-Colonialism, Communism and the Nigerian
    Trade Union Congress* (M.Soc.Sci. dissertation, University of Birmingham,
    February 1972), pp. 18–38.
24. 'Trade Unions and Industrial Relations', *IULC Policy Statement* (1963).
25. *Constitution of the NTUC* (Lagos n.d.) Article 1:7.
26. 'The Political Struggle of the Working Class' *IULC Policy Paper* (1963).
27. 'Policy Paper on Politics', *NTUC Policy Paper*, 2nd Revolutionary Con-
    vention, December 1965.
28. See Waterman, P. *Working Class and Revolutionary Trade Unionism in Nigeria*
    (Mimeographed paper, 1968), p. 35.
29. *Advance* (NTUC Weekly Newspaper), 18 August 1965.
30. Waterman, P. op. cit., 1972, p. 45.
31. Weeks, J. 'The Impact of Economic Conditions and Institutional Forces

on Urban Wages in Nigeria', *Nigerian Journal of Economic and Social Studies*, November 1971, 13 (3), p. 323.

32. Coleman, J. S. *Nigeria: Background to Nationalism* (Berkeley and Los Angeles: University of California Press, 1963), p. 255.

33. Weeks, J. loc. cit.

34. *See* Cohen, R. 'Nigeria's Labour Leader No. 1: Notes for a Biographical Study of M. A. O. Imoudu', *Journal of the Historical Society of Nigeria* 1970, 5 (2).

35. *Report of the Tudor Davies Commission into the Cost of Living in the Colony and Protectorate of Nigeria* (London: HMSO for the Colonial Office, No. 204, 1946), p. 10.

36. 'ACSTWU to Chief Secretary to Government, Lagos', 22 March 1945. *Collected papers on the 1945 General Strike*, Ghandi Library, University of Lagos.

37. 'Acting Chief Secretary to ACSTWU', 2 May 1945. *Collected Papers on the 1945 General Strike.*

38. Coleman, J. S. *op. cit.*, p. 257.

39. Melson, R. *Marxists in the Nigerian Labor Movement: a Case Study of the Failure of Ideology* (Ph.D. thesis, MIT, 1967).

40. ibid.

41. *West Africa* (London), 30 June 1945.

42. Melson, R. op. cit.

43. Sklar, R. L. *Nigerian Political Parties* (Princeton: Princeton University Press, 1963), p. 60 footnote.

44. *West Africa* (London), 1 September 1945, reporting on a House of Commons Debate.

45. Coleman, J. S. op. cit., p. 259.

46. *Tudor Davies Commission*, Para. 98, p. 27.

47. ibid., Para. 105, p. 30.

48. *West African Pilot* (Lagos) 4 September 1945, cited by Melson, R. op. cit., p. 260.

49. Coleman, J. S. op. cit., p. 260.

50. *Tudor Davies Commission*, Para. 83. p. 23.

51. Ananaba, W. op. cit., p. 228.

52. ibid., p. 237.

53. Which side could claim the kudos for initiating the committee is still disputed. For a ULC view *see* ibid., pp. 228–39. For a NTUC view *see* Bassey, S. W. *Review of the Development of the Nigerian Trade Union Congress* (Mimeographed n.d.), pp. 13, 14.

54. For this and other quotes from the JAC memorandum *see* Melson, R. 'Nigerian Politics and the General Strike of 1964' in Mazrui, A. A. and Rotberg, R. I. *Protest and Power in Black Africa* (New York: OUP, 1970), pp. 780, 781.

55. *Daily Sketch* (Ibadan), 1 June 1964.

56. This was especially true of Port Harcourt. Schwarz, W. *Nigeria* (London: Pall Mall Press, 1968), p. 24.

57. *Daily Sketch* (Ibadan), 8 June 1964.

58. Goodluck, W. 'Nigeria and Marxism', *African Communist*, 1964, No. 19, p. 55.

59. *Daily Sketch* (Ibadan), 1 June 1964.

60. *Daily Sketch* (Ibadan), 4 June 1964.
61. Details of the settlement are tabulated in full in Melson, R. op. cit., 1970, p. 783.
62. 'Annual Report of the General Secretary at the Eighth Conference of the TUC', 19–23 March 1948. Cited by Melson, R. 'Political Dilemmas of Nigerian Labour', *African Studies Association (USA) Conference Pape* (Mimeographed, 1967), p. 7.
63. Sklar, R. L. op. cit., p. 149.
64. Cited in ibid., p. 151.
65. Post, K. W. J. 'The National Council of Nigeria and the Cameroons', in Mackintosh, J. P. *et al. Nigerian Government and Politics* (London: Allen & Unwin, 1966), p. 420.
66. Sklar, R. L. op. cit., p. 271.
67. Nigerian National Alliance, *Manifesto of the NNA for the Federal Election of 1964*, p. 12.
68. United Progressive Grand Alliance, *Manifesto for the 1964 Federal Election*, p. 11.

CHAPTER 6

The Wage Bargain in Nigeria

The Legal and Institutional Framework for Industrial Relations

Nigeria inherited from the Colonial government a predilection in government circles for a system of industrial relations based on voluntary principles, which has only recently been undermined by the pressures of the war economy. The ILO conventions relating to the freedom to associate, organize, and bargain collectively, were ratified under the Colonial government and later incorporated in legislative acts.[1] An incentive to giving the conventions legislative backing was provided by the reformist Colonial Development and Welfare Act of 1940 which made the payment of grants subject to the implementation of certain trade union rights.[2] The legislation itself was based largely on British models. As an ILO survey noted:

> The principal characteristic of the legislation specifically designed to protect and guarantee the right of association in the British territories is that it is based on models largely determined by United Kingdom law and practice and intended to enable trade unions to pursue their objectives with legality, subject to certain safeguards.[3]

Included in these 'safeguards' were a more stringent definition of what constituted intimidation, and provision for the compulsory registration of trade unions. The Trade Unions Ordinance of 1938, like similar Ordinances in Sierra Leone (1940), the Gold Coast (1941), and Kenya (1943), provided for such registration and gave legal definition as to what constituted a trade union. In the Nigerian Ordinance this was described as:

> . . . any combination whether temporary or permanent, the principal purposes of which are the regulation of the relations between workmen and masters, or between workmen and workmen, or between masters and masters whether such combinations would or would not, if this Ordinance had not been enacted, have been deemed to have been unlawful combination by reason of some one or more of its purposes, being in restraint of trade.

The inclusion of the 'masters and masters' phrase allowed many employers' associations (fifty by 1964 alone) to register under the act. Members of the police force and the prisons service were however, specifically barred from organizing a trade union and the Chief Fire Officer, Ibadan, advised me in 1968 that his men too had been denied the legal right to organize a trade union. Despite these exceptions, the regulations were sufficiently permissive to allow free registration of unions in other areas of government employment.

So far as the determination of wages was concerned the Federal government, like its colonial predecessors, laid great stress on their support for a system of free negotiation and collective bargaining between employer and employee. The then Federal Minister of Labour declared his faith in such principles when addressing the 1955 International Labour Conference:

> Can the various types of collective bargaining familiar to older industrial societies thrive in the different conditions of under-developed countries today? This is an important question which in the view of my government permits of only one answer. We have followed in Nigeria the voluntary principles which are so important an element in industrial relations in the United Kingdom . . . Compulsory methods might occasionally produce a better economic or political result, but labour–management must, I think, find greater possibilities of mutual harmony where results have been voluntarily arrived at by free discussion between the two parties. We in Nigeria, at any rate, are pinning our faith on voluntary methods.

In the same speech the Minister did, however, qualify his approval of the voluntary principle by supporting government intervention which was 'carefully restricted to those fields where collective bargaining is either non-existent or ineffective'.[4] Even in these areas the government has in the past shown extreme reluctance to intervene in the wage determination process. As early as 1932 there existed legislative provision (in Ordinance 17 of 1932) for the Governor-in-Council to alter wage minima that were unreasonably low. No minimum wages were, however, fixed until 1944, following the more comprehensive legislation of the previous years, when new wages rates were prescribed for tailoring establishments in Lagos. Besides the 1943 legislation, government power to fix wages was further supplemented by the Wage Boards Act of 1958. By 1964 the power to prescribe minimum wage levels under these acts had been invoked on only nine occasions for individual trades and occupations in Lagos, while outside Lagos administrative wage setting was also infrequent, occurring on four occasions in the Jos Minesfield and once in the rubber-tapping industry in Benin.[5] As B. C. Roberts and L. Grefie de Bellecombe note, the Wage Boards were in any case seen as merely temporary expedients:

> It was certainly the intention of the labour advisers to the Colonial Government that (Wage Boards) should only be established in the absence of effective voluntary machinery and that in their functioning they would be a preparation for an eventual transformation to a Joint Industrial Council.[6]

In addition to the Wage Boards, provincial wage committees were from 1937 allowed to lay down minimum wages in the area of their jurisdiction. Never widely applied, they have now fallen into disuse except in some parts of the Northern states. It was not until 1964 that the government was forced to apply a comprehensive, though not uniform, set of wage levels throughout the country as part of the settlement following the 1964 general strike.

In the past Nigerian governments have also shown an aversion from intervening during the course of a trade dispute, although the Trade Disputes (Arbitration and Inquiry) Act (cap. 201) provided for the formal appointment of a Conciliator, Arbitration Tribunal, or Board of Inquiry, in the event of deadlock between the parties. Mediation was only undertaken by the Ministry of Labour with the consent of both parties to the dispute.

In May 1968 the exigencies of the war situation and the anticipation of increased strike action were thought compelling reasons for the government to issue a decree which imposed compulsory arbitration (at the pleasure of the Commissioner of Labour) in any dispute which lasted longer than seven days. The Trades Disputes (Emergency Provisions) Decree (No. 21 of 1968) was defended by the Commissioner of Labour in view of the need to develop 'a united and concerted effort of the entire community in order to crush Ojukwu's rebellion'. It was not, he claimed, 'intended to be a permanent feature of our system of industrial relations'.[7] While the decree seems to have had some effect in reducing the number of strikes in the later months of 1968, the subsequent years showed increases in the number of strikes and a dramatic increase in 1971 when, though the decree remained in force, the civil war was over and pent-up wage demands found expression in strike action. The powers of intervention that the Ministry assumed do none the less seem to have had some effect in keeping at a low level the number of man-days lost through industrial action. (See graph of *Strikes and Man-days Lost*, below, p. 195.)

Despite the Commissioner's assurance that the Ministry's intervening powers were temporary measures, an Industrial Arbitration Tribunal was set up in 1970 to determine wages referred to it by the Commissioner and to settle the interpretation of collective agreements or the terms of settlement of any trade dispute. On this occasion the Commissioner inaugurated the body by maintaining that it 'was a very important development in the industrial relations system of Nigeria' and left open the question of its permanence.[8]

Accompanying the past preference for voluntarism in wage negotiation, was the importation of what were thought to be appropriate structures and institutions within which industrial relations were to be conducted. Whitley Councils, covering senior clerical and technical staff in the government services, were established throughout the federation. One year after they were established (in 1948) they broke down temporarily, and though some wage negotiations were conducted through the Whitley Council machinery in 1952, in general their functions have usually been limited to consultation on peripheral issues concerning employment conditions, rather than the presentation of wage demands. In industrial establishments, the Department (later, the Ministry) of Labour, since its inauguration in 1942, strenuously tried to persuade employers to set up standing committees for joint consultation. Again, as in the British model, these are meant to deal with routine matters such as staff welfare, factory safety, hygiene, canteen food, etc., on the basis of friendly suggestions and recommendations from both sides of industry. The Ministry's efforts have met with a measure of success in the larger establishments dominated by expatriate capital, but meetings of consultative committees tend to be formal and infrequent. In addition there remains a good deal of suspicion as to the purposes of such machinery. As an Annual Report of the Ministry of Labour lamented:

> In many cases, it appeared to be still widely believed by employers that to consult workers would affect, in an adverse manner, the presumptive sanctity of management's authority and prerogative; that such a practice would undermine discipline if management plans for improvement should be subject to criticism by subordinates. Many trade union leaders, on the other hand, also seemed to entertain doubtful fears that joint consultation in industry would vitiate trade union influence and activities.[9]

While the joint consultative committees are only operative at the plant level, more recently there has been a greater success in establishing joint industrial councils at the industry-wide level. The Minesfield Joint Industrial Council has been of some importance in implementing collective agreements, and joint industrial councils have also been firmly established in the rubber, shipping, building, civil engineering, and banking industries. The formation of joint industrial councils in the last-mentioned areas was paralleled by the various amalgamations that the unions promoted across company lines – an amalgamation of nine bank unions occurred, for example, in June 1965.[10]

Collective bargaining has worked to some extent in the joint industrial councils, in most of the large industrial firms, and to a much lesser degree in public corporations and government services. In general, however, collective bargaining is only a minor factor in the adjustment of rates of pay for the country as a whole, notwithstanding the Ministry of Labour's enthusiastic panegyrics of its virtues. A typical statement in the 1963/4 Annual Report refers to the Ministry's continuing:

> ... its traditional policy of encouraging the development of independent, healthy, virile organisations of workers and employers for the purpose of regulating industrial relations between themselves without the intervention of a third party. To this end the establishment of machinery for mutual consultation and the settlement of disputes by direct joint negotiation and collective bargaining was encouraged.[11]

The use of collective bargaining in the large expatriate-owned firms can be attributed at least as much to the ethnocentricity of the managements as to the Ministry's injunctions. Despite its widespread use in this sector of the economy, in the main, the crucial decisions about wages have been taken, as will be argued, through the setting up of governmental commissions and committees to review wages, and through debate in the political arena. Though having a rather greater success in recent years, a staunch advocate of the British model, T. M. Yesufu, writing in 1962, conceded the general failure of the voluntarist principle:

> An examination of the working of individual machineries of joint consultation and collective bargaining leaves no doubt that, in far too many cases, very little more than passing success can yet be recorded.[12]

One of the major reasons why 'free' bargaining systems have not yet taken root is the fact that the unions, like unions in other underdeveloped countries, either through their own organizational weaknesses, or because of the objective conditions of the labour market, are inherently unequal partners to the bargain. Since 1961, an attempt to redress the imbalance by providing the unions with a more stable financial base has been made through the introduction of a 'check-off' system. Though the deduction of union dues from the workers' pay provides the unions with an assured income, the negative effects of the check-off – the undermining of the unions' independence, and a tendency towards inefficient organization and oligarchic leadership – are already visible in some Nigerian unions. The check-off now operates in over a hundred firms, but again, unlike Kenya and Tanzania where the check-off is a legal requirement, the voluntaristic principle has prevailed and a check-off order can only be issued once the consent of both the employer and the union is obtained. The individual member has the further right not to permit a deduction from his wage packet. One union leader described the attitude of some of his members towards the check-off system as 'lamentable' and complained that many members were giving 'flimsy excuses' for not signing their authorizations.[13]

In general the institutional and legal framework of bargaining that has been established in Nigeria can be seen as encapsulating the form, rather than the substance, of industrial relations. As such it closely corresponds to the broader discrepancy existing in other areas of social life (outlined in Chapter 1) between the constitutional, legal, and normative *mores* inherited from the colonial government, and the real behaviour patterns. The substantive issues that divide wage-earners on the one hand from employers and government on the other have an existence far removed from the recognized system of industrial relations, while the unions, the employers, and the government continue to give formal adherence to the system.

T. M. Yesufu argues that the meagre success of the inherited pattern is not in itself a reason for its rejection. As he puts it: 'If previous attempts to improve industrial relations in Nigeria through the educative process have not shown all the results that might have been expected, it is not because such efforts have been misdirected; it merely emphasises the magnitude of the work to be done.'[14] Equally, it may be argued that a mode of wage determination peculiar to Nigeria has emerged within the interstices of the formal structure, and has itself begun to acquire an institutionalized character. The check-off system and the increased use of joint industrial councils have certainly helped to make the prospects of collective bargaining on a large scale more realistic, while the recent inroads into the inherited framework of industrial relations are foretokens of the government's increased willingness to intervene in the settlement of disputes. Neither of these two developments is, however, in itself likely to reshape fundamentally the process of wage determination through periodic wage commissions, a process which is described below.

Incomes, Wage Movements, and Strike Patterns

Two cardinal features of income distribution in Nigeria are immediately discernible. One is the large differential between the wages received by an unskilled labourer and the salary enjoyed by high-level manpower. The ratio of a messenger's pay to that of a permanent secretary is, for example, about 1:30, compared with a ratio of 1:12 in Britain. The difference is further accentuated by the generous allowances given to high-income earners and by the extremely poor provision of social welfare services in Nigeria. The second feature concerns the differences in income between the peasant farmer and the wage-earner. Consideration of this differential has frequently provided the arena of debate within which any justification for increased wages is set.

While few would question that skill differentials in Nigeria are large by standards obtaining in the industrialized world, it is probable that, as Festus Olufemi Fajana argues, 'they are narrower than the differentials prevailing in other African countries'.[15] Fajana does not specify which other African countries he is thinking of, and clearly his generalization would not apply to several countries in Southern Africa, but in his careful examination of the Nigerian data (until 1967) he argues that by and large Nigerian wage differentials have been successively compressed:

> The years 1951, 1954, 1957, 1959/60, and 1964 were ones of substantial compression of skill differentials in Nigeria. In the period immediately preceding or succeeding these years, skill ratios either remained stable or fluctuated (in most cases in a downward direction).[16]

To explain the degree of compression, Fajana posits two hypotheses, the first concerned with the operation of market forces, the second with the operation of 'institutional' forces. The first hypothesis is dismissed on the grounds that a competitive explanation is inadmissible where, with a few temporary exceptions, the market for unskilled labour has been suffering from a growing surplus while that of skilled labour has been marked by continuous relative shortage. Dr. Fajana comes down heavily on the side of 'institutional' factors and in particular 'the influence of government actions and policies'.[17]

Not only have government actions and policies been instrumental in compressing wage differentials; they have also, as will be demonstrated, been of decisive importance in the movement of wage levels generally. Before documenting this, and describing the exogenous influences on government decisions, some discussion of rural–urban differentials is in order. Statistical comparisons between the two groups are extremely difficult to make, and despite a widespread acceptance of the view that the gap between the two groups is immense, serious reservations to this view should be expressed. A comparison of money incomes is meaningless where rent, transport, and food are all considerable items in the expenditure of urban wage-earners, while these items are either free or of lesser importance to the person living in a rural area. Moreover, Douglas Rimmer shows that in several studies comparing rural incomes to urban wage-incomes the ratio of dependants is assumed to be the same in both communities (i.e. one dependant for each person with income).[18] This assumption is decisively contradicted by the evidence of at least one survey. Guy Pfefferman, in a study based on a sample of 188 permanent industrial wage-earners, showed that, despite low absolute levels of remuneration, the average number supported by a wage-earner was 9·6 and there were several instances where dependants numbered over twenty.[19] As Douglas Rimmer argues:

> Whatever the representativeness of Pfefferman's findings may be, it is clear that, once the possibility is admitted of the ratio of dependants to income-earners being generally higher in wage-earning communities than in rural communities, the existence of a net differential in favour of wage employment no longer necessarily implies a higher average standard of living in wage-earning communities.[20]

An argument along these lines is highly challenging to much of the conventional wisdom of development economists who often assume that the wage-earners are an unjustifiably privileged group. It is challenging also to some left-wing theorists, who, following Fanon, have suggested that an 'aristocracy of labour' exists in African countries.[21] If there are any labour aristocrats around, they do not comprise the bulk of the permanent wage labour force, who are unskilled labourers with low levels of remuneration and real personal incomes closely comparable to a rural dweller. (In the Nigerian case unskilled labourers constitute 70% of total wage labour as Table 2.6, p. 54 above, indicates.) Given their recognition of continuing ties of blood and kin, as Douglas Rimmer comments, 'theirs is the aristocracy of *noblesse oblige*, not of high living'.[22]

Some of the underlying fallacies of the labour aristocracy thesis have been convincingly exposed by Gavin Williams, who maintains:

> The 'labour aristocracy' thesis argues first of all that *marginal* increments to workers' money wages are gained at the expense of the peasantry. This view is based on the following revealing assumptions. Firstly it assumes that increased wages cannot be met out of the profits of entrepreneurs (which is ridiculous in the case of capital-intensive factories employing relatively cheap labour) or out of the consumption of the elite. Secondly, it assumes that cuts to real wages would lead to a transfer of resources to the peasantry in the form of increased crop prices, lower taxes and an improvement of rural services rather than by a transfer of resources to the surplus-expro-

priating classes. In fact, a decrease in the rate of exploitation of the rural producer (does not) depend on an increase in the rate of exploitation of the urban worker . . .[23]

A disjunction of interest between the peasantry and the working class is thus not as obvious as it may appear at first sight. Links persist and the living conditions of both groups may not be all that dissimilar. In the colonial period the government indeed consciously and rigorously attempted to maintain a parity of income between peasants and workers. This meant in effect the adoption of a low-wage policy, the preference for which was explicitly canvassed in a Colonial Office document as early as 1905.[24] The justification for paying low wages did not, however, rest primarily on grounds of social equity, but rather relied on spurious economic arguments. It was assumed that workers would prefer leisure to income once they had achieved a certain standard of living and reached economic 'targets'. A backward-bending supply curve of labour was thought to result; the supply of labour drying up as wage levels increased. In fact the targets that workers set themselves were much more elastic than the colonial administrators realized (or were prepared to admit), and there appears to be solid evidence to support the view that wage-earners responded favourably to monetary incentives once these were offered.[25] As in the notion of labour commitment, it is also necessary when discussing labour supply to remember that the type of labour offered – on public works, roads, and railways – was hardly the most attractive or remunerative. Daily labouring never paid more than 9d. a day in Lagos until 1937 (when a 1/- minimum was set), and during the depression paid 4d. a day or less in the North.[26]

Despite these 'objectively' low wages successive wage commissions insisted that wage rates had to be determined in relation to incomes of non-wage-earners. In the case of the Miller Committee (1947), where the reference group was 'other urban dwellers', the principle of a low-wage policy was defended in these terms:

. . . as the qualifications of persons appointed to the lowest grades of the unestablished staff and therefore their potential earning capacity are in general the same as those possessed by the majority of the adult male population, it would be *incorrect* to provide them with a local purchasing power greatly in excess of that of the non-wage-earners among whom they live and may continue to live.[27]

Seventeen years later what the Miller Committee thought incorrect was enshrined as a basic element of social justice by the

Morgan Commission of 1964, though this time the farmers were the reference group:

> If the income of the farmer is as low as, or lower than, the prevailing wages of the labourer we have no doubt that he must, like the labourer, be living in conditions of penury. Accordingly, the *correct* approach is not to deprive the labourer of his rights to a reasonably decent standard of living.[28]

Whatever the grounds that the commissioners involved for deciding on the justifiability (or otherwise) of a wage award, it is beyond dispute that the role of government commissions is crucial in the movement of wages. Because the government is the country's largest employer, wage awards in the public sector are bound to have an effect on the general wage level. Equally saliently, changes in the rates of pay in the public sector spread to the private sector by what has been called 'the demonstration effect'. As W. M. Warren writes:

> The year-by-year evidence of the Labour Department's Annual Reports testifies to the general stability of rates in the private sector between major government awards (and the widespread readjustments following them).[29]

Given the tendency for private industry to follow in the footsteps of the government sector, the movement of wages over the country as a whole can be discerned to some extent at least by an examination of the changes in the rates of pay for a significant group of public employees – the unskilled labourers in Lagos. There are, of course, severe limitations to an assumption of this kind. It should be remembered, first, that wages in Nigerian-owned private firms are considerably lower (ranging from 25% to 40%) than in the private sector as a whole. Second, there are regional variations in the indices of real and money wages for places outside Lagos. No official general wage index for the country as a whole exists and it is only through an intricate extrapolation from various statistical sources that John Weeks has recently been able to provide some comparative data for several Nigerian cities. In general the indices of real wages of unskilled labourers appear to be higher in Benin, Ibadan, and Enugu, and lower in Port Harcourt, if the Lagos index is used as a basis for comparison.[30] Thus, while Table 6.1 below can indicate the magnitude of the relative changes in wage levels from year to year it does not exactly reflect comparable levels in other Nigerian cities. The Lagos index is cer-

tainly the most representative in that over a quarter of all wage-
and salary-earners are employed there, but the regional variations
should be borne in mind when examining the data in the table.
Table 6.1 provides ample evidence of the prevalent mode of wage
determination in the public sector i.e. nearly all the wage increases
(and all the major ones) coincide with the awards made by
specially constituted governmental wage committees and commissions and do not reflect continuing wage adjustments made
through the formally established industrial relations machinery.

Thus, following the report of the Bridges Committee in 1942,
a 50% increase in the cost-of-living allowance to government
employees was granted. A further increase of 50% was awarded
after the 1945 General Strike on the recommendation of the Tudor
Davies Commission. In 1952, the wages rates were raised by 30%
by administrative fiat, when it had become clear that the increase
in the cost of living in the previous few years had depressed the real
wages of the workers by about 20%.

The decision of the Western Regional government in 1954 to
raise the minimum wage rates of its employees to 5/- a day (an
increase of nearly 100%) acted as a catalyst to the grant of smaller
awards made on the recommendation of the Gorsuch Commission,
by the Federal and other Regional governments in the next year.[31]
The Western Regional government went its own way again in
1959/60 when it decided to appoint a separate commission under
Justice Morgan. Simultaneously the wages and salaries of employees of the Federal, Eastern, and Northern governments were
reviewed by a commission under the chairmanship of Justice
Mbanefo. Taken together, the Mbanefo and Morgan Commissions (of 1960) awarded wage increases to unskilled labourers of
the order of 15%–20%.[32] In 1964, the Morgan Commission recommended substantial increases in wage rates. The government's
White Paper considerably cut down the commission's awards, but
the settlement of the General Strike resulted in about a 30%
increase in wages. Finally, following the successive reports of the
Adebo Commission in December 1970 and August 1971, further
increases were granted amounting to about a 30% rise in wage and
salary levels.[33]

In looking at the movements of wages over the years one may
argue that wage-earners have been fortunate in maintaining or
enhancing their real wages to the point where as Peter Kilby has
noted, '. . . real wages in the organised sector have increased at
about twice the rate of *per capita* GNP'.[34] On the other hand, the

TABLE 6.1

Changes in Real and Money Wages for Unskilled
Government Labourers in Lagos, 1939–70

Year	Wages Rates in sh. per diem	Money Wage Index	Lagos Cost of Living Index	Real Wages
1939 (= 100)	1/0	100	100	100
1940	1/0	100	—	—
1941	1/0–1/3	106–125	—	—
1942+	1/9–2/0	175–200	151	116–132
1943	2/0	200	167	120
1944	2/0	200	163	123
1945+	2/2–2/5	214–238	176	122–135
1946	2/7	258	—	—
1947	2/7	258	—	—
1948	2/7	258	—	—
1949	2/7	258	—	—
			Lagos Consumer Price Index	
1949 (= 100)	2/7	100	100	100
1950	2/8	103	133	77
1951	3/0	115	140	82
1952+	3/4	129	131	98
1953	3/5	132	136	97
1953 (= 100)	3/5	100	100	100
1954+	3/9	109	105	104
1955+	4/8	137	108	127
1956	4/8	137	117	117
1957	4/8	137	119	115
1958	4/8	137	119	115
1959	4/8	137	124	110
1960+	5/10	171	132	129
1961	5/10	171	139	123
1962	5/10	171	145	118
1963	5/10	171	145	118
1964+	5/10–7/8	171–221	148	139–150
1965	7/8	221	153	144
1966	7/8	221	167	132
1967	7/8	221	162	137
1968	7/8	221	165	134
1969	7/8	221	179	123
1970	7/8	221	196	112

Sources:
(i) E. J. Berg, 'Real Income Trends in West Africa', in M. J. Herskovitz and M. Harwitz (Eds.) *Economic Transition in Africa* (Northwestern University Press, 1964), pp. 204, 205, 219, 220.
(ii) W. M. Warren, 'Urban Real Wages and the Nigerian Trade Union Movement', *Economic Development and Cultural Change,* October, 1966 15 (1), pp. 26, 27.
(iii) Official *Annual Abstracts* and *Quarterly Digests of Statistics.*
(iv) *Conclusion of the Federal Government on the Report of the Morgan Commission,* Sessional Paper No. 5 of 1964.
(v) J. Weeks, 'The Impact of Economic Conditions and Institutional Forces on Urban Wages in Nigeria', *Nigerian Journal of Economic and Social Studies,* November 1971, 13 (3), pp. 313–39.
(vi) Official *Economic Indicators* (Federal Office of Statistics). For later years, a draft copy available at the Federal Ministry of Labour was used.

Notes:
(1) The government's award to unskilled labourers in 1964 was £120. The *per diem* rate was calculated on the assumption that there are 26 working days per month.
(2) The dual rates indicated in 1941, 1942, 1945, and 1964 are due to the retroactive wage awards made in those years.
(3) Crosses indicate the years of the major government awards.
(4) There are slight disparities in the consumer price index in the period 1953–63 between the official figures and those extrapolated from sources (i) and (ii) after conversion to the 1953 base year. The official figures have been used. Slightly larger disparities exist between the consumer index derived from source (vi) in the period 1964–70 and the figure derived from John Weeks's real wage index (source (v)). In these cases Weeks's figures have been preferred.

Morgan Commission of 1964 was followed by six years when the money wage remained unchanged while the rise in prices wiped out the real gains that the settlement of the General Strike of 1964 brought. While real wages have improved again subsequent to the Adebo Commission, John Weeks maintains that in the period 1960–70 the movement of wages '. . . places Nigerian wage-earners near the bottom of the league among former British colonies for the decade'.[35]

The demonstration effect of the wage determination process in the public sector can be seen in the established strike patterns in the country, which has, as W. M. Warren puts it:

. . . the unusual characteristic of showing a rise in the number of strikes following a major wage award instead of preceding it, owing to the widespread attempts of employees in the private sector to raise their rates in step with those of government employees.[36]

Table 6.2 and the graph on the following pages illustrate the patterns of industrial protest since 1940.

TABLE 6.2

Strikes and Man-days Lost, 1940–71

Year	No. of Strikes	No. of Man-days Lost	Year	No. of Strikes	No. of Man-days Lost
1940	1	n.d.	1956–57	30	61,297
1941	6	n.d.	1957–58	49	63,400
1942	11	13,878	1958–59	53	73,095
1943	6	26,300	1959–60	54	70,862
1944	9	5,541	1960–61	69	160,478
1945	13	1,800,000	1961–62	58	57,303
1946	10	132,000	1962–63	45	53,039
1947	28	132,000	1963–64	62	94,907
1948	20	n.d.	1964	170+	±1,300,000
1949–50	46	577,000	1965	125	238,679
1950–51	19	286,351	1966	59	54,165
1951–52	38	20,243	1967	66	80,171
1952–53	26	59,847	1968	32	46,137
1953–54	33	26,874	1969	53	101,202
1954–55	30	12,166	1970	50	54,051
1955–56	43	901,600	1971	143	217,648

Sources:

(i) H. A. Tulatz, *Die Gewerkschaftsentwicklung Nigerias* (Hanover, 1963), p. 127.

(ii) T. M. Yesufu, *An Introduction to Industrial Relations in Nigeria* (London, 1962), p. 57.

(iii) *Annual Reports* of the Ministry of Labour.

(iv) P. Kilby, 'A Reply to John F. Weeks's Comment', *The Journal of Developing Areas*, October 1968, 3 (1), p. 21.

(v) Author's calculations from Ministry of Labour files.

Notes:

(1) Up to 1948, calendar years; thereafter from 1 April 1949 to 31 March 1950, etc.; from 1964, calendar years.

(2) The estimated figure for 1964 requires some explanation. One official estimate indicated only 253,460 man-days lost. This figure excludes however, the man-days lost in the General Strike of 1964 and the 'Election Strike' in December of that year. The man-days lost in the June strike alone were given by the Minister of Labour as 934,615. (*See* P. Kilby op. cit., 1968, p. 21.) To this figure has been added the official estimate exclusive of the General Strike plus an estimate for the December 1964 strike.

(3) Data collection appears to have improved briefly after January 1965, so rather than confusing the 1964–5 picture further, I have reverted to tabulating the Ministry's figures by calendar year.

(4) Only the figures for the years 1950–60 can be regarded as reliable (*See* P. Kilby op. cit., 1968, pp. 20, 21.) Figures from 1965 have been gathered from the Ministry's files and are accurately tabulated. However, on account of the disturbed conditions in the country under-reporting may have occurred from late 1966 onwards.

The data presented in Table 6.2 confirm in general the picture described by W. M. Warren, though certain intricacies of the data need to be explained. The incidence of strikes and the number of man-days lost do not always run in harness. The two most obvious discrepancies, in 1945 and 1971, are explained as follows. In the first case the General Strike of 1945 was recorded as a single strike, while due to the widespread nature of the action the number of

Graph of Strikes and Man-days Lost, 1940–71

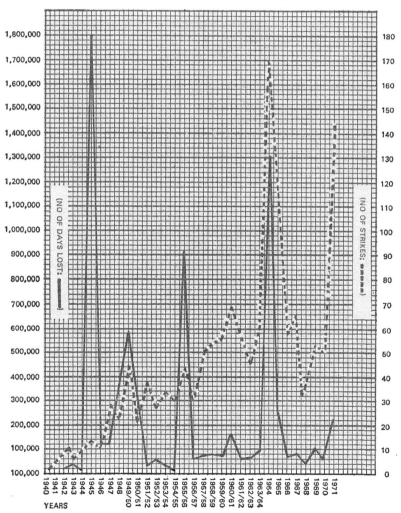

Sources: As for Table 6.2.

man-days lost was very large. In the second case it is probably the case that the powers of intervention assumed by the Ministry of Labour reduced the duration of strikes (thus lowering the number of man-days lost), without significantly affecting their frequency. In other years the amount of industrial dissatisfaction usually coincides or immediately follows the years of major governmental awards. Thus strikes or days lost reach noticeable peaks in 1945 (the year of the Tudor Davies Commission), in 1955/6 (the Gorsuch Report), 1960/1 (the Mbanefo and Morgan Commissions), 1964 (the Morgan Commission) and 1971 (following the Adebo awards). In effect the establishment of a wage commission crystallizes the issues around which industrial action is organized and may indeed serve (in the immediate term at any rate) to generate, rather than appease, industrial protest. The 'demonstration effect' is particularly seen in the private sector where the whole vocabulary of workers' activity is replete with references to the government commissions – workers presenting demands to their employers for 'their Gorsuch', 'their Morgan' or 'their Adebo'. It is also the case that the general interest in trade union activity (as evidenced e.g. by the growth in membership figures) coincides to a great extent with the degree of industrial protest. As can be seen in the graph presented in Chapter 4 (above, p. 130) trade union recruitment goes up most dramatically in 1964 and 1971, precisely those years of the greatest incidence of strikes.

It is now necessary to pull some of the threads of this section together. First, while it has been acknowledged that wage differentials in Nigeria are large, it has been suggested that they have been compressed over the years by the effects of government actions. Second, serious doubts have been expressed about the extent of the real differential between wage- and salary-earners and those outside this sector, though the importance of this comparison for decision-takers has been emphasized. Third, the movement of wages has been examined, showing in particular how crucial the government-appointed wage commissions are in wage determination. Finally, it has been argued that the level of industrial action correlates broadly with the setting up of government wage commissions. In all this, the centrality of the government's role in distribution of income has emerged. What has not been explicitly treated is the influence of other agencies and forces *on* government decisions. In particular, in terms of the focus of this book, what importance does organized labour have in the wage determination process?

Trade Unions
and the Wage Bargaining Process

Whatever the real gains of the Nigerian workers, the precise role of the trade unions in affecting wage levels has been a subject of a heated and complicated controversy in the academic literature.[37] While the sources of the views of the major protagonists to this debate have been fully annotated in the previous reference, I can only indicate the major lines of disagreement here.

Both Elliot Berg and John Weeks argue that government wage decisions may be made for reasons unconnected with trade union pressure. Berg suggests that the 'range of causal forces' which may be present is fivefold: (a) ideological or moral sentiments connected with social justice which motivates the ruling élite towards meeting the 'minimum needs' of the workers; (b) a response to unorganized dissatisfaction manifested by rioting or demonstrations; (c) a pre-emptive increase designed to assuage possible political dissent or undercut the labour movement from using such dissent for its own purposes; (d) an attempt to win friends for the ruling group among the workers or trade union leaders and (e) direct union pressure. The last is flatly discounted by Berg when he says that in the period 1939–60, 'unions had little effect on wages'.[38]

I propose to discuss these 'causal forces' in sequence. The view that there exist moral or ideological sentiments which incline the ruling group to social justice is paralleled in John Weeks's assertion in his earliest article that:

> One can build a 'model' of wage determination in the Nigerian context which is consistent with union weakness and this strike pattern [i.e. that there is a rise in strikes after a government wage award]. For humanitarian, institutional and ideological reasons the government commissions a major wage review about every five years.[39]

'Institutional' factors are for the moment ignored. As regards humanitarian, ideological, and moral considerations, one can hardly deny that there is a strong tradition of paternalism, inherited from the colonial government, which manifests itself in the social welfare work of the Ministry of Labour and in the Ministry's attempts to implement basic standards of hygiene, comfort, and safety in the workplace. But for these considerations to be the major determinants of wage awards, in the first place one might expect to find some kind of consistent social philosophy involving concepts of income redistribution or equity operating in the minds of the members of the successive wage commissions, and secondly one might expect to find such considerations uppermost in the minds of the political leadership responsible for the appointment of the commissioners. It would be unduly cynical to disparage the lofty moral sentiments that occasionally appeared in the reports of the wage commissions. As has already been noted, the Miller Committee and the Morgan Commission, 1964, *did* invoke grounds of social justice to defend their recommendations, but the two commissions were glaringly inconsistent in their application of the concept of social justice, the first commission arguing that social justice required a low-wage policy, the second that it required precisely the opposite. Besides, the commissioners were not above judiciously mixing their moral sympathy with the workers with a plea to the self-interest of the rulers. The mixed motivations at work are nowhere more evident than in the report of the Tudor Davies Commission which contains several declamatory passages of this kind. Quoting John Morley, the Commission maintained:

> 'Wise statesmen are those who foresee what time is thus bringing and try to shape institutions and to mould man's thought and purpose in accordance with the change that is silently surrounding them.'

And again:

> . . . the Trade Unions should receive every help and encouragement from Great Britain to develop along proper trade union lines. The alternative will be their being swallowed up and converted to political uses in a wider demand for self-government and independence i.e. their drifting finally and irrevocably into the hands of the politicians.[40]

In short, neither consistency of ethical outlook, nor unadulterated moral sympathy with the workers, can be established in the case of the wage commissioners. Certainly in the 1964 settlement and in most other wage settlements too, it would be unrealistic to quote statements like the Morgan Commission's approval of paying a living wage to workers, out of the context of the political events that surround the setting up of this commission. For the government the moral injunctions of the Morgan commissioners counted for very little. The settlement of the June 1964 strike, which was broadly in the unions' favour, was, in all essential respects, a political bargain, and owed nothing to ideological and moral considerations. The Minister of Finance and Chairman of the settlement committee gave a nice indication of his own moral philosophy, when, in answer to a critical speech by a trade union Member of the House of Representatives, S. U. Bassey, he attacked Bassey on personal grounds, then declared: 'It is stated even in the Bible that to those that have, more shall be given, and from those that do not have shall be taken even the little they have.'[41]

In the earlier period it is on prima facie grounds unlikely that charitable motives can be ascribed to government actions. Colonial governments are hardly noted for their gratuitous benevolence in the matter of government expenditure, and many colonial officials subscribed firmly to the view that higher wages were needless or even positively harmful. After the devolution of power to Nigerian politicians it appears that official statements regarding the necessity of holding down wages in the interests of 'development' are far more frequent than any commitment to a 'fair wage' policy. In reality this formulation of the 'state interest' turned out to be little more than a camouflaged attempt by the political leadership to secure the major portion of the benefits of development for themselves. Considering the damning evidence of the press accounts, probes, and various commissions of enquiry, into the assets of the politicians of the First Republic that have been published since the coup, there must be grave doubt whether the character of most of their policy decisions, let alone their wage decisions, was related to ideological or humanitarian considerations.

Elliot Berg's next set of causal forces – a response to unorganized dissatisfaction, a pre-emptive increase to assuage potential dissent, and a political gambit – all depend on the degree to which it is possible to separate the potential or real political influence of workers and the urban population at large, from the political influence of the unions themselves. Weeks makes a similar point in this way:

> The fact that the government in power seeks to woo wage-earners by raising wages does not by itself imply that trade unions are powerful. The mere existence of an urban wage-earning proletariat, unorganized and amorphous, may be sufficient to sustain real wages out of real or imaginary fears of this group.[42]

But if government fears are real, clearly the workers must have political influence; if imaginary they must be thought to have such influence, which, in its effects on the decision-making process, amounts to the same thing. According to this line of argument, then, workers have political influence, but trade unions may not. The distinction drawn between trade union pressure and wage-earner pressure is, however, as Warren has argued in his rebuttal to Berg, difficult to sustain, 'in any situation where the trade unions have any considerable following and public presence, and in which, therefore, the influence of either the one or the other cannot be assessed without analysing the interaction between them'.[43] Berg and Weeks do, however, have a substantial point here in that they implicitly raise the problem of assessing the precise sources of dissent, and analysing the mediating role that the unions play in amplifying, channelling, co-ordinating, or perhaps on occasions damping down, such dissent. It would be quite false to picture the unions as always being at the forefront of opposition to the government; indeed in some circumstances, like those obtaining during the civil war, the union centres found it politic to profess civic responsibility and attack wildcat strikes and other spontaneous demonstrations of worker dissatisfaction. It is also the case that on many occasions the unions, or more exactly their leadership, have not *initiated* wage demands but rather have given expression to demands that have emanated from the membership, or from previously unorganized workers. It does seem to be the most common case, however, that once a perceived injustice is felt and articulated, the unions have in the past provided a convenient instrument for aggregating and directing public manifestations of discontent. Thus it is impossible to point to a single demonstration, strike, grievance, or demand of national importance, that the workers have initiated without the trade unions becoming critically involved at some point.

That the unions' mediating role is of central importance can be demonstrated in two ways. First, so far as the workers are concerned the unions do have some relevance, as trade union recruitment rises at the exact moments when wage demands are being made. Why join the union if there is little expectation that it will help in the presentation of your demands? Secondly, though this is a more negative point, it would be much more convincing to the proposition that worker political influence is separable from union influence, if one could point to consistent or important initiatives by Nigerian governments, Federal, Regional, and State, to head off social discontent by appealing, so to speak, above the heads of the trade unions, to the wider urban masses. Provision of such basic facilities as public sanitation, water taps, low-cost housing, or paving, is notoriously meagre in Nigerian cities. Had the various governments raised the priority of such problems, it would have provided an ideal way of undermining the capacity of and the faith placed in the unions 'to deliver the goods'. Such a strategy is of course still open to the political class. In sum, however, I would argue that it is an unconvincing position to hold that in the past Nigerian governments took, or could take, cognizance of the discontent of wage-earners or the 'unorganized and amorphous proletariat' without at the same time taking cognizance of the influence of the unions in validating, facilitating, or sometimes generating, such discontent.

The view that governmental wage concessions may be designed to undercut an attempt by the unions to capitalize on popular discontent, or more positively to win friends among the workers or union leaders, is certainly more than plausible, but this would seem to argue *for* the view that trade unions influence wage decisions rather than (as Berg apparently believes) against it. The whole distinction between organized pressure by the unions *per se* and more indirect pressure, through the unions' 'threat potential', is revealed as tenuous. For if decisions on wages were indeed made on the basis of what the unions 'might do' these decisions are, it is reasonable to argue, a response to union pressure. Incidentally, Berg has perhaps unwittingly touched on a basic methodological problem for those who are behaviouralists by persuasion. For if 'activity' is to be the basic datum of social science, how does one simultaneously account for the existence of inevident activity in a 'becoming' or 'potential' stage.[44] Berg is quite right to raise the theoretical problem of 'proving' or measuring the influence of such latent forces, but he undermines his own case by acknowledging that the ruling group perceives the necessity, desirability, or expediency, of winning the support of the unions or their leaders.

Having discussed the other possible causal forces at work, and argued that in at least one case Berg has implicitly recognized the 'union factor' influencing governmental decisions, it is now possible to return to the major theme, i.e. the centrality or otherwise of direct trade union pressure in the process of wage determination. Here the weight of the negative case rests on the period 1939–60, where, in Berg's words, '. . . trade unions are a minor factor in wage determination'.[45] It would be useful initially to separate two issues (*a*) how important is union pressure in influencing the government to establish a wage commission? and (*b*) how far is it possible to identify a 'union factor' at work in wage decisions taken without immediate threats or demands made by the unions?

As regards the first issue, I have already spent considerable time on illustrating how successive wage commissions have shifted wage levels upwards and are expected by workers in the public and private sectors alike to do so. In other words, from the unions' point of view the battle is virtually won once the commission is set up, and though some comments are made later about the style of bargaining that the unions engage in with the commissions, for my present purposes I have confined myself purely to the question, 'Did organized labour induce the governments concerned to set up a wage commission?' In nearly all cases there is considerable evidence to suggest a direct link between trade union pressure and governmental response. The Tudor Davies (1945) and Morgan (1964) Commissions were appointed directly as a result of a General Strike or the threat of a General Strike. In the case of the 1942 Bridges Committee, it was established immediately after the COLA agitation led by Michael Imoudu (see Chapter 3 above) in a context where the number of strikes increased from one in 1940 and six in 1941 to eleven in 1942, while the cost-of-living index rose precipitously. The number of trade unions equally rose from fourteen in 1940 to eighty in 1942, while the unions were engaged in serious attempts to set up a central labour organization, attempts which finally succeeded in August 1943.[46] As regards the 1959 and 1960 wage commissions, no one has seriously questioned T. M. Yesufu's argument that:

> . . . the Trade Union Congress spearheaded a general demand for wage increases, using the workers' votes in the impending general elections as bait to the various political parties. The parties greedily swallowed the bait and all the Governments of the Federation promised to review wages and salaries.[47]

The cases of major wage awards that remain are those of 1952 and 1954/5, neither of which, it should be stated immediately, resulted as a consequence of direct and immediate trade union initiatives, but stemmed rather from governmental decisions. Consideration of these two cases provides a convenient focus to shift the debate on to the second issue that was raised: can we find a union factor affecting a government decision of this kind? Here the divergence of opinion is, on the surface, most acute. Readers may perhaps forgive the indulgence of personalizing the argument at this stage – not because my own position is unique, but because the intricacies in the argument of the several writers involved cannot fairly be summarized without the risk of misrepresentation. On the one hand, I argue that in the awards of the early fifties we are back in the area of 'pre-emptive' decisions and 'potential' dissent, that there are good and logical reasons why the governments concerned should have acted as they did and that these reasons can plausibly be connected with 'political factors' connected finally with 'union pressure'. On the other hand, John Weeks is of the view that 'economic factors', especially those connected with the labour market, provide a more fruitful explanation of the movement of wage levels in these years and more generally. The error of the 'political' explanation is thought by John Weeks to lie in the confusion of form and substance. He writes:

> The argument of Cohen and those who agree with him fails to draw the crucial distinction between the *forms* or *mechanisms* of wage setting and the underlying forces of wage determination. His argument deals only with the mechanism of wage determination in Nigeria, which he correctly identifies as political, but by thus restricting himself, he is diverted from the causes of wage movements which are economic.[48]

This is an apparently broad area of disagreement, and it may be useful to establish some common ground first. I concur with John Weeks that economic factors prescribe limits beyond which autonomous intervention by the unions in influencing wage movements can be considered insignificant. It would indeed be foolhardy to argue that the political leverage of Nigeria's trade unions is so great that they can 'hold the country to ransom'; extracting in wage settlements a sum so grossly disproportionate to the country's wealth that they have in the past seriously undermined the capacity of the government to foot the bill. On the other hand, the trade unions have been able to mobilize sufficient political resources to put in a competitive bid for whatever wealth is available for redistribution, and this has often occurred at the expense of other claimants. This view is probably not very different from Weeks's argument that '. . . while trade unions have pressed the wage level to the upper boundary of these [economic] limits at times, they have not been able to significantly affect the limits themselves'. Trade unions, in short, cannot affect the governments' *ability* to pay, because they, like other Nigerian institutions, cannot determine commodity prices which provide the bulk of government revenues. Fear of the unions or a desire to win support from organized labour may, however, affect the government's *willingness* to pay, assuming its ability to do so.

In the 1952 case, it can be argued that the colonial government's brief adherence to a concessionary wage policy, reflected in the 1952 awards, was an attempt to remove the political teeth from the trade unions and set the seal on the dissociation of the unions and the NCNC, a relationship which, after 1950, had little hope of attaining its former solidarity. In the latter year the attempted assassination of the Chief Secretary to the government by a labourer in Posts and Telegraphs department, coincided with a bid to oust the supporters of the Zikist movement from their strong positions in the trade unions and in party politics. The colonial government and the establishment politicians were moving towards a position of diarchy and the devolution of power to the Regions. In such a situation the existence of a radical nationalist movement with contacts in the unions was an embarrassment to both parties. The link-up between the CPP and the TUC following the General Strike of 1950 in the Gold Coast might have provided a further warning to the colonial authorities. The unsuccessful strike of mercantile workers in 1950 and the defection of some moderate union leaders to the ICFTU camp in 1951 provided the opportunity for the government to cut the ground from under the radicals' feet. Though the argument here is purely speculative, the precipitating factor in deciding the government to proffer a carrot might have been the proposal by the radical-controlled Railway Workers' Union to form a new central body early in 1952. Certainly immediately after this initiative the government moved unusually quickly to raise wages. It by-passed the wage-committee structure set up by the Miller Committee and granted substantial increases by administrative fiat.

John Weeks, in discussing the 1952 award and other wage awards of the early fifties, allows that 'political forces are not rejected' but considers that these emerge in response to economic conditions. In particular he points to the changed conditions of the labour market, the period before the wage increases (1947–51) being marked by a virtual freezing of money wages in the government sector while simultaneously the sources of governmental revenue, derived from the dramatic increases in the prices of primary commodities, rose considerably.[49] One consequence of this was, as Weeks argues, to make the possibilities of rural employment as attractive as government employment in the cities. Market conditions alone, he argues, dictated that the supply price of urban unskilled labour needed to be increased to ensure a flow of labourers comparable to the pre-1947 supply.

It is doubtful, however, whether there was an urban labour shortage of serious dimensions. The government report of 1952 which Weeks quotes to the effect that government and private business were finding it difficult to recruit labour and maintain labour stability is acknowledged as 'vague' and was to some degree a perennial complaint which recurs frequently in government reports. Crucial to the argument is that whereas in 1951 the Financial Secretary to the Legislative Council indicated in very strong terms the government's unwillingness to commit itself to any further award beyond the 12% it had already offered, the government later changed its mind. In 1951 the Financial Secretary had this to say:

> In endeavouring to meet the just claims of the service the government has gone to the limit which its finances can justify. There can be no prospect of increasing the allowance and the government is determined to hold the line against pressure for increases in basic wages and salaries. The government trust that private employers of labour will follow the same policy.[50]

Despite this commitment to 'hold the line' the Department of Labour's annual report of the following year included a government promise to review the 12% award, despite a low incidence of industrial unrest.

How is this change of heart to be explained? It was argued earlier that, though the evidence is speculative, the government may have been interested in preventing any possibility of the unions' allying with the established nationalist movement. This remains a possible explanation. Assuming that the changes in the terms of trade between town and countryside were as serious as Weeks argues, a second explanation of the wage awards is that they were an attempt to restore favourable (i.e. to the employer) conditions to the urban labour market. Nor, of course, are these explanations mutually exclusive. The data are too uncertain to support unequivocally one notion of causality rather than another. Suppose, however, for the sake of argument that Weeks's 'labour market' interpretation was favoured, one would have thought that the negative effects on the urban labour supply of rural prosperity were, given the circumstances of considerable labour mobility, just as evident in 1950/1 (when the government said that they

would not pay more) as in 1951/2 (when they promised a reconsideration of the wage rates). Perhaps, it may be argued, it took a
while for the urban labour shortage to become visible and appre-
hended by policy makers. If this is accepted, the labour market
hypothesis becomes a possible explanation for the Lagos awards of
1952 and for the other wage increases in the early fifties in Western
Nigeria that Weeks mentions.[51]

In the 1952 awards I think it is right to conclude that the political explanation is a 'case unproven'. But to extend the notion of a
perceptual time-lag on the part of decision makers to the awards of
1954/5 is impossible: and *this* award can, I believe, be largely
explained by political factors. Why? First, if the awards were
simply designed to increase the supply of available urban labourers,
the Western Regional government could have achieved this object
by using the mechanisms of the Regional and Provincial Wages
Committees; second, by paying far less than they in fact offered;
and third, by acting *sooner*. The awards of October 1954, as the
Annual Report of the Department of Labour was not slow to
point out 'marked an important departure from the long established "Miller" system of wage determination in this category'.
The report also quotes a fact-finding committee of the Federal
government as recommending the minimum of government intervention in wage settlements. The recommendations continued:

> . . . Any other policy would seem likely to lead to political influences
> and considerations entering into the determination of wages with
> effects that might be ruinous economically . . .[52]

What political influences were in play at the time? The most
important was the precarious electoral situation that the Action
Group found itself in. Contrary to a commonly expressed view that
the small number of wage-earners must of necessity preclude their
importance in electoral politics, the 1954 award is (with the awards
of 1959/60) the clearest example of parties attempting to win and
use worker support for electoral purposes. As Peter Kilby points
out,[53] elections are often lost by margins less than the absolute
number that organized labour represented. Moreover, the low
absolute numbers of union members have to be set against the
distribution of this 'constituency' in key urban areas and the
'spread effect' of workers' opinions to other sections of the electorate. In the 1951 Regional election the Action Group had defeated
the NCNC at the polls by a comfortable margin, but it had always
held a precarious base in Ibadan, whose predominantly Muslim

indigenes identified the Action Group with the native settler Christians from Ijebu province. In 1952, a political organization, the NCNC – Mabolaje Grand Alliance, unified a body of support which seriously threatened the Action Group's hegemony in the Western Region. The Ibadan District Council was decisively lost to the Alliance in March 1954, while the Federal Elections later in the year again showed a clear defeat for the Action Group in the West. W. M. Warren, in his rejoinder to Berg, has provided extensive evidence that both the NCNC and the Action Group were interested in appealing to the working-class vote, at both the national and Regional levels and that a number of meaningful initiatives were undertaken by the NCNC to retain working-class support.[54] In addition, the ULC leader, H. P. Adebola, used his seat in the House of Assembly as a platform to push the NCNC into a pro-worker position. He was aided by Adelabu, leader of the Mabolaje, who had a considerable following in Ibadan.

The decision of the Action Group to raise minimum wages can therefore be convincingly presented as a bid to avert electoral defeat, by swinging the wage-earner and wage-earner influenced vote behind the government. Once the Western government had committed itself to a higher minimum award, the other governments of the Federation, fearful of the possibility of being outflanked by the populist protestations of the Action Group, had little alternative but to follow suit. The Gorsuch Commission was accordingly appointed in 1955.

Thus in both major wage awards where trade union pressure for a commission was not directly involved, there appear to be some reasons for the governments concerned acting in response to the unions' 'threat potential'. How then do we 'prove' that the governments would not have acted in the way they did in any case, perhaps in response to economic pressures connected with the labour market? In the case of 1954/5, I believe that it is possible to isolate the 'political factors' involved in the timing of the awards, the amount granted, the mechanisms used to implement the settlement, and the recognition that political pressures *were* involved by the Federal government. Taken together with the analysis of electoral politics in the West at that time, there would seem to be a convincing set of reasons to assume political causality. In the case of the 1952 awards the political evidence is much more speculative, and determining factors concerned with the labour market need to be given considerable weight.

The degree of influence that the unions have in determining

wages in Nigeria is not a subject that is open to precise measurement. I have argued that union pressure can be directly linked to the decisions of governments to set up nearly all the wage commissions, and that where union pressure was not involved there were either possible or probable reasons for the governments concerned to wish to attract support or deflect dissent from workers and their unions. At the same time prevailing economic conditions should not be discounted in providing a favourable and permissive factor without which wage increases would either have been less dramatic or very difficult to entertain at all.

As to conditions in the labour market, I would not wish to question John Weeks's careful examination of the relevant data which suggests that there were broad correspondences between wage levels and conditions in the urban labour market. He shows, for example, how in 1946–50, when a surplus supply of labour existed, wage levels remained constant, how by 1950/1 this surplus was absorbed and wages were adjusted upwards in the next years, and how again in the period 1956–9, when an excess of labour recurred, wage levels were once again constant.[55]

There still seems to be a fundamental question of showing that wage decisions were determined by, rather than simply moving more or less in harmony with, shifting conditions in the labour market. Nigeria's economy, like all but the most ideal-type *laissez-faire* model, is not a self-regulating mechanism in which governments are totally passive agents of wider economic forces.[56] These forces prescribe the parameters of choice and response – but choice there was in the decisions to establish wage commissions, in the timing of wage awards, in the amount of wage increases granted, and, in some cases in the fact that there were any increases at all. It would of course be a happy concatenation of circumstances if at one and the same time a government had the ability to pay wage increases, helped to restore favourable conditions to the labour market, appeased possible discontent, responded to union pressure, and relieved a humanitarian conscience about the less fortunate members of society. In this case everybody would be right and there would be no need to make fine distinctions between the prominence of each of these factors, between contingent and necessary explanations, between mechanisms and causes. An eclectic view has its merits in a debate of this kind, but this does not remove the obligation to take a clear stance if a researcher's reading of the evidence shifts him in a particular direction. In sum, my view is that the factors that have the most frequent and most consistent explanatory value in looking at the process of wage determination are those associated with union pressure, political sensitivity to potential urban discontent, and attempts to win political support from trade unionists and their allies.

The Style of Wage Bargaining

There exist no formal provisions – legal or constitutional – for the setting up of regular wage commissions and no ministerial statements regarding their desirability. In fact, as has been argued earlier in this chapter, there is an institutional prejudice against this method of wage determination, the Ministry of Labour and the government continually stipulating their commitment to the process of voluntary negotiation and collective bargaining at the industry, occupational, or local, levels. Why then has this form of semi-institutionalized bargaining grown up? As far as the unions are concerned their style of wage bargaining is a response to the logic of their position in the economy and administration, and an attempt to redress their industrial weakness by whatever political influence they can muster. W. M. Warren describes the operative system in these terms:

> Time and habit have re-inforced this *modus operandi* [i.e. wage-setting by tribunals], but above all, underlying its stabilisation has been the continued weakness, especially financial, of individual unions, and the continuing delicate, albeit fluid, political situation. If the trade union movement itself has helped to create this pattern of wage-fixing, so has the movement in turn become adapted to it and thus further strengthened it. Successive administrations have envisaged the Nigerian trade union movement as conforming to the British model . . . Instead, however, the emphasis has been on public campaigning of a semi-political (or even directly political) character and on sympathetic or general strikes, the effect of which is to side-step the weaknesses of the individual unions and transform industrial action into political action.[57]

Translating economic grievances into political demands usually means that the unions run through a spectrum of political action; petitions, representations, and appeals to public opinion. The last is the most effective weapon in the trade unions' political arsenal. Sedulous attention is paid to the building up of the 'justness' of the unions' case in the press, which in turn further galvanizes workers' demands for a wage review. All the newspapers, perhaps because of the character of their readership, give good coverage of labour disputes, usually report the press conferences of the union centres, and often carry articles by union leaders.

Once the government has actually committed itself to establishing a wage commission, the negotiating responsibility invariably falls on the shoulders of a few unions or leaders who have in the past shown themselves able to articulate a widely held grievance. Individual unions rarely feel strong enough to make their own demands to their employers; instead they add their voices to the periodic clamour for a fresh deal for the wage-earners as a whole, and transfer the onus of bargaining to the militant few. Thus, in the past, only those trade union leaders who have the ability to ride or lead the crest of workers' opinion have continued to occupy prominent positions in the labour movement; and they survived because of their ability to act as crowd-pullers and propagandists, rather than administrators and organizers.

It is notable that in the agitation for a wage review and in the representations made to the commissions the more radical trade union leaders come to the fore, while the more moderate leadership (i.e. those in the ULC and the NWC) have to run faster to keep in the same place. By way of a corollary, in a period of labour quiescence the relative strengths of the LUF/NTUC and the NWC/ULC leaderships show an opposite trend, with (especially) the ULC's superior organizational strength and healthier financial situation giving it the edge in the competition for affiliates. In short, what counts in a 'confrontation situation' is the trade union leader's political style and his populist idiom. Michael Imoudu's continued popularity is a notable example of this proposition. Even before his recent withdrawal from the labour scene, he had little to do with the day-to-day running of his union and was (even by his own account) difficult to work with. On the other hand, in government/union clashes he displayed in full measure the requisite dramatic flair. In a demonstration during the 1964 General Strike he confronted the police ranks halfway across Carter Bridge in a red track-suit, and a Russian fur cap, apparel he described as his 'fighting kit'. Imoudu himself immodestly described his role to me in these terms: 'When the workers fight the government, I lead, the others follow.'

Describing how the leading trade unionists are able to use their propagandist abilities to influence the press and public opinion, Peter Kilby indicates how the formal bargaining system is circumvented:

> When the demands for a wage hike and the climate of opinion reach a certain point, the politicians (specifically the prime minister and his ministers-in-council), not the civil servants in the ministry of labour order that a tribunal be established. And it is trade unionists who provide the bulk of the testimony which goes to make up the tribunal members' notion of a fair wage award.[58]

An examination of the list of organizations which have made representations to the commissions (appended to each report) demonstrates that over the years certain unions have assumed a vanguard role. Checking through the list of submissions to the Morgan Commission (1964), for example, shows that there were about ten submissions from unions in the governments or public corporations to every one from unions in private industry. Unions in the railways, the ports, the post office, the public works department, and the civil service, almost invariably assume the negotiating responsibility for a wider circle of unions. It is no coincidence that most of the prominent trade union leaders have their stronghold in this group of unions. Imoudu organized the Railway Workers' Union, Adebola the Railway and Ports Transport Staff Union, Nzeribe was general secretary of the Post and Telegraphs Workers' Union; while Goodluck has unions in the Public Utility and Public Works Departments. Moreover, the most militant unions are usually those that operate in the most strategic areas of the administration and economy where they are in a position to cause a greater degree of disruption by the withdrawal of their labour.

It may be argued that the disruptive effects that the unions can cause are, considering the number of unionized workers, of minimal importance. But the union's power in this regard must be seen in the light of the susceptibility and sensitivity to pressures of this kind by the government and the political class. Government receptivity would clearly be greatest in situations where electoral contests are operative, a situation that has not obtained in Nigeria since 1966. How successfully then did the unions survive and adapt to Nigeria under military rule? Chapter 7 is concerned with this theme.

NOTES

1. Specific declarations of application and acceptance were made with regard to 'The Right of Association Convention' (1947), 'The Freedom of Association and Protection of the Right to Organize' (Convention 87 of 1948) and 'The Right to Organize and Collective Bargaining' (Convention 98 of 1949) Anon. 'The Influence of International Labour Conventions on Nigerian Labour Legislation', *International Labour Review*, July 1960, 82 (1), p. 29.

2. Roberts, B. C. *Labor in the Tropical Countries of the Commonwealth* (Durham, N. Carolina: Duke University Press, 1964), pp. 187, 188.

3. International Labour Office, *African Labour Survey* (Geneva: ILO, 1962), p. 223.

4. Ministry of Labour, *Quarterly Review*, June 1955, p. 562.

5. Ministry of Labour, *Annual Report*, 1963/4, Appendix VII, p. 111.

6. Roberts, B. C. and de Bellecombe, L. G. *Collective Bargaining in African Countries* (London: Macmillan, 1967), p. 57.

7. *Sunday Post* (Lagos), 5 May 1968.

8. *African Labour News* (Lagos), 1–15 June 1970.

9. Ministry of Labour *Annual Report*, 1963/4, p. 130.

10. *See* Etukudo, A. J. *Multi-Employer Bargaining: Industrial Relations in the Banking System of Nigeria* (Ilfracombe: Arthur Stockwell Ltd, 1971), p. 72.

11. Ministry of Labour, *Annual Report*, 1963/4, p. 57.

12. Yesufu, T. M. *An Introduction to Industrial Relations in Nigeria* (London: OUP, 1962), p. 57.

13. *Spark* (Quarterly magazine of the Western District of the Railway and Ports Transport and Clerical Staff Union of Nigeria), January 1973.

14. Yesufu, T. M. op. cit., p. 176.

15. Fajana, F. O. *Wage Differentials and Economic Development in Nigeria: 1947–1967* (Ph.D. thesis, University of London, 1971), p. 59.

16. *ibid.*, p. 48. It is interesting to note that the evidence Dr. Fajana cites is in marked contrast to the view that the Morgan Commission accepted. In their report the Commissioners argued that as a result of the previous government Commissions '. . . the differences between the wages and salaries at the bottom and those at the top have tended to widen.' *Report of the Commission on the Review of Wages, Salaries and Conditions of*

Service of the Junior Employees of the Government of the Federation and in Private Establishments (Hereafter, 'The Morgan Commission'), Lagos, 1964, p. 11.

17. ibid., p. 91.

18. Rimmer, D. *Wage Politics* (Occasional Paper, Faculty of Commerce and Social Science, University of Birmingham, No. 12, February 1970), pp. 34, 35, 56.

19. Pfefferman, G. *Industrial Labour in Senegal* (New York: Praeger, 1968), pp. 160–70.

20. Rimmer, D. op. cit., p. 57.

21. The economists' conventional view is widespread and does not need to be extensively annotated. For one example *see* Lewis, W. A. *Reflections on Nigeria's Economic Growth* (Paris: OECD, 1967), p. 42. The 'Labour Aristocracy' thesis has been propounded most notably by Giovanni Arrighi and John Saul. It should be noted that they themselves have doubts about the adoption of the term and consider it may 'generate confusion'. In addition they apply the term only to an 'upper stratum' of wage workers; the lower stratum is only 'partially proletarianised as, over their life-cycle, they derive the bulk of the means of subsistence for their families from outside the wage economy . . . we therefore feel justified in considering (them) part of the peasantry'. *See*, for these quotations, Arrighi, G. and Saul, J. S. 'Nationalism and Revolution in Sub-Saharan Africa' in Miliband, R. and Saville, J. *The Socialist Register, 1969* (London: Merlin Press, 1969) pp. 158, 159. My rejection of this view lies in my belief that there exist a large number of permanent wage earners who are 'fully proletarianized', but earning wages that are considerably below any income that a 'labour aristocrat' might conceivably enjoy.

22. Rimmer, D. op. cit., p. 58.

23. Williams, G. *The Political Economy of Colonialism and Neo-Colonialism in Nigeria* (unpublished paper), p. 18. Emphasis in original.

24. Hopkins, A. G. 'The Lagos Strike of 1897: An Exploration in Nigerian Labour History', *Past and Present*, December 1966, 35, pp. 145, 146.

25. Some of the fallacies surrounding the idea of a backward-bending supply curve of labour are discussed by A. G. Hopkins ibid. *See also* Byl, A. and White, J. 'The End of Backward-Sloping Labour Supply Functions in Dual Economies', *Cahiers Economiques et Sociaux*, March 1966, 4 (1), pp. 33–42.

26. Hughes, A. and Cohen, R. *Towards the Emergence of a Nigerian Working Class* (Occasional Paper, Faculty of Commerce and Social Science, University of Birmingham, Series D, No. 7, November 1971), p. 51.

27. *Report on Unestablished and Daily-Rated Government Servants* (Lagos: Government Printer, March 1947), Emphasis added.

28. *The Morgan Commission 1964*, p. 10. Emphasis added.

29. Warren, W. M. 'Urban Real Wages and the Nigerian Trade Union Movement', *Economic Development and Cultural Change*, October 1966, 15 (1), p. 24.

30. Weeks, J. F. 'The Impact of Economic Conditions and Institutional Forces on Urban Wages in Nigeria', *The Nigerian Journal of Economic and Social Studies*, November 1971, 13 (3), Table IV B, p. 331.

31. *Report of the Commission on the Public Services of the Governments of the Federation of Nigeria, 1954/5* (Lagos: Federal Government Printer, 1955).

32. See *Review of Salaries and Wages: Report by Commission appointed by Governments of the Federation, the Northern Region, the Eastern Region and the Southern Cameroons* (Lagos: Government Printer, 1959) and *Morgan Report on the Commissions for the Review of Wages and Salaries in the Public Service of the Western Region* (Ibadan: Government Printer, 1960).

33. *First Report of the Wages and Salaries Review Commission* (Lagos: Federal Ministry of Information, 1970) and *Second and Final Report of the Wages and Salaries Review Commission, 1970–1971* (Lagos: Federal Ministry of Information, 1971).

34. Kilby, P. *Industrialization in an Open Economy: Nigeria 1945–1966* (London: Cambridge University Press, 1969), p. 281.

35. Weeks, J. F. 'The Impact of Economic Conditions', 1971, p. 337.

36. Warren, W. M. op. cit., p. 34.

37. A brief guide to the controversy is as follows: The view that trade union pressure *is* central to the determination of wages was put forward both by Bill Warren (Warren, W. M. 'Urban Real Wages and the Nigerian Trade Union Movement', *Economic Development and Cultural Change*, October, 1966, 15 (1), pp. 22–36) and Peter Kilby (Kilby, P. 'Industrial Relations and Wage Determination: Failure of the Anglo-Saxon Model', *The Journal of Developing Areas*, July 1967, 1 (4), pp. 489–520). Arguing that there were other factors involved, or that trade union pressure was inconsequential, Elliot J. Berg and John Weeks joined debate with Warren and Kilby respectively. Berg's views were originally set out in 'Urban Real Wages and the Nigerian Trade Union Movement 1939–1960: a Comment' published as an occasional paper by the Centre for Research on Economic Development, University of Michigan; and subsequently published in *Economic Development and Cultural Change*, 1969, 17 (4), under the same title. Weeks, drawing partly on Berg's occasional paper, provided a critical comment on Kilby's article in 'A Comment on Peter Kilby: Industrial Relations and Wage Determination', *Journal of Developing Areas*, October 1968, 3 (1). Both Warren and Kilby were allowed the opportunity of rebuttal, the former in 'Urban Real Wages and the Nigerian Trade Union Movement 1939–1960: Rejoinder', *Economic Development and Cultural Change* 1969, 17 (4), the latter in 'A Reply to John F. Weeks's Comment', *Journal of Developing Areas* October 1968, 3 (1). This writer's own views were set out in a note entitled 'Further Comment on the Kilby/Weeks Debate', *Journal of Developing Areas* 1971, 5 (2) to which Weeks and Kilby have replied in the same issue of the journal. While referring only marginally to the previous terms of the debate, John Weeks has provided a substantial extension of his views in 'The Impact of Economic Conditions and Institutional Forces on Urban Wages in Nigeria', *Nigerian Journal of Economic and Social Studies*, November 1971, 13 (3), pp. 313–39.

38. Berg, E. J. op. cit., 1969, pp. 605, 607, 608.

39. Weeks, J. F. op. cit., 1968, p. 12.

40. *The Tudor Davies Commission*, 1945, pp. 13, 27.

41. *House of Representatives: Debates*, 5 April 1965, Column 609.

42. Weeks, J. F. op. cit., 1968, p. 10.

43. Warren, W. M. op. cit., 1969, p. 624.
44. Weinstein, L. 'The Group Approach: Arthur F. Bentley', in Storing, H. J. *Essays on the Scientific Study of Politics* (New York: Holt, Rinehart, & Winston, 1962), p. 159.
45. Berg, E. J. op. cit., 1969, p. 615.
46. *See* Warren, W. M. op. cit., 1966, p. 26; Coleman, J. *Nigeria: Background to Nationalism* (Berkeley and Los Angeles: University of California Press, 1963), p. 256, and Tables 4.5 and 6.2 above. For a contrasting view, which still allows the possibility that trade union activities explain wage awards between December 1941 and July 1942 *see* Weeks, J. F. 'The Impact of Economic Conditions', 1971, p. 323.
47. Yesufu, T. M. op. cit., 1962, pp. 143, 144.
48. Weeks, J. F. 'Further Comment of the Kilby/Weeks Debate: an Empirical Rejoinder', *The Journal of Developing Areas*, 1971, p. 165.
49. ibid., p. 168 et. seq.
50. Department of Labour *Annual Report*, 1951/2.
51. Weeks, J. F. 'Further Comment', 1971, p. 170, footnote 20.
52. Department of Labour *Annual Report*, 1954–5, Para. 20.
53. Kilby, P. op. cit., 1968, p. 23.
54. Warren, W. M. op. cit., 1969, pp. 620, 622.
55. Cf. Weeks, J. F. 'The Impact of Economic Conditions', 1971, p. 335.
56. I do not want to suggest that John Weeks believes this. Indeed he does explicitly talk about 'institutional forces' and 'institutional mechanisms'. My difficulty is that I don't know what he means by this unless it is 'governments', 'wage commissions', and 'trade unions'. At one point he says economic and 'institutional' forces are interrelated and that the economic forces set limits in which institutional mechanisms operate, at another that the role of both *government* and trade unions is 'somewhat overstated'. I would agree with the first proposition, but not with the second. *See* Weeks, J. F. 'The Impact of Economic Conditions', 1971, pp. 313, 314.
57. Warren, W. M. op. cit., 1966, pp. 32–3.
58. Kilby, P. op. cit., 1968, p. 24.

CHAPTER 7

Trade Unions Under Military Rule

Military Intervention in Nigeria: the Unions' Response

The coup of 15 January 1966 was greeted with an undisguised jubilation over much of the country – nowhere more than among the working class of the country. This was to be a blow for social justice, the end of 'chop chop' administration – even, some said, 'the end of politics'. The General Strike of 1964 and the subsequent election fracas had helped to delineate a popular enemy, a political class apparently hell-bent on preserving their power and appropriating the lion's share of the available wealth against all comers. Operating even in the minds of the coup leaders was a simplistic belief that once the political power of the politicians had been destroyed all else would follow. The half-cock nature of the January 15 events and the realities of holding power soon shattered this naïveté. General Ironsi's assumption of control at the centre was in the nature of a counter-coup, designed to destroy the abortive populism of the Nzeogwu coup, and ultimately succeeding in this.

To explain fully the background and reasons for the military intervention would involve a substantial historical diversion, for, as Antony Kirk-Greene suggests, 'The permutations of result and causality threaten to stretch back to before the name "Nigeria" was coined.'[1] I will merely note that the election crises of December 1964 and October 1965, the dispute over the census figures and the 1964 General Strike, all provided threats to the fragile legitimacy that the independence leadership was able to establish. The political motivation of the young majors represented in a broad sense a continuing strand of opposition among the deprived groups of Nigeria to the machinations of the political class. Though disaffected elements in the trade unions and the more radical UPGA supporters had nothing to do with the planning or execution of the coup, the intentions of the majors reflected, in an unorganized and inchoate fashion, the vision of a reformed Nigeria that was to be found in these groups. The common linking argument was that the political class could only be smashed by an alliance of 'progressive' forces. Awolowo and his section of the AG, far from the seat of Federal power and dispossessed of his regional power base, was interested in creating just such a trans-regional block of support. Few of the left elements, in SWAFP, in the NTUC, and among little coteries of intellectuals, were entirely confident of Awolowo's revolutionary credentials, but most saw him as the only civilian leader who could possible rally, in and out of prison, sufficiently wide support to make the notion of an organized political opposition credible, if not likely. For the young majors effecting a 'revolution from the top' was, as many other seriously intentioned revolutionary leaders have discovered, an even more difficult task. Only Majors Nzeogwu and Emmanuel Ifeajuna [2] were sufficiently close to the sources of political opposition to rally their support, and *their* links were tenuous enough. Moreover the coup itself was a failure in its primary objective, for the majors were unable to seize control in all the important *loci* of political power. Despite the marked inter-generational gap between the coup-makers and their senior officers, and the initial radical political demands of the coup leaders, ultimately Nzeogwu allowed authority to return to the senior command. He justified his abnegation of power in a subsequent interview by claiming that: 'I was being sensible. The last thing we desired was unnecessary loss of life. If I had stuck to my guns there would have been a civil war and as official head of the army (Ironsi) would have split the loyalty of my men.' [3]

For a while the close telescoping in time of the coup and counter-coup, and the need for Ironsi to go along with the popular groundswell, disguised the character of the Ironsi regime. He made a half-hearted attempt to unite the trade unions behind his government, but the splits in the labour movement had gone too deep to be healed by anything less than unity enforced by military decree. For the unions this was a golden opportunity gone to waste. The Ironsi government was a desperate improvisation, a child of circumstance, whose power rested on sufficiently shaky foundations for the workers, had they acted quickly under a united leadership, to gain some kind of voice in the decision-making process. As one might expect from the tortuous history of the labour movement, the union leadership was incapable of producing any such initiative. While conscious of the possibilities of co-operation with the military authorities, the union centres made no sustained attempt to forge labour unity or to adopt a common programme. Even the NTUC, whose political leanings might have provided an ideological apparatus to analyse seriously the possibilities of a trade unions/military alliance, did little more than offer homilies on the direction that Ironsi's government should take:

> . . . The Military Government must move in the direction and best interest of the workers, farmers and toilers of Nigeria. Conscious effort must be made to root out foreign domination of Nigeria's economy. The Military Government needs time and the peoples confidence to accomplish this. It should be made impossible for the old politicians or any group of politicians in the future to commercialise politics again. It is to bring about this that the Military Government should address itself. And this can be realised in partnership with organised labour. The leadership of labour should be recognised by the Military Government, and the formulation of plans . . . must be done with their active and conscious co-operation.[4]

In the event Ironsi fell back not on the support of the unions, but on a power base that would have been more familiar to his civilian predecessors, his fellow Ibo in the civil service and the officer corps. The promulgation of the so-called 'unity decree', the effect of which would, it was felt, allow the Ibo a competitive advantage in the jostling for civil service appointments, finally undermined his credibility. All his policies were now re-examined in the light of ethnic preferences, and many in Nigeria espoused the view (not supported by the historical evidence) that Nzeogwu and Ironsi were all along in collusion in an Ibo conspiracy to take over the Federation.

Whether this was a genuinely held belief or a convenient one, it provided a sufficiently attractive explanation of Ironsi's political ineptitude to arouse the ethnic passions of large numbers of Northerners, who in an uprising, almost certainly manipulated by the old NPC leadership and the Northern civil servants whose job security at both Regional and Federal levels was threatened, attacked the Ibo community in the North. After the killings of May 1966 the army itself, particularly at the command level, was gradually sucked into the maelstrom of ethnic animosities. For the Ibo officers garrisoned with troops of other ethnic origins, the next few months provided a nightmarish experience, and for fear of their own troops few slept easy at night.

The coup of July 1966, in which Ironsi and the Governor of the West were assassinated, was generated in this kind of atmosphere. Unlike in January, the coup-makers were largely rank and file Northerners supported by their NCOs and the coup was clearly a pro-Northern one. Brigadier Ogundipe, the Yoruba Chief of Staff, was unable to meet the mutineers' demands for (a) Northern secession or a repeal of the 'unification' decree, and (b) a return to the *status quo ante* 15 January.[5] Nor was he able to restore order. He resigned his command and left Nigeria. Control of the situation passed to Lt.-Col. Gowon who had earlier been sent to negotiate with the rebellious soldiers and was in fact taken prisoner by them. His speech of 1 August, when he assumed power, stopped just short of announcing a Northern secession, but he included a statement that, 'I have come to believe that we cannot honestly and sincerely continue in this wise, as the basis for trust and confidence in our unitary system of government has been unable to stand the test of time.'[6]

For the Ibo élite the July coup was a decisive blow to their hopes of holding or gaining a favoured place in the Federation.[7] Lt.-Col. Ojukwu refused to recognize Gowon's authority, while many Ibo professionals and academics living in the West and North began adding their voice to those who advocated that the East should 'go it alone'. With the September/October massacres in the North demands for secession became more vociferous, and continued despite the attempts of the military leadership to patch up some kind of settlement to the crisis at Aburi, Ghana, in early 1967. After the grim killings in the North, thousands of refugees, including many Ibo who had staffed the railways, posts and telegraphs, and other public corporations, in the North, fled to their home towns or those of their nearest relatives. To the support of the Ibo academics, officers, and civil servants, who had advocated secession previously, was added some kind of mass base from this second group of refugees, especially when the Federal Government procrastinated on the issue of compensation for refugee workers.

After the failure of the Aburi talks the army leaders had to take sides in the forthcoming ethnic struggle. Those Ibo officers who had not yet returned to the East defected to Ojukwu and abandoned their units, leaving only a handful of Ibo officers in the Federal army. Most of the original coup leaders were imprisoned in the East, too popular for Ojukwu to kill and too dangerous to be allowed unfettered movement. Nzeogwu was clearly mortified at the turn of events. In a letter to Tunji Otegbeye, the leader of SWAFP, written on the eve and the day of secession, he lamented:

> I am writing to you at a momentous occasion in our country's history, but with sadness at the turn of events in the political arena . . . The control of all information media by the local capitalists and national bourgeoisie, who manipulate our feuding war lords, has sublimated the political sins of national disintegration and a return to the tribe . . . In our lethargy, we shall be witnesses to the renting asunder of the national fabric and the biting away of large chunks of our territory by monarchs of reaction and tribal mob leaders . . . (on 31 May) With the proclamation of Independent Republic of Biafra, I am still optimistic that we can reach a reasonable solution to the emergence of extreme nationalism.[8]

What optimism Nzeogwu continued to have related probably to the belief among some of the radicals that there could be an alliance of the 'progressive' South against the 'reactionary' North. If conflict there had to be, so the reasoning went, let it be class, rather than ethnic conflict. These plans were only partly in agreement with those of the established Biafran leadership, though several of the coup-leaders (including one Yoruba Lt.-Col.) fought on the Biafran side in the belief that their plans could be made compatible with Ojukwu's aims. Nzeogwu himself was killed in battle fighting as a Biafran soldier on the Nsukka front, while Ifeajuna and Banjo (the Yoruba officer concerned), were executed by a Biafran firing squad, after having defied Ojukwu's orders concerning the defence of the Biafran-occupied Mid-West.[9]

But the left-group in the army had no strong links with the unions, who might have provided some kind of inter-Regional base of support. And within the unions too, the pressures of inter-ethnic hostility soon manifested themselves. For the Ibo trade union leaders outside Biafra the problem of dual loyalty was an especially painful dilemma. More than the army, whose national character was lost in successive waves of suspicion and hostility between officers and men, the trade unions had to some extent retained their inter-ethnic character. Many – probably the majority – of trade union general secretaries were Ibo, organizing workers of mixed or different ethnic origin. On the one hand were the calls of kinship and common suffering; on the other a measure of commitment to working-class solidarity, their own jobs, and the trade union centres in Lagos. For Ibo trade union leaders in the North, the choice was made for them. Machet-wielding rioters did not distinguish between worker, trader, or clerk, as they rampaged through the *sabon garis*; in Kano at least, as I was able to observe, the offices of the trade unions showed evidence of having been abandoned in haste. The Ibo trade union leaders in the North who survived joined the other refugees.

Though it is doubtful whether any concessions from the Federal government could have made a difference at this stage (late 1966), the demand for compensation for the Eastern workers was put up by the Eastern leadership as a test of the sincerity of the Federal government's dove-like protestations. Although the Federal government maintained, with some reason, that paying the money to the Eastern region treasury was merely a way of allocating money to the leadership to buy arms (both sides were arming clandestinely) the leadership in the East was able to use the non-payment of compensation as a convincing proof of the Federal Government's perfidy.

Those Ibo trade union leaders in the West, Mid-West, and Lagos who decided to stay in their jobs tried to arrange support for the Eastern workers in their claims for compensation and the back payment of wages and salaries, and pleaded with their centres to do the same. The ULC announced the creation of a special fund to help workers fleeing from the disturbed areas of the country.[10] This was a partial response to the urgings of the Western District Council of the ULC whose Ibo Secretary, Mr. E. U. Ijeh, showed considerable courage in consistently pressing for compensation. In a letter to Gowon, dated 26 October 1966, Ijeh and others claimed that:

> All along since the episode in which fellow Nigerians are killing their kith and kin, disorganising the economy of the country, straining the cordial relationship among the people of this country, sustaining piracy, gangsterism, ruthless and most grievous massacre of innocent citizens and horrible arson, we as workers had remained completely restrained and resilient in this matter only to pray fervently for a peaceful solution . . . We are convinced that the priority to the current impasses appear to have been overlooked. To our

mind, priority No. 1 should be to make an interim arrangement for the relief of the victims of the current situation.[11]

Ijeh, distressed by the lack of support shown by the Lagos office of the ULC (which he described as a 'gross betrayal'), himself travelled to the East to speak to the ULC affiliates and union leaders. He found the leaders on the verge of open revolt. Mr. Amobi of the Eastern District Council slapped a copy of the English journal, *West Africa*, on the table and attacked the ULC for bad faith and blatant discrimination against Eastern workers. In the article referred to, which was a 'Portrait' of Borha, the ULC General Secretary, Borha is quoted as rejecting accusations that the ULC had shown little sympathy for the plight of the Eastern workers, but he also stressed the national character of the ULC, claiming that, 'We can't say to the North, go to hell, for the sake of East.'[12] By the beginning of 1967 it was clear to Ijeh that the ULC's Lagos leadership had decided that to profess open support for the claims of the Eastern workers was politically unwise.

Within the East, the pressures for severing ties with Lagos were accelerated when, late in 1966, Philip Alale, a young radical who had been educated in Moscow and at Nkrumah's Ideological Institute at Winneba, organized the Eastern Nigerian Youth Movement, and attempted to bring several unions under its sway.[13] Several unions in the East had already begun to move away from their Lagos affiliations, refused to transfer the agreed portion of their dues, and were loosely grouped in the Eastern Nigeria Council of Trade Unions. Finally, Ben Udokporo, who was in charge of the ULC's Eastern District Council, announced on the same date as the declaration of secession the formation of a Biafran Trade Union Confederation (BTUC) under whose aegis most of the Eastern unions, whatever their previous affiliation, were organized.

By the time of secession, in May 1967, the labour movement had been profoundly affected by the pressures of ethnic politics. There was never complete fragmentation along ethnic lines, nor even as great a fragmentation as occurred in the civil service and the army, but the flight of Ibo workers and a number of Ibo trade union organizers did seriously damage the capacity of the unions to organize across ethnic lines. The leadership of trade unions in the Northern States passed firmly to Northern hands, the Lagos centres lost (until the war ended) their Eastern affiliates, while ethnic tensions within the leadership of the Lagos unions, which were never a serious factor previously, now became more import-

ant. Many Ibo general secretaries none the less continued throughout the war period to work in Federal territory, but some that I
talked to were anxious and ambivalent about their position and
felt with some justification that they were regarded with considerable suspicion by the Federal authorities.

Military/Union Relations
during the Civil War

For a couple of months after the Biafran declaration of secession
on 30 May 1967 there was little military activity and something of
a 'phoney war' existed. In July and August 1967, however, the Federal troops opened fronts in the south and north of the secessionist
state, while Biafran troops launched an attack into the Mid-West.
If the military lines remained fluid, the political lines on both sides
of the battleline hardened as the unions came under increasing
pressure to conform to the stated political purposes of the military
governments.

In Biafra, Ojukwu's appeals for solidarity in the face of a
common danger did not go unheeded. Indeed, the workers in
Port Harcourt, traditionally a militant group, organized a demonstration in favour of secession. After Biafra had declared itself
independent, Ben Udokporo, the BTUC, leader was given the title
of Labour Adviser and accorded a consultative status in the
Biafran administration. Faced with the immense devastation that
took place in Biafra, the unions barely had a recognizable presence
apart from the rest of the Biafran people. From a reading of
Ojukwu's memoirs it appears that no special consideration was
given to their interests,[14] and there is no available evidence that
the unions did other than conform to the urgings of the Biafran
leadership.

On the Federal side, the important ULC leaders had, as I have
indicated earlier, made their policy choice as early as 1967.
Henceforward they conspicuously disassociated themselves from

the activities of their Eastern affiliates and swung their ideological pronouncements solidly behind the Federal government's line even to the point of announcing a no-strike policy for the duration of the war. While the pressures to toe the 'patriotic' line were no doubt great, for many trade union secretaries in the ULC, Ibo and non-Ibo alike, the announcement of this policy was regarded as a serious tactical blunder by Adebola which tied their hands in any competition with the NTUC should militancy increase at the grass-roots level. It provided part of the reason why Adebola lost the presidency of the ULC at the annual conference of the centre in mid-1969.

A similar test of loyalty within the other centres to their Eastern members or to the Federal government took place. For the NTUC leaders the conflict was easier to resolve, for their ideological posturings dictated a pro-Federal stand. The NTUC's position on the war corresponded closely (as in much else) with the official Russian line. Ojukwu, like Tshombe, was identified as the pliant client of his neo-colonial masters, being used to destroy from within, a country which, if united: 'would perpetually constitute a threat to imperialist domination in the continent'.[15] The contradiction between support for the Federal government's efforts to crush the rebellion and at the same time support for workers' militancy was resolved by sleight-of-hand argument. It was not the workers who were the saboteurs of the national effort, on the contrary *they* were dying on the battlefield; but the management, who, said one NTUC leader, were 'doing everything possible to divert the attention of the Federal Military government from the immediate task of keeping Nigeria together'.[16] It was the management who were exploiting the patriotism of the workers by refusing to raise wages; it was they who were provoking the unions into rash actions so that they could disrupt trade union activities. On one occasion, Wahab Goodluck (the NTUC President) went as far as suggesting that private companies, with interests in Biafra, were deliberately fomenting industrial action:

> The possibility cannot be ruled out that the increase in labour unrest is calculated to divert the attention of the Federal Government from the war front. It is a common knowledge that those who are supporting the rebels are those who are equally having branches of their companies in the parts which are under the Federal Military Government.[17]

A far more likely explanation for the increase in industrial action in the early months of 1968, is that sections of the working class were feeling the effects of war shortages and special taxation and were no longer prepared to acquiesce tamely in their leaders' protestations of patriotism and civic responsibility. It was a characteristic feature of the whole war period that national labour leaders lost credibility and influence while grass-roots militancy grew and flourished.

As it became more apparent that the end of Biafra was to be a protracted affair, workers in the Federal area expressed more immediate concern with the decline in their living standards rather than with the task of keeping Nigeria one. The official consumer price index for Lagos showed a steady rise from 1964, when the last general wage increases were granted, and rose dramatically in 1969 and 1970. (See Table 6.1 p. 192 above). As well as a decline in purchasing power, following the introduction of import restrictions there were absolute shortages of imported items, including those like tomato paste, dried fish, and rice, customarily within the price range of the low-income groups. It was also apparent to the casual visitor to the markets that the shortages of imported goods had severely reduced the profit margins of the traders, and that they were trying to recoup their losses by increasing prices on local items. According to a report in the *Daily Times* (4 August 1968):

> Prices of essential commodities in Lagos markets have been inflated. Prices of food items like gari, yam-flour, corn, stockfish, palm and groundnut-oil at the local markets are known to have risen by as much as 50%. Traders have also increased the prices of milk, ovaltine and other beverages, toothpaste and tinned tomatoes.

The ability of the lower-paid workers to pay for their daily needs was also limited by the introduction of a compulsory savings scheme (described as a National Reconstruction and Development Scheme) which involved the deduction of 5% from all salaries and wages, over and above the contributions (about 5%) to the National Provident Fund. A few months after the introduction of the scheme, and probably in response to the industrial unrest, the lowest-paid workers were exempted from their contributions, being required only to contribute a flat rate of 10/- a year. The contributions continued to be deducted from the income of those earning above £480 per annum; the bottom ranges of this group having been particularly hard-hit by Decree 65 of 1966 which placed the tax burden squarely on the shoulders of the middle and lower (though not lowest) income groups. A married taxpayer earning about £500 per annum had his tax liability increased from £5 to £25 (a 400% rise), while those with an annual income exceeding £5,000 a year only incurred a 3·9% increase in liability.[18]

Industrial action was, for the most part, taken by workers who saw the prosecution of the war as secondary to their own interests and claims. In specific industrial disputes this led to a marked antipathy between the local leadership at the place of work and the representatives of the union centres. Though the full manifestations of this did not become apparent until after the war, grass-roots initiatives were also present during the prosecution of the military conflict. One example is the strike in April 1969 of 4,000 workers in the Western State Water Corporation, who were agitating for better conditions of service, increased wages, and improved medical facilities. The strike went on for several days against a background of public hostility to the workers and threats by the Military Governor. The strike leaders expected no aid, moral or economic, from the union centres and refused to accept mediation from this source.[19] Northern workers had shown fourteen months earlier that they too were not prepared to abnegate their right to strike in the face of verbal injunctions by the military leadership to maintain industrial peace. A threatened sit-down strike by members of the Fibre Textile Workers' Union in Jos was followed by the detention of eight strike leaders (arrested by the police, but, so a Jos union leader told me, later taken to a military camp for twenty-three days). This action provoked the textile union into a strike in protest against the arrest of its leaders. Once again, the local representatives of the union centres were apparently not involved.[20] This pattern, it may be remarked, is unusual in Nigeria, as the competition for affiliates normally means that the union centres are attracted to a local dispute like bees to a honey-pot, hoping, if the union is not firmly committed to one or other centre, to gain its adherence.

Union militancy was also on at least two occasions caused by the arrogant behaviour of soldiers, either returning from the front or based in the Lagos garrisons. After several instances of soldiers beating up conductors when they were asked for their fares, the Amalgamated Union of Lagos Municipal Bus Workers threatened disruptive action if the military authorities did not prevent the 'frequent manhandling' of their members and give them assurances of their safety within forty-eight hours. The Jos Taxi Drivers' Union similarly came out in response to 'molestation' by soldiers.[21]

The agitation during early 1968 led directly to the promulgation of Decree 21 of 1968, the Trade Disputes (Emergency Provisions) Decree, effective from the beginning of June, which severely restricted the right to strike. Although the promulgation of this order damped down the increase in industrial action, dissatisfaction was so widespread that the Federal Commissioner of Information and Labour had to threaten 'irresponsible workers' whose unions 'struck either in defiance or ignorance of the provisions of the new decree' with 'firm treatment'.[22]

If the workers were not entirely prepared to come to heel, it was no fault of the union centres. The NWC and the LUF had the overwhelming number of their affiliates in Federal territory, and both joined the other centres in expressions of political solidarity with the Federal government. Adebola for the ULC claimed that it was 'the binding responsibility of all the workers in the country to make the task of the military government easy', while Goodluck (of the NTUC) argued that the current situation demanded 'a high sense of responsibility from everybody to ensure the bouyancy of the nation's economy'.[23] A May-Day message in the NWC magazine waxed more lyrical:

> In this trying period of emergency, ours is a message of love, hope, hard work and sacrifice. Whatever may be our estate and calling, the incontrovertible fact is that we are first and foremost citizens of Nigeria; and as Nigerians, the honour and destiny of this country must supersede all other considerations. It is therefore against this sacred and patriotic background that we hereby fervently exhort you to bestir yourself as you had never done before and contribute your modest but genuine quota – your very best to the noble effort and struggle now going on . . .[24]

But whereas the ULC and NWC gave more or less open-ended commitments to the preservation of industrial peace for the duration of the war, the leaders of the NTUC were careful to point out that they still had unfulfilled demands which had at some point to be met. The statements of Goodluck and Bassey (the NTUC's General Secretary) were carefully tempered by obeisance, but now and then a sharper barb was visible:

> Cheaper transportation is yet a dream. I am not unmindful of the titanic task of the Federal Military Government, yet the non-implementation of the Housing Scheme cannot be defended . . . The NTUC has carefully studied recent economic measures and wishes to give its full support to a policy which it regards as noble and patriotic. However the Congress wishes to express its misgivings in what it believes to be 'an Economic Mirage Mission'. For those who have

followed the economic setback that was sweeping the USA as a result of her vandalistic war in Vietnam would realise that not a cent shall come out from the Yankees.[25]

The NTUC leaders also made clear that they expected the military leaders to act as a 'corrective' régime whose task was to bridge the disparity in incomes, and that failure to act on this issue would, at some later stage, produce (as they put it) 'industrial upheaval'. In point of fact the increase in industrial militancy had already, as has been noted, pushed the government into issuing a decree which emasculated the unions' right to strike. Nor did the military leaders confine themselves to imposing legal restraints on the unions. Once the Federal government was fully committed to crushing Biafra, it showed little hesitation in clamping down on dissidents. Several 'security risks' were incarcerated, including Gogo Nzeribe, an Ibo leader of LUF, who, as I was reliably informed, was beaten to death while in official custody during December 1967. Although many unionists who had heard rumours of his fate expressed disquiet in private, it is a testimony to the prevailing fear that no union leader felt confident enough to protest publicly.

Two military Governors in particular demonstrated a personal interest in maintaining industrial peace. In January 1968, when a strike of Western State Marketing Board workers was in the offing, Brigadier Adebayo advised union leaders to desist from any strike action as any such attempt would be regarded as an 'act of sabotage'. In a more threatening tone he added, 'I trust that nobody will be foolish enough to bring severe consequences upon himself by causing trouble.'[26] In the Mid-West Lt.-Col. S. Ogbemudia went beyond a mere threat and intervened in person during a sit-down strike by 4,000 workers in the Mid-Western Nigerian Development Corporation. According to a local informant, supported partly by a press account,[27] the Governor strode into the premises of the corporation and uninhibitedly beat several workers with his swagger stick while ordering them to return to work. They did.

While these incidents, together with the legal restrictions imposed on strikes, demonstrate that the military were prepared to use the repressive apparatus at their disposal to suppress demands from the unions, they should not be taken as representative of the character of military/union relations throughout the civil war. The unions on occasions provided a supportive role to the policies of the Federal government, especially in the sphere of foreign relations. Here, demonstrations by the unions against the role of foreign powers in the civil war were tolerated, or positively encouraged, particularly when the Federal government wished to contrast for propaganda purposes its popular support as opposed to the undemocratic base of 'Ojukwu and his rebel clique'. 'Incursion by Bloody Swede von Rosen Must be Stopped', 'RIP British Diplomacy', 'Pope, Get Out of Civil War', and 'Down with French Intrigue' read the posters on two such union-led demonstrations.[28]

Though it has been suggested that the policies of the military régime soon showed evidence of having moved far beyond the 'purgative' aims of the original coup-makers, there seems little doubt that the military régime was still at the end of the war regarded by many workers as being rather less corrupt and self-seeking than that of the politicians of the First Republic. Gowon's personal popularity was considerable, and a good deal of trust was placed in his promises of a programme of economic and social reconstruction after the war.

Dissension in the Labour Centres

Even before the end of the war tensions within the leadership of the labour movement came to the surface. These tensions were partly related to the role of the union centres *vis-à-vis* the Military government, a role which was thought by many rank-and-file members and some local leaders to express too great a compliance to the injunctions of the military leadership to maintain civil order. Workers complained that the centres were becoming increasingly isolated from their constituent unions and the rank-and-file membership, that their leadership was too closely tied to the interests of the foreign international bodies and that the activities of the centres were themselves becoming more and more irrelevant to the needs of the workers.

The leadership of the union centres had in fact remained remarkably stable since the Ibadan Conference in 1962. The first crack in the dominance of the old Lagos leadership came in September 1969 when the ULC's veteran leader, H. P. Adebola, was displaced from the Presidency by Mallam Yunusa Kaltungo. At the biennial general meeting of the centre vigorous accusations and counter-accusations were made concerning which side was most in the pay of the Americans. Adebola went to the lengths of inserting a large advertisement in the press stating that 'I, Alhaji H. P. Adebola have never been paid any salary or allowance in lieu of salary or honorarium by the ICFTU, AALC or the ULC.'[29] The assailed President suggested that the movement against his leadership was directed by George F. McCray, Director of the AALC, who had been asking questions as to whether 'the ULC will unite with the communists'. Adebola retorted, 'The (proposed) unity is between Nigerians and Nigerians, not between Americans and Russians.'[30] The vote, however, went decisively against Adebola; only seventeen out of about 250 delegates voted against the executive's decision to suspend him from office. His rival, Mallam Kaltungo, had neatly patched up an alliance of established and respected labour leaders, union bureaucrats in the centre (who were indeed receiving money from American sources), and delegates who represented a more militant strand of opinion in some of the affiliated unions. Faced with such an alliance Adebola had no alternative but to mend his fences as decently as he could. He congratulated George F. McCray for attending the conference of the ULC and proclaimed that he hoped all would 'forget the past and rally round the present leadership'.[31] Subsequent to this conciliatory statement Adebola was made Life Patron of the ULC. The alliance that Kaltungo built between the different shades of opinion and interest in the ULC was to survive for only two years, when at the next biennial conference in September 1971 Emmanuel Ijeh led a walk-out from the conference.

But this anticipates the story. Within the NWC also the leadership was under attack towards the end of 1969. In December of that year a Revolutionary Reform Committee under the leadership of J. U. Akpan and J. Uzor took over the centre and suspended the official leadership, including N. Chukwurah, on the grounds of 'maladministration'. Chukwurah refused to defend himself against this charge, and at the Fourth Extraordinary Emergency Convention of the NWC he and others were expelled –

though this time the grounds stated were that the old leadership 'only paid lip-service to labour unity'.[32]

The crisis of confidence in the established leadership of the labour movement was especially acute in the NWC and ULC, but the election of new leaderships in these organizations was symptomatic of a much more deep-rooted disenchantment with the failure of the centres to present a united face to the Military government. Michael Imoudu, individualistic as ever, left the LUF to its own devices (he was formally expelled in January 1971) and pushed the idea of unity through a hastily established body called the Workers' Unity Committee. Other manifestations of dissent were evident in the disaffiliation of individual unions from both the NTUC and the ULC. In March 1970 a number of unions, including the traditionally militant National Union of Seamen, left the ULC, while the 4,400-strong Shell-BP & Allied Workers' Union similarly disaffiliated from the NTUC because they wished to be members of a 'single national front'.[33]

Under pressures of this kind the leadership of the LUF, NTUC, ULC, and NWC came together in a United Committee of Central Labour Organizations (August 1970). The parallels with the 1963/64 situation were apparent to all. If the leaders of the central bodies were to retain their influence in the movement they had to go along with the groundswell of workers' opinion. They had done this with considerable success in the Joint Action Committee, but in 1970 and 1971, unlike 1964, the intensity of workers' feeling was such that the role of UCCLO became confined to making representations of a general kind to the Adebo commission, while union executives and local leaders carried out industrial protest at a local level quite without reference to the union centres.

Again as in 1964, the unions were divided as to whether UCCLO could be used as a basis for a permanent single central body. While there has always been a strong body of workers' opinion that would support the creation of a single congress, it was clear that the entrenchment of institutional interests had gone too far for pressures of this kind to have any force on the leadership of the centres. Even the leadership of the Labour Unity Front, which, it should be remembered, was set up initially not as a rival body seeking affiliates, but as a non-aligned group of unions pressing for unity among the other centres, made no attempt to argue for the establishment of a unified or federated body. Michael Imoudu quite rightly argued that 'the LUF had violated the principle on which it was founded' and tried to group another set of unions to press his case for 'unity first' – but by 1971 Imoudu was a spent force in labour politics and had little chance of leading a significant body of opinion.

The final organizational crisis that needs mention here is that which affected the ULC at its conference in September 1971 in Benin City. The conference took place against a background of continuing agitation regarding the recommendations of the Adebo Commission (discussed below). 'Official' statements and counter statements issuing ultimata to the Federal Military government and then withdrawing them, all added fuel to the flames, but the conference debate – if the raucous assembly, walkouts, and stage-managed ballots can be called that – centred around the usual divisive issues, namely accusations of corruption and the link with the ULC's foreign supporters. The various parties to the divide, basically Kaltungo and Odeyemi on the establishment side and the 'rebels' Ijeh and J. O. James on the other, became adept at issuing nebulous and confusing press statements as to the cause of the disagreement, so to sort out the kernel of truth from the chaff of propaganda designed for public consumption becomes especially difficult. The 'rebel' side seems to have been almost exclusively geographically centred on the old Western State District Council (now called the Southern Zonal Council) of the ULC. They argued that the leadership of the national ULC was not militant enough over the Adebo awards, that large sums of money emanating from foreign sources were unaccounted for, and that the leadership in Lagos had become bureaucratic and unresponsive to the demands of the district organizations. On the establishment side, Kaltungo argued that foreign sponsorship of the ULC had in any case dried up, so that there was no question of the Southern Zone not getting its fair share of ICFTU money. Ijeh and J. O. James were dismissed as being 'careerists and confusionists'.[34] They ultimately led a walk-out from the Benin Conference and left the old leadership on its now somewhat shaken pedestal. Emmanuel Ijeh's threat to create a rival splinter body does not appear to have been taken seriously by the ULC leadership, and once the Commissioner of Labour had refused to grant Ijeh's group a consultative status, the chances of creating yet another central labour organization withered away.

The Adebo Awards
and Trade Union Action

The sudden collapse of Biafra in January 1970 produced a deep sense of relief in Nigeria that the nightmare of civil war was over. The ending of the war also, however, took the lid off pent-up dissatisfaction within the labour movement and strident demands for a wage review were now made. As an editorial in the Lagos magazine *Afriscope* (November 1971) maintained, 'In the heat of the war it was relatively easy to keep the workers quiet but after January 1970 all hell nearly broke loose. Emergency or no, the workers clearly signalled that "enough is enough".'

The establishment of the Commission to review wages and salaries, under the chairmanship of Chief Adebo, in July 1970, was partly a response to the strident demands of the unions, but also clearly reflected the government's own concerns. Despite the bonanza of increased oil revenues, the economy had been seriously distorted by the effects of the prolonged war effort. Business confidence was low and the Federal government hoped to open up new areas for the deployment of foreign investment capital. Production levels in several manufactured goods, like soap, detergent, and cement, had fallen well below 1965 levels, while simultaneously the cost-of-living indices for the major cities had soared. The few half-hearted attempts at price controls which the Federal and State governments embarked on made little impact on the inflationary pressures in the economy, and none at all on the continually rising food prices. A wage and salary review was therefore seen not only as a means to assuage discontent but as an opportunity to stimulate the national economy and reorient the supply of consumption goods and services from the constraints of a war economy.[35]

At the same time the Adebo commissioners recognized that they had a special obligation to meet the needs of the lower-income groups who appeared, as in 1964, conscious of the fact that some members of the military and their associates had managed to corner a fairly healthy slice of the market in war supplies and take advantage of the administrative disruption during the previous few years. The commissioners made explicit mention of this grievance in their first report:

> ... the increase in the cost of living is a reflection of that sacrifice that has to be made in the interest of national security. Such sacrifice would be easier to bear, however, if it was seen to fall equitably on all sections of the population, such that the least sacrifice was made by those in the lowest income group. From some of the representations made to us, it is clear not only that there is intolerable suffering at the bottom of the income scale, but also that *the suffering is made even more intolerable by manifestations of affluence and wasteful expenditure which cannot be explained on the basis of visible and legitimate means of income.*[36]

The Commission had in fact taken written evidence from about six hundred trade unions and staff associations, and oral evidence from many other organizations and individuals. The range of people and organizations wishing to present their cases to the Commission exceeded by far those approaching any of the earlier Commissions and may in fact be regarded as the most significant attempt at the consultation of public opinion that Nigeria had witnessed for several years. The United Committee of Central Labour Organizations submitted a detailed and wide-ranging set of claims 'on behalf of all categories of workers in the public and private sectors of Nigeria'. The Committee demanded, *inter alia*, a minimum award of £48 10s, with percentage increases at the bottom of the scale of 380%, the abolition of the daily wage system and the differences in pay as between zones in the country, and the harmonization and rationalization of wages, salaries, and conditions of service, in the public and private sectors.[37]

In December 1970 the Commission decided to recommend an interim award backdated to 1 April (the unions had asked that it be back-dated to 1 January 1970) of 1/7 per day for the daily-paid workers and £2 a month for the wage- and salary-earners who were paid less than £500 a year. The Commission also recommended that 'the private sector should make similar adjustments to its workers in comparable circumstances'.[38]

It was precisely this recommendation that the private employers should follow suit that provoked furious disagreement between unions, employers, and the government. I have shown in Chapter 6 how the 'demonstration effect' of awards in the public sector was usually followed by agitation by unions in the private sector designed to secure similar increases. But this was the first occasion on which the commissioners' recommendations were given explicit sanction by the government, which at first announced its approval of the increments for *both* private and public sectors. Adrian Peace maintains that the government changed its mind on its blanket approval for the interim awards after representations had been made by the Nigerian Employers' Consultative Association on behalf of the leading West European expatriate concerns. The Commissioner of Labour, Chief Enahoro, now issued a statement that those expatriate companies which since 1964 had paid wage increases based on the cost of living were now exempt from compulsory payments. The difficulty was, as Peace argues, to distinguish those payments that had been made on the basis of increased productivity or on some other criterion, from those that had been made on the basis of a rise in the cost of living. Frequently, of course, several criteria were used and the unions and employers may have had different notions as to the basis on which bargaining took place and settlements were reached.[39]

The vacillations of the government, the feeling that it had knuckled under to pressure from expatriate interests, and the belief by some workers that they had been cheated of their just increments, led to an explosive industrial situation. The number of officially recorded strikes rocketed from thirty-two in 1968 (the lowest number recorded since 1956), to fifty-three in 1969, fifty in 1970, and 143 in 1971. (See Table 6.2, p. 194 above.) And it should be noted that this level was reached despite the annual renewal of the decree severely restricting the legal right to strike and providing penalties for those who incited strike action. If anything, the official statistics do not reveal the full extent of industrial actions, for demonstrations of workers' solidarity during 1970 and 1971 often involved short work-stoppages and other demonstrations of a mercurial kind. As Adrian Peace, who was conducting research in Lagos at the time, writes: '. . . faced with further prevarication over a decision by both management and government representatives, go-slows and strike action in certain factories quickly escalated into widespread strikes and lockouts throughout the Lagos area.'[40]

In its intensity and scope the outburst of industrial unrest was quite without precedent in Nigeria and quite beyond the power of the established trade union leadership to control. Workers often circumvented the ban on strikes by other often ingenious action. The Singer Machine factory in Lagos was occupied; while three textile mills were 'junked' by the workers – who smashed windows and weaving looms and overturned the cars of the management when they failed to pay the Adebo awards.[41] Stoning of the management occurred on several occasions in factories that Peace researched in Lagos, and on one occasion a manager was imprisoned until he had signed a document promising to pay the Adebo awards. Conductors and drivers for the Lagos Municipality, fearing the consequences of overt strike action, deflated the tyres of the buses standing at the depot. Even groups that had no clear connection with the awards also started demanding 'their Adebo' – perhaps the most pathetic case concerned five hundred lepers at a colony in Bende Division who demanded that the doctor heading the settlement should be dismissed while they paraded around carrying placards saying 'Pay us our Adebo Awards.'[42]

It is difficult to assess how fundamental a challenge to the power structure of Nigerian society these protests were. Clearly workers were aware that their actions involved a wider critique of the social inequalities in society at large, and that this implied a struggle which transcended the boundaries of the industrial system alone. Adrian Peace, who feels that the protests indeed concerned the position of workers in the overall social structure, quotes a young Ibadan worker (earning £15 a month) to this effect:

> This is our right, the £2 (a month) increase, and we shall fight for it to the end. What does the government think it can do to us, the workers and the other poor people . . . We have paid new taxes, we have paid National Provident Fund and in the war we paid extra taxes to fight the Biafrans. Then there are all the duties to the Government on imports so that the costs go up again. The war has ended but how would we know when there has been no improvement for us?[43]

On the other hand, workers still placed considerable trust in the members of the Adebo Commission itself, whom they often depicted as honest, sincere, and socially concerned individuals, whose recommendations were being tampered with by 'politicians' (a pejorative description which they applied to some military leaders as well as the Commissioner of Labour) under pressure from employer interests. The UCCLO memorandum included a plea that probably reflected a general view of the commissioners:

> We implore you also to look into our demands . . . like men of peace who are men of humanity, conscious at all times of the supreme obligation to temper policy by the avoidance of suffering by man, woman and child . . . All of you are regarded by workers as avuncular figures . . . By making recommendations that will improve their lot

you will identify yourselves with their suffering and justify the confidence reposed by them in your Commission.[44]

It was certainly the case that the demands of the workers were received with considerable sympathy by the commissioners and that the workers were occasionally able to drive a wedge between the Commission and some of the members of the Federal government. More significantly, however, the new burst of militancy began in a literal sense to frighten the management, dividing them among themselves. Rumour has it that hair-raising tales of stonings and machine-breaking replaced the polite after-dinner talk about the failings of the domestic help, and some of the richer expatriate concerns began to sue for peace. It has been argued elsewhere in this book that large foreign firms were not in any case overwhelmingly concerned with labour costs as this was a minor part of total production costs, through the capital-intensive character of their industries. Once some employers began to negotiate or capitulate on an individual basis the demands of workers in other private firms grew louder and the employers' castle of cards more or less collapsed. The formal announcement by the Commissioner of Labour that all employers in the private sectors would have to pay the Adebo Awards in full, regardless of any previous individual awards, set the seal on the workers' victory.

In August 1971 the Adebo Commission produced its second report.[45] Though containing many important and detailed recommendations concerning grading, the structure of the civil service, and the re-organization of the trade unions into industrial groups, the Commission's recommendations on wages were simple. A modified system of zoning was suggested to take account of the variations in the cost of living, while the revised wage rate for unskilled labourers in Lagos was raised to 10/- per day (a slight increase on the interim award). All in all, the Commission had raised the wage and salary rates by about 30%, though the extent of the differentials between the top and bottom of the scale had not been compressed significantly. The government agreed to the wage recommendations without demur.[46]

By the beginning of 1972 the agitation surrounding the Adebo reports had begun to die down, but by forcing the Military government to accede to their demands, rather than the demands of the employers, the workers of Nigeria had provided a show of force that surprised many and that may have significant implications for the future civilian rulers of Nigeria.

NOTES

1. Kirk-Greene, A. H. M. *Crisis and Conflict in Nigeria: A Documentary Source-book. Vol. 1 January 1966–July 1967* (London: Oxford University Press, 1971), p. 13.
2. See First, R. *The Barrel of a Gun* (London: Allen Lane, 1970), p. 298.
3. Luckham, A. R. 'The Nigerian Military: Disintegration or Integration', in Panter-Brick, S. K. (Ed.) *Nigerian Politics and Military Rule: Prelude to the Civil War* (London: The Athlone Press for the Institute of Common-wealth Studies, 1970), p. 69.
4. *Advance*, NTUC Newspaper, 11–18 February 1966.
5. Kirk-Greene, A. H. M. op. cit., p. 54.
6. ibid., p. 54.
7. See Asika, U. *No Victors: No Vanquished* (Lagos: East Central State Information Office n.d.), p. 74.
8. Letter to Otegbeye. Reproduced (partly in facsimile) in *Advance*, 13–19 August 1967.
9. Some details of the radicals' plans and their practical possibilities are discussed in Cohen, R. 'A Greater South: or What Might Have Happened in the Nigerian Civil War', *Occasional Paper*, Faculty of Commerce and Social Science, University of Birmingham Series C, No. 22, February 1971. But cf. St. Jorre, J. de, *The Nigerian Civil War* (London: Hodder & Stoughton Ltd., 1972), p. 135.
10. *Nigerian Worker*, ULC Newspaper, December 1966.
11. 'Nigeria at the Crossroads: Dynamic Approach Imperative', *ULC Western District Council* (Mimeographed: 26 October 1966).
12. *West Africa* (London), 17 December 1966, p. 1457. Ijeh's account of the incident is derived from an interview, February 1968 and a typewritten document which he prepared at the time – 'Plain Truth on the Current Labour Situation'.
13. Whiteman, K. 'Enugu: the Psychology of Secession', in Panter-Brick, K. (Ed.) op. cit., p. 126, footnotes 45, 46.
14. Ojukwu, C. O. *Biafra: Selected Speeches with Journals of Events and Random Thoughts* (New York: Perennial Library, 1969). But *see Selected Speeches*, pp. 13, 4 for the pre-war period when a salary and wages review was promised by Ojukwu.
15. *Advance*, NTUC Newspaper, 18–24 February 1968.
16. *Sunday Times* (Lagos), 11 February 1968.
17. Goodluck, W. O. 'An Address to the Second Annual Conference of the Lipton of Nigeria Workers' Union', NTUC files, 20 January 1968.
18. *Nigeria Year Book*, 1968, p. 149.
19. Personal Observation, and *see also Daily Times*, 30 April 1969.
20. *Sunday Times* (Lagos) 25 February 1968.
21. *Daily Times* (Lagos), 27 June 1968; *New Nigerian* (Kaduna), 11 May 1968.
22. *Daily Sketch* (Ibadan), 19 November 1968.
23. *Daily Times* (Lagos), 8 October 1968 and *Sunday Post* (Lagos), 17 November 1968.

24. *The Voice of Labour*, NWC publication, May 1968, p. 4.
25. NTUC *Press Release*, (NTUC files), January 1968.
26. *Daily Sketch* (Ibadan), 24 January 1968.
27. *Daily Times* (Lagos), 5 October 1968.
28. Reports in the *Sunday Times* (Lagos), 29 December 1968 and the *Daily Sketch* (Ibadan), 4 June 1969. *See also* for another example *New Nigerian* (Kaduna), 7 January 1969.
29. *Morning Post* (Lagos), 3 September 1969.
30. *Morning Post* (Lagos), 21 August 1969.
31. *Nigerian Tribune* (Ibadan), 22 September 1969.
32. *West African Pilot* (Lagos), 17 December 1969; *Nigerian Tribune* (Ibadan), 18 February 1970.
33. *Morning Post* (Lagos), 16 March 1970.
34. Information on the Benin Conference from a trade union informant. *See also Sunday Times* (Lagos), 12 September 1971 and *Morning Post* (Lagos), 10 September 1971.
35. *First Report of the Wages and Salaries Commission, 1970* (Lagos: Federal Ministry of Information Printing Division, 1970) p. 11.
36. ibid. Italics in original.
37. *Equitable Demand for Economic Growth and National Prosperity* (Ibadan: UCCLO, 1970), p. 36.
38. *First Report of the Wages and Salaries Commission*, p. 15.
39. Peace, A. *Towards a Nigerian Working Class: the Lagos Proletariat as a Political Élite* (Draft paper for Conference at the University of Toronto, April 1973). My thanks to Adrian Peace for allowing me to quote from this paper.
40. ibid.
41. *Daily Times* (Lagos), 29 January 1971.
42. *Sunday Post* (Lagos), 13 June 1971.
43. Peace, A. *Industrial Protest at Ikeja Nigeria* (Conference Paper, British Sociological Association, March 1972), p. 14.
44. *Equitable Demand for Economic Growth*, p. 42.
45. *Second and Final Report of the Wages and Salaries Review Commission, 1970–1971* (Lagos: Federal Ministry of Information Printing Division, 1971).
46. *White Paper on the Second and Final Report of the Wages and Salaries Review Commission, 1970–1971* (Lagos: Federal Ministry of Information Printing Division, 1971).

CHAPTER 8

Labour and Politics in Africa: A Comparative Perspective

Labour and Nationalism in Colonial Africa

Before returning to the major focus of this study, and presenting some conclusions regarding the role of organized labour in Nigerian politics, it may be worth while to set the Nigerian experience into a continent-wide perspective and examine some comparative evidence from other African countries.

As in Nigeria, it is only too easy to identify the factors that militate against the growth of large, highly structured, well-organized unions in other African countries. The wage-earning force is but a small percentage of the population (Nigeria's 3·2% compares with percentages ranging from about 2% to 14%), the numbers of unionized workers even smaller.

The difficulties of organization are accentuated by ethnic, religious, racial, and linguistic differences, the high proportion of migrant labour, employer hostility, and the frequently low level of political and economic consciousness. Moreover, owing to the general phenomenon of a rural/urban drift, particularly after the 1930s, these factors are operative in a situation where the supply of labour is usually far in excess of the demand. To this list can be added features that are particularly notable in Nigeria – endemic centrifugal tendencies at the central level, an indifferent or corrupt leadership, the predominance of 'house' or 'company' unions, and over-dependence on foreign trade union support.

In an industrial environment the conclusion would be obvious – trade unions could only have a low degree of bargaining power and would consequently be unable to effect a change in favour of their objectives (defined, simply, in terms of a rise in real wages, an amelioration of working conditions, and an increase in the social benefits accruing to the workers). In many African countries the answer is more ambiguous. If the wage rates obtaining in African countries are considered in relation to *per capita* income and in relation to the normal money income of the peasant (and without taking income redistribution into account), workers appear to have been reasonably successful in maintaining or enhancing real wages. Though the extent of the differential with non-wage-earners may, as has been argued in Chapter 6, be exaggerated by using over-simplified aggregated statistical comparisons, it has become an orthodoxy of development economists and left-wing writers alike that wage-earners in Africa are in a comparatively favoured position. Frantz Fanon, for example, writes:

> It cannot be too strongly emphasized that in the colonial territories the proletariat is the nucleus of the colonised population which has been most pampered by the colonial regime. The embryonic pro-letariat of the towns is in a comparatively privileged position . . . because of the privileged place which they hold in the colonial system [they] constitute also the 'bourgeois' fraction of the colonized people.[1]

While describing the proletariat as 'bourgeois' borders on fatuity, it is nevertheless true that wage- and salary-earners taken together have often effected upward changes in wages and salaries that have borne little relationship to the prosperity of the country concerned. Wage- and salary-earners in Dahomey, for example, who are supported by nearly two-thirds of the national income, have on several occasions precipitated a change in government when their share of the national wealth was threatened by govern-mental measures. Other events in the last few years can similarly be cited to illustrate the apparent strength of organized labour. In Upper Volta and the Popular Republic of the Congo union agita-tion has helped to depose the ruling groups – only, however, to have them replaced by military rulers. In Zambia, African Copper-belt workers have defied a wage-pegging programme and effected sharp upward revisions of wages and salaries.[2] In 1961 at Sekondi-Takoradi Ghanaian dockworkers ignored the 1958 Industrial Relations Act banning strikes and organized the first major popular demonstration against Nkrumah's régime.[3]

Clearly, in trying to assess whatever strength African organized labour has, the key cannot be in their industrial strength or economic power: for the reasons adduced earlier, they have a little. Instead, an explanation must lie in the particular conditions – economic, social, and political – which give African unions a greater bargaining power than their numerical significance and organizational viability would otherwise indicate.

In what then do these conditions consist? First, so one argument runs, in the pre-independence period the association of the unions with African nationalist movements politicized their activities and gave them a certain political leverage when the nationalist leaders came to power. A detailed refutation of this view has been attempted by Elliot J. Berg and Jeffrey Butler.[4] They dismiss generalizations about the political role of labour in underdeveloped countries as 'a kind of conventional wisdom', and consider that:

> . . . what is most striking about the political role of labor movements in the countries of Tropical Africa is their failure to become politically involved during the colonial period, their limited political impact when they did become involved, and their restricted role after independence.[5]

This analysis is especially cogent with regard to the degree and consistency of support that African unions gave to the nationalist movements in the pre-independence period – though their generalizations must be treated with care. Only in Kenya and Guinea, so they argue, can an intimate union-party relationship be adduced. In Nigeria, the collaboration between the TUC and the NCNC effectively ended in 1950; in the Gold Coast, after the strike called in 1950 by the TUC in support of the CPP's positive action campaign, a significant part of the union movement (especially those unions on the docks and in the railways) tried to preserve trade union independence from the party; in the French Cameroons, because of a strong ideological orientation by the unions (deriving from a close connection with the metropolitan parties and unions), the union movement was, for the most part, hostile to the claims of the major nationalist party. In other parts of French West Africa, however, the French permissiveness regarding the participation of civil servants in politics, and the ideological heritage of the metropolitan unions, produced a series of informal party-union alliances and to a large extent an interlocking leadership. But, even here, so Berg and Butler maintain, '. . . the pattern of union-party relations failed to develop along clear-cut lines of alliance and collaboration.'[6] Support for the Berg/Butler thesis has been advanced in Roger Scott's work on trade unionism in Uganda, where, he comments: 'Unions in Uganda were never deeply involved in party politics or the "struggle" for independence.' and later avows that:

> . . . the pattern of relationships in Uganda between the trade unions, the nationalist political parties and the independent government fits in with the controversial Berg-Butler thesis regarding the political impotence of trade unions in Africa.[7]

Berg and Butler's views have all the attraction of a polemic against a well-worn orthodoxy, but a careful reading of their own arguments suggests many reservations to their initial hypothesis. They have discussed at length only the cases of Guinea, Kenya, Nigeria, Ghana, Northern and Southern Rhodesia, and the French Cameroons. The first two countries, as Berg and Butler acknowledge, correspond to the pattern of union/party interaction; in all the other countries, even on their own evidence, there have existed periods of close – though intermittent – co-operation between nationalist parties and unions. Other qualifications are threaded between the stronger statements. In Nigeria during 1945–50, 'one segment of the labor movement threw itself into political activity', in Zambia 'in the beginning informal ties were close', in Southern Rhodesia 'the growing labour movement and the growing nationalist movement at first entertained friendly relations with each other', etc.[8]

While any generalizations which point to a hand-in-glove relationship between African unions and parties in the pre-independence period must now be set aside following the work of Berg and Butler and of Scott, the problem remains why so much effort is made to disprove an orthodoxy which is itself so tenuous. Quite simply, it is by no means clear that the political role of organized labour can, or should be, measured by the intensity of its relationship to a nationalist party. It is not an obvious proposition that a lack of constant co-operation is evidence either of political apathy or political impotence; on the contrary, it may attest to a degree of political sophistication. For the unions to stand consistently shoulder to shoulder with parties deriving their power base from traditional rulers or from members of the political class was tantamount to giving up any claim to represent the working class. Many unionists were also conscious of the need to preserve a power base independent of the nationalist movement even where they were in accord with common anti-colonialist objectives. This tendency could stem (a) from the concern of a union to the left of the established party to maintain a possible left-oppositional role, (b) from the attempt by a right-wing union to prevent incorporation as a wing of an ideologically centralizing party, or (c) from a more nebulous desire to cling to the principle of 'free' trade unionism and not have intra-union affairs infected by political conflicts and divisions emanating from outside the unions. Tom Mboya maintained that the political stance of the Kenya Federation of Labour was dictated by just such considerations:

> The question which has to be constantly reconsidered is where you draw the line between identification with the national movement and subordination to their political designs . . . (if political strikes are called only by the central trade union federation) . . . it gives you also a better opportunity to negotiate with the nationalist movement on a firmer footing, with no risk of one union being played off against another, or a union supporting this or that political faction.[9]

Far from its being necessary to evaluate the political role of labour in terms of its overt links with nationalist parties, I would argue that action undertaken by workers in defence of their class interests can have significant political implications even where nationalist parties are ineffective or proscribed. The role of the Kenya Federation of Labour during the Emergency and the tremendous impact that the activities of the Industrial and Commercial Workers' Union (1921–4) had on subsequent political developments in South Africa, are but two examples to illustrate this proposition.[10]

Berg and Butler often engage in retrospective definitions about the political or other meaning of workers' activities, and particularly strike action. Although, for example unions in French Africa are described as being 'continually embroiled in disputes with the government' and their energies as being 'devoted to pressure against the State', their objectives are defined as 'essentially economic' and not political in 'the proper sense of the word'.[11] Even if the problem of assessing what is 'properly political' is ignored, it is important to realize that the actors concerned gave a political meaning to the activities of organized labour. As Ioan Davies writes with respect to strike action in colonial times:

> Initially trade union attempts to gain recognition through strikes were seen by the colonial rulers as political, especially when the strikes were directed against the main employment agency – the government or a public corporation. It did not take much for a

colonial government to jump to the conclusion that any strike of government employees was subversive. That many strikes were so categorised, indeed, led African politicians and some trade unions themselves to see the strike as a political weapon.[12]

While self-definition, consciousness, and perception by the actors involved, may not necessarily explain everything, it is a dimension that needs to be added to the evaluation of an outsider. The political role of African labour in the pre-independence period sometimes involved a direct link with nationalist parties, but more often involved a set of short-term and loose alliances for immediate objectives, with the unions having considerable organizational independence. Even, however, where this was the case, union actions were often seen as political and had important political implications both for the colonial governments and for the nationalist politicians concerned.

Sources of the Political Influence of African Trade Unions

Whatever influence the unions derive from their pre-independence activities must clearly be the subject of a detailed empirical investigation in each country – certainly the degree to which they were politicized by the nationalist struggle is an important, though perhaps not crucial, datum for evaluating their post-colonial role. The Nigeria data cited in Chapter 5 suggest a fairly close parallel in the political aspects of the 1945 and 1964 General Strikes: it is possible that past struggles survive as folk memories in the minds of union members and may provide a basis for action notwithstanding the formal act of independence.

The political influence of the unions must also, however, be set in the 'real' social context in which the unions operate. Most African societies have exhibited discontinuities and weaknesses in political institutions, imperfectly formed party structures (or the absence of parties), defects in the supporting bureaucracies, gaps in the means of communication and control, and a lack of well organized interest groups other than the army. In this situation, the trade unions represent – for all their deficiencies – a relatively co-ordinated and articulate pressure group.

The capacity of the nationalist élites to draw all groups in the population into a common system of political values, which existed to some degree while there was a common colonial enemy, diminished drastically after independence. In the post-colonial situation, parochial interests, often based on primordial ties, re-asserted themselves and led to the development of an unintegrated or 'syncretic' society.[13] This development often reflected the incapacity of African ruling groups to distribute goods, services, and opportunities, such as would reduce the sense of deprivation of one community, one ethnic group, one region, one socio-economic interest, relative to another. The stated intention of many African leaders to subsume traditional interests into a common cluster of nationalist values, was more often an ideological mask or an affirmation of hope than a reflection of reality. To slip into the functionalist's jargon for the moment, if the political institutions of a society are breaking down or lack legitimacy, if the decision-makers are insensitive to demands, or if the demands are un-aggregated and anomic in character, the capacity of the system to manage change peacefully will be dangerously diminished. In societies that can be so categorized, it follows that any functionally specific group, like organized labour, that exhibits a high degree of efficiency and organization relative to the system as a whole, stands a chance of extracting its demands at the expense of the less 'specific' sectors of the society at large.

The army is, of course, the group most prone to show its teeth in such a situation, but the trade unions, too, have strong potential capacity to intervene politically. Political intervention by the army and trade unions may, of course, not be mutually exclusive. The role of the unions in the overthrow of unpopular governments in Dahomey, the Sudan, and the Popular Republic of the Congo may be mentioned in this respect, but it was the army alone which had the means of permanent control. In fact it may broadly be generalized, as S. P. Huntington argues, that the military is distinguished from other social groups by its ability to assume political control immediately:

> ... while other social forces can pressure the government, the military can replace the government. Monks and priests can demonstrate, students riot, and workers strike, but no one of these groups

has, except in the most unusual circumstances, demonstrated any capacity to govern.[14]

It is none the less true that a large-scale strike in Africa often has a political significance wider than the special claims of the wage earners, but may instead represent a fundamental attack on the failure of the system to 'deliver the goods'. Roger Murray's assessment of the potential significance of the Brazzaville pattern (Popular Republic of the Congo) provides an interesting argument along these lines. He claims that:

> The 'egoistic' oppositional action of urban wage-workers (and peripheral self employed) can debouch into a genuine critique of the power system of post-colonial clientage – if the confrontation is sufficiently *sharp* and *sustained* and if it is relayed in groups with a wider social vision and programme (revolutionary intellectuals).[15]

Another factor making for the potential strength of African trade unions is the strategic position they occupy in the economy'and administration. As the concentration of the political struggle often takes place in urban environments, and sometimes only in the capital cities, the geographical concentration of unions in urban environments means that the unions are well placed to give voice to their demands. If the number of unionists relative to the number of urbanized inhabitants of a country is measured, rather than comparing their number to the total population, the numerical importance of the trade unions becomes more significant. Moreover, as the government and public corporations are almost invariably the most important employers of labour in African countries, any major industrial action has implicit political consequences. The crucial importance of the government sector in providing employment in nearly all African countries can be indicated by the data provided in Table 8.1.

In its capacity as employer there is no reason to suppose that the government would react differently from any other employer trying to keep the wages of its employees below a certain level. Where a substantial portion of the national wage bill is provided by the government, ruling groups often argue that it is all the more necessary to save on the cost of labour in order that governmental revenue be invested in the vaunted development programmes. Failure to cope with a successful strike affects both the government's pocket and its prestige. In many cases, African governments have been too weak to prevent, or have directly connived at, exorbitant salary structures at the top levels of government and administration that were inherited from the colonial era.

Because workers tend to be most highly organized in the crucial service industries, such as the railways, posts and telegraphs, and docks, as well as in the bureaucracies which service governmental programmes and on whom the executive has to place almost

TABLE 8.1

*Estimated Employment in the Public Sector in
Selected African Countries*

Country	Year of Data	Estimated Employment in Public Sector	
		In Thousands	% of Total Wage Employment
Dahomey	1961	16	44
Mali	1961	14	73
Mauritania	1963	6	43
Uganda	1962	89	40
Nigeria*	1964	220	40
Ghana	1960	190	35

Source: For Nigeria, *Annual Abstract of Statistics*, Federal Office of Statistics, 1966, p. 22. For other countries, B. C. Roberts and L. G. de Bellecombe, *Collective Bargaining in African Countries*, 1968.
Employment in public works not included
* Excludes public corporations

complete reliance, the unions have additional leverage. Where modern skills are at a premium, the support of some small sections of organized labour may be necessary to fulfil basic 'pattern maintenance' goals. Only in this respect, and only for the limited numbers of the intendant classes that are organized by trade unions, is the labour aristocracy thesis (criticized in other respects in Chapter 6) upheld.

The unions, despite their small numerical strength, have, as we have argued in the Nigerian case, a considerable propaganda strength, and influence the political opinions of a sizeable number of people outside the union structure. Such influence derives from the social position of the workers (a theme that has been pursued earlier) and their location in the process of political communication. Living in an urban environment, it is they who have the most ready access to the mass media, they who are to be Lucian Pye's 'responding citizenry' without whom the modernizing values stressed by the élite groups can have little or no meaning.[16] To contain the political tensions that developmental goals give rise to, it becomes necessary to involve the functionally specific groupings in the urban situation in the political process. The failure to do so has implicit consequences for the country's political stability. As Lucian W. Pye writes:

> . . . from a communication point of view it is possible to relate the problems of the development of the mass media, the organisation of political articulation and the expression of interests, and the formation of collective opinions with the individual's reactions to the challenge of new ideas, his grouping with conflicting values, and his search for new perspectives – and to demonstrate that all these complex problems underlie the general problem of political consensus.[17]

Workers not only have to be convinced of the genuineness of the developmental and modernizing values of the élite in their own right, but they also act as communicators and opinion leaders in the villages of their origins which they influence by visits, through family relations, and through the activities of tribal organizations (with which the unions may share a dual allegiance). In many cases political opinions are formulated at the place of work and through the activities of the unions. The wage-earners become, as it were, the cybernetic links or transmission belts in the system of communication. It is true that the élite groups in many African societies still have a strong connection with the traditional segments of the society, but (as many studies of the new élite since independence have shown) there has been a growing sense of group solidarity among the élite groups, and a growing alienation from the more traditional ties and from lower-income urban groups. Though this is less true of Nigeria than of some other African countries (for example, Zaire) the wage-earners are residentially segregated, living in the commercial, market, or industrial areas, while the élite are generally found in modern estates; the workers obtain their goods and services from local artisans and petty traders, while the élite patronizes the foreign stores.

The life situation of the worker also predisposes him to hold distinct social attitudes and to take collective action, despite the often-repeated argument that the worker is comparatively privileged in relation to the peasant. The worker is most prone to the socially disruptive effects of urbanization and industrialization. He is often the victim of overcrowded cities with inadequate transport facilities, housing shortages, poor sanitation, incompetent police forces, and sometimes (as happened in Guinea and Ghana) breakdowns in the network of food distribution. Moreover, despite the proliferation of voluntary associations in Africa based on the tribal or kin group which alleviate the worst effects of the transplantation to a new environment, the worker has been wrenched from traditional social controls in the sense that these no longer provide an answer to the more impersonal disciplines of urban living. His experiences in the new *milieu* may introduce an element of tension and frustration into his formerly stable family and group relationships. In a tribal community where labour power was not sold, there was no sharp distinction between work and other activities; membership of the community brought security in the event of sickness, disability, or old age. As J. I. Roper notes: 'The worker was rarely an isolated or independent individual, he found his place within an age group, a kin group, or a craft group.'[18] Not surprisingly, labour movements are the focus for the discontent that the new situation gives rise to. The fact that, despite all this, the worker may still see himself in an advantageous position *vis-à-vis* the unemployed town drifter or the peasant, may only increase his desire to hang on to what he has, and stave off the 'threat' from below.

Another factor making for the political influence of the unions is that many national labour movements have tried to maintain economic resources independent of party or government control by allying themselves to one or other of the international trade union bodies. The affiliation of national centres to the international bodies often has a negative aspect, for the assurance of financial support, patronage, and scholarships, leads to a tendency to neglect grass-roots organization and the building up of viable trade union structures. However, it is possible that in some cases the support that the international bodies have given to the individual centres has allowed them to preserve a measure of autonomy which has enabled them to stand out against governmental control and direction of their activities.[19]

The international bodies also politicize the unions in a more intangible way. The Cold War ideologies that accompany the work of the ICFTU, the AALC, and WFTU; the Pan-Africanist bias of AATUF; and the anti-Nkrumahist origins of ATUC, all interact on the policies and predilections of African trade union leaders, and provide them with a critical awareness of African and international political issues. In several cases this leads to an abject acquiescence (at least publicly) to the foreign policy motivations of the international bodies. A Kenyan trade union delegate to the AALC's conference at Geneva in 1967 piously declared: 'Many Americans have told me that Irving Brown (the Executive Director of the AALC) is the best Ambassador they have in Africa', while the Deputy Secretary-General to the Mauritanian Workers' Union claimed that: '. . . in the vocabulary of the workers of Mauritania and the workers of the United States, the words "rupture" and "diplomatic" do not exist.'[20] Similar declarations of loyalty from those unions that are affiliated to the WFTU can be cited. The President of the NTUC enjoined the members of a visiting trade union delegation from the Soviet Union to enjoy the warmth of Nigeria's climate as it symbolized 'the inestimable warmth of the hearts of millions of Nigerian workers, farmers, the government and the people'.[21] While statements of this kind may indicate simply the desire not to cut off a lucrative source of aid, the ideologies of the international bodies do provide the trade union leaders with a degree of political consciousness, which makes them among the most politically articulate individuals in African societies. During the period of the emergency in Kenya, Mboya was able to use his contacts with the ICFTU to attack the British Government's conduct, while in post-colonial Africa the influence of the international bodies has often made of the trade union leaders the strongest advocates of radical Pan-Africanist or 'neutralist' foreign policies.

Several factors have been enumerated which provide the sources of the political influence of African trade unions – the association of nationalist and labour movements or the degree to which the unions had a political presence outside the nationalist movement, the relative weakness of the political systems in which unions operate, the strategic position that the unions have in the political and economic systems of African countries, their propaganda strength and influence outside the union structure, the political attitudes that arise out of the life-situation of the worker, and the influence of the international trade union bodies. These factors, taken together, go a long way towards explaining the *pre-disposition* for political involvement that many African unions manifest. While these factors provide a sufficient explanation of why many union actions take on a political colouring, a necessary explanation also lies in the politicization of the wage bargain itself. Extensive comment on the nature and extent of political wage bargaining has been made in Chapters 5 and 6, and there is no

need to repeat the theoretical arguments relating to this characteristic behaviour pattern here. Suffice to say that while the intricacies
of the bargaining relationship and the actual or potential threat
that individual unions represent may reveal large variations, it
appears that the constraints on the operation of 'free' or collective
bargaining systems are similar throughout African countries.

Organized Labour
in Post-Colonial Africa

In comparing the role and performance of Nigeria's trade unions
with other unions in post-colonial Africa, the judgement (written
in the early sixties) of Elliot Berg and Jeffrey Butler again provides
a convenient starting point:

> The unions in Tropical Africa were of even less significance after
> independence, than they had been before . . . Almost everywhere
> on the continent, labor organisations were taken over by the govern-
> ing parties . . . The labor movement, if not completely subordinate
> to the party, is at least pliable and responsive to party pressures.[22]

Roger Scott similarly writes that 'unions in Africa are no longer
independent institutions but are increasingly responsive to the
politics enunciated by national political leaders'.[23] Fortunately it
needs little elaboration to question these views for they have been
decisively contradicted by subsequent events. The most notable
displays of union strength in recent years – in Upper Volta, the
Sudan, Dahomey, the Popular Republic of the Congo, Zambia,
and Nigeria – have already been mentioned, while further serious
trials of strength between government and unions have taken place
in Senegal, the Ivory Coast, and Ghana. Overt political ideologies
and slogans have been adopted during periods of labour agitation,
and riots, processions, demonstrations, have occurred in many
African countries. On the other hand, all the precedents cited so
far illustrate that while the unions may provide an important

source of political dissent, they do not have the means of permanent control. Indeed, in all the cases where unions have seriously challenged the power of incumbent governments and helped to secure their downfall, the army has climbed to the seat of power on the shoulders of the trade unions. For this reason, and also because of the fact that the greatest militancy has often been displayed by the higher échelons of wage-earners (clerks, civil servants etc.), one should not be misled into thinking of the trade union demands as part of an incipient proletarian revolution.

Even where there has been no overt and serious conflict between government and labour, the picture of union subordination does not apply in every case. Many unionists, it is true, have had their militancy blunted by government employment, party office, and a fat salary. Others have entered into productivity deals or (in rare cases) profit-sharing schemes with their employers, or like Nigeria's ULC offered support to the government in exchange for progressive labour legislation, consultation on development policy, or the initiation of a check-off system. But to suggest a one-to-one relationship of dominance and subordination, as between government and labour, belies the complexity of the relationships that have emerged in the post-independence years, and underscores the very real difficulties that the political leadership has in containing union demands. By way of illustration, the Tunisian ruling party, the Neo-Destour, has consistently tried to bring the Union Générale des Travailleurs Tunisiens under control, first, by changing the leadership of the centre, and later through developing industrial cells of the party. Despite this, the UGTT has openly criticized the development plan of the party, and, in December 1962 attacked its centralizing tendency, while in the same breath denouncing the conspirators involved in an abortive plot against Bourguiba.[24] In Morocco and the Sudan, the unions, in Ioan Davies's judgement, '. . . have proved themselves important focal points of discontent',[25] despite the attempts of the party and military leaders to exercise control by alternative placatory and repressive measures. In his study of the relations between the United National Independence Party (Zambia's governing party) and mining workers on the Copperbelt, Robert Bates refers to the 'low level of success achieved by the government's policies toward mine labour' and argues that 'Zambia has been unable to reverse the private preoccupations of its workers'.[26]

In one sense it is not surprising that the capacity of the ruling parties to overcome or co-opt organized labour was stressed by

Chart of Union/Party Relationships in Selected African Countries

---

| *1. Integration* | *2. Partnership* |

Description of relationship: Union integrated in party.

Example: Tanzania.

Characteristic rationale: 'The Tanganyika Federation of Labour was seen to represent the special interest of a minority of the population seeking to extract maximum concessions for its members at the cost of the economic development of the nation.'[a]

Function of the unions: To increase productivity and discipline the work force. 'The objective of the five year plan can never be achieved without the active co-operation of organized labor.'[b]

Characteristic features of the relationship: Special representation of unions in party apparatus. Interlocking leadership, or control over appointment of union functionaries. The Secretary-General and Deputy Secretary-General of the TFL were appointed by Nyerere.

Similar Examples: Nkrumah's Ghana, Guinea.

Evidence of conflict: In Guinea, a crisis situation in 1961, thereafter little conflict. In Ghana, always strong pockets of resistance to party control as the Sekondi-Takoradi strike illustrates. In Tanzania, the TFL accused of harbouring mutineers after the 1964 army mutiny. A new union centre, the National Union of Tanganyikan Workers, created with the Minister of Labour as General Secretary.

Description of relationship: Recognition of some degree of union autonomy, but close co-operation expected in development programmes.

Example: Kenya.

Characteristic rationale: 'The rights of industrial workers must be fully protected as development takes place and much of this work can be left to responsible unions ... but ... the government cannot permit the existence of more than one central organization.'[c]

Function of the unions: Welfare benefits for members, administration of housing schemes, training programmes, consultation on development issues.

Characteristic features of the relationship: Legislation providing for compulsory arbitration and conciliation procedures where the unions are unable to resolve issues through accepted bargaining processes.

Similar examples: Ivory Coast, Tunisia.

Evidence of conflict: In the Ivory Coast, large strike by one union centre in 1959 ('For three days Abidjan was in chaos').[d] Attempt to move to an integrated relationship largely unsuccessful. Trade unionists involved in a 'plot', 1963. Student/worker strikes in 1969. In Tunisia, periods of marked hostility between unions and party.[e] In Kenya, after a period of 'regular conflict'[f] between 1960 and 1965, the unions came under increasing government influence.

Sources: (*a*) W. H. Friedland, 'Co-operation, Conflict and Control: TANU-TFL Relations, 1955–1964', in A. A. Castagno and J. Butler, *Transition in African Politics* (New York: Praeger, 1967); (*b*) United Republic of Tanzania, *Report of the Presidential Commission on the Establishment of a Democratic One Party State* (Dar es Salaam: Government Printer, 1965), p. 26; (*c*) *Text of Kenya*

3. Independent:
Allied to Opposition Group

Description of relationship: Unions exist independent of the ruling group, though not necessarily independent of opposition groups or foreign benefactors. Ruling groups either choose not to, or are not in a position to, challenge this autonomy.

Example: Morocco.

Characteristic rationale: Independence, the unions argue, has brought benefits only to a small clique. The trade unions must act to redress the situation.

Function of the unions: To act as agencies attempting to redistribute income in a more egalitarian fashion. To challenge the legitimacy of the ruling group. To help to promote alternative foci of political power.

Characteristic features of the relationship: Periods of intense hostility between government and unions.

Similar example: Albert Margai's Sierra Leone.

Evidence of conflict: In Morocco after 1959, the Union Marocaine du Travail was always in the vanguard of resistance to Hassan II. This was especially evident after the UMT allied itself to the Union Nationale des Forces Populaires, led by Ben Barka. In Margai's Sierra Leone, close union co-operation with the opposition All People's Congress, now in power.

4. Independent:
Normally Non-Aligned

Description of relationship: Government tolerance of, or indifference to, union autonomy, usually because the unions are thought not to represent a permanent or serious political threat.

Example: Nigeria.

Characteristic rationale: Government tolerance expressed in terms of an adherence to the principles of 'free trade unionism'. Union independence defended in terms of the 'right' to organize freely.

Function of the unions: Narrowly conceived in terms of representing their numbers and engaging in bargaining with employers (who may, of course, also include the government or public corporations).

Characteristic features of the relationship: The government may take a paternal interest in regulating the registration and 'proper' functioning of unions. Legislative controls are, however, likely to be few. Hostility may occur, but this is not necessarily followed by attempts at governmental control.

Similar examples: Many including Uganda, Zaire.

Evidence of conflict: Unions may, on occasions (as in the 1964 strike in Nigeria) pose a political threat to the ruling group.

Government Sessional White Paper on African Socialism and its Application to Planning in Kenya (London: Africa Centre Ltd, 1965), pp. 44, 45; (*d*) I. Davies, *African Trade Unions* (Harmondsworth: Penguin, 1966), p. 157; (*e*) W. A. Beling, *Modernisation and African Labour: A Tunisian Case Study* (New York: Praeger, 1965), Chapter 6; (*f*) I. Davies, op. cit., p. 168.

Berg and Butler. In common with many other studies undertaken in the early sixties, their arguments rested on the root assumption that political parties were likely to prove more vigorous and solid institutions than subsequent events have shown to be the case.

In the years immediately following independence, many Africans themselves seemed inclined to accept the legitimacy of the ruling parties. Parties were able to effect a measure of control over most interest groups, or reassert such control, even where (as in the Tanganyika mutiny of 1964), power had clearly slipped from the ruling party's hands. With the large number of military take-overs in succeeding years, often taking place with ludicrous ease, few scholars can now believe that the power of the parties was (and to a large extent *always* was) anything much more than an empty shell. In retrospect it has become evident that the web of relationships that existed between the ruling parties and other elements in the political process was far more complex – and involved a large number of intermediary and transactional bargains which diluted the message and impact of the parties and lent the parties legitimacy only for a series of tangible favours and rewards.

The picture of party ascendancy and union clientage is, in short, much too simple-minded to explain the variety of union/party relationships that materialized in post-colonial Africa. These relationships include, certainly, those of party control but they also encompass relationships of partnership or of a degree of union independence. The range of relationships that exist, or existed prior to military intervention, may be indicated, if in rather ideal form, by the chart on pp. 254–5.

Although such summary judgements of relationships that are constantly in flux are liable to be overtaken by changing circumstances the data presented does illustrate that parties have not entirely managed to contain the political influence of unions, even where they have made a strenuous attempt to do so. The description of the various types of relationships can perhaps be regarded more accurately as 'ideal types' which present the basic range of alternative union/party interactions. Thus even where (as in Tanzania) I have described the union as being integrated in the party, this indicates the formal or aspirational type of interaction within which there may still exist a degree of union independence.

But while I have concentrated in plotting party/union relationships in post-colonial Africa, the unions have demonstrated that they may under some circumstances have considerable political leverage even under military governments. Such leverage as they do have can initially be described by reference to a protrayal of some characteristics of underdeveloped societies. In defining his concept of a 'praetorian society' Samuel P. Huntington refers to the 'general politicization of social forces and institutions'. He goes on:

> All sorts of social forces and groups become directly engaged in general politics. Countries which have political armies also have political clergies, political universities, political bureaucracies, political labour unions and political corporations . . . In under-developed societies the military are concerned not only with pay and promotion, although they are concerned with that, but also with the distribution of power and status throughout the political system. Their goals are general and diffuse as well as limited and concrete. So it is with other social groups.[27]

If it is possible so to group generically all major institutions in a praetorian society, it is possible too to strike analogies in the behaviour of some of these institutions. In Africa there are a number of surface similarities between the army and organized labour. Both organize across ethnic or regional frontiers, both evince a degree of corporate consciousness (produced by training or common attachments to national symbols in the case of the army, and common work experience in the case of organized labour), and both are substantially excluded from the network of patronage that the independence politicians established.

But there the similarities usually end. There *are* cases in Africa where the army, as a path to political power or once it has assumed power, has consciously attempted to rest its political base on a wider section of the population. It is also probably true to assert that where the political base of the army is insecure (either because it rests on no significant civilian base and its 'egotistical' character is therefore exposed, or because there are divisions in the ranks of the army itself), the unions may perform an important political role. To illustrate these varieties of union/military relations, I propose to discuss briefly three cases.

A. POPULAR REPUBLIC OF THE CONGO SINCE 1963 – 'THE ARMY WIDENING ITS APPEAL'

In 1963 the Youlou régime was brought down amidst demonstra-tions, strikes, and conferences, organized by the *jeunesse* and the trade unions. The army's refusal to fire on the crowds assembled outside the Presidential Palace compelled Youlou to resign after the 'Three Glorious Days'.[28] The army (who were the agents of the transfer of power) preferred not to participate directly in the provisional government (the Commandant of the Gendarmerie was the only vaguely military man in the Cabinet) and instead the political initiative passed to the Mouvement National Révolutionnaire (MNR) which had grouped the elements involved in the Three Glorious Days. In August 1968 Major Ngouabi attempted to force to a climax a conflict of interest between the youth wing of the MNR and the Peoples' Militia (trained by the Cubans), on the one hand, and the army proper on the other. Early in 1969 he succeeded in capturing power and immediately started to outflank the previous government in his appeals to the trade unions, awarding pay-increases of up to 40% to low-income workers and up to 20% for middle-grade civil servants. His clear attempts to push the army along a revolutionary road may often comprise little more than empty rhetoric (his, for example, was the first government in Africa to recognize the National Liberation Front in Vietnam), but he has succeeded in gaining the adherence of sections of the MNR to his régime. The army, which numbered 700 men in mid-1963, has indeed considerably altered its character with the incorporation of 1,000 members of the MNR's youth wing. The combined military forces are now described as the People's National Army.

B. THE SUDAN SINCE 1958 – 'AN INSECURE ARMY'

General Abboud, almost certainly in response to a plea from the Prime Minister, a former army brigadier, took over power in November 1958 amid demands to include another coalition partner in the national government. Popular pressure was organized by the Communist Party and found expression in the unions and among students and the Gezira tenants. As Ruth First argues, 'Organized political opposition on a number of fronts under the leadership of left-wing forces . . . in time pierced the myth of the army's invincibility',[29] but the splits within the army, between varying alliances to the different brands of religious orthodoxy, and different generations of officers and career rivals, finally precipitated the collapse of the military junta in November 1964. For a while it looked as though the forces of the left, including the trade unions, might ally with some young army radicals, but army rule was to be supplanted instead by a series of shifting coalitions between the pre-1958 politicians. A constitutional crisis in 1968 gave a fresh chance to the alliance of the Free Officer movement in the army and the left oppositional groups. This time the *coup d'état* of May 1969 placed in power a group of officers publicly committed to a radical change in Sudanese society and who included in their Council of Ministers several left leaders connected with the popular risings of the previous nine years. The Sudanese experience showed that the army found it impossible to hold on to the reins of power without itself becoming infected by the schisms in civilian politics that provided the original justification for intervention. Political events during 1971 and 1972 when many of the left-wing elements were attacked, do, however, seem to show that a determined and ruthless army command may be able to free itself from some of the civilian forces that brought it to power and solidify its position as a separate 'estate'.

C. DAHOMEY – 'THE UNIONS AS POLITICAL ARBITERS'

For my purposes I shall have to ignore René Lemarchand's warning that Dahomey's 'political problems are tortuous and do not lend themselves to facile analysis'.[30] Despite the changes in party labels, since 1951 political alliances have been centred on three Regional power blocs, Abomey in the South-West, Porto Novo in the South-East, and the North. These Regions were respectively the fiefs of Dahomey's three most powerful politicians – Ahomadegbe, Apithy, and Maga. The division of the country into these Regional blocs, which were more or less balanced in relative power, made the control of Cotonou crucial to the outcome of any conflict. Here the usual factors adduced to explain the sources of the political influence of trade unions in urban centres come most forcibly to the fore. Cotonou does not form part of any of the Regional power blocs, but it provides essential services for all three. It is the centre of whatever educational, commercial, industrial, and administrative, activity Dahomey has. Here, too, the unions are organized, with a history of militancy among the working class (dating back to 1923 in the case of the dockers) and an almost total coverage of the civil service and salariat. Since independence there have been eight heads of state, three Republics, and a number of coups (some events are ambiguous), the first taking place in October 1963 and the last in March 1973. In each of these changes it apparently made little difference whether the contestants for power were military men or politicians – they all had, if they were to capture power, to come to terms with, or offer concessions to, the unions. As René Lemarchand maintains:

> It is only a slight exaggeration to say that whoever controls Cotonou controls Dahomey, and no political faction of note has thus far been able to control Cotonou without the support of the unions.[31]

In the case of Nigeria, the splits in the army do not run deep enough for the Sudanese pattern to emerge, while the unions cannot muster the strategic power of their Dahomeyian counterparts. The pattern of military/union relationships in Nigeria seems instead to represent a more general case where, whatever the claims to popular legitimation that are made at the time of the coup, these soon abate as the military rulers fall back on political forces that politicians relied on, or increasingly entrench themselves as a separate power bloc, moving perhaps to some kind of informal alliance with the bureaucracy.

In reviewing the role of trade unions in post-colonial Africa, the substantive arguments are unlikely to be encompassed in a series of continent-wide pronouncements, but instead need to be made in detailed studies of the degree of political influence, latent and actual, that a particular set of unions can bring to bear, the situations in which any such influences may be significant, and finally in the susceptibility of individual African governments to union pressure. In the analysis of these problems, the Nigerian experience, used as a case study, may have valuable insights to offer.

Organized Labour and Political Stability in Nigeria: some Conclusions

Wherein lies the political influence of Nigeria's trade unions, and what effect does or may that influence have on the political stability of the country? Even to use the word 'stability' in the Nigerian context is problematical. Nigeria never was the 'model democracy' that some British colonial administrators were wont to claim they had left behind. The conduct of the 1959 election, immediately prior to independence, already showed in genesis the corruption, rigging, and system of spoils that had their full-blown manifestation in the subsequent attempts to secure a popular mandate to govern. The succession of crises that marked the years of civilian rule have been discussed in our first chapter; but these crises pale by comparison both in scale and in the extent of human suffering with what Nigeria's peoples endured after the intervention of the military in politics. Coup and counter-coup, massacres, and finally civil war – the dry prose of the academic cannot possibly express the poignancy and meaning of these events.

It is this failure, a hundred times more than any methodological objections that may be raised, that calls into question the work of systemic or systemic-functionalist theorists. For at a high level of abstraction, and the higher the easier, it is always possible to erect a model of a continuing system. In some formulations it appears that systemic breakdown only occurs if a population is totally obliterated. Except in this unlikely event, systems never apparently cease to exist, they merely have different 'capabilities' to manage change, or different degrees of vulnerability to political pressures. Analyses of this kind have been given explicit formulation by the categories of appraisal of a system's vulnerability that Gabriel Almond and G. Bingham Powell adopt.[32] Using their terminology for the moment, it appears that Nigeria has little 'extractive capability' to draw fully on its human and material resources, as its bureaucracy is either so weak or so corrupt that it cannot fairly administer a savings scheme, or collect taxes from all the inhabitants, or provide an adequate transport network to export the country's produce. Its 'regulative capability' to organize a system of control over the behaviour of groups or individuals is, perhaps in common with all but the most totalitarian societies, of a limited character. With soldiers-turned-thugs having to be shot in public as an example to others, Nigeria may be worse off than most. Its 'symbolic capability' to draw all the groups in the population into a common system of political values can hardly be considered high when a large minority of the society apparently did not even wish to claim association with the Nigerian polity. Finally, its 'responsive capability', i.e. in systems terminology, the relationship between inputs and outputs or how demands are channelled, processed, and fed back into the system, must have fused at the point of reception and transmission, as institutional breakdown was all too apparent to both actors and observers immediately after the first years of Nigeria's independence.

Clearly, on virtually every score Nigeria is in a parlous condition of 'political underdevelopment'. Yet precisely because of the abstract perspective of analyses of this kind, they can tell us little about how people comprehend this condition and how they react to it. To understand *these* questions a quite different perspective is needed – a multi-faceted assessment of what chance each bidder (be it ethnic group, social stratum, organization, or individual) stands in the permanent competition for goods, resources, and control. For the basic manifestation of underdevelopment is the ephemerality and scarcity of goods and resources, and this overriding condition determines the behaviour of the bidders. When the stakes of the game are so high that they are seen as, and may indeed involve, survival, the intensity and persistence of conflict is inevitable. Moreover underdevelopment, as A. G. Frank in particular argues, is not a natural state like original sin, but a *process* which involves the systematic reduction of some groups' chances by other 'overdeveloped' groups, both national and international.[33]

What this book has attempted to do is to look at the chances of one stratum in the society, the wage- and salary-earners, and one set of organizations, the trade unions, and assess their performance and possibilities in relation to other segments of the society. Naturally the over-arching capacity of the system to manage the rules of play between the bidders as well as the constraints imposed by the under-development of Nigeria, are important data, and in this respect the occasional successes of trade union struggle, the fairly high effectiveness of the organizations that represent labour, and the degree of corporate consciousness that the wage- and salary-earners evince, are all positive factors to be set against the *relatively* low managerial capacity of the system as a whole.

But all too often the use of an abstraction like a 'system' translates into a crude notion of the state as neutral referee and arbiter, providing the structure and staging-ground for the interaction between the players. This the state never is, and in few places more visibly so than Nigeria. The apparatus of the state is itself one of the resources for which the bidders – notably the politicians, the bureaucrats, and the soldiers – are in competition. For the control of *this* resource the trade unions stand little chance, but in their bid for power the élite groups need allies and a certain measure of popular support or acquiescence. It is in this transactional and bargaining area that what political resources the unions have are traded for tangible goods and favours.

What then do these resources comprise? First, the success of the unions in adapting to, and partly helping to create, a mode of wage bargaining that is fundamentally political in character. As has been argued in Chapter 6, occasionally the need for electoral support has meant that the parties have attempted to buy worker or worker-influenced votes. But this mode of bargaining is not entirely dependent on the presence of an electoral system – the trade unions were able to derive leverage from the colonial government's wish to separate industrial from political issues in 1945 and in the early fifties. Again in 1970 the unions were able to plead that their restraint and sacrifice during the war period now merited a fresh reconsideration of their wage claims. Narrowly considered, trade union pressure alone does not explain the grant of wage increases: on the side of the government, there may well be a realization that discontented groups may be made less radical and offer less of a future threat if their demands are assuaged by periodic concessions. Again, these concessions are made more easily in a period of relative economic prosperity – as in the early fifties when the prices of primary commodities were high, or in the post-civil war period when governmental resources from oil substantially increased the government's 'ability to pay' increased wages.

Secondly, the unions have managed in the past to channel the grievances of a group wider than the confines of their membership. This is partly due to the sociological characteristics of the working class itself and the complex overlapping relationships it has with members of the urban population employed in the 'informal' sector of the economy and with the peasantry. More concretely, I have shown how in conflict situations with the government in 1945 and 1964 the unions for a time became the focus for oppositional elements and challenged the authority of the government itself

(Chapter 5). Perhaps too much should not be made of the potential ability of the unions to act as counter sources of legitimacy. There are latent conflicts of interest between the urban subproletariat and the labour force employed in the formal sector, which are only temporarily mitigated by the recognition of traditional obligations; while the union's capacity to sustain a strike on purely political issues is limited, as the 'election strike' of 1964 indicated (Chapter 5). On the other hand one may speculate that with the return to civilian rule, this aspect of the union's power may have a renewed importance. The unions alone continue to have a multi-ethnic leadership and organization, unlike the intendant class and the military, whose national character has been severely undermined by the events of the civil war. Ethnic quotas became in effect the guiding principle for recruitment to the state bureaucracies, while the army has reorganized the location of its installations in accordance with some recognition of ethnic parity. As opposed to this, the union centres seem to have been able to reintegrate their affiliates in the Eastern states without too much trouble, while in the West and Lagos many Ibo trade union leaders and workers continued in their jobs throughout the war period.

This ability to organize across ethnic lines may be of renewed importance, especially if a future devolution of power to civilians includes a requirement that parties need to have a measure of support in several states of the Federation. Politicians may find in the unions convenient instruments for gaining access to a section of popular support wider than their own ethnic group. As possible straws in the wind, it may be noted that Aminu Kano, Joseph Tarka, and Chief Awolowo, all established or rising stars in the competition for who shall inherit power, have been making increasingly populist noises and speaking on trade union platforms. There is also some evidence that a left-wing ginger group, formerly organized in the AG, is resurfacing with the participation of some who were previously inolved in shifting the AG towards a more radical position. The unions may well be in a position of trading their mediating role for some recognition of their objectives.

Finally, in the longer term, the structural changes in Nigerian society must themselves work towards the consolidation and increasing coherence of groups, based on an economic interest rather than ethnic sentiment. The bloody civil war and increased ethnic consciousness that resulted therefrom may on the surface seem to deny this proposition, but less noticed has been the simultaneous integration of the military élite into the top echelons of the political class. The small indigenous bourgeoisie profited considerably from the war restrictions on imported manufactured goods and they, together with the top bureaucrats, have decided material interests in common with the military brass. At the level of the working class, on the other hand, new initiatives of a radical kind were involved in the agitation surrounding the Adebo awards in 1970 and 1971 (Chapter 7). The growth of grass-roots unionism, irrespective of the claims and activities of the central labour organization, would seem to attest to the growth of a new degree of economic solidarity based on the work-place and local organization.

There is little doubt that the oil revenues, and the increased attractiveness of Nigeria as an investment outlet for foreign capital, have given considerable breathing space to the government, allowing it, for example, to maintain a standing army at very nearly civil war strength. But should it become politically or economically necessary to run down the army, demobilized soldiers will add considerably to the number of political discontents. If they, together with the more radical unions and politicians anxious to win popular appeal, manage to achieve some kind of alliance, a new political force of some considerable dimension may yet appear on the Nigerian political scene.

NOTES

1. Fanon, F. *The Wretched of the Earth* (London: MacGibbon & Kee Ltd., 1965), p. 88.
2. See Bates, R. H. *Unions, Parties and Political Development: A Study of Mineworkers in Zambia* (New Haven & London: Yale University Press, 1971).
3. See Drake, St. C. and Lacey, L. A. 'Governments vs. the Unions', in Carter, G. C. (Ed.) *Politics in Africa: Seven Cases* (New York: Harcourt, Brace & World, Inc., 1966).
4. Berg, E. J. and Butler, J. 'Trade Unions', in Coleman, J. S. and Rosberg, C. G. *Political Parties and National Integration in Tropical Africa* (Berkeley and Los Angeles: University of California Press, 1964), pp. 340-81.
5. ibid., p. 340.
6. ibid., p. 357.

7. Scott, R. *The Development of Trade Unions in Uganda* (Nairobi: East Africa Publishing House, 1966), p. 179.
8. Berg, E. J. and Butler, J. op. cit., pp. 344, 346, 353.
9. Mboya, T. *Freedom and After* (London: André Deutsch, 1963), pp. 195, 196.
10. See Amsden, A. H. *International Firms and Labour in Kenya: 1945–1970* (London: Frank Cass & Co. Ltd., 1971), pp. 30–44 and Kadalie, C. *My Life and the ICU* (London: Frank Cass & Co. Ltd., 1970). Introduction by Stanley Trapido. For further elaboration on this point *see also* Allen, C. 'African Trade Unionism in Microcosm: The Gambian Labour Movement, 1939–1967', in Allen, C. H. and Johnson, R. W. (Eds.) *African Perspectives* (Cambridge: Cambridge University Press, 1970).
11. Berg, E. J. and Butler, J. op. cit., p. 365, footnote 85.
12. Davies, I. *African Trade Unions* (Harmondsworth: Penguin, 1966), p. 95.
13. Zolberg, A. R. 'The Structure of Political Conflict in the New States of Tropical Africa', *American Political Science Review*, March 1968, p. 71.
14. Huntington, S. P. *Political Order in Changing Societies* (New Haven and London: Yale University Press, 1968), p. 217.
15. Murray, R. 'Militarism in Africa', *New Left Review*, July–August 1966, No. 38, p. 46.
16. Pye, L. W. *Communications and Political Development* (Princeton: Princeton University Press, 1963), p. 9.
17. ibid., p. 11.
18. Roper, J. I. *Labour Problems in West Africa* (Harmondsworth: Penguin, 1958), p. 23.
19. Beling argues this in the case of the Tunisian labour movement. Beling, W. A. *Modernisation and African Labour: A Tunisian Case Study* (New York and London: Praeger, 1965).
20. Afro-American Labour Centre, *Report of the AALC Conference held at Geneva, June 1967* (New York: the AALC, 1967), pp. 33, 39.
21. *Advance* (NTUC Newspaper), 16–22 March, 1969.
22. Berg, E. J. and Butler, J. op. cit., p. 341.
23. Scott, R. 'Are Trade Unions Still Necessary in Africa?', *Transition*, October–November 1967, No. 33, p. 29. *See also* this author's reply in *Transition*, February–March 1968, No. 35, pp. 11–12.
24. Beling, W. A. op. cit., p. 107 et seq.
25. Davies, I. op. cit., p. 142.
26. Bates, R. H. op. cit., p. 1.
27. Huntington, S. P. op. cit., p. 194.
28. *See* Murray, R. op. cit., pp. 38, 40 and *Africa Report* October 1963, p. 22.
29. First, R. *The Barrel of a Gun* (London: Allen Lane, 1970), p. 252 et seq.
30. Lemarchand, R. 'Dahomey: Coup within a Coup', *Africa Report*, June 1968, p. 46.
31. ibid., p. 47.
32. Almond, G. and Powell, G. B. *Comparative Politics: A Developmental Approach* (Boston and Toronto: Little Brown & Co., 1966), Chapter 6.
33. *See*, for example, Frank, A. G. *Capitalism and Underdevelopment in Latin America* (New York and London: Monthly Review Press, 1969).

Appendix

University Workers' Survey

A. A NOTE ON PURPOSE AND METHODOLOGY

The purpose of the survey was to examine the background and investigate the attitudes of a small group of workers towards their union, their fellow-workers and their position in society. An attempt was made to assess the extent to which the respondents evinced a corporate identity, and further questions were directly linked to their political views. The sample for the survey consisted of seventy members of the Ibadan University Workers' Union. The union was selected partly because of accessibility and good relations with the officials of the union, and partly because (unusually) in Ibadan, it provided a good spread of occupations ranging from technical and clerical workers to manual ('general') labourers. The union at the time had over a thousand members on the books, but the General Secretary identified about 280 members who were committed at least in the minimal sense that they attended meetings and evinced some interest in union activities. It was thought that the administration of a schedule to a quarter of them would provide a sufficient sample size. A pilot study of thirty members was made to test the clarity of the questions and the amount of time that would be needed for completing each schedule.

I was greatly helped in framing the questions by the set of surveys conducted by Robert Melson and reported in his Ph.D. thesis *Marxists in the Nigerian Labour Movement: a Case Study of the Failure of Ideology* (M.I.T., 1967) from which eleven 'attitude' questions were derived. No attempt was made to compare the results obtained, as the University Workers' Survey slightly altered the text of most of Melson's questions. Dr. Melson's findings on political attitudes are, however, summarized in Chapter 4 of this study.

An attempt was made to divide the population by skill (with the aid of union officials) and introduce a random element by asking union officials to select every second man on their prepared lists. Checking this later showed that randomness was not entirely established – the union officials concerned simply asked for volunteers. This has undoubtedly meant that a systematic bias in the sampling has occurred either towards more active members of the union (i.e. those who would be concerned enough to answer questions) or towards more work-shy members who might have relished the prospect of wasting an hour or so.

Unreliability was also introduced in that, despite vigorous pleadings that no one who had participated in the pilot survey should return to answer the revised schedule, familiar faces reappeared – perhaps as many as fifteen. In the event only five questions were substantially altered, so perhaps this factor is of little importance.

University students were used as interviewers, the format of the interview being students sitting side by side with respondents filling in questions as they were answered. In at least one case, where a set of five responses was depressingly similar, interviewer bias almost certainly occurred and the schedules had to be discarded.

The effect of these remarks on the methodology employed should be apparent: little reliance should be placed on the scientific status of the survey. Though it has been thought sufficiently valid to tabulate percentage responses in each category, given the statistical limitations in applying correlation coefficients to small samples, however expertly administered, it has not been thought rigorous enough to try to establish (by the use of Chi-squared tests, etc.) any positive or negative relationship between the responses offered.

B. SCHEDULE ON WORKERS' ATTITUDES

(*i*) *Number of Questions*
(*ii*) *Abbreviated Question and Responses*
(*iii*) *Number of each Response*
(*iv*) *Percentage of each Response*
(*v*) *Number of Responses*

(*i*)	(*ii*)	(*iii*)	(*iv*)	(*v*)
1.	*Age*			
	20–29 years	24	35	
	30–39 years	14	20	69
	40–49 years	15	22	
	50 years and over	16	23	
2.	*Occupation/grade*			
	Technical/foreman	18	26	
	Labourer/apprentice	17	24	70
	Artisan/craftsman	17	24	
	Clerical/skilled	18	26	
3.	*Pay* (monthly)			
	£8–£14	16	23	
	£14–£20	24	34	
	£20–£26	11	16	70
	£26–£32	8	11	
	£32 and over	11	16	
4.	*Place of birth*			
	Ibadan	9	13	
	Other large town or city	25	33	70
	Small town or village	36	51	
5.	*Ethnic affiliation*			
	Yoruba	28	41	
	Hausa/Fulani	3	4	
	Ibo	7	10	
	Ibibio	6	9	68
	Ijaw	4	6	
	Bini	6	9	
	Other	14	21	
6.	*Length of residence in Ibadan*			
	Under 2 years	6	9	
	2–5 years	9	13	70
	5–10 years	12	17	
	10 years and over	43	61	
7.	*Children: where educated*			
	Ibadan	33	47	
	Birthplace	11	16	70
	Other/not applicable	26	37	

(i)	(ii)	(iii)	(iv)	(v)
8.	*Retire to*			
	Ibadan	8	11	
	Birthplace	44	63	
	Other	5	7	70
	Don't know	13	19	
9.	*Use of, or ownership of land in birthplace*			
	Yes	49	73	67
	No	18	27	
10.	*Frequency of visits to birthplace*			
	Once or twice a year	40	57	
	Three or four times a year	5	7	
	More than four times a year	13	19	70
	Never	7	10	
	Not applicable	5	7	
11.	*Sends money home?*			
	Yes	57	81	70
	No	13	19	
12.	*Amount sent home*			
	Large amount (10% plus of income)	32	56	57
	Small amount	25	44	
13.	*Membership of tribal association?*			
	Yes	34	49	69
	No	35	51	
14.	*Has voted at his trade union meeting*			
	Yes	39	59	66
	No	27	41	
15.	*Spoken with general secretary?*			
	Yes	46	69	67
	No	21	31	
16.	*Knows trade union centre to which his union is affiliated?*			
	Yes	27	39	70
	No	43	61	
17.	*Can name leader(s) of the NTUC?*			
	Yes	49	70	70
	No	21	30	
18.	*Can name leader(s) of the ULC?*			
	Yes	54	78	69
	No	15	22	

(i)	(ii)	(iii)	(iv)	(v)
19.	*Education*			
	Lower primary	13	19	
	High primary (standard VI)	28	40	
	Secondary	15	21	70
	No schooling	9	13	
	Technical training (exclusive of other education)	5	7	
20.	*Regards general secretary as:*			
	Same sort of man	21	31	
	More important man	34	50	68
	One of the 'big men'	4	6	
	Less important man	9	13	
21.	*Regards an army officer as:*			
	Same sort of man	14	21	
	More important man	33	51	65
	One of the 'big men'	16	25	
	Less important man	2	3	
22.	*Regards a civil servant as:*			
	Same sort of man	26	38	
	More important man	21	31	68
	One of the 'big men'	13	19	
	Less important man	8	12	
23.	*Party supporter or member?*			
	Not interested in party politics	17	24	
	NCNC ⎫	19 ⎫	27 ⎫	
	AG ⎬ UPGA	24 ⎬ 50	34 ⎬ 72	70
	Other UPGA ⎭	7 ⎭	11 ⎭	
	NPC or other	3	4	
24.	*Are workers getting a fair share?*			
	No	65	93	70
	Yes	5	7	
25.	*Are trade union leaders in Lagos to be trusted?*			
	Yes	6	9	
	No	39	56	70
	Sometimes	25	35	
26.	*Why trade union disunity?* (Open Question)			
	Ideological differences	21	17	
	Leadership struggles	50	41	
	Government foments or provokes disunity	13	11	
	Some unions support government, some do not	12	10	121

(i)	(ii)	(iii)	(iv)	(v)
	Other reasons	12	10	
	Unions *are* united in goals and spirit	6	5	
	No reasons/don't know	7	6	
27.	*Newspapers read?*			
	Doesn't read newspapers	29	43	
	Privately owned	20	29	68
	Government owned	9	13	
	Workers' newspaper	10	15	
28.	*How can workers improve their position?* (Open Question)			
	Fostering labour unity	21	24	
	Having labour representatives or party in government	9	11	
	Striking	29	34	
	Working harder	6	7	86
	Replacing present leaders	8	9	
	Supporting government of the day	2	2	
	Take over government	5	6	
	Don't know/other	6	7	
29.	*Trusts politicians?*			
	Yes	4	6	
	No	58	83	70
	Sometimes	8	11	
30.	*Trusts army officers?*			
	Yes	18	26	
	No	27	39	69
	Sometimes	24	35	
31.	*Attitude to workers' political party*			
	In favour	30	45	67
	Not in favour	37	55	
'32.	*Considers ethnic factors enter into election for union office?*			
	Yes	6	9	70
	No	64	91	
33.	*Would send money to workers in war areas?*			
	Yes	48	73	
	No	12	18	66
	Already do through tax etc.	6	9	
34.	*Loan: would ask:*			
	Union	4	6	
	Fellow worker	17	25	68
	Friend not working with him	16	23	
	Relative/Tribal associate	31	46	

(*i*)	(*ii*)	(*iii*)	(*iv*)	(*v*)
35.	*Believes children will be in better job?*			
	Yes	65	94	69
	No	4	6	
36.	*Would be happy to work with Ibos?*			
	Yes	68	99	69
	No	1	1	
37.	*Why did you join your union?*			
	(Open Question)			
	Fight for workers' rights	41	42	
	Fight for better wages	32	33	
	'United we stand, divided we fall'			
	and variants	8	8	98
	Job security	7	7	
	Thought it compulsory	4	4	
	For help when in difficulties	2	2	
	No definite motive	4	4	
38.	*Notion of Socialism* (Open Question)			
	Fair distribution of wealth	43	27	
	Taking care of the poor	20	13	
	Everybody treated on merit	15	9	
	Workers in control of government	14	9	158
	To be friends, trust each other, to			
	be polite, hospitable, brotherhood	41	26	
	Everybody enjoys life	12	8	
	No clear notion, doesn't know	13	8	

Appendix 2

Nigeria's Labour Leader No. 1: Notes for a Biographical Study of M. A. O. Imoudu by Robin Cohen[1]

Michael Athokhamien Ominus Imoudu's life virtually spans the whole history of active trade unionism in Nigeria. He has organized one of the most militant unions in the country, the Railway Workers Union, which provided him with a popular base to project his personality into the labour movement as a whole. He has been involved in political and industrial action directed against the colonial government, and inspired the labour movement with his confrontations with the authorities. His dramatic march on the governor's residence in 1942, demanding for the workers a cost of living allowance, and his subsequent exile to a remote part of the Mid-West provided one of the greatest *causes célèbres* of the nationalist struggle. He has continued to enjoy a good deal of prestige among the working people of Nigeria, and has played a prominent role in the fusion and fissure of the various trade union centres in the country.

In terms of a narrative account of his life, Imoudu has been badly served. There exists one clumsy attempt at biography published in 1957,[2] in which little reliance can be placed on the details provided.[3] This work, which can only euphemistically be called a biography, is as much a vehicle for the author to write about anything he chooses, as it is a 'life history'. An exegesis on the qualities of leadership provides an opportunity for Omo-Ananigie to include brief notes on (inter alia) Ovid, Galileo and Carpernicle (sic), Julius Caesar, Thomas A. Kempis and Our Lord Jesus Christ. The fact that Imoudu was exiled to Auchi, provides an excuse for an elaborate description of Etsakor history and traditions as well as a discussion (with illustrations) of the wild animals, birds 'gnats and other winged insects in the jungles' that provided the ecological backdrop to Imoudu's period of exile.[4] For all the irrelevant eclecticism, Omo-Ananigie's booklet conveys something of the spirit of veneration that many workers have accorded Imoudu. As the preface has it:

> In short, the man, Imoudu, removed usual obstructions from labour front; madeusal (sic) labour deficiencies good and remunerative, and rendered comprehensive awards to all grades of working-classes in Nigeria. Henceforth, the Hero, Imoudu, gave labour a new square deal between the employers and employees for the first time in the History of labour movement in this country.[5]

> What scholastic account could better the description of Imoudu's reception in Lagos after his release from restriction? Imoudu was paraded about on a white horse through the streets

> packed full with full cosmopolitan crowds of sightseers and merrymakers, including schoolboys, ex-soldiers, market-Guildswomen, all wage earners, pensioners, money-lenders, Omolanke men, Brickmakers, including independent artists, artistes, artisans, Bookbinders, Printers, Carpenters and also Ministers of Religion and Ministers of State, Jurists, Legislators, Actuaries and Auctioneers.[6]

Other sources for a study of Imoudu's life are extremely scanty. One major difficulty is that Imoudu has kept very few documentary materials. These were either removed by the police in successive raids, or destroyed by himself in anticipation of such raids. In this respect the police in the post-independence period have been no less assiduous than their colonial predecessors. A few primary materials are, however, extant. A letter in the Macaulay Papers, dated 1 May 1941, illustrates how Imoudu attempted to elicit the support of market women in trying to keep prices down:

> Our dear mothers, [the letter begins], you should not be surprised to receive this letter [for] ... God help us unless we unite our voices to enable the Europeans to increase our monthly pay in a better way. It is your cooperation that we (wish to) pledge in this matter and the cooperation of our wives, children, senior and junior brothers and our relatives, many of whom are members of

the Women Marketing Association in Lagos and suburbs. ... Our downfall at work is your downfall too. Whatever affects the eye, will also affect the nose; in fact, you, our mothers. God help all of us.[7]

In 1947, M. C. K. Ajuluchuku reproduced in pamphlet form 'an imaginary conversation' between Imoudu and Governor Boudillon, where righteousness confronts arbitrary authority in the manner of a medieval passion play. There seems to be a distinct, possibility that this pamphlet was produced directly under Imoudu's inspiration; the unusual form the tract takes may have meant that Imoudu was not anxious to have a further brush with the authorities.[8]

Other primary sources of interest include a pamphlet history of the Railway Workers Union,[9] and three policy statements either written by, or attributed to, Imoudu. The first is a mimeographed speech that Imoudu made in 1964 commemorating the Russian revolution,[10] the second a dossier of the evidence supposedly given by Imoudu to the Morgan Commission set up by the Federal government in 1963 to consider possible wage increases.[11] Finally, following the successful outcome of the June 1964 general strike, Imoudu published his own analysis of the problems of achieving unity in the Nigerian labour movement.[12] These he succinctly identifies as:

1. Materials interests;
2. Structure and quarrel over unions like women over men or men over women;
3. Treachery and betrayal;
4. Embezzlement;
5. Fight for leadership;
6. Government recognition;
7. International relations; and
8. The question of ideology.[7]

The programme also includes an open letter to Tafawa Balewa. which denounces the political class in these terms:

> The ideas of our political leaders is (sic) a mixture of Feudalism, Capitalism, Socialism and Tribalism and this puts the whole country in a mock, mess and confusion. Some political leaders suggested Democratic, Pragmatic and Fabian Government. We all know some

of these suggested names have been obliterated from the globe and yet some Nigerian leaders are still parading these dead names.[13]

Besides these rather fragmentary sources, the major published sources are contemporary newspaper and magazine accounts that relate to Imoudu himself, or describe his influence on the labour movement. Especially instructive are the accounts of the 1945 general strike in Nigeria given in the *West African Pilot*, at a time when Imoudu was on the executive of the NCNC and the Trade Union Congress part of the organizational structure of the party. Conventional narratives of Nigerian Trade Union history include references to Imoudu's role,[14] though none is based on any original material derived from Imoudu himself.

Dr Robert Melson has, however, interviewed Imoudu in connection with his study on Marxists in the Nigerian labour movement.[15] Imoudu emerges as a somewhat irascible and footloose youth. His father was a travelled soldier who had seen service in East Africa and Imoudu early ran away from his village to broaden his horizon. Although he was brought back to Ora, when his parents died in 1922, he became a houseboy in the home of a relative who was a linesman on the railways. Imoudu travelled with his relation to Benin, Sapele, Warri, Onitsha and other cities in the East. In the course of his wanderings, he learnt fluent Ibo, became a Catholic (he subsequently disavowed any religious leanings), and was educated up to Standard VI level at Agbor and Warri Government Colleges.

In 1928,[16] Imoudu arrived in Lagos jobless, and joined the ranks of the unemployed for a year until he secured work as a daily labourer at 3/– a day. Work as a linesman in the Posts and Telegraphs Department, was followed by his apprenticeship as a turner on the railway in which he served his qualifying seven-year term. His political consciousness was aroused by the arrogant behaviour of a white foreman, and his early experience may have had something to do with his later agitation against whites in the Railway Corporation management, culminating in the violent 'Emerson Must Go' demonstration of 1959.[17]

His fulminations against authority had more to it than a racial character, as his attitudes to the post-independence political leadership and to his fellow trade union leaders show. Even those labour leaders with whom he shares a measure of political conviction have found him a headstrong consociate. Wahab Goodluck and S. U. Bassey who joined Imoudu in setting up the Independent United Labour Congress in 1962 soon fell out with him, and Goodluck subsequently discounted any possibility of collaborating with Imoudu by describing him as being 'too undisciplined to work with'. His relationship with the more conservative elements in the labour movement have had an even more tempestuous character. T. A. Bankole, who fell victim to Imoudu's habit of appealing to the rank and file over and above the heads of the established leadership, recounts his experience of a mass meeting of railway workers in 1945:

> Without allowing some moments for reflection, Mr Imoudu, apparently bewildered by the prevailing quiet, overtook me upon the rostrum, and with a stentorian voice, counteracted the effect of my reasoned appeal in the following terms: 'I am the President·and owner of the Railway Workers' Union throughout Nigeria, and I am going to speak for you. Am I not going to speak for you? (Shouts of Yes, Yes.) Negotiation has failed. We are going on strike. ...' After re-echoing the last sentence of Mr Imoudu's declaration the men sprang frantically upon their feet and staring at me shouted thief, thief, you have been bribed; the Government has bribed you.[19]

At the level of central organization, Imoudu's temperamental qualities have often been blamed for the failure of the labour leaders to subsume their interests in a single organization. This view certainly oversimplifies the complex issues generating trade union disunity;[20] but, at the very least, Imoudu's tendency to go it alone when he disagrees with the character or leadership of a central body has not helped matters. One such occasion was the break-up of the TUCN in April 1960. Imoudu, virtually the lone radical in a conservative leadership, had strong grounds for suspecting that his colleagues were working behind his back in an endeavour to secure affiliation to the International Confederation of Free Trade Unions, and were in fact receiving money from that organization. When he threatened to take the matter to a conference of affiliated unions, the central working committee warned Imoudu that he might be suspended and called upon him to attend a conference in Kano. With dubious constitutionality Imoudu sacked the working committee, called his own conference to a meeting in Lagos, and thereby inaugurated yet another central organization.

Clearly, only a man with considerable influence among the rank and file can afford to put himself out on a limb so often and still retain a following. His popularity derives partly from his labouring background, which stands in marked contrast to the petty bourgeois origins of the other prominent trade union leaders. Again, unlike the other leaders, he has not been as closely involved in prising money out of international organizations in Moscow, Washington and Brussels (despite a brief visit to Moscow in 1960); money, moreover, from which the workers receive little discernible benefit. Nor has his life-style altered dramatically as a consequence of his leadership role, though it would be fatuous to assert that he has received no material advantages from his elevated position.

Imoudu also has in large measure the 'common touch', which he displays through his oratory and flamboyant dress, beside which the other leaders strike a pale comparison. Ananaba records one incident when he addressed a meeting in the garb of a juju priest and brandished a horse tail fan, 'which his followers and admirers believed to be the secret of his power and iron will'.[21] He reached even greater heights in the 1964 strike when he led the workers across Carter Bridge in Lagos, sporting a Russian fur cap and a red track suit which was described as his 'fighting kit'.

Imoudu himself proclaims that, 'When I lead, I lead from the front!'[22] However, the increasing viability of other trade union organizations and Imoudu's advanced age will soon oblige him to take a back seat. There has already been a move to displace him from the Railway Workers' Union, and Imoudu has recently accepted a traditional title in his home town. One can only hope that before he passes completely from the scene, someone will undertake the task of making his reminiscences part of the public record.

NOTES

1   Reprinted from the *Journal of the Historical Society of Nigeria, Vol. V, No. 2, June 1970.* The present author, while researching into the political role of Nigeria's trade unions, came across many references to Imoudu's role in Nigerian labour history. He has also had occasion to conduct a long interview with Imoudu in Lagos. These research notes are offered for publication in the hope that some other researcher will be inspired to interview Imoudu in depth and write a detailed biography. The need for someone to undertake such a study within a short time should be made apparent. Imoudu is senescent, with failing health and eyesight; his memory should be tapped while there is still a chance for him to help elucidate a fascinating area of Nigeria's history.

2   P. I. Omo-Ananigie, *The Life History of M. A. O. Imoudu: Coeur de Lion*, Pacific Printing Works, Lagos, 1957, 90pp.

3   For example, Imoudu's birth date is given as 20 November 1906. It is, according to Imoudu, 15 September 1902.

4   Other eccentricities include the quoting of six verses of Gray's Elegy, a list of local tax statistics, a section headed 'The Etsakor Farmer's Lot (Remember Lot's Wife)', and a detailed itinerary of the NCNC tour of Nigeria in 1946 (Imoudu was one of the delegates).

5   Omo-Ananigie, op. cit., p. i.

6   Omo-Ananigie, op. cit., p. 12. Omolanke men are hand-cart pushers.

7   Letter addressed to Mesdames Pelewura and Lagunju, President and Vice-President of the Womens' Trader Association and signed by Messrs lmoudu and Adediran of the Railway Workers Union. Original (in Yoruba) in the *Macaulay Papers*, Vol. V, no. 11, lodged in the Ibadan University Library.

8   M. C. K. Ajuluchuku (pseud), *Imoudu vs Governor: Imaginary Conversation*, 1947.

9   L. Emejulu, *A Brief History of the Railway Workers Union of Nigeria*. n.d.

10 M. lmoudu, *Speech at the 41st Anniversary of the Great October Revolution on behalf of the Nigerian Working Class* (mimeographed) 1964. Robert Melson gives the reference, though no extant copy was found by the present author.

11 *Imoudu Before the Morgan Commission*. Lagos. 20th Century Press. n.d. 1964 (?)

12 M. lmoudu, *Programme for the Unification of One Central Labour Organization*. Lagos, 20th Century Press, July 1965.

13 M. Imoudu, *Programme* ... p. 2.

14 M. Imoudu, *Programme* ... p. 10.

15 A detailed, though pedestrian history of trade union development can be found in H. A. Tulatz, *Die Gewerkschaftsentwicklung Nigerians*. Verlag für Literatur und Zeitgeschehen. Hanover 1963. (Especially Chapters IV and VI); see also W. Ananaba, *The Trade Union Movement in Nigeria*, Hurst and Co., London, 1969. (Chapters III, V and X).

16 R. F. Melson, *Marxists in the Nigerian Labour Movement: A Case Study in the Failure of Ideology*. Unpublished Ph.D. thesis submitted to MIT, January 1967. Some details that follow are derived from this source.

17 In Melson's Account, 1929, Emerson being the expatriate manager of the Nigerian Railway Corporation.
18 Interview with Goodluck. July 1968.
19 T. A. Bankole, *The 1945 Strike: Background Review*, quoted by W. Ananaba, op. cit., p. 54.
20 For one view on this thorny problem, see R. Cohen, 'Why Trade Union Disunity', *Nigerian Opinion*, Vol. IV, nos 4–6, April–June 1968.
21 W. Ananaba, op. cit., p. 54.
22 Interview with Imoudu, July 1968.

Bibliography

I. BOOKS, PAMPHLETS, AND BOOKLETS

Africa Research Group *The Other Side of Nigeria's Civil War* (Cambridge, Mass: ARG, 1970).

Akpala, A. *The Prospects of Small Trade Unions in Nigeria* (Enugu: 1963).

Alexander, R. J. *Organized Labor in Latin America* (New York: Free Press, 1965).

Allen, C. 'African Trade Unionism in Microcosm: the Gambia Labour Movement, 1939–1967' in Allen, C. and Johnson, R. W. (Eds.) *African Perspectives* (Cambridge: Cambridge University Press, 1970).

Allen, V. L. *Trade Unions and the Government* (London: Longmans, 1960).

Almond, G. A. and Powell, G. B. Jnr. *Comparative Politics: A Developmental Approach* (Boston and Toronto: Little Brown & Co., 1966).

Amsden, A. *International Firms and Labour in Kenya: 1945–1970* (London: Frank Cass & Co., 1971).

Ananaba, W. *The Trade Union Movement in Nigeria* (London: C. Hurst & Co., 1969).

Anderson, C. W., von der Mehden, F. R. and Young, C. *Issues of Political Development* (Englewood Cliffs: Prentice-Hall Inc., 1967).

Andreski, A. *The African Predicament* (London: Michael Joseph, 1968).

Apter, D. E. (Ed.) *Ideology and Discontent* (New York: Free Press of Glencoe, 1964).

Arrighi, G. and Saul, J. S. 'Nationalism and Revolution in Sub-Saharan Africa' in Miliband, R. and Saville, J. (Eds.) *The Socialist Register* (London: Merlin Press, 1969).

Asika, U. *No Victors, No Vanquished* (East Central State Information Office, n.d.).

Austin, D. *Politics in Ghana: 1940–1960* (London: OUP, 1964).

Awolowo, O. *My Early Life* (Lagos: John West Publications, 1968).

Bailey, F. G. *Stratagems and Spoils* (Oxford: Basil Blackwell, 1969).

Banton, M. *West African City: A Study of Tribal Life in Freetown* (London: OUP, 1957).

Barbe, R. *Les Classes Sociales en Afrique Noire* (Paris: Economie et Politique, 1964).

Bascom, W. R. and Herskovits, M. J. (Eds.) *Continuity and Change in African Cultures* (Chicago: Chicago University Press, 1959).

Bates, R. H. *Unions, Parties and Political Development: a Study of Mineworkers in Zambia* (New Haven and London: Yale University Press, 1971).

Belling, W. A. *Modernisation and African Labour: A Tunisian Case Study* (New York and London: Praeger, 1965).

Berg, E. J. 'Rural Income Trends in West Africa 1939–1960' in Herskovits, M. J. and Harwitz, M. *q.v.*, 199–240.

Berg, E. J. and Butler, J. 'Trade Unions' in Coleman, J. S. and Rosberg, C. G. (Eds.) *q.v.*, 340–81.

Bottomore, T. B. *Social Classes in Modern Society* (London: George Allen & Unwin, 1965).

Braibanti, R. and Spengler, J. J. (Ed.) *Tradition, Values and Socio-Economic Development* (Durham, N. Carolina: Duke University Press, 1961).

Breese, G. *Urbanisation in Newly Developing Countries* (Englewood Cliffs, N.J.: Prentice Hall Inc., 1966).

Buchanan, K. M. and Pugh, J. E. *Land and People in Nigeria* (London: University of London Press, 1965).

Carter, G. C. (Ed.) *Politics in Africa: Seven Cases* (New York: Harcourt, Brace & World Inc., 1966).

Castagno, A. A. and Butler, J. *Transition in African Politics* (New York and London: Praeger, 1967).

Cohen, A. *Custom and Politics in Urban Africa* (London: Routledge & Kegan Paul, 1969).

Cohen, R. 'Class in Africa: Analytical Problems and Perspectives' in Miliband, R. and Saville, J. (Eds.) *The Socialist Register 1972* (London: The Merlin Press, 1972) 231–55.

Coleman, J. S. *Nigeria: Background to Nationalism* (Berkeley and Los Angeles: University of California Press, 1965).

Coleman, J. S. and Rosberg, C. G. *Political Parties and National Integration in Tropical Africa* (Berkeley and Los Angeles: University of California Press, 1964).

Comhaire, J. 'Economic Change and the Extended Family' in Van den Berghe, P. L. (Ed.) *q.v.*

Dahrendorf, R. *Class and Class Conflict in Industrial Society* (London: Routledge & Kegan Paul, 1965).

Davies, I. *African Trade Unions* (Harmondsworth: Penguin, 1966).

Drake, St. C. and Lacy, L. A. 'Government versus the Unions' in Carter, G. C. (Ed.) *q.v.*

Dudley, B. J. *Parties and Politics in Northern Nigeria* (London: Frank Cass & Co., 1968).

Dumont, R. *False Start in Africa* (London: Sphere Books Ltd, 1968).

Eckstein, H. and Apter, D. E. *Comparative Politics: A Reader* (New York, Free Press of Glencoe, 1963).

Emejulu, L. *A Brief History of the Railway Workers Unions of Nigeria* (Lagos: n.d.).

Epstein, A. L. *Politics in an Urban African Community* (Manchester: Manchester University Press, 1958).

Etukudo, A. J. *Multi-Employer Bargaining: Industrial Relations in the Banking System of Nigeria* (Ilfracombe: Arthur Stockwell Ltd, 1971).

Fallers, L. A. 'Social Stratification and Economic Processes' in Herskovits, M. J. and Harwitz, M. (Eds.) *q.v.* 113–32.

Fanon, F. *The Wretched of the Earth* (London: MacGibbon & Kee, 1965).

Fawzi, S. *The Labour Movement in the Sudan* (London: OUP, 1957).

First, R. *The Barrel of a Gun* (London: Allen Lane, 1970).

Fraenkel, M. *Tribe and Class in Monrovia* (London: OUP, 1965).

Frank, A. G. *Capitalism and Underdevelopment in Latin America* (New York and London: Monthly Review Press, 1969).

Friedland, W. H. *Unions and Industrial Relations in Underdeveloped Countries* (Ithaca: New York State School of Industrial and Labour Relations, 1964).

―― 'Cooperation, Conflict and Control: TANU-TFL Relations: 1955–1964' in Castagno, A. A. and Butler, J. *q.v.*

Friedland, W. H. and Rosberg, C. G. (Eds.) *African Socialism* (Stanford: Stanford University Press, 1964).

Galensen, W. (Ed.) *Comparative Labor Movements* (Englewood Cliffs, N.J.: Prentice-Hall, 1953).

―― (Ed.) *Labor and Economic Development* (New York: John Wiley & Sons, 1959).

―― *Labor in Developing Countries* (Berkeley and Los Angeles: University of California Press, 1963).

Galletti, R., Baldwin, K. D. S. and Dina, I. O. *Nigerian Cocoa Farmers* (London: OUP, 1956).

Geertz, C. (Ed.) *Old Societies and New States: The Quest for Modernity in Asia and Africa* (New York: Free Press of Glencoe, 1963).

Hailey, Lord *African Survey* (London: OUP, 1957).

Hawkins, E. R. *Road Transport in Nigeria: A Study of African Enterprise* (London: OUP, 1958).

Herskovits, M. J. and Harwitz, M. (Eds.) *Economic Transition in Africa* (London: Routledge & Kegan Paul, 1964).

Hodgkin, T. *Nationalism in Colonial Africa* (London: Frederick Muller, 1956).

―― *African Political Parties* (Harmondsworth: Penguin, 1961).

Huntington, S. P. *Political Order in Changing Societies* (New Haven and London: Yale University Press, 1968).

Jones-Quartey, K. A. B. *A Life of Azikiwe* (Harmondsworth: Penguin, 1965).

Kadalie, C. *My Life and the ICU* (London: Frank Cass & Co. Ltd., 1970), Introduction by S. Trapido.

Kassalow, E. M. *National Labor Movements in the Post-War World* (Evanston, Illinois: Northwestern University Press, 1963).

Kerr, C., Dunlop, J. T., Harbison, F. and Myers, C. A. *Industrialism and Industrial Man* (Cambridge, Mass: Harvard University Press, 1960).

Kilby, P. *Industrialisation in an Open Economy: Nigeria 1945–1966* (Cambridge: Cambridge University Press, 1969).

Kirk-Greene, A. H. M. *Crisis and Conflict in Nigeria: A Documentary Sourcebook Vol. 1 January 1966–July 1967; Vol. 2 July 1967–January 1970* (London: OUP, 1971).

Kornhauser, A. (*et. al.*) *Industrial Conflict* (New York: McGraw Hill, 1954).

Laswell, H. *Politics: Who Gets What, When, How* (New York: Meridian Books Inc., 1958).

Legum, C. *Pan-Africanism: A Short Political Guide* (New York and London: Praeger, 1965).

Lenin, V. *On National and Colonial Questions* (Peking: Foreign Languages Press, 1967).

Lewis, W. A. *Reflections on Nigeria's Economic Growth* (Paris: Organization for Economic Co-operation and Development, 1967).

Little, K. *West African Urbanisation: A Study of Voluntary Associations in Social Change* (Cambridge: Cambridge University Press, 1965).

Lloyd, P. C. (Ed.) *The New Elites of Tropical Africa* (London: OUP for the International African Institute, 1966).

—— *Africa in Social Change* (Harmondsworth: Penguin, 1967).

Luttwak, E. *Coup d'Etat: a Practical Handbook* (Harmondsworth: Penguin, 1969).

Luxemburg, R. *The Mass Strike: The Political Party and the Trade Unions* (Colombo, Ceylon: Young Socialist Publication, 1964).

Lynd, G. E. (pseud.) *The Politics of African Trade Unionism* (New York and London: Praeger, 1968).

Mabogunje, A. L. *Yoruba Towns* (Ibadan: Ibadan University Press, 1962).

—— *Urbanisation in Nigeria* (London: University of London Press, 1968).

Mackintosh, J. P. (*et. al.*) *Nigerian Government and Politics* (London: Allen & Unwin, 1966).

Mayer, P. *Townsmen or Tribesmen: Conservatism and the Process of Urbanisation in a South African City* (London: OUP, 1961).

Mboya, T. *Freedom and After* (London: André Deutsch, 1963).

Melson, R. 'Nigerian Politics and the General Strike of 1964' in Rotberg, R. I. and Mazrui, A. A. (Eds.) *q.v.*, 771–7.

Mercier, P. 'Problems of Social Stratification in West Africa' in Wallerstein, I. (Ed.) *q.v.*, 340–58.

Meynaud, J. and Saleh-Bey, A. *Trade Unionism in Africa* (London: Methuen, 1967).

Millen, B. H. *The Political Role of Labor in Developing Countries* (Washington: The Brookings Institution, 1963).

Mitchell, J. C. *The Kalela Dance*, Rhodes-Livingstone Paper No. 27 (Manchester: Manchester University Press, 1957).

Moore, W. E. 'The Social Framework of Economic Development' in Braibanti, R. and Spengler, J. J. (Eds.) *q.v.*

—— 'The Adaptation of African Labor Systems to Social Changes' in Herskovits, M. J. and Harwitz, M. (Eds.) *q.v.*, 277–97.

—— *The Impact of Industry* (Englewood Cliffs, N.J.: Prentice-Hall, 1965).

Morgenthau, R. S. *Political Parties in French-Speaking West Africa* (Oxford: Clarendon Press, 1964).

November, A. *L'Evolution du mouvement syndical en Afrique occidentale* (Paris and The Hague: Mouton, 1965).

Nyerere, J. *Ujamaa: Essays on Socialism* (London: OUP, 1968).

—— 'The Role of African Trade Unions' in Sigmund, P. E. *q.v.*, 202–5.

Ojukwu, C. O. *Biafra: Selected Speeches with Journals of Events* (New York: Perennial Library, 1969).

—— *Random Thoughts* (New York: Perennial Library, 1969).

Omo-Ananigie, P. I. *The Life History of M. A. O. Imoudu: Coeur de Lion: Labour Leader No. 1* (Lagos: Pacific Printing Works, 1957).

Ossowski, S. *Class Structure in the Social Consciousness* (London: Routledge & Kegan Paul, 1963).

Ottenberg, S. 'Ibo Receptivity to Change' in Bascom, W. R. and Herskovits,

M. J. (Eds.) *Continuity and Change in African Cultures* (Chicago: University of Chicago Press, 1959).

Padmore, G. *Pan-Africanism or Communism: The Coming Struggle for Africa* (New York: Denis Dobson, 1956).

Panter-Brick, K. (Ed.) *Nigerian Politics and Military Rule: Prelude to the Civil War* (London: The Athlone Press, 1970).

Payne, J. L. *Labor and Politics in Peru: The System of Political Bargaining* (New Haven and London: Yale University Press, 1965).

Peil, M. *The Ghanaian Factory Worker: Industrial Man in Africa* (Cambridge: Cambridge University Press, 1972).

Pfeffermann, G. *Industrial Labor in Senegal* (New York: Praeger, 1968).

Phillips, C. S. Jnr. *The Development of Nigerian Foreign Policy* (Evanston: Northwestern University Press, 1964).

Plotnicov, L. *Strangers to the City: Urban Man in Jos, Nigeria* (Pittsburgh: University of Pittsburgh Press, 1967).

Post, K. W. J. *The Nigerian Federal Election of 1959: Politics and Administration in a Developing Political System* (London: OUP for the Nigerian Institute of Social and Economic Research, 1963).

—— *The New States of West Africa* (Harmondsworth: Penguin, 1968).

Post, K. W. J. and Vickers, M. *Conflict and Control in an Independent African State: Nigeria 1960–1965* (London: Heinemann, 1973).

Pye, L. W. *Communications and Political Development* (Princeton: Princeton University Press, 1963).

Rex, J. *Race Relations in Sociological Theory* (London: Weidenfeld & Nicolson, 1970).

Roberts, B. C. *Labor in the Tropical Territories of the Commonwealth* (Durham, N. Carolina: Duke University Press, 1964).

Roberts, B. C. and de Bellecombe, L. G. *Collective Bargaining in African Countries* (London and New York: Macmillan and St. Martin's Press, 1967).

Roper, J. I. *Labour Problems in West Africa* (Harmondsworth: Penguin, 1958).

Rotberg, R. I. and Mazrui, A. A. (Eds.) *Protest and Power in Black Africa* (New York: Oxford University Press, 1970).

St. Jorre, J. de *The Nigerian Civil War* (London: Hodder & Stoughton Ltd, 1972).

Schatz, S. P. *Economics, Politics and Administration in Government Lending* (Ibadan: OUP for the Nigerian Institute of Social and Economic Research, 1970).

Schwarz, W. *Nigeria* (London: Pall Mall Press, 1968).

Scott, R. D. *The Development of Trade Unions in Uganda* (Nairobi: East African Publishing House, 1966).

Sigmund, P. E. (Ed.) *The Ideologies of the Developing Nations* (New York and London: Praeger, 1963).

Sklar, R. S. *Nigerian Political Parties: Power in an Emergent African Nation* (Princeton: Princeton University Press, 1963).

—— 'The Ordeal of Chief Awolowo' in Carter, G. M. (Ed.) *q.v.*, 119–65.

Smith, M. G. *Government in Zazzau* (London: OUP, 1960).

—— 'Pre-Industrial Stratification Systems' in Smelser, N. and Lipset, S. (Eds.) *Social Structure and Mobility in Economic Development* (Chicago: Chicago University Press, 1966).

Smock, D. R. *Conflict and Control in an African Trade Union: a Study of the Nigerian Coal Miners' Union* (Stanford: Hoover Institution Press, 1969).

Sokolski, A. *The Establishment of Manufacturing in Nigeria* (New York and London: Praeger, 1965).

Southall, A. (Ed.) *Social Change in Modern Africa* (London: OUP, 1961).

Storing, H. J. (Ed.) *Essays on the Scientific Study of Politics* (New York: Holt, Rinehart & Winston Inc., 1962).

Sufrin, S. C. *Unions in Emerging Societies: Frustrations and Politics* (New York: Syracuse, 1964).

Tedjasuknana, I. *The Political Character of the Indonesian Trade Union Movement* (Ithaca, New York: Cornell University Press, 1958).

Toyo, E. *The Working Class and the Nigerian Crisis* (Ibadan: Sketch Publishing Co., 1967).

Tulatz, H. A. *Die Gewerkschaftsentwicklung Nigerias* (Hanover: Verlag für Literatur und Zeitgeschehen, 1963).

University of London, Institute of Commonwealth Studies *Collected Seminar Papers on Labour Unions and Political Parties* (London: University of London, 1967).

Van den Berghe, P. L. (Ed.) *Africa: Social Problems of Change and Conflict* (San Francisco: Chandler, 1965).

Wallerstein, I. (Ed.) *Social Change: The Colonial Situation* (New York: John Wiley & Son Inc., 1966).

Warmington, W. A. *A West African Trade Union* (London: OUP, 1960).

Webb, S. and B. *Industrial Democracy* (London: Longmans, Green & Co., 1897).

Weber, M. *Economy and Society: an Outline of Interpretive Sociology*. Edited by Roth, G. and Wittich, C. (New York: Bedminster Press, 1968).

Weiner, M. *The Politics of Scarcity: Public Pressure and Political Response in India* (Chicago: Chicago University Press, 1962).

Wells, F. A. and Warmington, W. A. *Studies in Industrialisation: Nigeria and the Cameroons* (London: OUP, 1962).

Whittaker, C. S. *The Politics of Tradition* (Princeton: Princeton University Press, 1970).

Williams, G. 'The Social Stratification of a Neo-Colonial Economy: Western Nigeria' in Allen, C. and Johnson, R. W. *African Perspectives* (Cambridge: Cambridge University Press, 1970).

Woddis, J. *Africa: the Lion Awakes* (London: Lawrence & Wishart, 1961).

Worsley, P. *The Third World* (London: Weidenfeld & Nicolson, 1964).

Yesufu, T. M. *An Introduction to Industrial Relations in Nigeria* (London: OUP for the Nigerian Institute of Social and Economic Research, 1962).

—— *Labour in the Nigerian Economy* (October Lectures, Nigerian Broadcasting Corporation, 1967).

II. ARTICLES

Anon. 'The Influence of International Labour Conventions on Nigerian Labour Legislation', *International Labour Review*, July 1960, 82 (1), 26–43.

Anon. 'Nigeria's Levellers', *Economist* (London), 13 June 1964, 1224–8.

Adio-Saka 'NTUC: The Case of the Kettle and the Pot', *Spear* (Lagos), November 1968, 10–12.

Aluko, S. A. 'How Many Nigerians? An Analysis of Nigeria's Census Problems 1901–1963', *Journal of Modern African Studies*, September 1965, 3 (3), 371–92.

Bascom, W. R. 'Yoruba Urbanism: A Summary', *Man*, December 1958, 58, (253), 190–1.

Berg, E. J. 'The Economic Base of Political Choice in French West Africa', *American Political Science Review*, 1960, 54 (2), 391–405.

—— 'Backward Sloping Labor Supply Functions in Dual Economies: the African Case', *The Quarterly Journal of Economics*, 1961, 25.

—— 'Socialism and Economic Development in Tropical Africa', *Quarterly Journal of Economics*, November 1964, 78 (4), 549–73.

—— 'The Development of a Labour Force in Sub-Saharan Africa', *Economic Development and Cultural Change*, July 1965, 13 (4), Part I, 394–412.

—— 'Urban Real Wages and the Nigerian Trade Union Movement 1939–1960: A Comment', *Economic Development and Cultural Change*, 1969, 17 (4), 604–17.

Bhambri, R. S. 'Second Development Plan: A Selective Appraisal', *Nigerian Journal of Economic and Social Studies*, 1971, 13 (2), 179–93.

Bispham, W. M. L. 'The Concept and Measurement of Labour Commitment and its Relevance to Nigerian Development', *Nigerian Journal of Economic and Social Studies*, March 1964, 6(1), 51–9.

Braundi, E. R. and Lettieri, A. 'The General Strike in Nigeria', *International Socialist Journal*, September–December 1964, 1 (5–6), 598–609.

Byl, A. and White, J. 'The End of Backward-Sloping Labour Supply Functions in Dual Economies', *Cahiers Economiques et Sociaux*, March 1966, 4 (1), 33–42.

Callaway, A. 'Nigeria's Indigenous Education: the Apprentice System', *Odu*, July 1964, 1 (1), 62–79.

—— 'Unemployment among African School Leavers', *Journal of Modern African Studies*, 1963, 1 (3), 351–71.

—— 'From Traditional Crafts to Modern Industries', *Odu*, July 1965, 2 (1), 28–51.

Central Asian Research Centre 'Soviet News on Nigeria: The Trade Unions', *Mizan*, 1961, 3 (11), 27–9.

—— 'Soviet Approaches to African Trade Unions', *Mizan*, 1965, 7 (7), 6–10.

Cohen, R. 'Nigeria's Labour Leader No. 1: Notes for a Biographical Study of M. A. O. Imoudu', *Journal of the Historical Society of Nigeria*, 1970, 5 (2), 303–8.

—— 'Further Comment on the Kilby/Weeks Debate' *The Journal of Developing Areas*, January 1971, 5 (2), 155–64.

—— 'Nigeria's Central Trade Union Organisation: a Study Guide' *Journal of Modern African Studies* 9 (3), October 1971, 457–8.

Deyrup, F. J. 'Organised Labor and Government in Developing Countries: Sources of Conflict', *Industrial and Labor Relations Review*, October 1958, 12 (1), 104–12.

Dudley, B. J. 'Marxism and Political Change in Nigeria', *Nigerian Journal of Economic and Social Studies*, 1964, 6 (2), 155–65.

—— 'Federalism and the Balance of Political Power in Nigeria', *Journal of Commonwealth Political Studies*, March 1966, 4 (1).

Egboh, E. O. 'The Early Years of Trade Unionism in Nigeria', *African Quarterly*, April/June 1968, 8(1), 59–69.

Fischer, G. 'Trade Unions and Decolonisation', *Présence Africaine*, October 1960 and January 1961, no. 34–5, 17–61.

Friedland, W. H. 'Paradoxes of African Trade Unionism: Organisational Chaos and Political Potential', *Africa Report*, June 1965, 10 (6), 6–13.

Gamba, C. 'New Patterns in Industrial Relations in Developing Countries', *Journal of Industrial Relations*, 1965, 7 (3), 298–313.

Geiss, I. 'Some Remarks on the Development of African Trade Unions', *Journal of the Historical Society of Nigeria*, 1965, 3 (2), 365–76.

Glantz, O. 'Class Consciousness and Political Solidarity', *American Sociological Review*, 1958, 23 (4), 375–83.

Goodluck, W. O. 'Nigeria and Marxism', *African Communist*, October/December 1964, No. 19, 49–59.

Gutkind, P. C. M. 'The African Urban Milieu: A Force in Rapid Change', *Civilisations*, 1962, 12 (2), 167–91.

—— 'The Energy of Despair: Social Organisation of the Unemployed in Two African Cities: Lagos and Nairobi', *Civilisations*, 1967, 17 (3), 186–211 and 1967, 17 (4), 380–402.

Harris, J. R. and Rowe, M. P. 'Entrepreneurial Patterns in the Nigerian Saw-milling Industry', *Nigerian Journal of Economic and Social Studies*, 1966, 8 (1), 65–79.

Hodge, D. G. 'The Intermediate Classes in Marxian Theory', *Social Research*, 1961, No. 28, 20–42.

Hopkins, A. G. 'The Lagos Strike of 1897: An Exploration in Nigerian Labour History', *Past and Present*, December 1966, No. 35, 133–55.

Hutton, C. 'Unemployment in Kampala and Jinja, Uganda', *Canadian Journal of African Studies*, 1969, 3 (2), 431–40.

Kilby, P. 'African Labour Productivity Reconsidered', *Economic Journal*, June 1961, 71 (2), 273–91.

—— 'Industrial Relations and Wage Determination: Failure of the Anglo-Saxon Model', *The Journal of Developing Areas*, July 1967, 1 (4), 489–520.

—— 'A Reply to John F. Weeks's Comment', *The Journal of Developing Areas*, October 1968, 3 (1), 19–26.

—— 'Further Comment on the Kilby/Weeks Debate: Final Observations', *The Journal of Developing Areas*, January 1971, 5 (2), 175–7.

Kilson, M. L. J. 'Nationalism and Social Classes in British West Africa', *Journal of Politics*, May 1958, 20 (2), 368–87.

Kiomene, S. E. and Kenegha, J. 'Nigeria Today', *4th International*, November 1966, 3 (4), 117–86.

Lemarchand, R. 'Dahomey: Coup within a Coup', *Africa Report*, June 1968, 45–68.

Lichtblau, G. E. 'Paradoxes of African Trade Unionism: The Dilemma of the ICFTU', *Africa Report*, June 1964, 10 (6), 18–19.

Lloyd, P. C. 'Craft Organisation in Yoruba Towns', *Africa*, January 1953, 23 (1), 30–44.

Luyimbazi, F. L. 'Trade Unions and Economic Planning in West Africa', *Civilisations*, 1966, 16 (2), 190–208.

Mboya, T. 'Trade Unions and Development', *Venture*, 1964, 16 (1), 11–13.

Melson, R. 'Ideology and Inconsistency: The "Cross-Pressured" Nigerian Worker', *American Political Science Review*, 1971, LXV (1), 161–71.

Murray, R. 'Militarism in Africa', *New Left Review*, July–August 1966, No. 38.

O'Connell, J. 'The Political Class and Economic Growth', *Nigerian Journal of Economic and Social Studies*, March 1966, 8 (1), 129–40.

—— 'Political Constraints on Planning: Nigeria as a Case Study in the

Developing World', *Nigerian Journal of Economic and Social Studies*, 1971, 13 (1), 39–57.

Ojedokun, O. 'The Changing Pattern of Nigeria's International Economic Relations: The Decline of the Colonial Nexus, 1960–1966', *The Journal of Developing Areas*, 1972, 6, 535–54.

Okediji, F. O. and Aboyade, O. 'Social and Economic Aspects of Environmental Sanitation in Nigeria: A Tentative Report', *The Journal of the Society of Health, Nigeria*, January 1967, 2 (1).

Oluwide, B. 'Nigerian Trade Unions in the Struggle for National Unity and Socialism', *Africa and the World*, June 1965, No. 9, 19–21.

Orr, C. A. 'Trade Unionism in Colonial Africa', *Journal of Modern African Studies*, May 1966, 4 (1), 65–81.

Otegbeye, T. 'The Revolutionary Movement in Nigeria', *World Marxist Review*, 1964, 7 (9), 32–7.

Peil, M. 'Aspirations and Social Structure: a West African Example', *Africa*, 1968, 38 (1), 71–8.

Rimmer, D. 'The New Industrial Relations in Ghana', *Industrial and Labor Relations Review*, January 1961, 14 (2), 206–26.

Sandbrook, R. 'Patrons, Clients and Unions: the Labour Movement and Political Conflict in Kenya', *Journal of Commonwealth Political Studies*, 1972, 10 (1), 3–27.

Schatz, S. P. 'Economic Environment and Private Enterprise in West Africa', *The Economic Bulletin of Ghana*, 1964, 6 (4), 42–56.

Scott, R. D. 'Are Trade Unions Still Necessary in Africa?', *Transition 33*, October/November 1967, 7 (2), 27–31.

Seibel, H. D. 'Some Aspects of Inter-Ethnic Relations in Nigeria', *Nigerian Journal of Economic and Social Studies*, July 1967, 9 (2), 217–28.

Sklar, R. L. 'Contradictions in the Nigerian Political System', *Journal of Modern African Studies*, August 1965, 3 (2), 201–13.

Smith, M. G. 'The Hausa System of Social Status', *Africa*, 1959, 29 (3), 239–52.

Smythe, H. H. 'Social Stratification in Nigeria', *Social Forces*, December 1958, 37 (2), 168–71.

Teriba, O. and Phillips, O. A. 'Income Distribution and National Integration', *Nigerian Journal of Economic and Social Studies*, 1971, 13 (1), 77–122.

Trachtman, L. N. 'The Labour Movement in Ghana: A Study of Political Unionism', *Economic Development and Cultural Change*, January 1962, 2 (1), 183–200.

Warren, W. M. 'Urban Real Wages and the Nigerian Trade Union Movement', *Economic Development and Cultural Change*, October 1966, 15 (1), 22–36.

—— 'Urban Real Wages and the Nigerian Trade Union Movement 1939–1960: Rejoinder', *Economic Development and Cultural Change*, 1969, 17 (4), 618–33.

Weeks, J. F. 'A Comment on Peter Kilby: Industrial Relations and Wage Determination', *The Journal of Developing Areas*, October 1968, 3 (1), 9–18.

—— 'Further Comment on the Kilby/Weeks Debate: An Empirical Rejoinder', *The Journal of Developing Areas*, January 1971, 5 (2), 165–74.

—— 'The Impact of Economic Conditions and Institutional Forces on Urban Wages in Nigeria', *Nigerian Journal of Economic and Social Studies*, November 1971, 13 (3), 313–39.

Zolberg, A. R. 'The Structure of Political Conflict in the New States of Tropical Africa', *American Political Science Review*, March 1968, 70–87.

III. OFFICIAL PUBLICATIONS

(a) By Trade Union Organizations

African Regional Organization of the ICFTU
   The Role of Trade Unions in Economic and Social Development Special Paper No. 8 (Lagos: June 1966).
   Princples of Wage Determination in the African Setting Special Paper No. 9 (Lagos: April 1967).
Afro-American Labour Centre
   Report of the AALC Conference in Geneva (New York: June 1967).
   Documents and Proceedings of the Regional Trade Union Economic Conference (Addis-Ababa: 14–22 September 1967).
Joint Action Committee
   Interim Reward Memo to all Members (Mimeographed, 22 October 1963).
   Workers' Viewpoint on 1964 Election (Ibadan: 1965).
Nigerian Trade Union Congress (and IULC)
   Constitution (Lagos: n.d.).
   Our Fight for Wages and Workers' Rights Publication No. 2 (Lagos: 23 January 1961).
   Documents relating to the 1st Revolutionary Convention of the Independent United Labour Congress (Hotel Majestic, Yaba: 2–4 August 1963).
   Documents relating to the 2nd Revolutionary Convention of the NTUC (Lagos: December 1965).
   Bassey, S. U. *Review of the Development of the Nigerian Trade Union Congress: 1941–1967* (Mimeographed, n.d.).
Nigerian Workers Council
   Constitution (Lagos: Mimeographed, n.d.).
   Declaration of Principles: A Programme of Positive Action (Lagos: 23 December 1962).
Trade Union Congress of Nigeria
   First Annual Conference of Delegates: Text of Resolutions passed (Kano: 20–22 April 1960).
   Workers of Nigeria: To-day Architects of an Independent Nigeria: To-morrow Builders of a better Nigeria (TUCN Manifesto, Lagos: John Okwesa & Co., 1 October 1960).
Trade Union Institute for Economic and Social Development
   Dialli, A. O. *Industrial Relations: The Trade Union Viewpoint* (Lagos: Mimeographed, n.d.).
   —— *A Decade of Constructive Union Action: The National Union of Bank, Insurance and Allied Workers in Perspective* (Lagos: Mimeographed, March 1968).
Union Générale des Travailleurs d'Afrique Noire
   Toure, S. *Report on Policy and Doctrine* (Paris: Présence Africaine, 1959).
United Committee of Central Labour Organisations
   Equitable Demand for Economic Growth and National Prosperity (Ibadan: 1970).

United Labour Congress
  A Programme for the Future (Lagos: 25 May 1962).
  General Secretary's Report of the First Annual Delegates' Conference (Lagos: Mimeographed, May 1963).
  Presidential Address to the First Annual Delegates Conference (Lagos: Mimeographed, 3 May 1963).
  Minutes of the Second Bi-Ennial Delegates Conference (Port Harcourt: Mimeographed, 2–4 July 1965).
  Nigeria at Cross Roads: Dynamic Approach Imperative Open letter to Lt. Col. Yakubu Gowon (Ibadan: ULC Western District Council, Mimeographed, 26 October 1966).
  Open Letter to All Heads of Military Governments of Nigeria and Military Administrator of Lagos (Ibadan: ULC Western District Council, Mimeographed, 5 May 1967).
  Quarterly Progress Reports of the Director of Organisation (Irregular) (Lagos: Mimeographed, 1967 onwards).
  Adeleke, A. *The Problems of Union's Leaders in Nigeria vis-à-vis the Government* (Lagos: Mimeographed, 14 September 1967).
  Ijeh, E. U. and James, J. O. *A Short Address presented by the ULC West District Council* (Port Harcourt: Mimeographed, 2–4 July 1965).
  Odeyemi, E. O. A. *Enemies of Free Trade Union Movement Launch Offensive on the ULC* (Lagos: Mimeographed, 9 May 1968).

(b) By Nigerian Political Organizations

Nigerian Labour Party
  Programme and Constitution (Lagos: Salaho Press, 1957).
Nigerian National Alliance
  Manifesto for the Federal Election of 1964 (n.d.)
Nigerian Peoples Party
  Introduction to the NPP Two Years Programme (n.d.)
  The New Nigeria: Programme of the NPP (Lagos: APN Ltd., 1 May 1961).
Nigerian Youth Congress
  Nigeria the way Forward: Policy and Programme of the NYC Adopted at the NYC First Annual Convention (Lagos: Ribway Printers, 2–3 September 1961).
Socialist Workers and Farmers Party of Nigeria
  Manifesto, 1964 (Lagos: Ribway Printers, 1964).
  Constitution (Lagos: Ribway Printers, n.d.).
  Otegbeye, T. *Ideological Conflicts in Nigerian Politics* (Lagos: 1964).
United Progressive Grand Alliance
  Forward with UPGA to Unity and Progress: a clarion call to all progressive forces (1964 Election Manifesto).
  Manifesto for the West Regional Parliamentary Election (Ibadan: 1965).

(c) By Governments (listed by year of publication)

Orde-Browne, G. St. J. *Labour Conditions in West Africa* (London: HMSO for the Colonial Office, 1941).
Report of a Committee appointed to consider the adequacy or otherwise of the rates of pay

of labour and of African Government servants and employees in the township of Lagos (Cost of Living Committee, Lagos: published for the Government by the Crown Agents, 1942).

Report of the Tudor Davies Commission into the Cost of Living in the Colony and Protectorate of Nigeria (London: HMSO for the Colonial Office, No. 204, 1946).

Harrigin, Sir W. *Report of the Commission on the Civil Services of British West Africa 1945–6* (London: HMSO for the Colonial Office, No. 209, 1947).

Report on Unestablished and Daily-rated Government Servants; Sessional Paper No. 8 of 1947 (Lagos: Government Printer, March 1947).

Report of the Commission of Enquiry into the Disorders in the Eastern Provinces of Nigeria (London: HMSO for the Colonial Office, No. 256, 1950).

Labour Administration in the Colonial Territories, 1944–1950 (London: HMSO for the Colonial Office, 1951).

Gorsuch, R. H. *Report (1954–1955) of the Commission on the Public Services of the Governments of the Federation of Nigeria* (Lagos: Federal Government Printer, 1955).

Conclusions of the Government of the Federation on (Gorsuch, R. H.) *Report of the Commission on the Public Services of the Governments of the Federation of Nigeria* (Lagos: Federal Government Printer, 1955).

Guide for Employers: Information on Labour Legislation and Wages Rates in Nigeria (Ministry of Labour and Welfare, Lagos: Government Printer, 1957).

Board of Enquiry into a Trade Dispute between the Elder Dempster Lines Ltd. and the Nigerian Union of Seamen (Lagos: Ministry of Labour, June 1959).

Review of Salaries and Wages: Report by Commission appointed by Governments of the Federation, the Northern Region, the Eastern Region and the Southern Cameroons (Lagos: Government Printer, 1959).

Revision of Salaries and Wages Rates in the Eastern Region Public Service (Premier's Office, Enugu: Government Printer, 1960).

Morgan Report on the Commission for the Review of Wages and Salaries in the Public Service of the Western Region: Sessional Paper No. 5 of 1960 (Ibadan: Government Printer, 1960).

Report on Employment and Earnings: Enquiry (Office of Statistics, Lagos: December 1961).

Report of the Coker Commission of Inquiry into the Affairs of Certain Statutory Corporations in Western Nigeria Vols. I–IV (Lagos: Federal Ministry of Information, 1962).

Kilby, P. *Development of Small Industry in Eastern Nigeria* (Enugu: Ministry of Commerce in Eastern Nigeria and USAID, 1962).

Manpower Situation in Nigeria: Manpower Studies No. 1 (Federal Ministry of Information, Lagos: National Manpower Board, 1963).

Nigeria's High Level Manpower 1963–1970: Manpower Studies No. 2 (Federal Ministry of Information, Lagos: National Manpower Board, n.d.).

Report of the (Morgan) Commission on the Review of Wages, Salaries and Conditions of Service of the Junior Employees of the Governments of the Federation and in Private Establishments (Lagos: Federal Ministry of Information Printing Division, 1964).

Conclusions of the Federal Government on the Report of the Morgan Commission: Sessional Paper No. 5 of 1964 (Lagos: Federal Ministry of Information Printing Division, 1964).

286 BIBLIOGRAPHY

National Development Plan, 1962–1968 (Ministry of Economic Development, Lagos: n.d.).

House of Representatives Debates: 1962, 1962 and 1965.

United Republic of Tanzania *Report of the Presidential Commission on the Establishment of a Democratic one Party State* (Dar es Salaam: Government Printer, 1965).

Government of Kenya *Text of Kenya Government Sessional White Paper on African Socialism and its Application to Planning in Kenya* (London: Africa Centre Ltd, 1965).

(Elwood) *Grading Team Report on Grading of Posts in the Public Services of the Federation of Nigeria* (Lagos: Ministry of Information Printing Division, April 1966).

National Standard Classification of Occupations (Lagos: Federal Ministry of Labour, 1966).

Second National Development Plan, 1970–1974 (Lagos: Government Printer, n.d.).

First Report of the Wages and Salaries Review Commission, 1970 (Lagos: Federal Ministry of Information Printing Division, 1970).

Second and Final Report of the Wages and Salaries Review Commission, 1970–71 (Lagos: Federal Ministry of Information Printing Division, 1971).

White Paper on the Second and Final Report of the Wages and Salaries Review Commission, 1970–71 (Lagos: Federal Ministry of Information Printing Division, 1971).

Quarterly Reviews of the Dept. and Federal Ministry of Labour, 1944–March 1968 (Lagos: Government Printer).

Annual Reports of the Dept. and Federal Ministry of Labour, 1940–1965/6 (Lagos: Government Printer).

Annual Abstracts of Statistics 1960–1967 (Lagos: Federal Office of Statistics).

Quarterly Digests of Statistics 1960–1967 (Lagos: Federal Office of Statistics).

(d) By International Bodies

Inter-African Labour Conference Report of the Sixth Conference CCTA/CSA Labour VI (61) 35, (March 1961).

International Labour Organisation
    Yearbooks of Labour Statistics (1968, 1969, 1971).
    African Labour Survey (Geneva: 1962).
    Calcott, D. *The Background and Conditions of Unemployed School Leavers in Three Rural Towns of the Western State of Nigeria* (Working Paper No. 61 prepared for Ministry of Economic Planning and Social Development, Western Nigeria. Geneva: 6 November 1967).

United Nations Economic Commission for Africa
    Report of the African Seminar on Labour Statistics (Addis-Ababa: 1954).

United Nations Economic and Social Council
    The Enlargement of the Exchange Economy in Tropical Africa (New York: 1954).
    Report from the Federal Republic of Nigeria to Regional Symposium on Industrial Development in Africa (Cairo: ECA and Centre for Industrial Development, January/February 1966).

IV. NEWSPAPERS AND PERIODICALS

Advance Bi-weekly, then weekly newspaper of the NTUC, Lagos.
African Labour News Fortnightly newspaper of the African Regional Organization of the ICFTU, Lagos.
Daily Sketch Daily newspaper, Ibadan.
Daily Times Daily newspaper, Lagos.
Inter-African Labour Institute Bi-monthly bulletin, London.
Morning Post Daily newspaper of the Nigerian Government, Lagos.
New Nigerian Daily newspaper, Kaduna.
Nigerian Employers' Consultative Association Monthly newsletter, Lagos.
Nigerian Opinion Monthly journal of the Nigerian Current Affairs Society, Ibadan.
Nigerian Tribune Daily newspaper, Ibadan.
Nigerian Worker, The Monthly newspaper of the ULC, Lagos (Discontinued).
Nigerian Yearbooks 1965–1971 (Lagos: Times Press Ltd).
Spark Quarterly magazine of the Railway and Ports Transport and Clerical Staff Union, Lagos.
Spear Monthly magazine, Lagos.
Sunday Post Weekly newspaper, Lagos.
Sunday Times Weekly newspaper, Lagos.
United Labour Congress of Nigeria: Information Monthly mimeographed newsletter of the ULC, Lagos.
Voice of Labour, The Monthly mimeographed journal of the Nigerian Workers' Council, Lagos.
West Africa Weekly journal, London.
West African Pilot Daily newspaper, Lagos.

V. OTHER SOURCES

(a) *Theses*

Fajana, F. O. *Wage Differentials and Economic Development in Nigeria: 1947–1967* (Ph.D. thesis, University of London, 1971).
Melson, R. F. *Marxists in the Nigerian Labour Movement: A Case Study in the Failure of Ideology* (Ph.D. thesis, Massachusetts Institute of Technology, 1967).
Oyemakinde, J. O. *A History of Indigenous Labour on the Nigerian Railway, 1895–1945* (Ph.D. thesis, University of Ibadan, 1970).
Waterman, P. *Neo-Colonialism, Communism and the Nigerian Trade Union Congress* (M.Soc.Sci. dissertation, University of Birmingham, 1972).
Williams, G. *The Political Sociology of Western Nigeria* (B.Phil. thesis, Oxford University, 1967).
Yesufu, T. M. *Problems of Industrial Relations in Nigeria with Special Reference to the Administration of Workmen's Compensation* (Ph.D. thesis, University of London, 1960).

(b) Mimeographed Material and Conference Papers

Awa, E. O. *Roads to Socialism in Nigeria* (Nigerian Institute of Social and Economic Research, Conference Paper, March 1962).

Bassey, S. U. *Review of the Development of the Nigerian Trade Union Congress 1941–1967* (Mimeographed paper, n.d.).

Berg, E. J. *Wage Structures in Less Developed Countries* Discussion Paper, University of Michigan, January 1968.

Buese, J. E. *The Role of Trade Unions in National Economic and Social Planning* (Bonn: Research Institute of the Friedrich-Ebert Foundation, n.d.).

Cohen, R. *Trade Unions and the Military in Africa: the Nigerian Case* (African Studies Association USA, Conference Paper, 1972).

Hart, K. *Informal Income Opportunities and the Structure of Employment in Ghana* (Institute of Development Studies, Brighton, Conference Paper, 1971).

Henderson, J. P. *Wage Negotiation and Legislation in Nigeria* (Michigan State University, Economic and Agricultural Development Institute, 9 December 1964).

Hughes, A. and Cohen, R. *Towards the Emergence of a Nigerian Working Class: the Social Identity of the Lagos Labour Force* (Occasional Paper, Faculty of Commerce and Social Science, University of Birmingham, Series D, No. 7, November 1971).

Melson, R. *Political Dilemmas of Nigerian Labour* (African Studies Association USA, Conference Paper, 1967).

Peace, A. J. *Industrial Protest at Ikeja, Nigeria* (British Sociological Association, Conference Paper, 1972).

—— *Towards a Nigerian Working Class: the Lagos Proletariat as a Political Elite* (Draft paper for a conference at the University of Toronto, April 1973).

Rimmer, D. *Wage Politics* (Occasional Paper No. 12, Faculty of Commerce and Social Science, University of Birmingham, 1970).

Seibel, H. D. *Labour in a Nigerian Industrial Firm: A Study of 200 Workers in the Nigerian Textile Mills* (Ikeja: April 1964).

—— *Industrial Labour in Nigeria* (Nigerian Institute of Social and Economic Research, 1964).

Storer, D. *The General Strike: Pressure Group in Action or Failure of Communication* (Seminar Paper, University of Ibadan, February 1966).

University of Ibadan *Papers* from the Joint Seminar of the Department of Economics and the Nigerian Institute of Social and Economic Research mainly concerning the Adebo Awards (November–December 1971).

Waldstein, N. S. *The Indigenous African Trade Union Movements of Nigeria, the Federation of Rhodesia and Nyasaland, French West Africa and the Belgian Congo* (Cambridge, Mass: Massachusetts Institute of Technology, April 1960).

Waterman, P. *Working Class Struggle and Revolutionary Trade Unionism in Nigeria* (Mimeographed Paper, 1968).

Weeks, J. *Employment and the Growth of Towns* (African Studies Association, UK, Conference Paper, September 1971).

Williams, G. *The Political Economy of Colonialism and Neo-Colonialism in Nigeria* (Conference Paper, July 1972).

Wober, J. M. *Psychological Factors in the Adjustment to Industrial Life among Employees of a Firm in (Sapele) Southern Nigeria* (Department of Social Anthropology, University of Edinburgh, September 1966).

Yesufu, T. M. *Labour in the Nigerian Economy* (Lagos: Nigerian Broadcasting Corporation, October Lectures, 1967).

(c) Typescripts, Papers, and Files

Central Trades Union Organizations in Western Nigeria 'An Address to the Military Governor of the Western Provinces' (Ibadan: 22 February 1966).

Chukwura, N. 'ICFTU Exposed! TUCN Crashes!!' (Lagos: the Author, 2 April 1962).

Dialli, A. 'The Income requirements of Nigeria's Workpeople Today: the Issues Involved' (Lagos: National Union of Bank, Insurance & Allied Workers Union, July 1970).

Federal Palace Hotel African Workers' Union 'Open Letters to the Federal Government' (Lagos: January 1962).

Goodluck, W. O. 'An Address to the Second Annual Conference of the Lipton of Nigeria Workers' Union' (NTUC Files, 20 January 1968).

Ijeh, E. U. 'Labour in a Quandary' (Ibadan: typewritten, 29 November 1966).

—— 'Plain Truth on Current Labour Situation' (Ibadan: typewritten, 29 December 1966).

Longe, J. O. I 'Government View of the Role of Trade Unionism in Nigeria' (Ibadan: Department of Adult Education and Extra-Mural Studies, n.d.).

Macaulay Papers 'Miscellaneous Documents Concerning Trade Unionism' Vol. V, No. 11 (Ibadan University Library).

Nigerian Trade Union Congress 'Miscellaneous Press Releases from July 1967– March 1968' (Lagos: NTUC files).

United Labour Congress 'Various files relating to the Activity of the Centre' (1967, 1968, early 1969).

University of Lagos 'Collected Papers on the 1945 General Strike' (Photocopies, Ghandi Library, University of Lagos).

Addendum to Bibliography (1981)

Aina, O. A. *Industrialisation and Class Formation in Nigeria, 1946–1975: An Examination of the Relationship between Industrial Development and Class Formation in Nigeria* (Ph.D. thesis, University of Sussex, 1980).

Akpala, A. 'Labour Policies and Practices in Nigeria', *Journal of Industrial Relations*, 1971, 13 (3), 274–90.

Ayoade, J. A. A. 'Federalism and Wage Politics in Nigeria', *Journal of Comparative Commonwealth Politics*, 1975, 13 (3), 282–9.

Davison, R. B. *Industrial Relations Decrees on Nigeria: Questions and Answers to Explain the Law* (Zaria: Ahmadu Bello University, 1977).

Diejomaoh, V. P. 'Industrial Relations in a Development Context: the Case of Nigeria' in Damachi, U. G., Seibel, H. D. and Trachtman, L. (Eds.), *Inaustrial Relations in Africa* (London: Macmillan, 1979), 169–200.

Etukudo, A. J. *Waging Industrial Peace in Nigeria* (N.Y.: Exposition Press, 1978).

Fapohunda, E. R. 'Characteristics of Women Workers in Lagos', *Labour and Society*, 1978, 3 (2), 158–71.

Gutkind, P. C. W. *The Emergent African Urban Proletariat* (McGill University, Montreal: Centre for Developing Area Studies, 1974).

Gutkind, P. C. W., Cohen, R. and Copans, J. (Eds.) *African Labor History* (Beverly Hills & London: Sage Publications, 1978).

Hinchcliffe, K. 'Labour Aristocracy – A Northern Nigerian Case Study', *Journal of Modern African Studies*, 1974, 12 (1), 57–67.

Hughes, A. and Cohen, R. 'An Emerging Nigerian Working Class: the Lagos Experience 1897–1939' in Gutkind, P. C. W., Cohen, R. and Copans, J. (Eds.) *q.v.*

Jackson, S. 'Hausa Women on Strike', *Review of African Political Economy*, May–August 1978, 13, 21–36.

Joseph, R. 'Political Parties and Ideology in Nigeria', *Review of African Political Economy*, May–August 1978, 78–90.

Lloyd, P. C. *Power and Independence: Urban Africans' Perception of Social Inequality* (London: Routledge & Kegan Paul, 1974).

Lubeck, P. 'Workers and Consciousness in Kano, Nigeria: a View from Below', in Sandbrook, R. and Cohen, R. (Eds.) *q.v.*, 139–60.

—— 'Labour in Kano since the Petroleum Boom', *Review of African Political Economy*, May–August 1978, 13, 37–46.

—— 'The Value of Multiple Methods in Researching Third World Strikes: a Nigerian Example', *Development and Change*, 1979, 10 (2), 301–320.

Nigeria, Federal Republic *Report of the Board of Inquiry into the Affairs of the Amalgamated Dockworkers, Transport and General Workers' Union* (Lagos: Federal Ministry of Information, 1971).

—— *Report of the Public Services Review Commission (Udoji Report)* (Lagos: Federal Ministry of Information, September 1974).

—— *Government Views on the Report of the Public Service Review Commission* (Lagos: Federal Ministry of Information, December 1974).

—— *Proceedings of the Tribunal of Inquiry into the Activities of Trade Unions (Adebiyi Proceedings)* (Lagos, 1976).

—— *Report of the Tribunal of Inquiry into the Activities of Trade Unions (The Adebiyi Report)* (Lagos: Federal Ministry of Information, 1977).

Osoba, S. 'The Phenomenon of Labour Migration on the Eve of British Colonial Rule: a Neglected Aspect of Nigeria's Social History', *Journal of the Historical Society of Nigeria*, 1969, 4 (4), 515–38.

Otobo, D. *Central Trade Union Organisation in Nigeria and the External Factor since 1945, a Critical Assessment* (D.Phil. thesis, University of Oxford, 1979).

Peace, A. 'The Lagos Proletariat: Labour Aristocrats or Populist Militants' in Sandbrook, R. and Cohen, R. (Eds.) *q.v.*, 281–302.

—— 'Industrial Protest in Nigeria', in Cohen, R., Gutkind, P. C. W. and Brazier, P. (Eds.) *Peasants and Proletarians: the Struggles of Third World Workers* (New York: Monthly Review Press, 1979), 418–40.

—— *Choice Class and Conflict* (Brighton: Harvester, 1979).

Remy, D. 'Economic Security and Industrial Unionism: a Nigerian Case Study' in Sandbrook, R. and Cohen, R. (Eds.) *q.v.*, 161–77.

Sandbrook, R. and Cohen, R. (Eds.) *The Development of an African Working Class: Studies in Class Formation and Action* (London: Longman, 1975).

Smyke, R. J. and Storer, D. C. *The Nigeria Union of Teachers: an Official History* (Algonac, Michigan: Reference Publications, Inc., 1977).

Waterman, P. 'Communist Theory in the Nigerian Trade Union Movement', *Politics and Society*, 1973, 3 (2), 283–312.

—— 'Conservatism amongst Nigerian Workers' in Williams, G. P. (Ed.) *q.v.*

—— 'Consciousness, Organisation and Action amongst Lagos Portworkers', *Review of African Political Economy*, May–August 1978, 13, 47–62.

—— *Wage Labour Relations in Nigeria: State, Capitalists, Unions and Workers in the Lagos Cargo-Handling Industry* (Draft Ph.D. thesis for Eramus University, Rotterdam, 1980).

Waterman, P. (Ed.) *Nigerian Labour Studies on Microfiche* comprising:

1. Nigerian Labour Archives of Chief O. A. Fagbeno, 1943–1975.
2. Labour in the Nigerian Press, 1976–1977 (in preparation).
3. The Lagos Port Labour Archive (in preparation).
4. The Nigerian Trade Union Tribunal of 1976.
5. Wage Labour Relations in Nigeria (an extended version of Waterman's draft Ph.D. thesis).
6. Labour and Labour Relations in Nigeria: a Classified Bibliography (in preparation).

All the above items are (or will be) available on microfiche from Inter Documentation Company, AG Poststrasse 14, 6300 Zug, Switzerland.

—— 'The Nigerian State and the Control of Labour: the Case of the Lagos Cargo-Handling Industry' in Collins, P. (Ed.) *Administration for Development in Nigeria* (forthcoming).

Weeks, J. F. 'Wage Policy and the Colonial Legacy – a Comparative Study', *Journal of Modern African Studies*, 1971, 9 (3), 361–87.

Williams, G. P. 'Political Consciousness among the Ibadan Poor', in de Kadt, E. and Williams, G. P. (Eds.) *Sociology and Development* (London: Tavistock Publications, 1974).

—— (Ed.) *Nigeria: Economy and Society* (London: Rex Collings, 1976).

Index

Aba, 2, 22, 118

Abeokuta, 22, 54, 56

Action Group (AG), 3, 4, 5–6, 7, 10; (1966) coup, 217; ideology, 8, 264; in the West, 11, 27, 44; internal divisions, 5–6, 14, 170–1, 174; oppositional role, 15; (1951) Regional election, 206–7; see United Progressive Grand Alliance

Adebayo, Brigadier, 228

Adebo Commissions (1970, 1971), 125, 128, 158, 191, 193, 196, 231, 232, 233–7, 265

Adebola, H. P., 76, 77, 78, 83, 169; and union internationals, 83, 105, 230; attacks on, 83, 98; on Joint Action Committee, 92, 93, 102; on unity, 124; on workers' responsibilities, 155; party candidate, 172; role in (1964) General Strike, 166–7; union organizer, 79, 211; United Labour Congress President, 87, 106, 122, 124, 125, 154, 207, 224, 227, 230

Advance, 94, 136, 157

African Civil Servants Technical Workers Union (ACSTWU), 71, 104; role in (1945) General Strike, 160, 161, 162, 163

African Regional Office/Organization (AFRO): connections with United Labour Congress, 151, 152, 153; distribution of finance, 123; formation, 83

African Trade Union Confederation (ATUC), 152, 250

African Workers' Union/Nigerian Labour Party, 174

Afriscope, 233

Afro-American Labour Centre (AALC): distribution of finance, 99, 230; educational assistance, 126, 152; (1967) Geneva conference, 251; ideology, 250; leadership, 230

Agriculture, 49, 128; as a source of wealth, 39, 40; employment in, 50, 51; revenue received from, 46

Ahmadu Bello, Alhaji (Sardauna of Sokoto), 4, 9, 11

Airways African Senior Staff Association, 114

Ajukchuku, M. C. K., 174

Akintola, Chief, 6, 7, 14, 171; leader of Nigerian National Democratic Party, 10, 11; opponents of, 17

Akpan, J. U., 111, 230

Alale, Philip, 222

Alexander, R. J., 145

Alkali (Islamic) courts, 17

All African Trade Union Federation (AATUF), 152, 250; affiliation of Gambian Labour Union, 99; distribution of funds, 83, 99; relations with Nigerian Trade Union Congress, 82; relations with World Federation of Trade Unions, 83

All-Nigeria Government Technical and General Workers' Federation, 72

For Product Safety Concerns and Information please contact our EU
representative GPSR@taylorandfrancis.com Taylor & Francis Verlag GmbH,
Kaufingerstraße 24, 80331 München, Germany

Printed and bound by CPI Group (UK) Ltd, Croydon, CR0 4YY
08/05/2025
01864397-0001